A
COLLECTION
OF SEVERAL
PIECES
OF
Mr. JOHN TOLAND,

Now first publish'd from his Original
Manuscripts :

WITH

Some MEMOIRS *of his* LIFE *and*
WRITINGS.

VOLUME II.

LONDON:

Printed for J. PEELE, at *Locke's Head* in
Pater-noster Row. M. DCC. XXVI.

THE
CONTENTS
OF THE
SECOND VOLUME.

A

THE CONTENTS.

AN APPENDIX,
Containing ſome Pieces found among Mr. TOLAND's *Papers.* Pag. 1

A

LETTER

CONCERNING THE

ROMAN EDUCATION.

WHEN I laſt had the happineſs, Sir, to be in your company, you may remember that we ſpent moſt of the afternoon about antient and modern Learning, which ſtill continues to be a very faſhionable ſubject (1) both in Books and Converſation. Yet, with all juſt regard to the famous advocates of either ſide, the Queſtion, in my opinion, ought not ſo much to have been, *who ſucceeded beſt in the ſeveral faculties,* (tho I wou'd not have this excluded) *as which kind of Learning excells, and is of greateſt uſe to mankind that of the old Greecs and the Romans, or that of the late Schoolmen and the preſent time?* Not that I wou'd make an odious compariſon

(1) *In* 1703.

between us and the Schoolmen, over whom
we have got many confiderable advantages :
but, I'm fure, the further we ftill proceed to quit
their language, and matter, and method, the
nearer we muft needs approach to thofe of the
Greeks and the Romans.   Nor can I imagin
that any men will fo far oppofe matter of
fact, or expofe their own judgment, as to
deny that all the perfections of the Moderns
beyond the Schoolmen have been revealed to
them by the Ghofts of the Antients, that
is, by following their rules, reading their
works, imitating their method, and copying
their ftile, which laft holds as true in profe as
in verfe.

THIS   ought not at all to be wonder'd
at, as if the Antients had been a different
race or fpecies of men from us, or that Greece
and Italy did formerly breath out more improving exhalations than at prefent, as fome
of the Heathens fancy'd their Oracles were
given rather in one place than another by an
infpiring vapor out of that particular fpot.
You may be certain, Sir, that I am difturb'd
with no fuch fancy : the Antients and we
are equal in our race and make, in the ftruc-
ture of our brains and our natural capacities :
'tis government and education that makes
all the difference ; liberty of fpeech, and
the rewarding of merit.   The rules of reafon
and good fenfe are eternal, the fame in all
ages and countries, and wherever equally cultivated

tivated they moſt certainly produce the like effect. But where men are reſtrain'd in their genius, debarr'd all freedom from ſuch and ſuch ſubjects, or branded and incapacitated for being of this or that opinion; there 'tis impoſſible there ſhould be any impartial ſearch after truth, or any real improvement of the underſtanding, any uſeful or new diſcoveries; and conſequently ſuch times and places muſt come infinitely ſhort of others that had an unlimited liberty, and all due encouragement. Can it be expected, for example, that the like extent of knowlege, the like mutual exerciſe of wits, or the like increaſe of diſcoveries ſhould obtain in thoſe countries where one ſort of Philoſophers alone are allow'd, and even thoſe oblig'd to ſpeak the language of their Prieſts, as in other countries where all Philoſophies were publicly taught, and where all Religions were equally tolerated, and no opinion of any kind diſcountenanced, nor any men branded, but thoſe who ſubverted the Government, or deprav'd men's Morals? and therefore it's no wonder why new Rome ſhould come ſo ſhort of the old, or why the preſent Greeks ſhould be Barbarians, whereas their anceſtors held all the world to be ſuch except themſelves. The difference is now as plain between England and Spain; which ſhows that time is not concern'd, and that liberty civil and religious is the cauſe of our knowlege, as their tyranny and inquiſition is that of their ignorance.

As for the several sorts of learning, some being common to the Antients and the Moderns, and some being peculiar to the one and to the other, I'll say nothing to you at present on so copious an argument. But *I was always persuaded, that, as to the persons who made a profession of learning, and as to the manner of teaching it to others, the Antients made a much better choice than the Moderns, and ought incontestably to have the preference.* Their learned men were <u>not the meanest of the people bred to letters</u>, or rather to various cants for a livelyhood; uncommon words and terms being as far from arts and knowlege as pedantry is from learning, or affectation and foppery from civility and good manners : but all the dignities and degrees of the sacred Priesthood itself, as well as the great posts in the Law, and all the offices in the State, were possest by men of distinguisht birth and fortune, and whose education was every way sutable. Among the Moderns, on the contrary, the noble and the rich quit the use of Letters as well as of arms to the meaner sort, thinking their knowlege should be carry'd about by their servants like their cloaths, tho' with this difference, that they will not use the one as they wear the other; whereby they render themselves obnoxious to be blindly led by their inferiors in opinions, as they shamefully put their possessions in their power whenever they are tempted to become the masters. This in our time has made the Arts
of

of peace and war hateful and contemtible, wheras being formerly plac'd in better hands and far nobler purpofes, they were neither mercenary nor oppreffive, but exceeding honorable and beneficial. They were not in the firft place cloifter'd up from fociety ; nor under the whips and fines, the fcanty dyet and barren lectures of fpeculative men, accuftomed to a retir'd and fedentary way of living : for fuch perfons are commonly ftrangers to the world, which (with the want of practifing mankind by the advantage of travelling) makes 'em imperious and auftere, vehemently ad_dicted to difpute, impatient of contradiction, noify and paffionate in converfation, and, what's worft of all, more concern'd to pre-poffefs the underftandings of their Schollars with thofe particular doctrines which make for the profit and credit of their own profeffion, than to fit them for bufinefs, to give 'em gentile accomplifhments, and to advance 'em in the liberal Arts and Sciences. But the Roman youth, after they came out of their nurfes and pedagogue's hands, were plac'd under the infpection of Companions rather than Mafters, men of univerfal learning, generous breeding, well vers'd in public proceedings and in the common affairs of life, their examples being as inftructive at leaft as their precepts. Forein languages they taught their difciples by converfation, and to be Critics in thofe as well as in their own by Grammar. You muft not fancy, Sir, that thefe were like the prefent Governors (as they call 'em) who in great men's houfes are but the next fort of ferving men after the Chaplain, and when they travel abroad are only the Stewards of their young Mafter's cafh, and confequently fuch flovenly pedants as to afford perpetual matter of laughter to their difciples, being neither capable to introduce thefe nor themfelves to the audience of Princes, to the diverfion of Courts, or into any creditable company.

BUT among the Romans, before the ruin of the Commonwealth, they invited Philofophers from Greece by ample rewards, or prevail'd on able perfons at home to undertake this province; befides very reputable conditions, they treated 'em always with the refpect that became men of learning and knowlege, whofe behaviour and politenefs their children were as carefully to imitate as to obey their directions in all parts of their conduct. They did not fill their heads with narrow, pedantic, and ufelefs notions, nor did they captivate their tender minds to blind authority, or implicitly fwear 'em to particular opinions; much lefs did they torment their memories with any wretched, unintelligible jargon: but cultivating their reafon, and leaving their judgments free, they taught them to difcourfe handfomly in private, to fpeak eloquently in public, to write perfpicuoufly, elegantly, and correctly; but, above all things, to underftand the Cuftoms, Laws, and Religion of their Country. The knowlege

knowlege of Mankind (a mighty art) they communicated to 'em by comparing antient History with the daily obfervations they made on ftrangers, their own acquaintance, and fellow-citizens. By reading the cuftoms and conftitutions of other places, they fhow'd 'em what in their own was blamcable or praifeworthy, what requir'd to be amended, added, or abolifht. They infpir'd them with an ardent paffion for Liberty, a true love and refpect for ftrict Laws, with an equal abhorrence of Tyranny and Anarchy : perfuading 'em to prefer death to flavery, and readily to expofe their lives and eftates in defence (not of any form indifferently) but of a Government which protected their perfons, preferv'd their property, encourag'd induftry, rewarded merit, and left their fentiments free. Such a government it was that they call'd their Country, and for this they thought it moft honourable to dy, whether it were fixt in temperate climates and happy fields, or among barren rocks and fands, under the coldeft or moft foggy air. For wherever they enjoy'd liberty, there they thought themfelves at home ; and indeed a fondnefs for any fpot of earth from the mere confideration of being born there, is not only a falfe notion of our Country, but, in my opinion, as childifh a prejudice as that of fome old Men, who order their dead bodies to be carry'd many hundreds of miles to be laid with their deceaft Progenitors, their Wives, or other Relations.

THE

THE Roman youth were taught manly and martial exercifes. By public games and prizes, as horfe-raceing, courfeing in chariots, wreftling, running, fencing, and the like, they were inur'd to bear fatigues, and bred to all heroic Virtues, which are very confiftent with the eafy, affable, and obliging carriage which they learnt at the fame time, and from the fame men. This made the Commanders in thofe days as famous for their learning as their valor, the fame perfons governing and obeying by turns, without any difference between the Soldier and the States-man, the Orator or the General. To this is owing not only their furprizing actions, noble refolutions, and powerful harangues; but in particular their admirable ftratagems of warr (proceeding from a perfect knowlege of human nature, acquired by Hiftory and Philofophy and which can never be practis'd by fuch as had no other education befides handling a mufquet or trailing a pike, treading perpetually in the common road of their appointed exercife, and who are only preferr'd to their pofts with refpect to their feniority, juft like the Fellows of a College. The favour of a Soverain can make any man a General, but not endow him with the leaft tincture of thefe arts; nor are they to be learnt in all the breeding of a Courtier. Soft foothing fpeeches will never pafs for orations, no more than cunning little tricks for ftratagems; and the managing of a

ball

ball is as different from the marſhalling of an army; as dancing is from fighting.

FROM want of conſidering the mixt capacity of the great men among the Romans, or rather for not underſtanding their manner of Education, which equally fitted them for the Forum and the Camp; even moſt of the learned of our time look on the Orations they read in their hiſtorians as never ſpoken, which is a great and unpardonable miſtake. A militia of free citizens is no leſs a commonwealth or politic body than the Senat and Aſſemblies they have left at home, and in which the next year they'll take their places, when others have their turn of going into the field. In the Roman armies they voted on many occaſions by their centuries in the camp, as well as about civil affairs in the city; and therefore the uſe of reaſon and perſuaſion was as neceſſary in the one place as the other; not that I affirm theſe Speeches were conſtantly deliver'd in the very words of the hiſtorians (which yet they often were) but only to that purpoſe: for it wou'd be too voluminous to inſert them always at length, when the ſenſe of them can be abridg'd into a narrow compaſs, which we ſee done by the beſt writers of our time in harangues, decrees, proclamations, and other public pieces which we very well know to be genuine. And, that I may ſay no more on this ſubject, the Hiſtorians, who, after this example, had ſtufft their works

with

with falfe Harangues, did not efcape the cenfure of the Antients, and the like authors little confider what they do among the Moderns :
but in compofing a Romance fuch a practice is
of a piece with the reft, and certainly allowable, being then an imitation of nature in a
free country, and not in danger of impofing
in any country on the readers.

THE Education of the Romans is likewife
the reafon why their youth enter'd fo early
on action, converfing with men from their
cradles, and not boys with boys , as among
us, till we arrive at manhood, when at length
we begin to think of learning the duties of
fociety ; but old age does generally overtake
us before we can half conn our leffon. The
fons of the Nobility or Patricians were admitted after a certain age to hear the debates
of the Senat, as the beft and only School,
where they cou'd learn how far extended the
liberty of the people, and what were the true
bounds to the power of the Magiftrate ; how
to imitate betimes the beft mafters in the art of
perfuafion, to obferve the orders, rules, and
methods of proceeding ; and to know what
behaviour was becoming towards their fubjects, enemies, auxiliaries, and allies, as well
as to form a right notion of all the feveral
interefts and parties in the Commonwealth.
The fons of the inferior Gentry and Commons, thofe of the Equeftrian and Plebeian
Orders, modeftly ftood for the fame ends by
the

the door ; and, such was the power of their virtuous Education and Discipline, that you scarce ever meet with any instances of their blabbing again in company what was propos'd or resolv'd in those august Assemblies, but on the contrary, very many commendations of their silence and discretion, tho, were any of 'em basely inclin'd, they might flatter themselves with no discovery from the multitude of their companions.

I cannot speak here, Sir, as I wou'd, of the Patrons which the Roman youth propos'd for their imitation amongst the most noted men of the Republic, observing all their words and actions, accompanying 'em to the Forum and the Senat, takeing notes from their public speeches or pleadings, attending 'em home to their houses, and paying to 'em the same reverence and gratitude as to their own parents. After the same manner they put themselves Voluntiers under the bravest Generals, to learn the art of war, not avoiding, but rather chusing the most dangerous expeditions, and they were actually oblig'd to make a certain number of campaigns, before they were capable of any Office whatsoever in the Government ; but all these particulars require a larger consideration than is consistent with the bounds of this Letter.

I am, Sir, &c.

DIREC.

DIRECTIONS

For breeding of Children by their Mothers and Nurfes, in two LETTERS, *written above two thoufand years ago.*

Introduction to the Letters.

N my Letter concerning *the Roman Education* I faid nothing relating to Mothers or Nurfes, as not falling naturally within my province. I remember Mr. LOCKE has been cenfur'd more than once by fome of our Pedants for takeing the Women's bufinefs (forfooth) out of their hands, and for being too converfant in the nurfery. But the impotent declamations of thofe odd creatures fhou'd never have deterr'd me, if that true lover of mankind had not exhaufted the fubject in his moft ufeful *Treatife of Education:* befides that this part is not fo arbitrary and fubject to variation, as what may be reckon'd the genteel or fafhionable Learning of different Countries; the right methods of breeding Children by their Mothers or Nurfes being the fame (however various the practice) in all times and places. Yet,

to

to gratify for once thefe fqueamifh Hyper-Critics, as well as to exhibit in a fmall compafs what is deliver'd by Mr. LOCKE in too many words (the grand fault of his book) I fhall give 'em this very part of Education from the hands they think moft proper ; fince the following Letters were written by two Ladies, of whom I think it fitting here to give fome fhort account.

THEANO was the dearly beloved wife of PYTHAGORAS, who, tho' not the firft wife man, yet the firft man that ever bore the title of a Philofopher. She was as learned as fair : and, after her husband's death, manag'd the Pythagoric School, with her fons TELAUGES and MNESARCHUS. 'Tis no wonder therefore that this Sect fhou'd be fo illuftrious from its very foundation for female Difciples, which were fo numerous, that PHILOCHORUS of Athens fill'd a whole volum with 'em : but neverthelefs it rais'd the wonder of Mr. MENAGE, that of all fects Women fhou'd be fond of the Pythagoric fect, which recommended and enjoy'd filence fo much. This piece of raillery is as infipid, as it is vulgar. THEANO, as I faid, was the firft and moft celebrated among the Pythagorean Ladies. She was afterwards call'd the Daughter of the Pythagorean Philofophy, which made fome other miftake her for the daughter of PYTHAGORAS himfelf. We have a remarkable inftance, how far Philofophy had

cur'd

cur'd her of the Superftition and vulgar errors
of her country, where, among other fuch
filly obfervations, people believ'd themfelves
polluted by touching dead bodies, and that
even man and wife muft perform certain
rites of purification after conjugal. careffes.
Now THEANO being askt by fome body,
within what fpace of time a woman might
be counted pure, after the embraces of a
man? She anfwer'd, *After her own hus-*
band immediately; after another man, never.
This THEANO then wrote the fecond of the
following Letters, and I need fay little more
of MUIA (who wrote the firft, the fubject
requiring this order) but that fhe was the
worthy offspring of THEANO and PYTHAGO-
RAS. It was queftionlefs an effect of her
education, no lefs than of her natural difpofition, that, while a maid, fhe appear'd in all
public affemblies at the head of the young
Ladies; and that, when a wife, fhe continu'd
at the head of the marry'd Women. She was
fo much admir'd for her prudent management, that her townfmen, the Crotonians,
converted her houfe into a temple of CERES;
and was fo remarkable for her elegant learning, that the avenue to this houfe was ftil'd
the MUSÆUM: a glorious example for Ladies
to imitate in both refpects. To be fhort,
thefe Letters are choice monuments of antiquity, and perfect in their kind, both with
refpect to the epiftolary ftile, and likewife as
to accuracy of thought.

I   LETTER

L E T T E R I.

CONTAINING

Directions for the Choice and Conduct of a Nurse.

M U I A *To* P H Y L L I S
Health.

OW you are become a Mother of Children, I give you the following advices.

CHUSE a Nurse every way fit for the purpose, but particularly a neat and modeft Woman, one that is not addicted to Wine or too much Sleep : for fuch a Woman is agreed by every body, to be the beft qualifi'd for bringing up Children without any fervil examples ; provided always that her Milk be kindly, and that fhe wholly refrain from her Husband for the time. For great ftrefs is to be laid on thefe matters ; fince the choice of a Nurfe, and her manner of tending us, is of moft evident and effential concern in the courfe of our whole lives. A good Nurfe will do every thing that fhe ought in its due feafon, not

giving

giving the breast, pap, or any other nourishment to the Child at random, and as often as he craves; but with a peculiar discretion, for this highly conduces to the infant's health : and if she will not suffer him to sleep whensoever he pleases, but when she judges him to want his natural rest, this likewise will not a little confirm his health. Let not the Nurse be a passionate Woman, nor a stammerer in her speech; neither let her be indifferent when or what she eats, but be discreet and sober in her meals. Let her further, if you can possibly compass it, be a (1) Greec and not a Barbarian. The best time to lay the Child to sleep, is, after he has sufficiently fill'd himself with Milk : for rest is not only most grateful to Children, but the digestion of such food is also most easy.

If any thing else besides Milk must be given him, let it be of the simplest sort. But Wine ought to be wholly deny'd him, as being naturally too strong and hot : or if he must have any, let it be very rarely, and such as

(1) This caution, as that about stammering a little before, is given to prevent Children (who are continually imitating every thing they see or hear) not only from acquiring any vicious habit in their manners, but even in their speech : As *CICERO* likewise says, that *it is a matter of great concern who they be whom any one hears every day at home, or with whom he must converse from a child ; how our Fathers, how our Masters, and how our very Mothers express themselves.* In Bruto.

comes

comes neareſt the conſiſtence of Milk that may be. His body muſt not be too often waſht : for the leſs frequent, and the more carefully prepar'd his baths are, the better. If he be ſent abroad to nurſe, let it be in a temperate air, neither too hot nor too cold ; as the ſituation of the houſe muſt not be too bleak, nor too cloſe. Let not the water us'd about him be over-hard or over-ſoft ; as his very ſwadling-bands, and what other cloaths he wears, muſt be of a middle ſort between coarſe and fine, yet ever juſtly fitted to his body : for nature does in all theſe things require a certain ſimplicity and economy, but no nicenefs or magnificence.

I have thought it not unuſeful to write theſe things to you at preſent, in hopes of a happy nurſery, perform'd as before preſcrib'd : but, God aſſiſting, we ſhall likewiſe in due time give ſuch proper directions as we can for the Education of the Child.

B   LETTER

LETTER II.

CONTAINING

Directions for a Mother how to manage her Children.

THEANO *To* EUBULA *Health.*

 am inform'd that you bring up your Children after a very nice and fond kind of manner. Now, it is the duty of a good Mother, not to cocker up her Children in Pleasure, but to accustom them to Modesty and Prudence. Take heed therefore, that you play not the part rather of one that flatters, than of one that loves them; for Pleasure being made, as it were, the foster-brother of Children, such a companion renders them intemperate and incorrigible. And what is it, pray, that can be afterwards more agreeable to Children, than the Pleasures to which they are us'd from the beginning? Wherefore care must be taken, my friend, that the Education of Children become not their Perversion: for 'tis a perversion of nature when their minds are abandon'd to Pleasure, and their bodies

to

to Voluptuoufnefs ; thus avoiding labour in the laft, and growing fpiritlefs in the firft. But Children ought to be timely inur'd to pains-taking and hardfhips, that, when afterwards they muft in good earneft fuffer pains or undergo fatigues, they may not turn the flaves of their paffions (over-rating Pleafure, and dreading Labour) but that, fcorning fuch poor prejudices, they may prefer Honour and Virtue to all things whatfoever, and continue ftedfaft in the purfuit of the fame. By confequence then, their Feeding is not to be too fumtuous or plentiful, nor their Pleafures too many or exquifite, nor their Paftimes too frequent or long : neither may they fpeak whatever comes uppermoft, nor always be themfelves the chufers of what they fhall do.

I am further inform'd that you are terribly frightn'd when your Child cries, and that you are at much pains to coax him again into fmiles ; tho' he fhou'd even beat his Nurfe, or tell your felf that you laugh impertinently : nay, that you make provifion of cooling things for him in fummer, and of warming implements in winter, with many other delicacies which poor folk's Children never experience, but are brought up at a much eafier and cheaper rate ; nor are they for all that of a flower growth, and for the moft part they enjoy a much better health. But you, on the contrary, educate your Children as if they were the pofterity of SARDANAPALUS,

B 2 ener-

enervating the natural vigor of Men by effemi-
nate Pleasures. What think you will become
of that Child, who, if he may not eat when
he lifts, strait falls a crying; or, if he may
eat, must have sweet and relishing things?
who faints away, if the weather be hot; and
shivers all over, if it be cold? who, if any
body chides him, will contend again? who,
if not serv'd at command, grows melancholy?
and falls into a morose humour, if delay'd
his meals? who shamefully indulges himself
in laziness, and whose behaviour is infa-
mously soft and indolent? Know then for certain, my friend, that such as begin their lives
in such dissolute sloath, seldom fail of becoming other men's servants in riper age.
Do your endeavour therefore to pluck up
those Pleasures in your Children by the roots,
practise upon them the hardy and not the
delicate method of Breeding, let them learn
to bear hunger and thirst, with heat and cold,
and to behave themselves civilly, not only to
their superiors, but also to their equals : since
thus they will acquire a certain ingenuous and
manly carriage, both when they are seriously
employ'd in affairs, and when they relax their
minds by necessary diversions. For believe
me, friend, labours to Children are in the
nature of preparatories towards the attaining
of perfect Virtue, and which having sufficiently imbib'd, they afterwards receive the
tincture of Virtue itself with much greater
facility. Take care then, my friend, that,

2

as

as ill-cultivated vines bear none or bad fruit, fo the tender rearing of your Children may not produce the mifchief of much vanity and difgrace.

C O N C L U S I O N.

CERTAIN Critics may think both thefe Letters fpurious, if they will; as they pronounce all the Grecanic Epiftles to be fuch without diftinction : but in the mean time I defy 'em to prove thefe Letters to be fo in particular, or (which is our main point at prefent) to write a couple of better or as good Letters upon the fame fubjects themfelves. The inftructions are never the worfe, come they from THEANO and MUIA, or from any Sophift or Grammarian that perfonated thofe excellent Ladies. But indeed the four Letters are evidently fpurious, which LEO ALLATIUS has publifh'd under the name of our THEANO, in his *Notes on the Life of* PYTHAGORAS. Befides their being written in the Attic, whereas thefe are in the Doric dialect (generally affected by the Pythagoreans) PLATO's mention'd in the laft of 'em, and his dialogue with PARMENIDES, contrary to all Chronology. There were other Women, and fome not unlearned, call'd by the name of THEANO ; fo that there may be no miftake in the name, tho' a very grofs one in the perfon.

I muft not forget to remark, that, according to the noble fimplicity reigning in the

moft

moſt ancient writings, the ſecond perſon **is**
always expreſs'd in our two Letters by *thou*
and *thee*: and ſo I ſhou'd have tranſlated,
were it not that Cuſtom (the only diſpoſer of
Languages) has made *you* to ſignifie in Engliſh
the ſecond perſon no leſs in the ſingular than
in the plural number, juſt as in Latin *ſe* ſignifies the third perſon in both numbers.

I ſhall here add two Letters which in my
opinion are little inferior to the former. One
from MELISSA to CLEARETA, and the other
from THEANO to NICOSTRATA, concerning
the behaviour of married women.

MELISSA *To* CLEARETA
Health.

YOU appear to me to abound of
your ſelf in all good qualities: for
the earneſt deſire you expreſs to
hear ſomething concerning the de-
cent behaviour of Women, gives fair hopes
that you purpoſe to grow old in a courſe of
Virtue. Now, it behoves a prudent and free-
born Woman, who is join'd to one Man according to the laws, to adorn herſelf modeſt-
ly, not magnificently. Let her dreſs be clean,
and neat, and convenient; but neither ſplen-
did nor ſuperfluous: for tranſparent or gorgi-
ous attire, and thoſe garments interwoven
with

with purple and gold, are to be rejected, and wholly left to Miftriffes, as inftruments whereby to allure and retain the more cuftomers. But the ornament of a Woman, whofe bufinefs is to pleafe one Man, does not confift in modes but in manners: fince 'tis the honour of a freeborn Woman to ftudy to pleafe her own hufband only, and not every one elfe that looks upon her. Inftead of Paint then, bear a blufh on your face, as a fign of modefty. Prefer probity, and neatnefs, and frugality, before gold and precious ftones : for a Woman of truly virtuous inclinations muft not place all her beautifying skill in adjufting her cloaths, but in the management of her houfe, and in complaifance towards her husband, the beft means to procure his favour. Indeed the Will of a husband fhould be an unwritten law to a good wife, whereby to govern all her actions; as fhe ought to think that obedience is the faireft and ampleft dowry fhe can bring with her: for more truft is to be put in the beauties and riches of the mind, than in thofe of the face or of a fortune ; fince malice or ficknefs may deftroy thefe laft, whereas the firft continues ftedfaft and ufeful till death.

Farewell.

B 4   THEANO

THEANO *To* NICOSTRATA
Health.

I have heard of your husband's extravagance, that he keeps a Miftrifs, and that you are jealous of him. But, my friend, I know a great many other men, that labour under the fame diftemper : for they are caught (it feems) by thofe women, and held faft, and depriv'd of their underftanding. In the mean while you are tormented both night and day, you abandon your felf to grief, and are ever contriving fomething or other againft him. But do fo no more, my friend : for the virtues of a wife lies not in watching her husband's actions, but in complaifance to his will, and this very complaifance obliges you to bear with his madnefs. He keeps company with a Miftrifs for his pleafure, and with a Wife for his convenience : but it is convenient not to mix evils with evils, nor to heap one folly upon another. Some faults there be, my friend, which are irritated the more by reproof, and which pafs'd over in filence are the fooner cur'd, as fire not blown is obferv'd to go out of itfelf : and therefore if he defigns to conceal his conduct from your knowledge, but that you are refolv'd to expofe by chiding his

weaknefs,

weakneſs, then he'll tranſgreſs openly, and
without ceremony; place not then your friendſhip in the careſſes, but in the merit of your
husband ; for in this lies the pleaſure of
Society. Perſuade your ſelf, that he goes
to his miſtreſs inſtigated by luſt, but that he
comes to you as a companion for life ; that
he loves you out of judgment, but her only
out of paſſion. But this laſt is of ſhort duration, as being ſoon ſatiated : 'tis ſuddenly begun,
and as ſuddenly ended. Thus a man, that is not
altogether profligate, will ſpend but little time
with a Miſtriſs : for what can be ſillier than that
inclination, in gratifying which a man procures
his own damage ? Moreover, he will at leiſure
reflect upon the ſhipwrack he makes of his fortune and of his fame : for no wiſe man will continue voluntarily in any fault to his own hurt.
Being therefore call'd upon by the rights he
owes you of marriage, and conſidering with re-
gret how his fortunes are impair'd, he'll thorow-
ly know thee at laſt, and, not able to bear
the diſgraceful remorſe of his crime, he'll
quickly reform. Do not you however, my
friend, be provok'd to lead a life anſwerable
to that of a Miſtriſs ; but diſtinguiſh your ſelf
by obedience to your husband, by care about
your family, by officiouſneſs to your acquaintance, and by natural affection to your children. Nor ought you even to be jealous of
the woman herſelf : for 'tis only commenda-
ble to have an emulation with virtuous women. Shew your ſelf (on the contrary) at all
times

times prepar'd for a reconciliation : for, my friend, noble qualities procure us the good will of our very enemies, and esteem is the effect of probity alone. Being only thus reprov'd by you, he'll grow the more asham'd, and be the sooner desirous of a reconciliation. Nay, he'll love you the more ardently, becoming conscious of his injustice towards you, as well as acknowledging the unblamableness of your life, and having receiv'd such a proof of your affection for him : for, as the end of bodily afflictions is pleasant, so the differences of Friends render their reconciliation the more agreeable. Be likewise pleas'd to make a parallel of the worst that may happen every way. When he's sick, you become sick too of course with grief ; if he suffers in his reputation, the world will make you likewise suffer ; if he acts against his interest, your interest as join'd to his, cannot escape unhurt : from all which you may learn this lesson, that in punishing him you punish your self. If, on the other hand, you get a divorce, and marry another man ; yet, in case he be guilty of the like practices, you must still marry another : for widowhood is not tolerable to young women. But you'll live alone, as if you were not join'd to any man ; you'll neglect your family, and ruin your husband : and I say, that you'll reap for your pains the plague of a miserable life. But you'll be reveng'd on his Mistrifs. She'll observe and avoid you ; or, if it comes to blows, a shameless woman will

be

be found a ſtout fighter. But 'tis a ſatisfaction to ſcold with one's husband continually : and what will you get by that ? for wranglings and contentions do not put an end to irregularity, but proportionably encreaſe the miſunderſtanding. What next then? you'll attempt ſomething againſt his perſon. By no means, my friend, Tragedy teaches us to maſter jealouſy by thoſe ſeveral repreſentations, in which Medea perpetrates her cruelties. But as hands muſt be refrain'd from ſore eyes, ſo do you get rid of this evil by taking no notice of it : for in being patient, you'll the ſooner extinguiſh his paſſion.

THE

THE
FABULOUS DEATH
OF
ATILIUS REGULUS:
OR,

A DISSERTATION *proving the re-*
ceiv'd History of the tragical Death
of MARCUS ATILIUS REGULUS
the Roman Consul, to be a Fable.

SIR,

THE second time I had the honour to
wait upon you at your Lodgings, I
found you reading CASAUBON'S
POLYBIUS, which occasion'd us to
discourse a while of History, and particularly
about that of this Author. Among several important observations you were pleas'd to make,
I could never afterwards forget the question
you propos'd to me about the tragical Death
of ATILIUS REGULUS, *Why* (1) POLYBIUS

(1) *Lib.* 1.

makes

*makes no mention thereof, when he is fo diffu-
five in the circumftances of his defeat and
captivity?* I was not afham'd to confefs then
that I had no folid anfwer to give; for as,
like the reft of mankind, I come to the knowledge of things fucceffively and occafionally:
fo I had no opportunity before that time to
enquire into this matter. Nor, perhaps, without that difficulty, fhould I have ever underftood fo much of it as I perfuade my felf now
I do. All true judges of Learning are fenfible, how beneficial good Converfation is
to the attaining of it. And I do now experience it, fince your undefign'd hints have
afforded me matter enough, without any
ftudied digreffions, for an extemporary and juft
Differtation.

A Note of PALMERIUS upon (2) APPIAN
directed me to a confiderable Fragment of the
24th book of DIODORUS SICULUS, which has
plainly convinc'd me, that the commonly receiv'd account of the death of ATILIUS is
nothing elfe but a female tattle, and a Roman
fable. And that you may not call in queftion
the authority of my Fragment, which I do
not know if ever you faw, I'll give you the
hiftory of it in a few words.

THE Emperor CONSTANTINUS, furnamed
Porphyrogennetus, the fon of LEO, and grand-

---

(2) *De bello Punico.*

fon of BASILIUS, having, contrary to the common genius of Princes, a more than ordinary inclination to Literature; was at the pains, whilft yet a minor, to difpofe under feveral heads, common-place-wife, whatever he was moft defirous to underftand : and made large collections out of all the Authors treating of them, that came to his hands. His labours of this kind amounted to no lefs than 106 Volumes, whereof only three are hitherto found and publifh'd; the firft by FULVIUS URSINUS, the fecond by DAVID HOESCHELIUS, both very learned men, and the third (which is ours) purchas'd at a vaft price in Cyprus by the learned FABRICIUS PEIRESCIUS, and publifh'd at Paris by the immortal ornament and promoter of Greek Erudition, VALESIUS, in the year 1631.

As for the genuinenefs of the Fragment we can't doubt of it; for our Emperor in his Collections is exact even to a nicety. The many paffages he has out of the extant Works of POLYBIUS, DIODORUS, JOSEPHUS and others, agree generally in terms with the copies we read every day, which leaves us no pretence of queftioning the reft, and excludes all other proof as fuperfluous.

AND for DIODORUS, he is univerfally own'd to be one of the beft and moft difinterefted Writers among the Ancients. He's none of thofe who only copy or contract a bulky

3   volume

volume or two, nor of such as obtrude precarious relations and conjectural inferences for matter of fact upon posterity. He's very unlike them who go no farther than their closets for materials, and he betrays no where the least partiality or mercenary end. He travell'd over a great part of Europe and Asia. He saw the most celebrated places mentioned in his works, and got authentick Memoirs concerning them upon the spot. He purposely liv'd a considerable while at Rome, then the Epitome of the Universe, where he could not miss of all necessary helps towards carrying on his great and useful design. Besides, he spent thirty years complete in making, for the ease and benefit of others, this curious Collection out of the most valuable Authors; and very fitly entituled it *The historical Library.* These particulars we learn from his own Preface. PLINY, after due commendations, calls it in the Proem of his natural History *The historical Libraries.* So it is cited in the plural by JUSTIN MARTYR, and EUSEBIUS, who likewise (3) says *That* DIODORUS *collected into one work the whole historical Library.* We need not wonder then if this industrious Author has preserv'd several matters not to be easily or in deed at all met with elsewhere; which serves but to make us more sensible of our loss in the best part of his labours.

(3) *Præparat. Evangelic.* lib. 1;

· I fhould now give you the Fragment with the Obfervations I made upon it. But to render the Difcourfe more natural and therefore more evident, I fhall firft relate the hiftory of ATILIUS, after which I'll offer my exceptions, then fhew the reafons of my diffent, and laftly fubjoin the whole Fragment with the addition of another.

I. After the two potent and emulous Republicks of Rome and Carthage had a long time with various fuccefs contended for the foveraignty of Spain, and the dominion of Scicily, Sardinia, and other Ifles of the Mediterranean; the Romans at length perceiving that their attempts were likely to prove fruftraneous, without more marine force and experience, (for the Carthaginians were undoubted mafters at fea) fitted out a great fleet of hatched veffels fuch as they never had before, and excellently well mann'd. They foon found by their fuccefs and recovering ftate, of what advantage good fhips and ftout feamen were like to be; which made them augment their forces that way more and more, as (4) POLYBIUS copioufly defcribes. Thus, flufh'd with fome late victories, and much relying upon their naval army, confifting of 140000 fighting men, they look'd no longer fo low as Scicily; but refolv'd to transfer the war into the enemies own country, fwallow-

(4) Lib. 1.

ing

ing in their hopes no meaner an acquisition than Carthage it self. In pursuance of this design MARCUS ATILIUS REGULUS and LUCIUS MANLIUS made a descent into Africa, after having beaten the Carthaginians at sea who endeavour'd to hinder their landing. The Punick commanders were ASDURUBAL, AMILCAR and BOSTAR, of which two last more hereafter. The Romans took in a short time several strong places, and, MANLIUS with part of the army and the prisoners returning to Italy, ATILIUS was left with the sole power of prosecuting the war; who, as fast as he could sit down before them, took from the Carthaginians (5) 200 towns, wasting the country to the very suburbs of their capital city, which made him brag, that he had seal'd the gate of Carthage, that none might escape. The poor Carthaginians were under a terrible consternation upon this stupendious progress of the enemies arms, and would readily conclude a peace upon any reasonable terms. But the (6) haughty ATILIUS, not knowing how to use his good fortune, propos'd such hard conditions as differ'd little from absolute slavery, which put the Africans to despair. But happily about this time arriv'd some Grecian mercenaries under XANTHIPPUS an expert and couragious Lacedemonian, who by the consent of the commanders themselves, to whose ill conduct the people attributed the Roman vic-

---

(5) *Appian. de bello Punico.*
(6) *See pag.* 18, &c.

C

tories, was set over all the forces, and shortly after totally routed the Romans, and took ATILIUS who became AMILCAR's prisoner. As soon as this defeat was known in Rome, they fitted out another fleet under the Consuls ÆMILIUS and FULVIUS, who at the Hermæan Promontory attack'd that of the Carthaginians and took all their ships being 114 with all the men on board 'em, and by consequence the (7) Generals AMILCAR and BOSTAR. So ASDRUBAL alone was left to manage the war by land.   Upon this last victory the Carthaginians sent their Ambassadors to Rome to treat of the peace, and ATILIUS their prisoner with 'em, upon oath to return if he could not persuade the Senate to grant their demands.   But he instead of this dissuaded them, and return'd with the Ambassadors, prepar'd to suffer for the good of his country whatever punishment the offended Carthaginians should inflict.   (8) CICERO with some others affirms that they cut his eyelids, and thrust him into a dungeon, where they constantly kept him awake in a certain machine till he dy'd. Others with (9) APPIAN say he was put into a barrel stuck every where full of sharp nails. (10) FLORUS has him crucify'd; and all tortur'd to death. This story has not only been thus transmitted to posterity by most of the Historians that

(7) *We hear no further of 'em in this War.*
(8) *Offic. lib.* 3.
(9) *De bello Punico.*
(10) *Lib.* 8.

wrote

wrote of the Roman affairs, but also still continues to be a celebrated example, in most
authors as well as familiar discourses, of fortitude, and greatness of mind.

II. But preserving the highest veneration
for the memory of this noble General's heroick actions, especially the love he bore to
his country, I'll make bold to give a very
different account of his end, which, from
the reasons you shall hear by and by, I think
was after this manner. After he did contrary to the instances of all his friends, so
gloriously return to Carthage, the Romans
having got into their hands AMILCAR and
BOSTAR at the Hermæan fight (as abovesaid)
to comfort his wife they committed them
(11) with other prisoners of the best quality
to her custody, to exchange them for her
husband, or detain them till he was let at
liberty. In the mean time ATILIUS dyes either
of some infirmity according to the course of
nature, or more probably being a high spi-
rited and proud man, he broke his heart for
the sudden and unusual disgrace he fell under.
But let this be as it will, I only maintain his
death was not violent. ATILIUS's children,
you may easily imagine, were extreamly troubled at their father's death in captivity and a
foreign land. But his wife was in despair,
refusing all consolation. She could not bear

(11) *Zonaras.*

C 2   the

the fight of a Carthaginian, and out of excefs of anger and grief, attributed the death of her husband to the negligence of his keepers. She therefore commanded her fons to ufe the captives as ill, which injunction they cruelly executed, as you'll fee in the Fragment. And tho' AMILCAR did frequently implore this enraged woman's compaffion, yet relentlefs to all his prayers, and the proteftations he made of the great care he took of her hufband whilft he was his prifoner; fhe continu'd to torment him till the matter was difcover'd to the Senate, who were, for this difhonour done to the Roman name, highly incens'd againft the mother and children. But fhe to excufe herfelf, and to avoid the imputation of cruelty among her neighbours and acquaintance, told them that fable of her husband's lamentable death, which was quickly fpread over the town by thofe women efpecially who came to comfort her; and who, 'tis likely, made this pretended tragedy the chief theme of their difcourfe at every goffipping. Thus it obtain'd credit firft among the women and vulgar; then it afforded the fubject of a Tragedy to the Stage, where it receiv'd all the advantage of fiction, that is allowable to Poets or Politicians; and at laft out of hatred to the Carthaginian name, it was commonly inferted by Hiftorians in their relations of that Punick War, and fo handed down to us.

III. My

III. My reasons for what I have here asserted are,

1. First, POLYBIUS's silence : for no Histo-
rian had better opportunities to know those
things than he.   He was SCIPIO the younger's
own tutor, and his companion too in his expeditions.   He was particularly present at the
destruction of Carthage by this great person ;
and there is such a connection between this
latter and the former Punick Wars, that a
man so familiar with the General, so learned
and curious as to write the history of both,
with much sincerity and no less accuracy,
could not be ignorant of so remarkable a circumstance, as the fate of ATILIUS must needs
be, if such a thing there were. Besides, (12) he
assures us himself, that he has gone over all
the particulars of ATILIUS's story, that those
who read it may thereby learn to become
better men, according to the vulgar saying,
*Happy is he who learns by the misfortunes of
others.*   Now, I refer it to the judgment of
every unbyas'd and thinking person, whether if POLYBIUS had this good intention towards mankind, as we have no reason to
doubt it, he would omit this common account of our Consul's death, if it had been
true ? Or whether he can be suppos'd to forget what he design'd so punctually to relate,
when in matters of little importance, where

(12) *Lib.* 1.

C 3   his

his word is no way engag'd, he's sometimes tediously circumstantial?

2. My second reason is the partiality of the first Historians, who treated of that Punick War, to wit, FABIUS and PHILINUS, *who,* says (13) POLYBIUS, *related not the truth to us with that sincerity they ought.* PHILINUS assures his reader that the Carthaginians manag'd all matters with unparallel'd wisdom, justice, and courage, and the Romans quite contrary. But FABIUS, as zealous for the credit of his countrey, gives PHILINUS the lye, and as much extolls the equity, prudence, and valour of the Romans, as he enlarges upon the cruelty, folly, and cowardise of the Carthaginians. POLYBIUS having occasion in another (14) place to correct one of FABIUS's voluntary mistakes about that war, has those fine words, which, one would think, were calculated for our times. *But why have I mention'd* FABIUS, *says he, and his history? not that I believe his narrative so like the truth as to gain belief from some. For what he writes in this place is so contrary to reason, that tho' I were silent, the readers will easily perceive the man's insincerity, which plainly enough discovers itself. But this I write to admonish those, into whose hands his history may come, that they judge not as the*

(13) *Lib.* 1.
(14) *Lib.* 3.

title

title of the book promises, but according to the nature of the things themselves. For there are some who rather consider him that speaks than what he says; and because they know the author liv'd in those times and was a Roman Senator, they forthwith receive whatever he delivers as most deserving of credit. But for my own part, as I would not have this author's veracity slightly call'd in question, so neither would I establish it in such a manner as to pin the reader's faith upon it; but rather that every one should chuse those things his judgment inclines him to believe. Thus far our Author.

Now, let this same FABIUS, or who else you please, be the first writer of this story, the next Roman author that mention'd it did probably copy him, as all the rest might one another without much enquiring into the original of the thing, which all the quotations in the world can render no truer than the first relation. I say not this as if I thought 'em always partial or fabulous. I acknowledge they were not so barren of truly brave and vertuous instances in their citizens to be fond of a fantastick Hero. But in matters of this nature which are establish'd by popular tradition, wherein religion or the honour of a nation are concern'd, and the belief whereof can have no ill consequences, 'tis not always safe, nor perhaps will it be thought so necessary to insist too nicely upon truth.

Modern

Modern as well as ancient Hiftories furnifh us with numerous examples to this purpofe. The brevity I defign permits me not to improve on my behalf the different accounts, that the authors give us of Regulus's torments. The laft of 'em is fufficient to punifh the blackeft crime, and it was impoffible for one to fuffer 'em all, being not only too many, but contrary to each other. There is fomething more than miftaking a word, or exaggerating Rhetorick in this variety. Vulgar Romance, which is made or embelifh'd at pleafure in all ages, and taking things upon truft, are the fofteft expreffions I can beftow upon it.

3. My third reafon is pofitive, and built upon the Fragment in which I chiefly confider three paffages.

1. Firft, Atilius's own wife (as you'll obferve) has nothing to lay to the charge of her illuftrious captives the Carthaginian Generals but a bare fufpicion that her husband dy'd for want of being well look'd after, or as fhe expreffes it, through (15) neglect. And do you think if there had been any thing in the famous Legend, but fhe would make them bloody reproaches upon this head?

2. Secondly, Amilcar with tears protefts that he in particular took all poffible care of her husband whilft his prifoner; nor would

(15) Ἀμελεία.

he

he fail to excufe others or lay the blame on the ftate where it fhould be, if there had been occafion for it. And tho' he fees he can by no means mollifie this mercilefs woman, and looks upon himfelf as a loft man ; yet he ftill calls God to witnefs his innocency, and, that for the thanks his care of their father deferv'd of ATILIUS's children, complains he's moft ungratefully repaid with exquifite torments.

3. Thirdly, the indignation of the Magiftrates againft the ATILII upon the difcovery of their barbarity, and their imputing all the fault to their mother; with the fpeedy care they took to burn the dead according to cuftom, and carefully to cherifh the living. Now, 'tis prefum'd, the Senate would not exprefs this high refentment if ATILIUS had perifh'd thro' violence or neglect. And had we the reft of this 24th Book of DIODORUS, we fhould, queftionlefs, hear the fact excus'd to the Carthaginians, or, at leaft, their complaints. But that, I fear, is irrecoverable with the reft of LIVY, POLYBIUS, TACITUS, APPIAN, MARCELLIN, and many others, (to fpeak nothing of entire authors) unlefs more of CONSTANTINE's collections be difcover'd in Greece, where, 'tis probable, they may be all ftill with much better Books.

THESE (as they clearly appear in the Fragment) feem to me reafons fufficient to convince

vince all ingenuous perfons, that the tragical ftory of the Death of REGULUS is partly invented, partly miftaken, and altogether a fable. I could add feveral other cogent arguments from the politicks and manners of the Carthaginians, with their dangerous ftate at that juncture, to give fo grievous a provocation to the Romans; but that I look upon more proofs as needlefs, when the matter of fact is already made fo evident.

IV. Now finally, to illuftrate the whole, and confirm our Differtation, I fubjoin the verfion of the *Fragment* itfelf, which is as faithful as you could make it elegant.

A Fragment of the 24th Book of DIODORUS SICULUS *in the collection and edition mention'd above.*

" BUT the mother of the (16) young men
" bearing heavily the death of her husband,
" which fhe attributed to neglect and care-
" leffnefs, commanded her fons to ufe the
" captives as ill as they could. Firft then,
" they were fhut into a fmall room fo nar-
" row that for want of place they were forc'd
" to conglobate their bodies, and lye round
" as beafts are wont to do. And then being
" deny'd food for five days, BOSTAR out of
" anguifh of fpirit, and hunger together, ex-

(16) *The Atilii.*

" pir'd.

" pir'd. But AMILCAR being endu'd with a
" fingular greatnefs of mind, altho' deftitute
" of all hope, yet kept himfelf up as well as
" he could, and did frequently beg compaffi-
" on from the woman with tears, telling her
" what great care he had taken of her huf-
" band. Yet he was fo far from inclining
" her to any fenfe of humanity, that the
" cruel woman did fhut up BOSTAR's carcafs
" with him five days longer, affording him
" in the mean time food enough to preferve
" life in him, to make him fenfible of his
" calamity and torment. But AMILCAR feeing
" now all hopes of mercy cut off from his
" entreaties calls JUPITER *the protector of*
" *ftrangers*, and all the powers that regard
" human affairs to witnefs; loudly exclaim-
" ing that for the thanks due to him he was
" rewarded with moft cruel torments. Now
" whether by the compaffion of the Gods,
" or fome good luck that brought him unex-
" pected affiftance, he dy'd not by thefe tor-
" tures : for when he was in the utmoft peril
" of his life, what by the noifome ftench of
" BOSTAR's body, and what by the other
" ftreights he was under, fome of his fer-
" vants coming to know of it told the thing
" to certain foreigners. Thefe, highly mov'd
" at the indignity of fuch wickednefs, fpee-
" dily difcover'd the whole matter to the
" Tribune of the people. And becaufe the
" fact appear'd extreamly barbarous, the Ma-
" giftrates fummon'd the ATILII before them,
" who

" who narrowly efcap'd capital punifhment
" for having infamoufly branded the Roman
" name with this mark of cruelty. More-
" over, the Magiftrates threatn'd them fe-
" verely if they did not hereafter take fpe-
" cial care of the captives. But they laying
" all the blame of the matter upon their
" mother, burnt the body of BOSTAR and fent
" his afhes to his country; and, delivering
" AMILCAR from his former mifery, they
" brought him by degrees to his ufual ftrength
" again.

SIR, you may remember I accus'd ATILIUS of mixing fome Pride with his many extraordinary Virtues; and diffuading the Peace at Rome, with his return to Carthage, are ftill fufficient to magnifie his name without the addition of a fable. This I did not therefore to leffen his character, which I defervedly admire; for there's fome bafe allay in the fineft gold: but I have great reafon to collect fo much from fome Authors, and am put out of all doubt by another judicious Fragment of the fame Book of DIODORUS, and out of the fame collection, whereof I give you this indifferent Tranflation.

The fecond Fragment.

" I hold it the duty of a Hiftorian (fays our
" Author) diligently to fet down and mark
" the manners and inclinations of the Com-

' manders

" manders on both fides.   For as by blaming
" the ill conduct of any, others may avoid
" committing the like faults ; fo on the other
" hand, the commendation of what is right-
" ly perform'd enflames the mind to purfue
" Virtue.   Now who would not juftly re-
" prehend the impudence and arrogance of
" ATILIUS REGULUS, who, not able to bear
" his good fortune, as if it had been fome hea-
" vy burthen, both depriv'd himfelf of great
" praife, and caft his country into mighty
" dangers? For when he had it in his power, be-
" fides procuring the glory of much clemency
" and humanity, to conclude a peace very glo-
" rious and advantageous to the Romans, but
" bafe and difhonourable to the Carthaginians;
" he fet light by all thefe confiderations, and
" proudly infulting over the misfortunes of
" the diftreffed, impos'd fuch hard conditions
" as mov'd the indignation of the Gods, and
" forc'd the vanquifh'd to act moft valiantly.
" Thus through the mifcarriages of this one
" man, there happen'd fuch a fudden change
" of affairs, that the Carthaginians, who, by
" reafon of their late defeat, had defpair'd of
" any fafety, now having unlook'd for fup-
" plies, quite routed the enemies forces : and
" the Romans, who, before were reputed to
" excell all the world in land fights, were fo
" difcomfited and fhatter'd as not to dare
" after this to venture a land battle with their
" enemies. Whereupon this war became more
" tedious than any of the precedent, and was
" con-

" converted into a naval one, in which in-
" numerable ſhips of the Romans and their
" allies, and above 100000 men periſh'd over
" and above what fell by land. Beſides, it
" coſt ſuch vaſt ſums of money as were thought
" ſufficient to entertain as great fleets tho'
" the war ſhould laſt fifteen years. Now the
" Author of theſe evils bore a large ſhare of
" them; for he obſcur'd his former glory
" with much greater infamy and diſhonour:
" and by his infelicity became a warning to
" others not to be puft up by ſucceſs. What
" is moſt to be noted, having cut off from
" himſelf that favour and compaſſion which
" is uſually beſtow'd upon the afflicted, he
" was forc'd to bear their reproaches and ſub-
" mit to their power, whoſe calamities he in-
" ſulted over a little before.

THUS, Sir, without favour or affection,
(you may be ſure) I have confuted this old
tradition; and remov'd all the cruelty from
Africa, where it lay ſo long, into Italy whoſe
title to it I find much better. There are many
other hiſtories as little queſtion'd as ever this
was, which, we are very certain, have not a
quarter ſo much ground nor probability to
recommend 'em for truth. And yet many
in the world place all their learning and ſomething more in the bare belief of ſuch childiſh
and old-wives fables. Truly we ſhall not envy them this ſublime knowledge, nor the refin'd ſpeculations it affords them. Nay, with

3   our

our confent they may not only value themfelves upon it, but laugh at our ignorance too, like PARSONS the Jefuit, who pleafantly, becaufe ferioufly, affirms in his anfwer to COOKE, that *one Papift of mean learning is more wife and knowing than an hundred Hereticks together. For the Heretick,* fays he, *is only guided by his own fenfe and reafon, but the Papift follows the learning and wifdom of his whole Church confifting of an infinite number of great men, and fo makes their learning and wifdom his own.* I wonder he might not as well conclude, that the pooreft Papift is more learned than a million of Proteftants, or than all the Popes themfelves, from thefe notable premiffes. But fuch is the admirable reafoning of our implicit-faith-men in every thing! They differ only about their fubjects whilft they perfectly agree in their difquifitions. But this is fo evident and you fo perfpicacious, that I need infift upon it no longer: and therefore fhall only add that with all imaginable affection, I am,

Sir,

You moft humble Servant.

OXON, *Aug. the* 6th, 1694.

SOME

SOME LETTERS
OF PLINY

Tranflated into Englifh.

To Mr. * * *

Sir,

I fend you fome Letters of PLINY, as a fpecimen of the Tranflation I am making of the whole; and defire your judgment on this Effay. I make no doubt but you will agree with me, that for what they call a happy turn, delicacy of expreffion, and fpeaking only to the bufinefs in hand, no modern comes near our PLINY, no more than in the variety of his fubjects, fuch as intrigues of ftate, points of literature and hiftory, queftions in natural philofophy, rural pleafures, the concerns of his friend, and fome trifles which he renders important. The fhort Notes I fhall add at the

foot

foot of every page will juſtifie my Tranſlation, which I endeavour to make as conciſe as his Latin, not comparable indeed with that of CICERO, but nothing behind him in ſenſe or matter. I conclude as he does in one of his Letters, that I give you this account, SIR, becauſe our mutual friendſhip requires you ſhou'd not only be made acquainted with all my words and actions, but even with my deſigns. Farewell.

Epſom Sept. 10.
1712.

TO SEPTIMIUS.
Lib. 1. *Ep.* 1.

YOU have frequently exhorted me, that, if I had written any Letters with more accuracy than others, I wou'd collect and publiſh them. I have made ſuch a collection, yet without obſerving any order of time (for I was not writing a hiſtory) but juſt as they happen'd to come each to hand. It now remains, that neither you repent of your advice, nor I of my compliance : which if we do not, will occaſion me to look out for theſe Letters I have thrown aſide as uſeleſs, and not to ſuppreſs thoſe I may write hereafter.

Farewell.

TO CANINIUS RUFUS.
Lib. 1. *Ep.* 3.

HOW fares Comum, my delight and yours? that country feat fo exceeding lovely? that gallery, where 'tis always fpring? that moft fhady grove of plane-trees, that canal, fo green and clear as a diamond? the lake hard by, which feems defign'd for a refervatory to fupply it? thofe firm and yet eafy walks? that bath which never wants the fun in his round? thofe large dining rooms for company, and thofe leffer withdrawing rooms for a few friends? how goes it with the drinking rooms? how with thofe bedchambers for night, and thofe antichambers for day? Do thefe poffefs and fhare you by turns? or are you 'hinder'd (as you were wont) with frequent excurfions abroad, by an over-earneft defire of encreafing your eftate? If thefe poffefs you, then are you eafy and happy: but if they do not, you are only one of many that admire 'em. Why do you not rather (for it is high time) commit thofe low and fordid cares to others, and apply your felf to books in that quiet and plentiful retreat? let this be your bufinefs and leifure, your labour and recreation: let ftudies employ your thoughts by day, and be the fubject of your dreams by night. Invent and finifh fomething, that may be perpetually yours: for the reft of your poffeffions will, after your death, fucceffively

fall

fall to the fhare of many owners; but if this once begins, it can never ceafe to be yours. I know how great a foul, and how fine a genius I exhort. Do you only endeavour to have as good an opinion of your felf, as others muft needs entertain of you, if once you are confcious of your own worth.

Farewell.

TO CORNELIUS TACITUS.
Lib. 1. *Ep.* 6.

YOU'll laugh, and you may laugh as long as you pleafe. I, that fame PLINY whom you know fo well, have caught three wild boars, and extraordinary fine ones. Who, you your felf? fay you. Yes, I my felf: but I fat by the toils, not fo as entirely to quit my eafe and quiet; for I had lying by me, not a hunting-pole and a lance, but a pocket-book and a pencil. I meditated fomething and noted it down, that, if I went home with empty hands, yet I might bring with me full pages. You'll fee no reafon to defpife this manner of ftudying. 'Tis wonderful, how the mind is roufed by the exercife and motion of the body. The woods and the folitude all around you, and that very. filence which is requifite in hunting, are great enticements to thinking. Whenever therefore you go a hunting hereafter, you may upon my authority carry with you a pocket-book and a pencil, as well as a pouch and a bottle.

You'll

You'll find that MINERVA does no lefs wan-
der upon the mountains, than DIANA.

TO . MINUTIUS FUNDANUS.
Lib. 1. *Ep.* 9.

'TIS a wonderful thing how reafonably
we act or at leaft feem to act, in the
city upon particular days ; but not fo every
day, nor many days together. For if you ask
any one, *what have you been doing to day?*
and that he anfwers, *I was to congratulate
with a friend for his fon's arriving to man's
eftate, I was prefent at a contract or a wed-
ding, one call'd me to be a witnefs to his will,
another to affift him in a law-fuit, another to
have my advice in fome other matter:* thefe
things will juft then feem neceffary offices;
but, if confider'd as done every day, they
muft appear to be pure lofing of time, and
you'll be convinc'd of it much more when
you retire into the country. For then I call
to mind, how many days I have fpent in
moft trivial affairs; which reflection I efpecially have, when, in my Laurentin villa, I read
any thing, or write, or even take care of my
body, the prop and fupport of the mind.
There I hear nothing of which I wou'd chufe
to be ignorant, nor fpeak any thing I wifh
unfaid again. No body detracts from me at
another man's table by malicious difcourfes,
and I find fault with no body but only with
my felf, when I can't write to my mind. I

2   am

am perplex'd with no fears, I am not dif-
quieted with any reports: I fpeak only with
my felf and my books. O upright and fincere life! O fweet and honourable leifure!
preferable (I had almoft faid) to any bufinefs
whatfoever! O fea! O fhore! you true and
private ftudying-place! how many things you
dictate to me? how many things you occafion
me to invent? Do you therefore, as foon as
ever you can, leave that noife, thofe vain
prattles, with all the pains you are at to fo
little purpofe, and betake your felf to ftudy
or recreation: fince 'tis better (as our friend
ATILIUS has no lefs learnedly than facetioufly
faid) for a man to be idle than to be bufy in
doing nothing.   Farewell.

TO FABIUS JUSTUS.
Lib. 1. *Ep.* 11.

'TIS a great while fince you have fent
me any Letters. I have nothing (fay
you) to write. Why then write this very
fame, that you have nothing to write; or at
leaft that with which our fore-fathers us'd to
begin, *if you are in health 'tis well, I am
likewife in health.* This will be enough for
me, for 'tis all in all. You'll think I am
jefting, but I defire it of you very ferioufly.
Let me know then what you are a doing, of
which I cannot be ignorant without the greateft uneafinefs.   Farewell,

D 3   TO

TO AVITUS.
Lib. 2. Ep. 6.

IT wou'd be both tedious, and to little purpose, to give you a particular account, how I (that am not wont to be every man's guest) shou'd happen to sup with a certain person, who in his own opinion is liberal and yet frugal, but to me appears to be at the same time both sordid and prodigal: for he order'd the richest dishes to be set before himself and a few friends, but the least and the cheapest before the rest of the company. He likewise order'd his wine, which was in very small bottles, to be distributed into three sorts; not to give us the liberty of chusing, but that we might not have the power of refusing: since one sort was for himself and us, another for his lower friends (for he has his friends by tires) and a third for theirs and our gentlemen. He that sat next me took notice of this management, and ask'd me whether I approv'd it. By no means, said I. Pray then, reply'd he, what method do you follow? Why, I order the same things to be serv'd to all that are at the table: for I invite people to a meal, but not to a reproach; and I equalize those in all things, whom I admit to my bed or my board. What, your Gentlemen too? Certainly: for then I look upon 'em as my companions, and not as my dependants. O, but this is expensive. Not

at

at all. How can that be? The reason is, because my gentlemen don't drink the same
wine as I, but I the same as they: and truly
if you be not very extravagant, 'twill be no
great burthen to share with others what you
use your self. 'Tis Luxury therefore that must
be moderated, and kept under as it were, if
you wou'd save charges; which is much better done by your own temperance, than by
the disgrace of others. But to what tends all
this? E'en that the boundless luxury of some
people may not, under the notion of frugality, impose on so hopeful a young Gentleman
as your self: and my affection for you requires of me, when any thing of this nature
happens, to precaution you by such an example what you ought to avoid. Remember
therefore, that nothing is more to be avoided than this new fellowship between luxury
and sordidness; which, as they are most pitiful things disjoin'd and asunder, so they are
much more contemptible when united.

Farewell.

TO CANINIUS.
Lib. 2. *Ep.* 8.

DO you study? or go a fishing? or ride
a hunting? or do all these together?
since our Larius gives you an opportunity for
'em all: for this lake affords plenty of fish,
the woods that surround it game, and that
most profound retreat study. But whether
D 4
you

you follow 'em all or any one thing, I cannot say, I envy you : neverthelefs 'tis a torment to me that I cannot likewife enjoy thofe things, for which I long with as much ardor as feverifh perfons do for wine, or baths, or fountains. Shall I never be able to break, if I cannot diffolve, thefe intolerable bonds ? I think I never fhall. For frefh bufineffes throng on the back of the old, before thefe are quite finifh'd : and the weight of my affairs is encreas'd upon me every day, like an addition of fo many cords and chains.

Farewell.

The beginning of PLINY's Letter to GALLUS, defcribing his Country Houfe near Laurentum.

Lib. 2. Ep. 17.

YOU admire why the Laurentin (or Laurens, if you'll have it fo) fhou'd fo extreamly delight me. But you'll ceafe your wonder, when you know the agreeablenefs of this Country Houfe, the conveniencies of the place, and the extent of the fhore on which it is fituated. Its diftance from the city is but feventeen miles ; fo that after having done all your bufinefs, you may arrive there before it be late or the fun is down. You come to it by more ways than one, for the way of Laurentum and that of Oftia lead

hither ;

hither ; but after travelling fourteen miles you quit the Laurentin, and after eleven the Oftian road. Leaving the one and the other you fall into a way that is fomewhat fandy, pretty deep and tedious for carriages, but to people on horfeback eafy and fhort. The profpect is vary'd from place to place, for by the woods you meet, the road is fometimes ftraighten'd, and fometimes again it grows extraordinary large acrofs moft fpacious meadows. You meet many flocks of fheep, with great herds of cows and horfes, which after winter thrive well and grow mighty fleek by the grafs of the downs, and the kindly warmth of the fpring. My Villa is large enough for all conveniencies, yet not coftly to maintain. There is, in the firft place, an entry which is plain indeed, but not flovenly : &c.

Here follows the defcription of the houfe, gardens, enclofures, &c.

The conclufion of the fame Letter.

ARE you now convinc'd that for good reafons I cultivate, inhabit, and love this retirement ? which, you muft needs be too much addicted to the city, unlefs you defire to fee ; and I wifh you may defire it, that to fo great and many ornaments of our little houfe may be added the higheft commendation from the honour of your company.

Farewell.

T O

TO CALVISIUS.
Lib. 3. *Ep.* 1.

I don't remember that ever I paſt my time more pleaſantly, than when I was lately with SPURINNA: inſomuch, I aſſure you, that, if it be my lot to grow an old man, there's none, whom in old age I wou'd ſooner imitate: for nothing is more methodical than that kind of life, and I am as much delighted with the orderly life of men, of old men eſpecially, as with the conſtant courſe of the ſtars. Indeed, hurry and confuſion are not wholly unbecoming young men, but all things ſtill and regular are expected of the old, in whom pains taking is of the lateſt, and ambition is ſcandalous. The rule I am going to tell you, is moſt conſtantly obſerv'd by SPURINNA, and theſe little things (little, if they were not daily practis'd) are reduc'd by him into a certain order and rotation as it were. In the morning he ſits for ſome time on his couch, at ſix a-clock he calls for his ſhoes, he walks three miles, and exerciſes his mind no leſs than his body. If he has any friends with him, they are entertain'd with excellent diſcourſes, but if not, ſome book is read; and this ſometimes when he has the company of his friends, provided they don't diſlike it. Then he ſits down a while, and ſo comes the book again, or a

2   diſcourſe

difcourfe that excells any book. Soon after
he mounts his chariot, and takes in his wife
of exemplary virtue, or fome of his friends,
as very lately my felf. O how amiable, how
fweet is that privacy! How much of antiquity will you learn there! Of what actions,
of what men will you hear! What precepts
will you be taught! tho' he prefcribes this
temperament to his own modefty, as never
to feem to dictate. After he has thus rode
feven miles, he walks another mile, and fits
down again, or betakes him to his clofet and
his pen : for he writes, and that in both
languages, Lyrics efpecially with a great deal
of art. They are wonderful foft, wonderful fweet, wonderful facetious : and their
graces are augmented by the probity of the
writer. When he's warn'd of the hour for
the bagnio (which in winter is eleven a-clock,
and one in fummer) if it be not windy weather, he walks naked in the fun. Then he
plays long and vehemently at tennis, for by
this kind of exercife, he likewife makes war
upon old age. After he has wafh'd he fits
down to table, but does not eat immediately : and in the mean time hears fomething
read with a diftinct and foft voice. His friends
may all this while freely do the fame things,
or whatever elfe they like better. At laft
comes in fupper, no lefs neat than frugal,
ferv'd up in old and upright plate. He likewife ufes Corinthian ware, with which he's
pleas'd but not betwitch'd. The intervals of
fupper

supper are frequently fill'd up by the performances of Comedians, that pleasure itself may
be season'd with wit.   Even in summer this
takes up a good part of the night, but is
tiresome to no body, the entertainment
being continu'd with a world of agreeableness.   Hence it is, that now after his seven
and seventieth year, he has the perfect use of
his eyes and ears ; hence it is, that his body
is brisk and active, and that he has nothing
of old age but experience.   For this kind of
life I pray, and act it already in my thoughts;
being resolv'd to begin it chearfully in good
earnest, as soon as my years may warrant me
to sing a retreat.   In the mean time I am
fatigu'd with a thousand labours, of which
the same SPURINNA is both my comfort and
example : for he likewise, as long as it was
dishonourable to do otherwise, perform'd the
usual duties, fill'd diverse magistracies, govern'd
provinces, and earn'd his present leisure by
a great deal of pains.   I therefore prescribe
to my self the self-same course and the self-
same end ; and give you an assurance of this
even now under my hand, that if you perceive me to go longer on in business, you
may plead this very letter of mine as a law
against me, and command me to be quiet,
as soon as I can avoid the imputation of
laziness.

Farewell.

.T O

TO CATILIUS.
Lib. 3. *Ep.* 12.

I Shall come to fupper to you : but I bargain now before hand, that it be fhort, that it be frugal, that it abound only in Socratic difcourfes, and that even of thefe there be no excefs. There are likewife certain duties belonging to the night, wherein CATO himfelf cou'd not be found imploy'd without blame, whom yet CAIUS CÆSAR fo reproaches as to commend him : for he reprefents certain, who met him blufhing, when upon uncovering his head, they difcover'd he was drunk; and then adds he, *you would think that* CATO *had furpris'd them, and not they* CATO. Could more authority be attributed to CATO, than that even drunk he appear'd fo venerable ? But let the time of our fupper be limited, as well as the preparation and the expence : for we are not thofe, whom our very enemies cannot cenfure without praifing us at the fame time.

Farewell.

TO LICINIUS.
Lib. 4. *Ep.* 30.

I Have brought you, as a prefent out of my country, a queftion very worthy of
your

your profound erudition. A spring rises in a hill, it runs thro' rocks, is receiv'd in a basin made by hands, and, interrupted there a while, it falls into the Larian lake. The nature of this Fountain is admirable. It increases and decreases thrice a day at certain floods and ebbs. This is plainly seen, and the experiment is try'd with extraordinary delight. You seat your self near it and eat there; nay, and drink too out of the fountain, for 'tis extream cold. In the mean while it does at certain and proportionable spaces of time fall or swell. You lay your ring, or any thing else, on the dry sand, the water comes towards it by degrees, and covers it; at last the ring begins to appear again, and is by little and little quite left by the water. If you stay long enough, you may observe the same thing a second and a third time. May there be any hidden breath, that sometimes opens the mouth and jaws of the fountain, and sometimes closes them again, according as by inspiration it rushes in, or by expiration 'tis forc'd out? as we see to happen in bottles, and in other vessels of that sort, which have not an open and ready passage: for they likewise, tho' inclin'd and held downwards, do by certain delays of the obstructing air (exprest in frequent gulpes) stop what's to be pour'd out of them. Or is the fountain of the same nature with the ocean? and by whatever cause this last is driven to the shores and swallow'd

back

back again, ſo this ſmall water is ſunk or
rais'd. Or as rivers, running into the ſea, are
by contrary winds and tides forc'd back towards their ſource, ſo is there any thing that
at certain times may drive back the ſtream of
this fountain? Or are the latent veins of ſuch
a certain capacity, that while they are collecting the quantity they loſt, the ſtream grows
leſs and ſlower, but quicker and greater when
the veins are full again? Or is there, I know
not what occult and imperceptible libration,
which when it is light, raiſes and forces the
ſpring; and when it is depreſt, ſtops and
choaks it? Do you ſearch the cauſes of ſo
great a wonder, for you are able: 'tis
enough for me, if I have clearly enough expreſt the matter of fact.   Farewell.

The Beginning of PLINY's Letter to APOLLINARIS, deſcribing his Tuſcan Villa.

Lib. 5. Ep. 6.

I Was pleas'd with your care and uneaſi-
neſs, when, having underſtood that I deſign'd to go this ſummer to my Tuſcan Country Houſe, you perſuaded me not to do it,
as thinking the place unwholſome. Indeed;
the coaſt of Tuſcany along the ſhore is foggy
and infectious, but this place is far diſtant
from the ſea, and ſtands juſt at the foot of
the

the Apennin, which is the healthieſt of mountains. And that you may be rid of all fear
on my behalf, take this account concerning
the temperature of the climate, the ſituation
of the country, and the agreeableneſs of the
Villa, which muſt needs be very pleaſing for
you to hear, and me to relate. The air in
winter is cold and ſharp, neither will it bear
or produce myrtles, olives, or ſuch other
plants as thrive by a perpetual warmth : but
it agrees with bay-trees, and ſometimes produces very green ones, but none decay oft-
ener than they do about the city. The ſummer is wonderfully temperate; and the air
is always in ſome kind of agitation, but which
occaſions breezes more frequently than winds.
This is the ſeaſon that you meet with many
old people, and that the youth ſee their
grandfathers and great grandfathers. You
may hear the old ſtories and diſcourſes of
our anceſtors, and, when you come hither
you'll think your ſelf born in the former age.
The proſpect of this country is extraordinary
fine. Imagin to your ſelf a certain vaſt am-
phitheater, and ſuch as nature alone is able
to form : then a large and ſpacious plain
incompaſt with hills, and the tops of thoſe
hills cover'd with lofty groves and antient
trees, which ſupply continual hunting, and
of diverſe ſorts. The ſides of the hills are
ſtock'd with coppice woods, among which are
mellow and clayiſh hillocks (for you can
ſcarce find a ſtone, tho' you purpoſely look
for

for one) which in fruitfulnefs are not inferior to any fields on the plains, and yield a plentiful crop, later indeed, but not lefs full or ripe. Below thefe the whole declivity is cover'd with vineyards, which give the fame uniform profpect on every fide; and fhrubs grow in abundance about the extremities, like a fort of fringe. Next come fields and meadows. The fields are fuch as can be only broken by huge oxen and ftrong plows, this moft ftiff earth turning up into fuch vaft clods as require nine breakings before they are tam'd. The meadows are befpangl'd and enamel'd with flowers, producing clover and other herbs, which are foft and tender as if they were always young : for they are all water'd with never-drying ftreams. Neverthelefs, where the greateft quantity of water is to be found, there is no marfh; becaufe, being fteep land, whatever moifture it cannot foak, glides down into the Tyber. This river, which is navigable, runs thro' the middle of the country, and carries all our productions to the city, tho' only in winter and the fpring : for it grows low in fummer, and leaves in its dry bed, the name of a great river, which it reaffumes in autumn. You'll be greatly charm'd if you behold the fituation of this country from the top of the hill : for you'll not imagin to fee land, but fome piece that is painted with the moft exquifite delicacy. With this variety, with this difpofition, the eyes are refrefh'd wherever they turn.

My Villa which ſtands towards the foot of the
hill enjoys as fair a proſpect as if it were on the
top : it riſes ſo eaſily and by ſuch ſlow degrees, that you find yourſelf got up without
perceiving that you mounted. The Apennin
is behind, but a good way off. In the moſt
ſtill and faireſt days there come breezes from
thence ; yet neither piercing nor impetuous,
but ſpent and out of breath by the diſtance
itſelf. The greateſt part of the houſe looks
towards the ſouth, &c.

A Court, Shade, and Wildernefs, in the ſame Deſcription and Letter.

Before this lovely front of the houſe, there
is anſwerable to the whole extent of it a
very ſpacious Court, wherein horſes are to
be manag'd, and may even run races in a
circular courſe. It is open in the middle;
which at one view wholly diſcovers it to
thoſe that are coming into it. It is planted
round with plane-trees, and theſe are ſo cover'd with ivy, that their lower parts are
green with its leaves, as the tops are with
their own. The ivy creeps up from the
trunks to the branches, and by paſſing over
from one tree to another, links 'em all together. The diſtances between them are fill'd
up with box, and they are lin'd quite along
behind with a hedge of bay, which joins
its ſhade to that of the plane-trees. This
court

court extending in a right line, is terminated in a femicircle, and changes its landíchape, being at the end furrounded and cover'd with cyprefs, occafioning there a clofer, more dark and gloomy fhade; tho' the open round fpots of this wildernefs (which are very many) receive the cleareft light, which makes rofes thrive here, and fo the coolnefs of the fhade is temper'd with the grateful warmth of the fun. All thefe numerous and various windings are at laft reduc'd to a ftraight line, and not in this plot alone, for there are feveral others feparated by allies, on either fide befet with box or rofemary. Here you have green parterres, and there compartments of box, which are cut into a thoufand figures, fometimes into letters denoting the name of the owner, and fometimes that of the gardiner. Among thefe there mount by turns pyramids of yew and the fhapes of trees loaden with fruit. But in fo regular a piece of art there ftill appears a ftudy'd negligence, with a fort of imitation of nature and the country, the middle fpace being adorn'd with dwarf plane-trees; befides which, there is ftore of foft and creeping acanthus, then feveral more figures, and a greater number of names.

E 2

TO

TO ANTONINUS.
Lib. 5.   *Ep.* 10.

THERE's nothing makes me more sensible how good your Verses are, than
when I strive to make the like: for as painters
can never reach the perfection of a fair and
faultless face; so I lagg, and fall short of your
original.   I therefore so much the rather exhort you to produce a great many more, which
all may passionately endeavour, but none, or
very few, be able to imitate.

Farewell.

TO MACRUS.
Lib. 5.   *Ep.* 18.

TIS well with me, because 'tis well with
you.   You have your wife with you,
and you have your son. You receive delight
from the sea, from the springs, from the
green trees, from the fields, and from a most
pleasant country-house: for indeed I cannot doubt, but that house is most pleasant,
which was the retirement of that man, who
was more, before he was made most happy.
Here in Tuscany, I both hunt and study,
which I do sometimes by turns, and sometimes both together: yet to this hour am

I not

I not able to decide, whether it be more difficult to take any thing or to write.

Farewell.

TO MAURICUS.
Lib. 6. Ep. 14.

YOU press me to come to your Formian Villa ; and I shall go, on condition that you put yourself to no sort of inconvenience, which is making the like bargain for my self, against your coming to me : for 'tis neither the sea nor the shore, but you, and ease, and liberty, that I would enjoy. Otherwise it were more elegible to stay in the city. We must do every thing according to our own or other folks humour : and this on my word is the nature of my stomach, that it can bear nothing but what's plain and unmix'd.

Farewell.

TO NEPOS.
Lib. 6. Ep. 19.

DO you know that the price of lands is risen, especially, near this city? The cause of this surprizing rise, which is the subject of much discourse, did at the last meeting of the Senate, occasion several most excellent speeches, importing, That *the candidates at elections should neither treat,*

E 3
nor

nor make prefents, nor lay out any money.
The two firft of thefe abufes were not lefs
exceffively than openly practis'd; and the
third, notwithftanding the care us'd to conceal it, was a thing taken for granted. Now
our friend HOMULUS, having diligently improv'd this unanimous agreement of the
Senate, mov'd for a refolution, that the Con-
fuls fhould be order'd to acquaint the Prince
with the defires of them all, and to pray him,
that according to his ufual vigilance, he
would correct this, as he had other diforders.
The Emperor affented, for he put a ftop to
thofe bafe and infamous expences of the candidates, by a law againft canvaffing, and oblig'd them to qualify themfelves by laying
out on land, a third part of their eftates;
efteeming it a very fhameful thing, as indeed
it was, that fuch as are defirous of this honour, fhould live in Rome and Italy, not as
their country, but as a lodging, or like travellers in an inn. The candidates hereupon,
outbid one another every where, and buy
up whatever they are inform'd is to be fold;
infomuch, that many now part with their
lands, who did not think of doing it before.
If you are weary therefore of your farms in
Italy, this is certainly your time of putting
them off to advantage, as well as of buying
in the provinces, while the candidates are
felling there to purchafe here.

Farewell.

T O

TO MACRUS.

Lib. 6. Ep. 24.

WHAT a world of difference there is, by whom any thing is perform'd : for the same actions are either extoll'd too high, or prest down too low, by the fame or the obscurity of the authors of them. I was sailing upon our Larian lake here, when an old friend of mine shew'd me a villa on the shore, and the very room hanging over the water. Out of that place (says he) did a woman of our borough precipitate herself together with her husband. I inquir'd the cause. Her husband (continues he) stunk with certain ulcers, which from a long disease he had contracted about the privy parts of his body. His wife, than whom none cou'd better judge of that matter, beg'd him to let her inspect the part affected to see if curable; she saw, she despair'd, she exhorted him to dye; and became herself the companion of his death, nay, and was the guide, the example, and the necessary cause of it : for she bound herself with her husband, and so tumbl'd into the lake. I, that am of the same town, never heard of this fact till very lately : not because it is less than the most famous deed of Arria, but because the woman herself is less.

Farewell.

TO FEROX.
Lib. 7. *Ep.* 13.

THE same letter informs me, that you study, and that you do not study. I speak riddles —— Yes for certain, till I tell you more distinctly what I mean. For it denies that you study, yet is so polite, that none but one who studies cou'd write it; or else happy are you above all mortals if amidst sloth and idleness you can finish such pieces.

Farewell.

TO FALCO.
Lib. 7. *Ep.* 22.

WHEN you know who and what my friend is, you'll wonder the less, that I so earnestly prest you to confer upon him the Tribuneship. But now, after you have promis'd me, I am at liberty to tell you his name, and to give you his character. 'Tis CORNELIUS MINUTIANUS, who, whether you regard his rank or his accomplishments, is the ornament of my country. Being nobly born, he abounds in riches, but loves books as if he were born poor. He is a most upright judge, a most indefatigable advocate, and a most faithful friend. When you are better acquainted with the man, who is equal to all honours, to

all

all titles (for I'll fay no more of the modefteft
perfon in the world) you'll be perfuaded 'tis
you yourfelf that have receiv'd the obligation.
Farewell.

TO RUFUS.

Lib. 7. *Ep.* 25.

O How much does the modefty of learned
men, or their love of quiet leften or
obfcure their fame! But we, when about to
fpeak any thing in publick or to rehearfe,
fear only thofe who have made their ftudies
known : whereas they who hold their tongue
perform thus much farther, in that they admire a noble work by their very filence.
What I write, I write from experience.
TERENTIUS JUNIOR, having moft honourably
acquitted himfelf in the horfe fervice, and
in the adminftration of the Province of Nar-
bon, retir'd to his own eftate in the country,
and preferr'd a moft profound tranquillity to
the employments that were ready to be heap'd
on him.   Having invited me to his houfe, I
confider'd him as an underftanding head of a
family, or as a diligent farmer, being ready
to difcourfe him on thofe fubjects, wherein
I thought him moft converfant ; and I begun
fo to do, when he by a moft learned fpeech
recall'd me to my ftudies.   How accurate
every thing ! How excellent his Latin ! How
pure his Greek ! For he's fo much mafter of
both,

both, that you wou'd always think he excell'd
in that language he's actually fpeaking.   How
much has he read? How much does he remember? You would fwear the man liv'd at
Athens, and not in a country feat.   But what
need of more words? He has encreas'd my
follicitude, and makes me ftand no lefs in fear
of thofe retir'd men, who may be reckon'd
a fort of farmers, than of thofe whom I
know to be the moft learned. I advife you to
the fame caution : for as in camps, fo in
letters, you'll find, if you carefully enquire
after them, a great many under a ruftic habit, who are arm'd at all points, and begirt
with a moft piercing wit.

Farewell.

TO MAXIMUS.
Lib. 7. *Ep.* 26.

I Was lately convinc'd by the indifpofition
of a friend, that we are beft when we
are fick : for what fick perfon is difturb'd with
avarice or luft? He purfues no amours, he
covets no honours, he neglects riches, and,
let him leave but ever fo little behind him,
he has enough.   Then he believes there are
Gods, and remembers himfelf to be a man.
He envies no body, he admires no body, he
defpifes no body, neither is he curious to
hear or is pleas'd even with fcandal.   His
thoughts are wholly fet on baths and fountains.

tains. The top of his cares, the top of his wiſhes is, that, after eſcaping his diſtemper, he may become ſleek and plump: which is to ſay, that he reſolves to lead an innocent and happy life for the future. What the Philoſophers therefore endeavour to teach in many words, nay in many volumes, I can thus briefly preſcribe to you and myſelf; that when we are well, we continue to be ſuch, as we profeſs our ſelves reſolv'd to be, when we are ſick.

Farewell.

TO ROMANUS.
Lib. 8. *Ep.* 8.

HAVE you at any time ſeen the well of CLITUMNUS? If you have not yet (and I believe not, ſince otherwiſe you had told me of it) ſee it now, as I have done of late, tho' it repents me I was too backward. There riſes a gentle hill, ſhaded with a grove of antient cypreſs-trees. At the bottom of this hill breaks out the Fountain, iſſuing by ſeveral ſprings, ſome greater and ſome leſs, and bubling up makes a baſon, which ſpreading wide appears ſo clear and tranſparent, that you may count the chips that are thrown in, and the pebbles that ſhine at the bottom. From thence the water is protruded not by any declivity of the place, but by its own quantity and weight. This fountain more-

over

over (that immediately becomes a large river capable of boats, which coming upwards, it forces down again and keeps back) is fo impetuous, that tho' it runs on plain ground, it bears along, without the help of oars, whatever is to follow its courfe. But you can difficultly get againſt its ſtream with all the help of oars and poles to boot. Both effeɗs are pleafant enough to thofe who are on the water for play and paſtime, exchanging labour for eafe, or eafe for labour, juſt as they change their courfe. The banks are cover'd with abundance of aſh and poplar-trees, which the pellucid river, as if they were drown'd therein, adds by refleɗion to the number of the green ones above. The coldnefs of the water may compare with fnow, nor is it inferior in colour. Hard by is an antient Temple, held in great veneration. CLITUMNUS himfelf ſtands clad in a Pretexta. The lots there ſhow him to be a prefent and a prophetical Deity. Several chappels are fcatter'd around it, and as many images of the God. Each has its peculiar devotion, with its peculiar name, and fome likewife their peculiar wells : for befides the greateſt, which is as it were the father of the reſt, there are others lefs, divided in their fources, but united in the river, which is paſſable by a bridge. This bridge is the bounds of what's facred and what's profane. 'Tis lawful above it only to fail, but below it, people may alfo fwim. The Hifpellates, on whom AUGUSTUS beſtow'd this

place,

place, do afford both bathing and lodging for
your money. Nor are there wanting country feats, which following the pleafantnefs of
the river, ftand on the brink of it. In a
word, there's nothing that will not afford
you fome delight: for you'll ftudy likewife,
and read various things by various perfons,
written on every pillar, on all the walls, to
celebrate this Fountain and its God. Moft of
'em you'll commend, but fome you'll defpife; tho' fo great is your humanity, that
you'll laugh at nothing.

Farewell.

TO URSUS.
Lib. 8. Ep. 9.

'TIS a great while fince I have taken a
book, fince I have taken a pen into
my hand. 'Tis a great while fince I knew
what is eafe, what repofe, what that flothful
indeed but delightful thing, to do nothing,
to be nothing: fo much am I render'd incapable, either to retire or to ftudy by the many
affairs of my friends! For no ftudies are fo
valuable, as to make us abandon the duty we
owe our friends, and which thofe very ftudies
command us moft religioufly to obferve.

Farewell.

T ☉

TO MAXIMUS.
Lib. 8. *Ep.* 19.

IN Letters confift both my joy and my comfort : for there's nothing fo joyful which by thefe is not made more joyful, nor any thing fo fad, which by thefe is not made lefs fad. Having therefore been out of order by the ficknefs of my wife, the danger of many in my family, and even the death of fome ; I have my refuge to books, as the only eafers of my grief, they teaching me to underftand adverfity better, and to bear it more patiently. Now you know it is my way to examine by the judgment of my friends, and particularly by yours, whatever I am about to publifh to the world. Do you therefore, if ever, be attentive in correcting the Book you'll receive by this letter ; becaufe I fear, left by occafion of my fadnefs, I have not been attentive enough my felf. I cou'd indeed fo far mafter my grief as to be able to write ; but yet not fo far as to do it with an eafy and chearful mind; for as fatisfaction from ftudies, fo ftudies proceed from mirth.

Farewell.

TO

TO GALLUS.

Lib. 8. *Ep.* 20.

THE fame things, to know which we begin long journies, and crofs the feas, we
neglect nearer hand and under our eyes : whether it be that nature has fo fram'd us, as to be
incurious of what's at home, and covetous of
what's remote; or that the defire of every
thing grows fo much the fainter, as the means
of obtaining them become eafier; or, finally, that we put off to another time our defign of feeing, what's in our power to fee as
often as we pleafe. Whatever be the caufe,
there are very many things in our own city,
and about it, which we never faw with our
eyes, nor ever heard with our ears; yet were the
fame in Greece, in Egypt, in Afia, or in any
other land fruitful of wonders, and valuing
it felf upon them, we fhould have heard, and
read, and feen them e'er now. Thus I have
lately both heard and feen my felf, what before I neither heard nor faw. My grandfa-
ther in law requefted of me, that I would
take a turn to vifit his farms near Ameria.
As I was walking over thefe, they fhew'd
me a Lake at the foot of a hill, going by the
name of Vadimon, and told me certain incredible things of it at the fame time. I
went ftrait to it. The lake is as round as a
wheel lying on the ground, equal on all fides,

4

no creek, no bay; but every thing propor-
tioned, even, and as if they had been hol-
lowed and fcoopt out by the hand of an ar-
tift. The colour of the water is lighter than
blue, and deeper than green; the fmell of
it is fulphureous, the tafte medicinal, and the
virtue of it is to confolidate fractures. It oc-
cupies but a fmall fpace, yet large enough
to feel the force of the winds, and to have
its furges fwell'd by the fame. There is no
boat upon it (for it is facred) but certain
graffy Iflands all floating in it, all defended
with reeds and rufhes, and fuch other things
as grow in fertile marfhes, or at the extremities of this very lake. Each of thefe iflands
has its proper figure and motion. The mar-
gins of all are bare, becaufe that being frequently ftruck againft the fhore, or one another, they reciprocally wear and are worn.
They are all equally high, and equally light;
for their roots fall flanting into the water,
after the manner of a keel. This figure may
be obferved on all fides, they being funk and
fufpended in the fame water. Sometimes
they are join'd and coupl'd together, and
refemble the continent : at other times they
are feparated by oppofite gufts of wind; and
not feldom floating fingly, when the water's
in a gentle motion. The fmaller often lye by
the fides of the greater, as lighters do by fhips;
and the greater and the lefs are often in
fuch a motion, as if they ftrove together,

I   or

or ran a race. Being driven back again into the fame place from whence they fet out, they enlarge the ground; and fometimes on this fide, and fometimes on that, they leſſen or increaſe the lake, and then only leave the compaſs of it entire when they keep in the middle. 'Tis well known, that cattle following the grafs, are wont to get upon thoſe iſlands, miſtaking them for the utmoſt bank, without perceiving the ground to be moveable till they are feparated from the fhore, and then grow afraid of the water all around them, as if they were fhip'd and tranſported; but foon getting out, as the wind happens to drive them, they no more perceive, when they come afhore, than when they went aboard. The fame lake difcharges it felf into a river, which, after being viſible a little while to the eye, is fwallowed into a cave, and runs deep under ground, and whatever's received by it before this deſcent, it preferves and brings out again at the other iſſue. I have written theſe things to you, as fuppofing them not lefs unknown nor lefs agreable to you, than they were to my felf; for nothing more delights you as well as me, than the works of nature.

Farewell.

TO GEMINUS.

Lib. 8. *Ep.* 22.

HAVE you not obſerv'd ſuch, as being ſlaves to all manner of luſts, are yet ſo angry with the vices of others, as if they envy'd them; and moſt grievouſly puniſh ſuch as they moſt diligently imitate: when nothing is more becoming even thoſe than lenity, who ſtand in need of no body's clemency. And indeed I look upon that man as the beſt and moſt faultleſs, who pardons others as if he always err'd; but yet ſo abſtains from errors, as if he wou'd never pardon. Let us therefore hold this as a maxim both at home and abroad, as well as in every condition of life, that we be implacable towards ourſelves; but eaſily reconcil'd, even to thoſe who cannot forgive any but themſelves: and let us fix in our memory what THRASEA the mildeſt, and for this very reaſon, the greateſt of men, was frequently wont to ſay, *who hates vices, hates men.* You'll be curious perhaps to know, what mov'd me to write this. A certain perſon of late——But we'll diſcourſe of this more to the purpoſe when we meet; tho' now that I think better of it, not then neither: for I am afraid, leſt telling that which I blame others for practiſing, cenſuring, reporting, ſhould be repugnant to the virtue I ſo earneſtly inculcate. Who therefore, or
what-

whatfoever he be, let him be forgot in filence: fince to make him remarkable, might
fhew fome example; but not to make him
fo, fhews much more humanity.

Farewell.

TO AUGURINUS.
Lib. 9. *Ep.* 8.

IF now I begin to praife you after being
prais'd by you, I am afraid left I fhould
be thought not fo much to fpeak my own
judgment, as to return you thanks. But tho'
I fhould be thought fo to do, I efteem all
your writings neverthelefs to be very fine, and
thofe to be the fineft that treat of us. This
proceeds from one and the fame caufe: for
you write beft when you write of your
friends, and I read as beft of all what concerns myfelf.

Farewell.

TO TACITUS.
Lib. 9. *Ep.* 14.

YOU neither applaud yourfelf, nor do
I write more out of refpect, than as
the fubject itfelf requires. Whether pofterity will have any regard for us, I know not,
but certainly we deferve it fhould have fome:
I will not fay for our wit (fince that were

F 2 arrogant)

arrogant) but for our ftudy, diligence, and even our defire to pleafe pofterity. Let us only perfift in the courfe we have begun, for tho' it has advanc'd but few to glory and fame, yet it has deliver'd a great many from forgetfulnefs and filence.

TO LATERANUS.
Lib. 9. *Ep.* 27.

I Have often before, but efpecially of late, perceiv'd how great is the power, how great the dignity, how great the majefty, nay, how great is the divinity of Hiftory. A certain perfon was publickly rehearfing a book full of truth, and referved part of it for another day. Hereupon the friends of fomebody came begging and praying him, not to proceed with his rehearfal: fo much afham'd are they of hearing what they did, who had no fhame in doing what they blufh to hear. The author however granted their requeft, for he had not given his word to read the reft. But the book, like the deed itfelf, does ftill remain, as it will for the future, and be read in all ages, fo much the more becaufe not ftraight publifh'd: for men grow impatient to difcover thofe things, that are kept back from their knowledge.

Farewell.

TO

TO RUSTICUS.
Lib. 9. Ep. 29.

AS it is more eligible to do any one thing in perfection, than many things indifferently; so it is to do many things indifferently, if you cannot do any one in perfection. This consideration has induc'd me to make a tryal of my abilities in various kinds of studies, having not confidence enough to confine myself to any in particular: and therefore when you read this or that thing of mine, you'll so pardon every one, as not being the only one. Shall the number of pieces be an excuse in the other arts, and the condition of studies continue more severe, where it is more difficult to succeed? But what do I talk of pardon, as if I were on the sudden grown ungrateful? For if you receive these last performances with the same courtesy that you did those I sent before, I may rather expect praise than pardon; tho' I for my part am well content with the latter.

Farewell.

TO GEMINUS.
Lib. 9. Ep. 30.

YOU do very often in person, as now by letter, praise your friend NONIUS to me,

F 3 me,

me, for being liberal to fome people : and I likewife praife him, provided it be not to them only. For I will have him, that is truly liberal, give to his country, to his kindred, to his wive's relations, to his friends, but I mean to his poor friends ; not as they, who chiefly prefent thofe, that are moft able to prefent again. I look upon fuch not to give away their own, but by their gifts (cover'd over with hooks and birdlime) to catch the goods of others. They are much of the fame difpofition, who take away from one what they give to another, and fo court the fame of liberality by avarice. But the firft thing to be done towards this, is to be content with one's own ; as the next is, to become a fort of confederate by turns with him, who maintains and cherifhes fuch as you know are truly in want. All which if NONIUS does, he's without doubt to be commended ; if only any one of 'em, he's lefs indeed, but ftill to be commended : fo rare a thing is even an example of imperfect liberality ! All men are feiz'd with fuch a vehement defire of having, that they may feem rather to be poffeft than to poffefs.   Farewell.

TO TITIANUS.

Lib. 9. *Ep.* 32.

WHAT are you doing? What are you about to do? I lead a moft pleafant,
that

that is, a moſt idle life.   For this reaſon I would willingly read, but not write, long letters ; the one as being idle, the other as being indolent : for nothing's more ſlothful than your indolent, or more curious than your idle folks.

Farewell.

TO CANINIUS.

Lib. 9. *Ep.* 33.

I Have happen'd upon a true ſubject, but very like a fiction, and worthy of that moſt luxuriant, moſt profound, and truly poetical genius of yours.   You muſt underſtand that I happen'd upon it, as ſitting at ſupper one and another were relating diverſe wonderfull things.   Great is the ſincerity of the relator : tho' I may ask, what is ſincerity to a Poet ? Yet the relator is ſuch as you would not ſcruple to credit, were you even writing a hiſtory.   In Africa is the colony of Hippo, near the ſea, and nearer to the town is a navigable lake, out of which there runs a gut like a river, which, as the tide happens to ebb or flow, is by turns carry'd off to the ſea or reſtor'd back to the lake.   Thoſe of all years are buſy'd in this place, as they delight in fiſhing, or ſailing, or ſwimming : but eſpecially the boys, who are allur'd hither by play or idleneſs.   To ſwim in the deepeſt water is among theſe matter of glory and cou-

F 4

rage ;

rage; and he's victor who leaves fartheft behind him both the fhore and his fellow fwimmers. In this contention a certain boy, bolder than the reft, fwom far beyond them; a Dolphin meets him, now gets before him, now follows him, next wheels round him, laftly gets under him, flides him off, comes under him again, and carries him all trembling firft towards the fea, then prefently turns towards the fhore, and reftores him to the land and to his companions. The fame of this thing fpreads thro' the colony: all run together, and look upon the boy himfelf as a miracle; they ask him queftions, they hear him anfwer, they report all again. Next day they flock to the fhore, they look towards the fea, or any thing that's like the fea. The boys fall to fwimming, he among the reft, but with more caution. The dolphin comes again at his ufual time, and approaches the boy. He flies with the others. The dolphin, as if he were inviting and calling him back, frisks above water, dives again, and dexteroufly performs diverfe wheelings and turnings. The like he did the fecond day, and the third, and feveral other days, till the fhame of fearing feiz'd upon thofe men bred to the fea: they come near him therefore, they play to him, and they call upon him; at laft they likewife touch him, and handle him, he tamely fuffering it all the while. This experiment encreafes their boldnefs. The boy efpecially, who made the firft tryal, fwims towards the
dolphin

dolphin as he was fwimming, he leaps upon his back, is carry'd and return'd, believes himfelf to be known and belov'd by him, and loves the creature on his part, neither of them fearing nor being fear'd. The boldnefs of the one and the tamenefs of the other encreafes, while the other boys fwim on the right and the left, encouraging and directing them. There accompany'd him (which is likewife a wonder) another dolphin, as if he were a fpectator and comrade : for he neither did nor fuffer'd any thing like the other ; but came and departed with him, as the boys did with the other boy. It looks incredible (yet is as true as the reft) that this dolphin, the play-fellow and carrier of the boys, us'd to be drawn upon the fhore, and, growing dry upon the fands in the heat of the day, to be rowl'd back again into the fea. 'Tis alfo well known, that OCTAVIUS AVITUS, the Legate of the Proconful, did, out of fuperftition, as he was thus lying on the fhore, pour a certain ointment upon him, frightn'd by the novelty and fmell of which he fled into the deep ; nor was he feen till after many days he appear'd languid and forrowful, yet foon recovering his ftrength, he repeated his former tricks and fervices. The magiftrates flock'd from all quarters to behold the fight, by whofe coming and ftay this fmall republick was burthen'd with new expences : and laft of all the place itfelf loft its former quiet and privacy. They agreed therefore to make away fecretly
with

with the caufe of this confluence. With what compaffion, with what exuberance will you bewail, adorn, and elevate thefe particulars! tho' you are under no neceffity of feigning or adding, fince it will be fufficient if the things that are true be no way dimi-nifh'd. Farewell.

TO SATURNINUS.
Lib. 9. Ep. 38.

I Muft commend our friend RUFUS, not be-caufe you intreated me fo to do, but be-caufe he moft highly deferves it : for I have read over his Book, perfect in all refpects ; tho' the love I bear him made it fo much the more agreeable. I judg'd however as I read : for they are not the only Critics who read to find fault.

Farewell,

A New

A NEW
DESCRIPTION
OF
EPSOM,
WITH THE
HUMOURS and POLITICKS
of the Place:
IN A LETTER TO
EUDOXA.

Scribetur tibi forma loquaciter & situs agri :
Continui montes, nisi dissocientur opacâ
Valle ; sed ut veniens dextrum latus adspiciat sol,
Lævum discedens curru fugiente vaporet.
Hor. Epist. 16. lib. 1.

MADAM,

 SINCE the place in which I pass
the summer was thought fit, on a
certain occasion you remember, to
be compared with my mistress, who
makes it summer wherever she is ; you desire,
that

that as I fhew'd you the picture of the one, I would likewife fend you a defcription of the other, and as like the original as may be. The right you have to every thing that is mine, makes this requeft a command; and therefore without any further difficulty or apology (ceremonies inconfiftent with rural fimplicity) be pleas'd to receive it as taken from the life at one fitting. But the performance is not fo eafy, efpecially in the manner, as is the promife of a thing. I am not ignorant, that you think correctnefs and elegance of ftile as neceffary to fet off the plaineft truth, as neatnefs of drefs and politenefs of manners are to recommend the moft beautiful woman: a flatternly negligence, or a tawdry affectation, being no lefs difgufting in the one than in the other. Yet as there are feveral forts of beauties, each having their peculiar charms, it is juft fo with writing. You know (without being one of thofe they call Virtuofo-Ladies) that there's the low and the fublime, the epiftolary, the hiftorical, the oratorial ftile, with many other fuch differences. And in this Letter I fancy you'll eafily agree, the ftile ought to be a little luxuriant, like the fubject it felf. Nay you have enjoin'd me as a task, to be rather turgid than fimple in a piece of ferious amufement, where, you fay, I ought to fhew my felf more a Poet than a Hiftorian, yet ftill keeping clofe to the truth of the latter. Befides, that even unerring nature puts on her gayeft apparel in

May,

May, and teaches us her children, by the example of the trees, of the plants, of the birds, and of every object that prefents it felf to our fenfes, to delight in the fame innocent variety; particularly in profpects, landfchapes, and the defcriptions of extraordinary places, fuch as I am now going to do my felf the honour of fending you.

EPSOM (1), a village in the county of Surry, much frequented for its moft healthy Air and excellent mineral Waters, is diftant about fourteen Italian miles from London-bridge, and twelve from Fox-hall. It is delicioufly fituated in a warm even bottom, antiently call'd Flower-dale, between the fineft Downs in the world on one fide (taking their name from the village of Banfted feated on their very ridge) and certain clay-hills on the other fide, which are varioufly checquer'd with woods

(1) The old Saxon name of this place was EBBESHEIM, which is to fay *Ebba's home* or Palace, fo called from EBBA, a Queen of this country: as afterwards EBBISHAM and EB's-HAM, the corrupt pronunciation of this laft word occafioning the prefent name of EPSOM. Surrey, and Suffex, with part of Hampfhire, made up the Kingdom of the South Saxons, founded by the valiant ELLA, next after that of Kent, and continued in his pofterity to ETHELWOLF, the firft Chriftian King, whofe Queen was EBBA, of whom THOMAS RUDBORNE, who wrote in the time of HENRY III. thus fpeaks in his *Manufcript Chronicle* in the COTTON Library (Nero A. 17.) *Regina vero nomine Ebbe in fua, id eft Wiccianorum provincia, fuerat baptizata. Erat autem GUS-TRIDI filia, fratris RUHERI, qui ambo cum fuo populo Chriftiani fuerunt.* Guilford was the fummer refidence of the South Saxon Kings.

woods and groves of oak, afh, elm, and beech, with both the poplars, the intoxicating yew, and the florid white-beam. The wyche-tree, the withy, the horn-beam, the bird-feeding quicken-tree, and the correcting birch, are not wanting. I need not mention the numberlefs copfes of hazel, thorn, holly, maple, and other trees and fhrubs of dwarfifh growth, that agreeably diverfify all this country : nor that, for the moft part, they are amoroufly clafpt in the twining embraces of ivy and honey-fuckles. The Downs, being cover'd with grafs finer than Perfian carpets, and perfum'd with wild thyme and juniper, run thirty miles in length, tho' under different appellations, from Croydon to Farnham : and for fheep-walks, riding, hunting, raceing, fhooting, with games of moft forts for exercife of the body or recreation of the mind, and a perpetual chain of villages within a mile of each other beneath, they are no where elfe to be parallel'd. The form of this our village, as feen from thence, is exactly femicircular; beginning with a Church, and ending with a Palace : or, left our ftile here fhou'd offend you, MADAM, it has a Palace for its head, and a Church for its tail. Mr. WHISTLER's far-confpicuous grove makes, as it were, a beautiful knot in the middle : as the road from thence to Wood-cote-green, may be call'd Midway-ftreet. EPSOM never miffes of the eaftern or weftern Sun, and is about a mile in length; the area, within
the

the bending of the bow or half-moon, being
a fpacious plain of corn-fields, fown with e-
very grain, and opening full to the downs.
To thefe ever-green mountains of chalk you
may out of every houfe infenfibly afcend,
without as much as a hedge to obftruct the
air or the paffage. Indeed the rifings are many times fo eafy, that you find your felf got
to the top, without perceiving that you were
mounting. From the circumference of the
femicircle there branch out two or three pleafant lanes, being the extremities of the roads
which lead to the town, from the flow de-
clivities of the neighbouring hills. Thefe
are prefer'd to the principal ftreet by fuch
as are lovers of filence and retirement; and
are known by the names of Clay-hill, New-
inn-lane, and Woodcote-green, in which laft
place your humble fervant has his hermitage.
There are other alleys and outlets of meaner
note. Among them I don't reckon the a-
venue leading up the hill to Durdans, the
Palace I juft now mention'd; nor yet Hudfon's-
lane, which I remember for the fake of Ep-
fom-court, that antient Saxon (2) feat (long
fince converted into a farm) the mother and
original

(2) In old writings its likewife call'd Ebbyfham-place; now
only a great name, and nothing more to be feen, but an oblong
fquare area rais'd higher than the other ground, on the fouth-eaft
of the houfe. Abundance of wrought ftone, of Roman bricks
and tiles are often dug up about the farm: and fome of the
fields do yet preferve the name of a Park.

original of our fubject. Now, all thefe by-places are fo feparated from each other by fields, meadows, hedge-rows, plantations, orchards and the like, that they feem to be fo many diftinct little villages, uniting into one confiderable town at the large ftreet, in the middle of which ftands the watch-houfe. As I wifh to fee this laft a more ftately edifice; fo I long to have the whole fpace about it, from the new-Parade down to the Spread-eagle, neatly pitch'd : confidering that flint-ftones are fo near, fo plentiful, and fo cheap.

Several perfons, who have chofen this fweet place of EPSOM for their conftant abode, are diftinguifh'd from the reft by their habitations, as they are either by their birth or fortunes. As Sir JOHN WARD's houfe on Clay-hill, Sir EDWARD NORTHEY's on Woodcote-green, and Mr. ROOTH's in New-inn-lane, whofe canal on the top of a hill, with the foft walks on both fides, and the green mounts at each end, are very delightful. But among feveral other fuch houfes, I fhall make particular mention only of two. The firft of thefe is Durdans, twice already mention'd; tho' the place is fo well known, that I need not fay any thing to fet off the grove, or the houfe, or the fituation. But it were to be wifhed, that the right honourable the Lord GUILFORD, owner, would on the eminence (which bounds his noble avenue from the downs) erect a ftone Pillar infcrib'd TO HEALTH AND LIBERTY,

3   as

as the air is the moſt pure in that place, and
unconfin'd, that can be. This pillar, after
the manner of the antients, will alſo ſerve
for a point of view according to the modern
way : and will be no leſs beneficial to the
town, nor leſs obliging to the company that
frequent it, than ornamental to Durdans.
Round the baſis ſhould be a ſeat of the ſame
ſtone for the Ladies, who own they have for
ſome time left off their laudable old cuſtom
of walking on the downs : not out of lazineſs
or love to gaming, as they are ſcandalouſly
aſpers'd ; but, as they themſelves more truly
affirm, from the want of a reſting place on
this charming ſpot, by them call'd Mount
Amoret. Nor ſeems indeed this ſpot to be
of common earth, but rather magic ground ;
for the perſons who have not walk'd three
evenings and three mornings (at the leaſt)
upon Mount Amoret, muſt not promiſe
themſelves any good from the air of Epſom :
neither husbands, if they are maids ; nor, if
batchelors, wives. The ſame is as true of
the mount in Aſhted Park, yet with this
difference ; that if there you take your rounds
either on horſeback, or in a coach, then
both the virtue of the place, and the merit
of all your actions, will prove without any
effect. The gladiator, in the middle of it,
kindly warns you of the danger. Not the
high-tufted trees nor the ſhort-bitten lawns,
not the gloomy coverts nor the lightſome
glades, not the open proſpects of APOLLO,

nor

nor the retired walks of DIANA can avail you any thing, if you survey 'em not all on foot.

The other house in Epsom that requires a special mention, is Mount Diston, so nam'd from the owner, and from the round hillock near adjoining, which, rising gently on all sides in a conic figure, terminates on the summet in a circle, which is a hundred foot diameter, and divided into four equal quarters. The round and cross walks of this circle are turf'd, and those triangular quarters planted with trees; which, after they are grown to their full height, will make a stately landmark over all this country. But tho' nothing seems more pleasing to the eye, than the near prospect of the town, or the distant prospect quite around, yet you mount still higher nine and twenty steps into an arbour or pavilion, on the top of an oak, that grows in the very edge of the circle, and whence your view is every way proportionably enlarg'd. Up to this circle there comes a double walk, divided by a range of trees from the best garden, yet of very easy ascent, three hundred and fifty five foot, which I call the north walk : and at the other end, there comes up to it likewise from the reservatory the south walk, three hundred and seventy foot; in both which the slopes seem wonderfully natural, yet artfully contrived. At the foot of the mount is a cross walk, from north-east to south-west, two hundred and ten foot, open at each end thro' handsom grills; and from the

the court before the house there goes a walk from north-west to south-east, five hundred and fifty five foot, including the breadth of the court. Behind the house is a magnificent double Terrass, the middle of each being gravel, and turf on the sides, (which may be adorn'd with ever-green dwarfs) three hundred foot long; and the semi-circular slope, with proper squares, in the middle of this terrass, is eighty foot broad: to which you ascend out of the garden ten steps, being five steps to each terrass, and then ten steps more from the upper terrass into the house; all these steps, as well as those in the fore-court, being of excellent Portland stone. From the terrass, which I have said is three hundred foot long, there is continued in a straight line over the side of the mount, directly towards the downs, a walk finely turf'd, as are all the rest (except one private sand walk, and one gravel-walk) six hundred and fifty foot. And it must be acknowledg'd that Mr. ACKRES, in laying out this hill, wherein nature was the chief guide that he followed, has done justice to his art: nor is it to be doubted, but his genius will still appear with greater advantage in the garden as soon as he goes about it; there being not a more beautiful or convenient piece of ground for such a use any where. Let others judge as they please of the house and the conveniences about it, I shall confine my self to the peculiar objects of my own delight, which will add not a little to the pleasures of this place.

But

But remembring, MADAM, that I am to defcribe a village, and not a fingle houfe, I muft needs fay, that even the Houfes of the very townfmen are every where mighty neat, built moft of 'em after the neweft manner, and extremely convenient, being purpofely contrived for the entertainment of ftrangers, and therefore beautify'd by the owners to the utmoft of their ability, to which the ruins of Nonfuch-palace have not a little contributed. The fronts are adorn'd throughout with rows of elm or lime-trees, in many places artificially wreathed into verdant Porticos, cut into variety of figures, and clofe enough wrought to defend thofe, who fit under fuch hofpitable fhades, from the injuries of the fun and the rain. Here fometimes breakfaft and fupper are taken, as at other times a chearful glafs and a pipe : for thefe vegetable canopies, in the very heat of the day, yield a grateful and refrefhing coolnefs, by the fanning breezes they collect from the delicate air of the downs. The fineft of 'em all is that which fhades the pav'd terrafs in the centre of the town, extended quite along before the chief tavern and coffee-houfe. By the converfation of thofe, who walk there, you wou'd fancy your felf to be this minute on the Exchange, and the next minute at St. James's ; one while in an Eaft-India factory or a Weft-India plantation, and another while with the army in Flanders or on board the fleet in the ocean. Nor is there any profeffion,

fion, trade, or calling, that you can mifs of here, either for your inftruction or for your diverfion. Fronting this our Forum (as I may well call it) there is another of thefe fhades, lately wrought over a pav'd walk of confiderable length, which I juft now call'd the New Parade. Behind the houfes are handfom tho' not large Gardens, generally furnifh'd with pretty walks, and planted with variety of fallads and fruit-trees ; which in feveral of 'em are all left free for the Lodgers. Such as neglect their gardens, find their error in the emptinefs of their rooms, as I wifh they ever may. Thus when you are on the top of the downs, 'tis one of the lovelieft profpects imaginable, to view in the (3) vale below fuch an agreeable mixture of trees and buildings, that a ftranger is at a lofs to know (as it has been obferv'd of my beloved city Leyden in Holland) whether it be a town in a wood, or a wood in a town.

One thing is wanting, and happy is the fituation that wants no more! For in this place, (notwithftanding the medicinal Waters, and fufficient of fweeter for domeftic ufe) are not to be heard the precipitant murmurs of impetuous cafcades ; there are no purling ftreams in our groves to temper

G 3

the

---

(3) This valley of Flower - Dale divides Walton and Hedley, and ends about a mile below Epfom, butting upon a hill on the other fide Ewell river.

the fhrill notes of the warbling chorifters, whofe never - ceafing concerts exceed B o- N o N c i N i and C o r e l l i : the woods are not frequented by the unhappy, that they may liften to the foft whifpers of fome gentle rivulet to beguile and mitigate their cares ; the vallies are not divided by the curling waves, and fporting whirl-pools of rapid rivers ; neither are the flowry meads reviv'd by gliding meanders, cool bubling fprings, or ftagnant lakes. I leave you to guefs, whether in thefe periods I defign'd to fhow how well read I am in bombaft-romance, or rather to refrefh the heated imagination, by exhibiting the various images under which water naturally delights us in the country. Ewell, an antient market-town within an eafy mile, has a moft plentiful fpring, the head of a cryftal brook; capable, were it here, to furnifh a thoufand ornaments and conveniences. And I am perfuaded from phyfical reafons, that the digging a trench of a reafonable depth, for a quarter of a mile (along the rivulet over Epfom-court-meadows) from the now-uncertain fprings in Church-ftreet, would quickly produce a ftream, that in three quarters of a mile farther fhould fall in with the other, and give it the more dignify'd name of Epfom-river. But this prefent defect (for I augurate an approaching remedy) is amply recompens'd by every thing befides.

The two rival Bowling-greens are not to be forgot, on which all the company by turns,

after

after diverting themfelves in the morning according to their different fancies, make a gallant appearance every evening (efpecially on Saturdays and Mondays) mufick playing moft of the day, and dancing fometimes crowning the night : as every new comer is awaken'd out of his fleep the firft morning, by the fame mufic, which goes to welcome them to Epfom. The Ladies, to fhow their innate inclination to variety, are conftantly tripping from one green to the other; and the Men are not more fure to follow 'em, than glad of the occafion, to excufe their own no lefs propenfity to change.

Here the Britifh beauties, like fo many animated ftars, fhine in their brighteft luftre ; not half fo much by their precious jewels and coftly apparel, as by the more pointed glories of their eyes. Here every old man wifhes himfelf young again, and the heart of every youth is captivated at once and divided between a thoufand deferving charms. A fairer circle was never feen at Baiæ or Cumæ of old, nor of late at Carels-bad or Aix-la-chapelle, than is to be admir'd on both the Greens and in both the Long-rooms on a public day. If the German baths outnumber us in Princeffes, we outfhine 'em in Nymphs and Goddeffes, to whom their Princes wou'd be proud to pay adoration. But not to diffemble any thing, bountiful nature has likewife provided us with other faces and fhapes, I may add, with another fet of drefs, fpeech, and behavior (not

G 4

to

to mention ages) ordain'd to quench the cruel flames, or to damp the inordinate defires, which the young, the handfom, and the accomplifh'd, might undefignedly kindle: fo neceffary is an antidote to love, where the difeafe is fo catching and fo fatal!

In the raffling fhops are loft more hearts than guineas, tho' CUPID be no where fo liberal as in England. And the greateft order, that in fuch cafes can be expected (however to me it be a rout) is preferv'd at the gaming-tables of every kind; where it is very diverting for a ftander by to obferve the different humors and paffions of both fexes, which difcover themfelves with lefs art and referve at play, than on any other occafion. There you'll fee a fparkifh young fellow of twenty five, fitting right over a blooming beauty of eighteen, but fo intent on gain and the dice, that he never exchanges a word or a look with her: while a little lower you may fmile at an old hunks, that loves his mony as well as any in the city, yet lofing it as faft as he plays, by having his eyes wholly off his cards, and fixt on a green girl of thirteen, that cares as little for any man there, as he does for his wife at home. The rude, the fullen, the noify, and the affected, the peevifh, the covetous, the litigious, and the fharping, the proud, the prodigal, the impatient, and the impertinent, become vifible foils to the well-bred, prudent, modeft, and good humour'd, in the eyes of all impartial beholders. Our Doctors,

tors, inftead of prefcribing the waters for the vapors or the fpleen, order their patients to be affiduous at all public meetings; knowing that (if they be not themfelves of the number) they'll find abundant occafion to laugh at bankrupt fortune-hunters, crazy or fuperannuated beaus, marry'd coquets, intriguing prudes, richly dreft waiting maids, and complimenting footmen. But being convinc'd, MADAM, that you diflike a malicious infinuation, as much as you approve an inftructive hint, I abftain from all particular characters; fparing even thofe, who fpare none but themfelves.

From this account it is plain we are not quite in Heaven here, tho' we may juftly be faid to be in Paradife : a place cohabited by innocence and guilt, by folly and fraud, from the beginning. The judicious EUDOXA will naturally conclude, that fuch a concourfe of all ranks of people, muft needs fill the fhops with moft forts of ufeful and fubftantial wares, as well as with finer goods, fancies, and toys. The Taverns, the Inns, and the Coffee-houfes anfwer the refort of the place. And I muft do our coffee-houfes the juftice to affirm, that for focial virtue they are equal'd by few, and exceeded by none, tho' I wifh they may be imitated by all. A Tory does not ftare and leer when a Whig comes in, nor a Whig look four and whifper at the fight of a Tory. Thefe diftinctions are laid by with the winter fuit at London, and a gayer eafier habit worn in the country : even

even foreigners have no reason to complain of being ill receiv'd in this part of the Island.

Religion, that was design'd to calm, does not ruffle mens tempers by irreligious wranglings: nor does our moderation appear by rude invectives against persons we do not know, no more than our charity does consist in fixing odious characters on such as unwillingly dissent from us. But, if at any time we must needs deal in extremes, then we prefer the quiet good-natur'd Hypocrite to the implacable turbulent Zealot of any kind. In plain terms, we are not so fond of any set of notions, as to think 'em more important than the peace of society. Curst be those Priests and Politicians (as they are sure to fall sooner or later a victim to good sense) who so industriously propagate discord and inhumanity in Britain! while in Holland (for example) tho' they differ, as all men must unavoidably do, in their sentiments of many things in Religion, and that they have opposite interests in the state; yet this is so far from exasperating, that it renders them more remarkably civil, as the certainest means to gain on each others persuasion, or at least on their good opinion. They are not branded there for their Creeds, nor their Faith ridiculously sollicited with promises of favor or preferment; which wou'd be an infallible method to bring all persons void of honor or conscience to make an open profession of their national religion, and then (what's worst

of

of all) to cover their infincerity with the furious pretext of zeal. Private advantage (believe me) but not the fear of God or the love of man, is the adequate, the true, the only fource both of Hypocrify and Perfecution : for a real perfuafion is as far from needing any fuch interefted baits, as an averfion to mens perfons for the fake of their opinions is from being a mark of judgment or grace. Neither ecclefiaftical favagenefs, nor political enthufiafm, follow thefe our beft allies from the coffee-houfe to the tavern, nor from the exchange to their own tables, no, nor even to church itfelf : and the man, of what color or profeffion foever, wou'd be counted no lefs unmannerly than ftrangely affuming, that fhou'd prefcribe to another what company he ought to keep. His own after that wou'd be no longer coveted, nor indeed eafily admitted. And I doubt not but fome fuch magifterial fawcinefs of old, was the original of a prefent wife cuftom, which makes it fcandalous for a fort of men (I will not name out of refpect) to be feen in taverns or coffee-houfes. This makes all people eafy. No dictators, no informers. The Dutch (in a word) are fo intermix'd and intermarry'd, that you can never guefs at their fect or party by public converfation ; and, to do it, you muft follow a man to his chapel or to his clofet : for all promifcuous difcourfes on thefe fubjects, are manag'd with the fame cheerfulnefs and indifference, that they do any other topics.

pics. If we muſt needs emulate the Dutch, for heaven ſake let's do it in theſe laudable reſpects, and not fooliſhly damn 'em for being more induſtrious than our ſelves. In the mean time, let the wiſe and well-meaning, the able and honeſt of all denominations, heartily join together to carry on the public cauſe, and mutually bear with one another's incurable differences or infirmities, becoming in this laſt reſpect perfect *Interpendants*. Let free-born Britons be the common deſignation for the future; and no diſtinction be known among us, but only of ſuch as are for civil liberty, toleration, and the proteſtant ſucceſſion, and of ſuch others as are for abſolute ſlavery, perſecution, and a popiſh pretender.

A juſt indignation at our ſenſeleſs quarrels has extorted this cenſure, like ſome epiſode in a Poem. But (that I may not digreſs too far, tho' in a place where you may ramble long enough without fearing to loſe your way) I am pretty ſure I ſhall be forgiven this tranſport for Unity by our Governor himſelf. So we uſually call, MADAM, a Gentleman of our ſociety here, that for good humor, good breeding, and good living, is eſteem'd by all thoſe who poſſeſs or underſtand theſe qualities. He's a profeſt enemy to all party-diſputes, he's the arbiter of all differences; and in promoting the intereſt of this town, which he has frequented for many years, 'tis plain that he looks upon virtue as its own reward. His choice of the place is

3

of

of a piece with his judgment in every thing : for as England is the plentifulleſt country on earth, ſo no part of it is ſupply'd with more diverſity of the beſt proviſions, both from within itſelf and from the adjacent villages, than Epſom. The nearneſs of London does in like manner afford it all the exotic preparatives and allurements to luxury, whenever any is diſpos'd to make a ſumptuous banquet, or to give a genteel collation. You wou'd think yourſelf in ſome enchanted camp, to ſee the peaſants ride to every houſe with the choiceſt fruits, herbs, roots, and flowers, with all ſorts of tame and wild fowl, with the rareſt fiſh and veniſon, and with every kind of butcher's meat, among which Banſteddown mutton is the moſt reliſhing dainty.

Thus to ſee the freſh and artleſs damſels of the plain, either accompany'd by their amorous ſwains or aged parents, ſtriking their bargains with the nice court and city Ladies, who, like Queens in a Tragedy, diſplay all their finery on benches before their doors (where they hourly cenſure, and are cenſur'd) and to obſerve, how the handſomeſt of each degree equally admire, envy, and cozen one another, is to me one of the chief amuſements of the place. The Ladies who are too lazy or too ſtately, but eſpecially thoſe that ſit up late at play, have their proviſions brought to their bed-ſide, where they conclude the bargain ; and then (perhaps after a diſh of Chocolate) take t'other nap, till what they

they have thus bought is got ready for din-
ner. Yet thefe rounds of the Haglers (which
I would have by no means abolifh'd, and
which may be call'd a travelling market) are
not incompatible with a daily fix'd Market in
the middle of the town, not only as a farther entertainment for the Ladies, who love
occafions of coming together, no lefs than
the men, but likewife becaufe a greater
choice of every thing may be had there, and
at all hours, than poffibly can be at their
doors : nor would it be more advantageous to
the meaner fort for cheapnefs, than convenient
for the neighbouring Gentry on many accounts.

The new fair during the Eafter holy-days,
and that on the twenty fourth of July, are
as yet of little moment, tho' capable in
time to be highly improv'd. Even VENUS
had a mole; and goffipping is the great
eft objection I have ever heard made to E P-
S O M. But befides that this is common to it,
with all places of narrow compafs, efpecially
places of public refort: fo, next to not deferving any cenfure at all, the beft remedy
is, not to mind the unavoidable chat of idle
people, who are generally fufferers in the
end. But what fence is there any where
againft ignorance and prejudice? When I have
known at Hampftead fome houfe-keepers fo
filly, as to let their rooms ftand empty, rather than to fill them with Jews : tho' thefe
people are known to give as good rates as
any other whatfoever, and that they are as

2

ready

ready to promote all the diverfions of the place˙ Yet, tho' ignorance and prejudice, as I faid' do thrive amain every where in the world ﹔ fo wife men will ever be eafy in fpite of both˙

So much for the Town. Nor is my pleafure diminifh'd by excurfions out of it: for no where has nature indulg'd her felf in grateful variety, more than in this canton. The old Wells at half a mile's diftance, which formerly us'd to be the meeting place in the forenoon, are not at prefent fo much in vogue ; the waters, they fay, being found as good within the village, and all diverfions in greater perfection. The view from the fertile Common in which they lye, is, as from every elevation hereabouts, wonderfully delightful; efpecially fo diftinct a profpect of London at fo great a diftance. But the fortuitous cure of a leprous fhepherd (an origin attributed to thefe in common with other fuch Wells) appears even hence to be fabulous, that they have never fince had the like effect : tho' otherwife thefe aluminous waters are experienc'd to be very beneficial in gently cleanfing the (4) body, in cooling the head, and purifying the blood; the falt, that is chymically made of 'em, being famous over all Europe. Yet the cold Bath, lately erected on the bottom of this pretended miracle, meets with as little encouragement, as the old ftory it felf does with belief; it not being the fafhion in this, as in fome other countries, to have all falutiferous

waters

(4) Infirmo capiti fluit utilis, utilis alvo. *Hor. Epift.* 16. *lib.* 1.

waters under the infpection of the parfon, or the protection of a faint. The hunting of a Pig there every monday morning, when the only knack confifts in catching and holding him up by the tail, is infinitely more becomeing the boys that perform it, than the fpectators that employ 'em. As for a cold Bath, Ewell would by much be the propereft place; fince, by reafon of the fpring, the water may not only be chang'd for every new comer, but a bafin be likewife made adapted for fwimming, which on fuch occafions was the practice of the antients.

But to fhift our fcenes: from the Ring on the moft eminent part of the Downs, where I have often counted above fixty coaches on a Sunday evening, and whence the painter muft take his view when he reprefents Ep-som, you may diftinctly fee nine or ten counties in whole or in part. Befides the imperial city of London, very many confiderable towns, and an infinite number of country-feats, you alfo fee the two Royal Palaces of Windfor and Hampton-Court. Within a mile and a half is the place, and only the place, where that other fplendid Palace of Nonfuch (5) lately ftood: a fit fubject of reflection for thofe, who are inclined to moralize on the frailty, uncertainty, and viciffitude of all things. You may from thence, further perceive with your glafs, the ruins

of

(5) A great part of it ftood in my own time, and I have fpoken with thofe that faw it entire.

õf the moſt antient Palace of Eltham in Kent,
and that of Oatlands in this ſame county of
Surry ; where was likewiſe the Saxon Royal
ſeat of Croydon, the modern one of Rich-
mond, the royal manor of Wokeing, with
ſeveral more of this rank, which ſhews the
good taſte of our former Kings. But not to
quit our Downs for any court, the great number of Gentlemen and Ladies, that take the
air every evening and morning on horſeback,
and that range either ſingly or in ſeparate companies over every hill and dale, is a moſt entertaining object. You can never miſs of it
on the fine grounds of the new orbicular
Race, which may well be term'd a rural
Cirque. The four-mile courſe over the Warren-
houſe to Carſalton, a village abounding in
delicious ſprings as much as we want 'em, ſeldom likewiſe fails to afford me this pleaſure :
having all the way in my eye (like ſome cy-
noſure) the tufted trees of the old Roman for-
tification (6) Burrough, properly ſituated to
crown the downs, and once in my opinion
reigning over all the groves. I except not
that of Durdans famous for love, nor even
Aſhted-mount the manſion of the graces. Sut-
ton and Cheam, tho' not too low, are yet in

VOL. II.   H   winter

(6) I am not the firſt that made BURGH a Roman fortreſs; for,
in the poſthumous edition of Dr. GALE's Annotations on ANTONINE's
Itinerary, it will be found there were Roman Garriſons, not only at Burrough (call'd by the Saxons Burgh from the old fort)
but likewiſe at Ben'sbury by Wimbledon, at Gatton, and ſuch
other advantageous poſts near the city NOVIOMAGUM on Wood-
cote-warren.

winter too (7) dirty; as Walton and Hedley are both too windy, too (8) woody, and therefore in summer too close.

This I insert for your information, noblest CHERUSCUS, to whom I'm confident EUDOXA will communicate this Letter; since you have wisely resolv'd (as you do every thing) to purchase a summer retreat, cost what it will, somewhere in this neighbourhood. But whether you gently step over my favorite Meadows, planted on all sides quite to (9) Woodcot-seat, in whose long grove I oftenest converse with my self: or that you walk further on to Ashted-house and Park, the sweetest spot of ground in our British world: or ride still further to the enchanting prospect of Box-hill, that temple of nature, no where else to be equall'd for affording so surprizing and magnificent an idea both of heaven and earth: whether you lose yourself in the aged yew-groves of Mickle-ham, as the river Mole does hide itself in the (10) Swallows beneath, or that you had rather try your patience

(7) The dirtiness of Cheam is not the fault of the place, which is naturally dry, but proceeds from the negligence of the inhabitants; from which imputation, I wish Epsom it self were wholly free.

(8) This objection is not like to continue long, since so many woods have been fell'd and grubb'd up of late, that the country is rather in danger of being left too bare: tho' the raising of wood for timber, or fuel, or shelter, or ornament, be the easiest thing in the world; and that we are no less bound to make this provision for posterity, than our Ancestors have done it for us.

(9) It belongs to the right honourable the Lord BALTIMORE.

(10) See the description of Box-hill.

patience in angling for trouts about Leatherhead: whether you go to fome cricket-match and other prizes of contending villagers, or chufe to breath your horfe at a (11) Race, and to follow a pack of hounds in the proper feafon: whether, I fay, you delight in any or every one of thefe, E P S O M is the place you muft like before all (12) others.

I that love the country entirely, and to partake in fome meafure of moft diverfions (except gaming) have fixt my refidence here; where I continue the whole fummer, and whither I withdraw frequently in winter. Nor are thefe I now nam'd my only inducements: for as I prefer Retirement to Solitude, and fo wou'd have it in my power to be alone or in company at pleafure, I cou'd be no where better fitted befides; every body meeting his acquaintance on the Bowling-greens, in the Coffee-houfes, in the Long-rooms, or on the Downs; and few vifiting others at their houfes unlefs particularly invited, or where friendfhip has made all things common. 'Tis otherwife among themfelves with chance-lodgers, who come purely for diverfion. In two or three hours time I can be at London, whenever I will, at my eafe; and, if I have no bufinefs in town, I can receive all the public news as well, and almoft as foon, at E P S O M: fe-

H 2 veral

(11) Banftead-downs are very famous for horfe-matches, as there is not a properer place in the world for this fport,

(12) Ille terrarum mihi præter omnes
Angulus ridet. *Hor. Od. 6. lib. 2.*

veral ftage-coaches going and returning every day, with town and country waggons more than once a week; not to mention the ordinary poft, that arrives every morning, Sundays excepted. Thus I remove at pleafure, as I grow weary of the country or the town, as I avoid a crowd, or feek (13) company.

Here then, EUDOXA, let me have Books and Bread enough without dependance, a bottle of Hermitage and a plate of Olives for a felect friend; with an early rofe to prefent a young Lady, as an emblem of difcretion no lefs than of beauty : and I inglorioufly refign (from that minute) my fhare of all titles and preferments to fuch as are in love with hurry, pay court to envy, or divert themfelves with care; to fuch as are content to fquare their lives by the fmiles or frowns of others, and who are refolv'd to live poor that they may die rich. Let fome therefore hide their aking fcars under laurels, or raife eftates to their children by ruining their clients, or fquander the gettings of their fathers in corrupting elections againft their country; while others kill whom they can't cure, or preach what they don't believe : but grant me, ye powers, luxurious tranquillity !

You

(13) Hæc mihi non procul urbe fita eft, nec prorfus ad urbem; Ne patiar turbas, utque bonis potiar : Et quoties mutare locum faftidia coguut, Tranfeo; & alternis rure vel urbe fruor.

Aufon. Edyl. 3.

You have here, MADAM, the defcription that you demanded of EPSOM, and my reafons for liking the place. But the main attractive is ftill unfaid. I have other Miftreffes that charm me in the neighbourhood, befide thofe which may be gain'd with fome addrefs and pains in a town fo well ftock'd with beauties. I make no queftion, but you'll prefently think, I mean the lonely Shepherdeffes on the wide downs, or the plain farmers daughters as they go to hay-making, to harveft, a nutting, a milking, or perhaps to turn in or out their harmlefs cattle: amours that Gods and Heroes have not difdain'd. This, I repeat it, will be your firft thought, which wou'd be uncivil in me to contradict. But I know your next reflection will be, that I allude to the nine Mufes, which meet me in every lawn and every grove, in every fhady bower and folitary glade. MINERVA is to be met on our downs as well as (14) DIANA: and if ever I go a hunting, 'tis always (as a learned Roman has recorded of himfelf) with a pocket-book and a pencil, that if I happen to take nothing, I may yet bring fomething (15) home. Nor is this all. To us lovers of the country, the lowing of oxen, the bleating of fheep, the piping of fhep-

H 3 herds

(14) Experieris non Dianam magis montibus quàm Minervam inerrare. *Plin. lib. 1. epift. 6.*

(15) Venor aliquando: fed non fine pugillaribus, ut quamvis nihil ceperim, non nihil referam. *Idem lib. 9. Epift. 36.*

THE
PRIMITIVE
CONSTITUTION
OF THE
CHRISTIAN CHURCH,

With an Account of the principal Controversies about Church-Government, which at present divide the Christian World.

CHAP. I.

The Occasion and Argument of the Work.

I.  INCE Religion, SIR, no longer signifies an institution that informs the mind, and rectifies the manners, but is become the distinguishing name of Sect and Party; happy is that man who is not so rigidly narrow, sour, uneasy, and censorious, as his Religion wou'd make him, if it be in a

suffering

suffering condition ; nor so intolerably insolent, vexatious, oppressing, and destructive, as if it has the countenance of authority. The one of these hates the man who excludes him from publick trust, he severely observes his failings, and watches an opportunity to shake off his yoke : the other will engross to himself all preferments, he unmercifully punishes the exposer of his actions, and keeps him down the more to prevent his revenge. Mutual exasperations must necessarily follow; then Persecutions, Depopulations, Tumults, and Wars. This makes it of the greatest consequence therefore to any good Government, that the principal members of it be, rightly inform'd, and have due notions, not only of what's true in speculation, but likewise of what's useful in practice, or beneficial to the society. And if they begin with the last, they may be sure to discover the first : for nothing that serves to lessen the quiet, peace, union, and happiness of men, can be true Religion; since one of its main ends (and perhaps the chiefest in this world) is to retain 'em the more effectually in their several duties.

II. BUT what disposes me more readily than my duty it self, SIR, to write on this subject for your satisfaction, is, that I cannot remember to have ever met with a certain Gentleman (whom I need not name or describe to you, and who has more opportunities than I to be about your person) but he
                                                    presently

presently magnify'd the Church, rail'd against Schifmaticks, or exprest his abhorrence of Hereticks. Nor, to do him justice, is he singular in this; for most other men talk with admiration of Ecclesiastical Discipline, and the Order of Priesthood, without which they believe that no Religion or community can subsist. That this opinion has long and largely reign'd, I acknowledge; tho', to speak freely, I do not for all that think the Clergy to be the Church, nor, where they differ from other men, to be any part of the Christian Religion. I do not admit the Church it self to be a Society under a certain form of Government and Officers; or that there is in the world at present, and that there has continu'd for 1704 years past, any constant System of Doctrine and Discipline maintain'd by such a Society, deserving the title of the Catholick Church, to which all particular Churches ought to conform or submit, and with which all private persons are oblig'd to hold communion. Much less do I believe that there was instituted in the Church a peculiar Order of Priests (tho' Christian Priests I do allow) no Priests, I say, whose office it is to instruct the People alone, and successively to appoint those of their own function, whether by the hands of one presiding Bishop, or of several equal Presbyters, Pastors, Ministers, or Priests of any degree or denomination. And least of all will I grant, that either Princes or Priests may justly damnify any person in his reputation,

reputation, property, liberty, or life, on the account of his religious Profeſſion ; nor lay him under any incapacities for not conforming to the national manner of Worſhip, provided he neither profeſſes nor practiſes any thing repugnant to human Society, or the civil Government where he lives.

III. THESE are not the means inſtituted by CHRIST and his Apoſtles, nor directed by true prudence to ſupport the dignity and power of Religion : neither is it difficult for any man, not partial or negligent, to find out thoſe means ; nor impoſſible to put them in execution, when diſcover'd. There is a vaſt difference between the Doctrine of CHRIST, and the methods appointed to propagate or to preſerve it. Now this is the very caſe : for it is not out of a regard to his ordination, degree or function (of all which in their places) that a Prieſt is reckon'd a Chriſtian ; but only as he believes the Doctrines, and practiſes the Duties taught by JESUS CHRIST ; which is common to him with all other perſons ; or otherwiſe none but a Prieſt cou'd be properly ſaid to be of any Religion. Yet ſince it became more advantageous to be a ſervant to the Church than one of its members, and more honourable to be a Prieſt than a mere Chriſtian ; Religion, by which they get no more than others, has been generally neglected by the Clergy ; and Diſcipline, wherein conſiſts all their power and profit, is made almoſt

moſt the ſole argument of their preaching and diſputes. Diſcipline, and not Religion, occaſion'd the Schiſm of the Eaſt and Weſt. Hence aroſe the firſt and principal conteſts betwixt the Papiſt and the Proteſtants: from the ſame cauſe proceeded the impoſitions of the Engliſh Hierarchy upon the Diſſenters from it; nor are the latter divided into Preſbyterians and Independents on any other ſcore. In a word, much the greateſt part of the inhuman barbarities, controverſies, and diviſions of Chriſtians, with nine parts in ten of the religious volumes they have written, owe their being to the oppoſite factions of Prieſts, and to their various forms of Church-Government.

IV. THUS while the Clergy are contending for their own ſuperiority and advantage, the Laity (as if they were afraid to ſuffer for their neutrality) warmly take ſides in a quarrel wherein they are not in the leaſt concern'd: only that the great point in debate is commonly about the likelieſt means of making themſelves ſlaves, without their perceiving it; or how to keep 'em in ſubjection, ſhou'd they grow weary of their chains. This is ſelf-evident in the diſpute about Occaſional Conformity, which divides our Nation at preſent, and is like to give us more diſturbance in time to come. Yet 'tis Diſcipline and not Religion, not Chriſtianity but the Church, that is the occaſion of thoſe unnatural heats, ſcandalous libels, bitter

bitter invectives, foul aspersions, malicious reports, and irreconcileable factions, which from thence have taken their rise, or that make it a new pretence to cover antient animosities. The worst part of the Episcopal Clergy endeavour most strenuously to bring all the grist to their own mills ; and the most ignorant among the Dissenting Ministers struggle as stoutly to keep back those by whose custom they get their livelihood : while the honest men on all sides make large allowances and concessions, without being violent or uncharitable in any thing .The honour and authority of both is nearly concern'd in the number of their adherents. Ambitious Statesmen stimulate and encourage the one, or protect and uphold the other (how indifferent soever they may be to the merits of the cause) as it contributes to serve their own private purposes, or to gratify the aims of the Prince. And all this while the People, who are the very play-thing and foot-ball of these cunning gamesters, are with much address made to believe, that their good and happiness is the grand matter in question ; each party pretending to be zealously espousing their interests, or, to be sure, the People wou'd not be such fools as to espouse theirs. Nevertheless, which ever side they defend or oppose, which ever faction they desert or embrace, they are neither more nor less Christians than they were before : they learn no new spiritual Doctrine, nor no new moral du-

3 ty ;

3

ty ;

ty; and consequently they become neither wifer nor better men.

V. WITH all this, SIR, be pleas'd to do juftice to thofe that deferve it, when you are fo prone to be merciful to offenders : for you are not to imagine that every man goes upon one or other of thefe falfe bottoms; and that thofe very perfons who defend the truth among us, are only in the right by accident. There are thofe in the Court, in the Senate, of the Church, of the Law, and in the Camp, in the capital City, and in all parts of the country, who are not the fervile flatterers, nor implicit followers of other mens Opinions; who feek neither profit nor applaufe, nor authority nor revenge : but who oppofe all arbitrary impofitions on the Underftanding or Confciences of men, from a generous affeftion to their own fpecies, out of a right knowledge of human nature, and for advancing the flourifhing ftate of the commonwealth. Not (as many do, who yet are not the worft rank of men) for temporary ends and politick accommodations, but from a deep and juft fenfe of impartial, full, divine, and eternal liberty. Thefe are the perfons to whom the nation is indebted for wealth and tranquillity at home, for power and reputation abroad : whereas the firft would foon be ruin'd, and the fecond be fooner loft, might thofe of narrow affeftions, bigotted notions, of fordid or ambitious inclinations, manage affairs,

affairs, and overbear the reft. Thefe are the men, who having receiv'd their light and knowledg from reafonable arguments, are not for converting others by dint of blows; who leave all parties their free choice, without being unfettled or indifferent in their own Faith; and who, tho' they act themfelves on true Principles, are often oblig'd to work on the prepoffeffions of their neighbours, to procure a majority in favour of truth. May they receive the excellent and unfpeakable rewards of Virtue! may their names and actions be faithfully tranfmitted to pofterity! and may their worthy examples be emuloufly follow'd by thofe of the prefent and the future time, by this nation, and by all the regions of the earth!

VI. BUT all other forts of men are fo tranfported by their paffions, or fo intent on their particular views and defigns, that they are deaf to whatever can be faid to 'em on this fubject. Intereft never confiders right or wrong, but power and advantage. And let a man offer the cleareft demonftrations, his pains will be thrown away on fuch as are guided more by prejudice or cuftom, than by reafon and convenience. But fince I write to one who profeffes a greater love for truth, than fondnefs for any Church or form in the world; who declares he'll never think himfelf too old nor too great to learn; and that he'll neither be afham'd nor afraid to change, whenever he

meets

meets with sufficient motives: I shall therefore with all imaginable plainness deliver my own sentiments, which I have not adopted out of singularity, since I have not sought renown by publishing them under my name; nor yet out of interest, since they are not the opinions to which rewards or preferments are annext; and least of all from education, since there's no place nor society wherein they are publickly taught. But I have, by a free enquiry and diligent application, learnt them from the dictates of right reason, from my own observations on the best governments in the world, and from the original Constitution of Christianity.

VII. AS I call all things by their proper names, so I endeavour to restore Words to their genuine significations, and to rescue them from sophistry, ambiguity, and obscurity. Many, without designing any fraud, impose on others by the expressions they use in an undetermin'd sense, and are by the same confusion alike deceiv'd in their turn. To employ terms sometimes one way, and sometimes another, pretending all the while to mean but one thing, is a dishonest artifice, a sophism in logick, and whereof the author must probably be ever conscious to himself. But to define your words, and to assign the idea you defend or oppose, is not only the fairest dealing, but also the safest; and, between unfeign'd enquirers after truth, 'tis the most

certain

certain way to fhorten controverfies, as well as for men to differ without breach of charity, without indecent language, or mutual difefteem. Where I agree with others, I think not my felf the lefs in the wrong merely for that, nor the more in the right where I difagree with them ; neither theirs nor my bare opinion being of any weight againft truth. And as no party wou'd be thought to maintain all my notions, becaufe they may like fome of 'em; fo I wou'd not be denominated from any party for approving them in certain things, whereas I may difapprove them in more. It is no fmall artifice to give nicknames in Religion, and to beftow an odious or a creditable title, according to the words in prefent fafhion : for what's the bugbear of one age is the honour of another; nay, what was twenty years ago the blackeft crime, is now in many cafes the brigheft merit : and the only thing to which moft are conftant, is, that if a man's not found within the pale of fome certain Sect, he's look'd upon by all as an outlying deer, which it's lawful for every one to kill. But notwithftanding my foreknowledge of this matter, yet, as I fhall not ambitioufly affume the name of any party, neither fhall I be concern'd what name they'll pleafe to impofe upon me, fo long as I know my felf to be a hearty well-wifher to mankind, a fincere lover of my country, and your no lefs faithful than dutiful Servant. Do me this juftice, SIR, and proceed.

CHAP. II.

Of the Chriſtian Religion.

I. WHEN JESUS CHRIST, the moſt reſplendent ſun of ſanctity, juſtice, and knowledge, begun to diſperſe thoſe thick clouds of ignorance which from the Jews and Gentiles had much obſcur'd the perfect truth, he engag'd his principal followers in the noble task of reſcuing men from the tyranny of cuſtom, fraud, and force : and (inſtead of ſuperſtitious practices, introduc'd by the fooliſh, and improv'd by the crafty ; inſtead of unintelligible theories, calculated as much for the authority of ſome, as for the ſubjection of others) he fixt the true notion of one God, and declar'd how he becomes propitious to rebellious man ; he taught repentance and remiſſion of ſins ; he injoin'd faith in himſelf as the MESSIAS and deliverer ; he brought life and immortality to light, and ſettl'd morality upon its juſt and natural foundation.

II. HIS Diſciples, with a zeal becoming the laſt commands of their divine maſter (who ſuffer'd an ignominious death for the glorious cauſe of truth, and for the ſalvation of mankind) perform'd their part with almoſt equal danger and ſucceſs. Theſe extraordinary perſons were from their ſeveral provinces call'd ſome Apoſtles, ſome Prophets, ſome Evangeliſts, ſome Paſtors and Teachers ; and

and fome by more of thefe names, as they were at certain times differently imploy'd, according to the feveral dialects of the places where they preach'd, or as fynonymous terms in the fame language and country. They were ty'd to no certain place nor conftant refidence, having generoufly undertaken, to the utmoft of their power, to diffufe the Chriftian Doctrine among all nations of the earth, and to provide effectual means for the prefervation of it wherefoever they planted it; tho' to the hazard of their own lives, and ready to feal the truth of it with their blood. When it came immediately out of their hands, it was no lefs plain and pure than ufeful and neceffary; and, as being the concern of every man, it was equally underftood by every body, as it was in reality promifcuoufly offer'd to all forts and degrees of men. CHRIST did not inftitute one Religion for the learned, and another for the vulgar. It is recorded on the contrary, that (1) *the common People heard him gladly*, that (2) *he preach'd the Gofpel to the Poor*; and he was not only follow'd by divers of the female fex, but alfo among the converts of P A U L are reckon'd (3) *of the honourable Women not a few*. This fuppofes that having a good difpofition, they eafily comprehended the evidence of the Chriftian Doctrine, which therefore they imbrac'd and

I 2   prefer'd

(1) *Mat:* xii. 37.
(2) *Mat.* xi. 5.
(3) *Acts* xvii. 12.

prefer'd to their own native but lefs edifying Religions.

III. AND certainly one of the moft diftinguifhing advantages of true Chriftianity is this, that neither poverty, nor want of letters, nor the hurry of particular callings, can hinder any perfon from acquiring it, without which it cou'd not be properly a perfect Religion : but rather on the fame foot with the ceremonial worfhip of the Jews, with the fecret myfteries of the Heathens, and with the abftrufe doctrines of the Philofophers; whereas it fupplies the imperfections of the firft, prevents the impofture of the fecond, and excludes the difficulties of the third. Not the borrow'd terms or pofitions of antient perplexing fophifters, not the barbarous jargon and idle diftinctions of later fcholaftick wranglers, neither the precarious hypothefes and nice fubtilties of conceited doctors, nor the pretended infpirations and ridiculous vifions of extravagant enthufiafts, were then erected into Articles of Faith. Truth was not then made the fport of chance, and tumultuoufly decided by the votes of factions ; nor any thing deliver'd for truth, but what vifibly tended to make men either the wifer or the better. Curious queftions about the Perfon of CHRIST were not fubftituted by his Apoftles to his Doctrines; the circumftantials were not made the fundamentals, nor the hiftory of Chriftianity transform'd into the effence

fence of the fame. That idolatry, thofe fables, this pomp and pageantry, were not fo
early father'd upon himfelf, which then he
was known actually to abolifh and deftroy.
Nor cou'd he be then reprefented as the
favourer of tyranny, or the founder of a
more formal, fuperftitious, and impofing
Priefthood than the Levitical, when he exprefly declar'd all his true followers (4) to
be *Kings and Priefts,* that is, the difpofers of
their own liberty and the minifters of their
own facrifices, as being voluntary members of
fociety, and the worfhippers of God in fpirit
and truth.

IV. AND here, as a moft tractable learn-
er, I wou'd addrefs my felf to thofe that are
more knowing, defiring information in this
point ; namely, to what purpofe any thing can
ferve, which does not render us either wifer or
better men than we were before? For what produces neither of thefe effects, cannot be comprehended, and therefore in that refpect is wholly ufelefs ; fince what we don't underftand cannot make us the wifer, and if we are not the
wifer, how can we be the better? But if this
be granted (as I can yet perceive no reafon why
it fhou'd not) then I wou'd again be inform'd
why nations, provinces, families, friends, and
acquaintance fhou'd be difturb'd, why all
union fhou'd be diffolv'd, affections divided,
laws fubverted, or governments unhing'd,

I 3   about

(4) *Rev.* i. 6.

about fuch things as no mortal can either conceive to himfelf or explain to others? as the
Judgments and Decrees of God; the manner
of his Subfiftence, of his will, or underftanding; the immediate State of departed Souls;
the Refurrection of the fame numerical body;
with other fubjects which are thought more
eafy, but which are not better known. Yet
hence in great part proceed the inhuman divi-
fions of Chriftians, tho' this be not the only
nor the greateft caufe : whereas nothing can
be wifer, plainer, truer, and confequently
more divine, than what CHRIST and his A-
poftles have propos'd about the means of reconciling God to finners; of purifying the
mind, and rectifying the manners; of illumi-
nating the underftanding, guiding the confcience, and directing particular duties; of con-
firming the hopes of recompence to the good,
and denouncing the dread of punifhment to the
bad; of propagating mutual love, forbearance,
and peace among all mankind; of cementing,
maintaining, and fupporting civil fociety.

V. THE whole Chriftian Religion was
fucceffively and occafionally committed to
writing by certain of the Apoftles, Evangelifts,
and other Difciples; and it fummarily confifts
in the belief and obfervation of the truths that
were taught by its founder JESUS CHRIST.
This, and this only, entitles men to the name
of Chriftians; not the prefcriptions of time
or fucceffion, not the fancy'd prerogatives of
any

any places or perfons. Whoever therefore receives the doctrines, and practifes the commands of the Gofpel, is a true Chriftian, however he came by his Religion ; whether under the difcipline of mafters, or by his own private induftry and ftudy. Nor can there be affign'd any good reafon in the world, why a man may not learn his duty, fettle his belief, and form the conduct of his life, by reading the volume entitl'd the NEW TESTAMENT, which contains the originals of the Chriftian Religion ; as another may regulate his perfuafion and manners, by reading the Dialogues of PLATO, which contain the fpeculations and morals of that Philofopher. To fay that to be a Platonift is an indifferent thing, but not fo of a Chriftian, is one of thofe unwary expreffions by which people know not what they mean themfelves. For if Platonifm be truth, none ought to be indifferent to it, unlefs where the matter of it is indifferent in itfelf ; nor even in fuch a cafe can any body be indifferent to a truth that is made evident to him, unlefs we cou'd believe or disbelieve as we pleafe, which is a thing in no man's power to do, whatever he may think fit to fay. And if Platonifm be falfe (as certainly in many things it is) then no perfon ought to be indifferent about imbracing a fyftem which he ought moft carefully to examin, left he be miftaken in his reafons, and confequenly mifled in his actions. But if it be meant that none fhou'd be com-

pell'd either to disbelieve or to profeſs Pla-
toniſm, or any other Sect of Philoſophy, the
ſame is as true of Chriſtianity ; the preaching of the Goſpel, and the conviction of con-
ſcience, being the only juſt and ordinary
means to propagate it. The ſpeculative Doctrines of it are offer'd to the light of internal perſuaſion, and the moral Precepts of it
are left to the care of external laws.

VI. I am not ignorant that, on the contrary, Chriſtians are pretended to be members of a form'd Society, into which they
are admitted by peculiar Rites, which muſt
be only perform'd by ſpecial Officers divinely commiſſion'd to that end, and to whoſe
Government all the members are to be in
conſtant ſubjection ; as they are to be juſtly
cenſur'd or expell'd, if they do not conform
to the laws by which thoſe officers claim their
authority. That this has been for more than
a thouſand years paſt, as it is at preſent, the
ſenſe of moſt (tho' not of all) Chriſtian Societies or Churches, however they may differ among themſelves as to the nature or extent of their Power, Ordination, or Function, I do moſt freely confeſs ; as, on the
other hand, I think I have good grounds to
affirm it not to have been ſo from the beginning, not to be the true intention of the
writings of the New Teſtament, nor to be
the moſt reaſonable ſenſe that can be put
upon them, and much leſs to follow from

4

thence

thence by any evidence or neceſſity. This is what I ſhall now endeavor to ſhew, and is the Argument of the following Chapters, wherein the proofs of it are to be ſought, and not here in the Introduction, as I my ſelf ſhall take no ſuch poſitive aſſertions for an anſwer from others.

VII. BUT before I begin this task, I think it not wide from my purpoſe to ſhew, how much nobler and more generous ideas ſome of (thoſe they call) the antient Fathers had of Chriſtianity ; conceptions, I ſay, much more worthy and juſt than many of them, who, in our times, are not a little proud to ſtile themſelves their ſons. But let it be always remember'd that I am none of thoſe froward and undutiful children, ſuch as they have all been without exception, that comply with the will of their fathers only when it ſuits with their own, but that roundly diſobey and reject it when it thwarts or contradicts their favorite notions, which is the conſtant practice of every party. And that this is no more than the naked truth, I deſire that Church, nay, or that one man in the world to be nam'd, who agrees with every thing in all the Fathers, or in any one Father whatſoever. What I am therefore going to alledge, is left to impartial conſideration, not from the authority of the perſons, but from the reaſon of the things themſelves, compar'd with the teſtimony of the Scriptures;

tures : for matters are come at present to that pass in the world, that I expect no thanks, but rather ill-will for what I have said in commendation of the Christian Religion ; especially from those (whoever they be) that have chang'd it into an art of gain, and a system of contention. Thus in the first preaching of it, such as glory'd in being the only true Church did most strenuously oppose its progress, and the Priests were of all others its fiercest enemies. Nor ought this to be reputed a wonder, since there is no such satyr in nature against Priest-craft as the Gospel of CHRIST ; which so exasperated the corrupt Priests of his time, that after growing weary of their captious disputes, malicious calumnies, invidious insinuations, opprobrious language, scurrilous reflections, false representations, and cruel persecutions, (the common and perpetual arts of the interested patrons of error) they never rested till they brought him at last to the scandalous death of the cross.

VIII. BUT not to digress : *Those who live according to Reason* (says (5) JUSTIN MARTYR) *are Christians, tho' they be reputed Atheists. Such among the Greeks were* SOCRATES, *and* HERACLITUS, *and all like to them: and such among the Barbarians were* ABRAHAM, *and* ANANIAS, *and* AZARIAS, *and* MISAEL, *and* ELIAS, *and many others, whose names*

(5) *Apol.* II. *Edit. Par. p.* 83.

names and actions, becaufe we think it tedious, we fhall not at prefent rekearfe. How much more charitable is this opinion, than that of almoft all Chriftians at this time and for feveral ages paft! who condemn SOCRATES, with all the pious, virtuous, juft, heroick, and excellent perfons among the antients, to eternal torments, notwithftanding their good works (which are gravely term'd fplendid fins) becaufe they did not believe what was never reveal'd nor propos'd to them, and therefore never requir'd nor made a part of their duty. If we do not agree with our Author that SOCRATES, and fuch others, were properly Chriftians, yet if we believe (as we cannot but do) that JESUS CHRIST taught a reafonable Doctrine, it feems to be fafer for us to follow thofe latitudinarian notions of JUSTIN, than the more narrow, rigid, and damnatory decrees of others; fince they are things, and not names, that determine worth, and that truth is the fame, whether it be partly or wholly difcover'd: befides that the obligations under the Gofpel and the Law of Nature differing but as from lefs to more, there might in fome fenfe, according to the meafure of their knowledge, be found true Chriftians in the world, (and the holy Patriarchs we take to be fuch) before (6) *the fulnefs of grace and truth* was reveal'd by CHRIST, from whom all that now offer a reafonable worfhip, bear the denomination of Chriftians.

IX. *AFTER*

(6) *Joh.* i. 14.

IX. *AFTER* SOCRATES (says (7) the same JUSTIN) *had diligently endeavour'd by sound Reason to make these things appear, and to draw men away from the Dæmons,* or false Gods, *those very Dæmons by the means of men delighting in wickedness* (the Sophists concern'd for their glory, and the Priests for their offerings) *so order'd matters, that he was put to death for an Atheist and irreligious person, giving out that he introduc'd new Deities. And they serve us after the same manner; for these things were not only confuted from Reason among the Greeks by* SO- CRATES, *but also among the Barbarians by Reason it self transform'd or become a Man, and call'd* JESUS CHRIST; *by whom we being perfuaded, maintain that the Dæmons who do these things, are not only not good, but also evil and impious; such whose best actions do not equal those of virtuous men: wherefore we likewise are nicknam'd Atheists. And we acknowledge, that in respect of those pretended Divinities we are Atheists, but not so of the most true God, the father of justice, and temperance, and all other virtues, without any mixture of evil.* 'Tis observable here how strangely men are misrepresented to the world by a prevailing faction, and made to hold those very things which they labour'd to destroy. SOCRATES, who intended to subvert the Doctrine of Dæmons, must himself have

(7) *Ibid. p.* 56.

have a familiar Dæmon; and while he establifh'd the *Dæmonium* or true God, 'tis prefently converted into a Dæmon or false God. This was likewife in divers refpects the very cafe of JESUS CHRIST, on whom thofe things have been fpurioufly charg'd, that he really defign'd to overthrow. We may further perceive how liberally the epithet of Atheift has been thrown in all ages on men void of Superftition, by the Priefts and by the rabble; tho' the Chriftians, who were fo much and fo unjuftly charg'd with this crime at the beginning, ought even for that very reafon to be more referv'd in imputing it to others, were they not likewife further reftrain'd by the charity they are enjoin'd, and by which they are ever to think the beft of every thing. And indeed there appears to be as much caufe in this age for fome body to make an Apology for learned men from being Atheifts, as NAUDÆUS did in the laft age from being Magicians; for this was the blackning cry of that time.

X. JUSTIN in other places fpeaks to the fame purpofe; and CLEMENS of Alexandria comes not behind him, when he fays, as from the mouth of the Apoftle PETER, that (8) *God gave us a New Teftament*, or manner of worfhipping him, *thofe of the Jews and the Greeks being antiquated. But we that worfhip him of late,* adds he, *in a third way, are Chriftians: for PETER clearly fhews,*

in

(8) *Stromat. lib. 6. Edit. Par. p. 636.*

in my opinion, that one and the same God was known by the Greeks after the manner of the Heathens, by the Jews in their own Jewish way, but of late by us in a spiritual manner. A little after he affirms, that what the Prophets were to the Jews, the same were the Philosophers to the Heathens ; *God raising up among the Greeks the most approv'd persons, and distinguishing them from the vulgar, according as they were capable to receive his favour, that they might serve for Prophets to their countrymen in their own language.* And lastly, he says, that *as the Preaching of the Gospel is now come in its due time ; so in their season were the Law and the Prophets given to the Jews, and Philosophy to the Greeks.*

XI. SOME other Fathers were of these comprehensive sentiments, among whom I do reckon LACTANTIUS. Tho' the best part of his *Divine Institutions* (for so he calls his Books) be childish declamation against the Philosophers, and pitiful plagiarism from CI-CERO ; yet one thing he has advanc'd (9) in the sixth Book, which creates me no small wonder, considering the temper of the man : for he asserts that tho' no particular person or party has taught the whole truth, yet that it is easy to shew that all the truth is divided among the several Sects of Philosophers. *Now,* adds he a little further, *if there were*

any

(9) *Edit.* Oxon. *p.* 621, &c.

any perfon that wou'd collect together and digeft into one body the Truth which lies fcatter'd among each of thefe, and diffus'd throughout their Sects, certainly this man wou'd not difagree with us. Then he fays, that none can perform this without the aid of Revelation; but that *if any fhou'd happen by chance to do it, he wou'd difcover a moft affur'd Philofophy: and that tho' he cou'd not defend thefe things by divine teftimonies, yet that truth wou'd recommend it felf by its proper luftre.* An admirable Apologift, fhall I rather fay a betrayer of Chriftianity? In the firft place, by all Truth he muft only mean all practical and moral virtues; fince the Philofophers knew nothing of the revelations or miracles either of the Jews, or of the Chriftians. Secondly, I deny to LACTANTIUS, that, unlefs affifted by Revelation, none can collect all thofe truths which are fcatter'd among the Philofophers. Is this a proper argument from a Father for the neceffity of Revelation? Or has he not forgot and contradicted himfelf in other places? For there's no reafon why the perfon who difcover'd two truths, might not add a third to 'em, to that a fourth, to this a fifth, and fo on. Now if any one of the Philofophers had written or invented ten or twenty of thefe truths (as feveral have done more) it is much eafier for another to digeft into one volume what they have all prepar'd to his hand, and left him only the labour of collecting: nor is this a

4   matter

matter that feems to require any other help, befides books, judgment, application, and time. If it fhou'd be objected that it was never yet done, this is more than can be warrantably affirm'd, without knowing all that ever has been done : tho', were it fo, it follows by no means from thence, that it fhall never be perform'd, fince every thing has its time of beginning; and it were extream folly to argue that nothing fhall be hereafter, which has no exiftence at prefent : which reafoning, had it been true yefterday, this Difcourfe had not been written to day.

XII. BUT leaving LACTANTIUS to the correction of thofe, who can be angry with the Fathers when they advance what does not relifh their own palats; I fhall conclude with the idea which MINUTIUS FELIX has given of Chriftianity, in his better Defence of it againft the Heathen CÆCILIUS. *Do you think, fays he, (10) that we conceal what we adore, becaufe we have no Temples or Altars? For what image can I frame of God, when if you rightly confider, man himfelf is his image? What Temple fhall I build for him, when the whole Univerfe, which he has made, is not able to contain him? And when I, that am but a man, can command a larger habitation, fhall I confine the Power of the divine Majefty within one fmall Shrine? Shou'd we not rather dedicate a Temple to him in our minds, and*

(10) *In Octavio. Edit. Lug. Bat.* p. 313.

and confecrate an Altar for him in our hearts?
Shall I offer thofe things in Victims and Sacri-
fices to the Lord, which he has created for
my ufe, fcornfully throwing back his gifts to
himfelf again? This were Ingratitude, when
the moft pleafing Sacrifices to him are a good
difpofition, a pure mind, and a fincere confcience.
Whoever therefore keeps himfelf innocent, he
prays to the Lord ; he that loves juftice, does
offer him Sacrifice : whoever abftains from
fraud, procures the favour of God ; and he that
delivers any out of diftrefs, makes him an a-
greeable offering. Thefe are our Sacrifices, this
is our divine Service : fo that whoever is the
honefteft man among us, him we alfo count the
moft religious. According to this model, the
Chriftian Worfhip does not confift (it feems)
in ftately Edifices, fumptuous Altars, numerous Attendants, gorgeous Habits, exquifite Mufick, or a curioufly contriv'd, expen-
five, and ceremonious fervice, fupported by
ample revenues and poffeffions. Were the
Religion of MINUTIUS believ'd or obferv'd,
there had been no Difputes about thefe or the
like temporal matters; no charge of impious facrilege on the one hand, nor profane
idolatry on the other ; no reviling accufations
of fuperftition or fanaticifm, of pageantry
or clownifhnefs : neither wou'd any room be
left for the boafted and affected mediums of
order, decency, and reverence, between thefe
two extremes. A man's behaviour, and not
the cant of a party, not the particular garbs

or cuſtoms of any place, but the goodneſs and ſincerity of his actions, wou'd be the real teſt of his Religion.

C H A P. III.

Of the Church, and the Diſtinctions thereof.

I. **B**UT the Chriſtian Religion is not the point in queſtion, 'tis the Chriſtian Church. The Church, the true Church, the pure Church, the Orthodox, the Catholick Church, are in every body's mouth; and therefore one wou'd think they muſt needs very well underſtand what they mean by the Church : tho', in reality, they have no fix'd idea to this word, nor any ſignification in which they all agree; and that particular notion, to which they are moſt inclin'd, I mean of a form'd Society with proper rites, officers, laws, and government, does no where occur in the New Teſtament, and is both unreaſonable and impoſſible in it ſelf. The original word, which we tranſlate Church, is *Eccleſia,* and denotes in the Greek laws and writers, any Aſſembly of men call'd together, as by a publick cryer, to hear an oration; anſwerable to the Latin word *Concio* for the ſame thing, from *concieo,* to ſummon or bring together. And hence it came to ſignify numbers of men, that aſſemble of themſelves at

known

known and ftated times, fuch as the meetings of towns and corporations, as the *Ecclefiæ* of Athens, of Lacedemon, and other
Republicks.

II. E C C L E S I A therefore in it felf is
but any publick Affembly in general, whether about civil, or religious, or other affairs
whatfoever; and whofe rules are either none,
or few, or many, or various, according to
the nature of the things to be debated, or
the different cuftoms of feveral times and
places. Thus it is generally us'd in the New
Teftament. But accuracy of Language not
being the bufinefs of the penmen of that volume, *Ecclefia* does likewife occur there (11)
for a tumultuous rabble got together by
chance, without any warrant from authority,
nor knowing why they came themfelves. And
in the fame place, that is, in the nineteenth
Chapter (12) of the Acts of the Apoftles, a
lawful Affembly, or *Ecclefia*, is oppos'd to
it. The Chriftians therefore call'd their own
Affemblies for worfhip or inftruction by this
name, not for any peculiar worth or energy,
but becaufe it was then the common word
for Affemblies or Congregations. It really
fignifies the fame thing with the Jewifh Synagogue, which is a fynonymous term: but
the firft Chriftians being reputed a Sect of

K 2   the

(11) *Act.* xix. 32.
(12) *V.* 39.

the Jews, they rather chofe to borrow the Language of the Heathens, left they fhould be thought to fymbolize with the former, or ftill to continue fuch. Thus Meetings are now oppos'd to Churches in England, which, after all, are but two words for the fame thing; namely, a place of affembling on a religious account. Yet the firft Chriftians were not fo fuperftitioufly nice in the diftinction of words, as their modern followers : for the Apoftle JAMES calls (13) the meeting of Chriftians a *Synagogue*, tho' the wary Tranflators have render'd it Affembly; and the Author of the Epiftle to the Hebrews expreffes (14) the affembling of Chriftians by the word *Synagogein*.

III. IN fhort, any Meeting or Society of Chriftians is promifcuoufly call'd *Ecclefia* in the New Teftament, let them come together about any bufinefs whatfoever. Thus it is put for thofe in the fame family, as the Church (15) in the houfe of PRISCILLA and AQUILA, that (16) in the houfe of NYMPHAS, and that (17) in the houfe of PHILEMON. So it occurs for the Chriftian Meetings of particular cities, and for the Chriftians of whole nations and provinces; as *the Churches*, that

is,

(13) *Ch.* ii. 2.
(14) *Ch.* x. 25.
(15) *Rom.* xvi. 3, 5.
(16) *Col.* iv. 15.
(17) *Philem.* 2.

is, the Christians of Rome, Corinth, Laodicea, *the Churches* (18) of Asia, the *Churches* of the Gentiles, and the like, which are expressions frequently us'd in PAUL's Epistles. From the proper signification of a Meeting at a certain time and place, the first Christians made *Ecclesia* likewise to signify all those of their persuasion, wherever dispers'd in the world, as being united in their minds or Religion ; but without any respect to the gathering together of their bodies into any definite place, or under any certain rules and oeconomy : as PAUL exhorts the Ephesian Husbands (19) to love their Wives, *as* CHRIST *loves his Church* ; and in such other general passages where it signifies all Christians, both they who teach, and they who are taught. In other passages it signifies the People as distinct from their instructors : so PAUL in the Acts of the Apostles exhorts (20) the Elders of Ephesus *to feed the Church* ; and in his first Epistle to TIMOTHY, speaking of the qualifications of an Elder, he says, (21) that *if he knows not how to rule his own House, he cannot take care of the Church of God.*

IV. BUT for the Pastors to signify the Church as distinct from the People, there's no shadow for such a meaning of the word in the whole New Testament. The only place alledg'd

(18) 1 *Cor.* xvi. 4. *Rom.* xvi. 19.
(19) *Eph.* v. 25.
(20) *Chap.* xx. 28.
(21) *Ch.* iii. 5.

ledg'd to this purpofe, is the celebrated *Dic Ecclefiæ* in MATTHEW's Gofpel, (22) where CHRIST directs, that if any man has a controverfy with his brother, and that the other will neither make it up by an amicable compofition, nor yet by the conviction of witneffes, then he's to tell the matter to the Church ; *but if he neglects to hear the Church,* fays CHRIST, *let him be to thee as a Heathen and a Publican.* Here it is moft obvious to all difinterefted lovers of truth, that this paffage concerns a civil injury, where, the offending brother refufing to give private fatisfaction, the difference was to be compounded by the Congregation, to whom the offended brother was to refer it ; which CHRIST moft wifely order'd 'em to do, to fave both the expences and further enmity of a law-fuit. And truly if the Clergy wou'd claim any thing from hence, it muft be the utter difcharging of other Judges, and the bringing of all civil caufes under their own cognizance and jurifdiction. Now that I have given the true fignification of this paffage, I defire thefe three Queftions to be confider'd : Why the Clergy fhou'd be meant here, when no other text does favour fuch an interpretation, and that *Ecclefia* is fo often put for the Laity, as Chriftians are corruptly diftinguifh'd ? Whether any ordinary and external Tribunal of Chriftian Bifhops, or other Churchmen, can be prov'd

(22) *Ch.* xviii. 17.

prov'd to have exifted then in the world? And why *tell it to the Church* fhou'd not be here underftood of the whole Congregation, as well as PAUL means the whole Congregation, when, in the firft Epiftle to TIMOTHY, (23) he fays, *Againft an Elder receive not an ac-cufation, but before two or three witneffes: them that fin rebuke before all, that others may alfo fear?* The places are exactly paral-lel, and need no further explication.

V. F R O M all this it clearly follows, that thofe who receive the Doctrine of CHRIST are Chriftians, that their affemblies are Churches; and if they will call their per-fuafion or fellow-believers the Church, or by a common figure give that name to the Houfe or Place of their meeting (as we fay the Chan-cery, the Court, the Exchange) there is no harm in all this, provided that in their fpeech and writing they carefully diftinguifh thofe fignifications; and that they let us always know which of them they mean, that there may be no equivocation or confufion. But the abufe of this word has occafion'd a world of extravagant notions and diftinctions, nei-ther warranted by Scripture nor Reafon. The Clergy call themfelves the Church, by which they mean a certain body, polity, or govern-ment; and tho' you fhou'd never fo ftrictly conform your felf to the Doctrine of CHRIST,

K 4   yet

(23) *Ch. v. 19, 20.*

yet if you oppofe the Clergy, you are faid to oppofe the Church, which makes their blind admirers imagine that you oppofe Chriftianity. The Difcipline and Ceremonies of a particular Sect are often call'd the Church; and if you neglect or diflike thefe, you are ftrait made an enemy to Religion; for which you may be fure to fuffer in your perfon or reputation, and generally in both. Sometimes a favourite - doctrine, as Paffive Obedience to the arbitrary will of Princes, the Divine Right of Epifcopacy or Presbytery, the Immerfion of adult perfons in Baptifm, or fome other particular opinion, is made the principal Diftinction of a Church. Then a Doubt is propos'd, Whether by the Church be meant an affembly of Men and Angels? Whether the Patriarchs and holy men of the Old Teftament, were not a part of CHRIST's Church? Whether Children be real members of the Church, and how? Whether the whole Church can ever err, or totally perifh? And whether the Paftors and the Sheep be not in a certain fenfe two Churches, whereof the firft is the reprefentative of the laft? But I have already remov'd the imaginary foundation of this reprefentative Church of the Clergy, and under the next head of *Synods and Councils*, I fhall demonftrate that there can be no fuch Reprefentation; where I fhall likewife examine the diftinction of particular Churches and the univerfal.

VI. NEXT

VI. NEXT the Church is divided into visible and invisible, which, if it be meant of a real and seeming persuasion, quadrates as well to all other Opinions or Societies, where the external profession is more diffusive than the internal sincerity : and if it be meant of the publick exercise of Religion, in opposition to a time when none in the world does or dares openly acknowledge it, then it's possible that at such a time there may be no person of that Religion ; or there's a plain demonstration, that this Religion is not a Society consisting of members under such a Government as they commonly call the Church. Another distinction of the Church is into militant on earth, and triumphant in heaven, to which the Romanists add the laborant in purgatory. And truly this last may be found as soon in the New Testament, as the representative Church of the Clergy, which may very properly be call'd militant, considering the fines, imprisonments, banishments, executions, ravages, devastations, wars and massacres it has so frequently occasion'd ; and still continues to practise wherever it has the power, for it seldom wants the will. But 'tis by a wonderful figure of speech that the Martyrs are stil'd the triumphant Church, for being worsted by their enemies ; and 'tis by a modesty no less singular, that others decline those triumphs till they cannot help it.

VII. THE

VII. THE Catholick Church is an un-scriptural expreffion, and fignifies all Chri-ftians, or nothing. It cannot mean any par-ticular fet of Opinions, for there is none wherein all Chriftians are agreed; much lefs do they all fubmit to any one kind of Go-vernment, tho' the Pope has fairly aim'd at a univerfal Monarchy under this Catholick pre-tence. And to fay, that it denotes the Or-thodox believers, is neither grammar nor fenfe: for, in the firft place, there may be errors fpread over all Chriftian Societies; and then among that great variety of Churches, which manifeftly differ in difcipline, rites, and doctrine, every one of them is Ortho-dox to it felf. So that if Catholick figni-fies Orthodox, God knows how many Ca-tholick Churches we fhall have. At leaft, if there be but one, it will be the true labour in vain to find it among fo many pretenders, if you take their own words for it; and let them e'en decide it as they pleafe, for names and titles are but empty things in comparifon of truth. Tho' the real notion of the Church be thus loofe and unfix'd among the admirers of it, as you'll better perceive in the follow-ing Chapter: yet they talk of nothing more commonly or pofitively than the extraordina-ry Prerogatives of the Catholick Church; by which they do not mean (or in the plaineft cafe they fpeak very myfterioufly) the Privileges of individual Chriftians, but the fancy'd excel-

lencies

lencies of an abstracted, and therefore an imaginary idea made up of no particular ideas; like all those charms, graces, and beauties, which the valiant DON QUIXOT ador'd in his belov'd DULCINEA, tho' he never set eyes upon her; and that indeed there was no such creature in being out of his own giddy brain.

C H A P. IV.

Of Synods and Councils.

I. THO' the vulgar notion of a Church does no where appear in the New Testament, yet so early are people accustom'd to fix that idea to the word, that, whenever they read there of particular Churches (as when PAUL, in (24) the first Epistle to the Corinthians, mentions *the Churches of God*, the divisions (25) in the Church of Corinth, and says, in (26) another place, that *the care of all the Churches* lies on his shoulders) they do not simply conceive the Societies of Christians in those places united in the same persuasion, but likewise as under a particular form and discipline of divine and unalterable Institution; as now the Church of England, the Church of Scotland, or the Lutheran Churches, are consider'd by their several professors. On the

---

(24) *Ch.* xi. 16.
(25) 1 *Cor.* xi. 18.
(26) 2 *Cor.* xi. 28.

the other hand, when they meet with the word Church intended in a general sense of all Christians, because they agree in the same Faith, as, in his first Epistle to TIMOTHY, PAUL says, That (27) *the Church of the living God is the pillar and ground of the truth*; then they imagine I know not, and indeed they know not, what universal Church, to whose Decisions all the particular Churches are to stand, by the power whereof they are to be govern'd, and in which they are all united, and made members of the same Society.

II. B U T I have already shewn that the word *Ecclesia* signifies no representative Church of the Clergy. I deny not but that in certain districts, as parishes, towns, provinces, and a whole nation, a select number of persons may meet by authority in a Christian Government; or by voluntary confederation in other countries, to agree upon the circumstances of time and place in their worship, or any other thing relating to their well-being and convenience. On such an occasion, when a numerous Society cannot without confusion meet together in one place, the light of nature has taught 'em to devolve the care of their transactions on a sufficient number, to whom they commit a fiduciary power, and of which their Pastors may or may not be, so as *all things be perform'd decently and*

3

(27) *Ch.* iii. 15:

and in good Order, as PAUL directs in the first Epiftle (28) to the Corinthians. Matters of this nature (as what habits of diftinction any fhall wear among 'em, what fafts they fhall appoint, what feftivals they fhall obferve, or what other regulations they fhall think neceffary) may be alter'd or abolifh'd as urgent caufes fhall appear; and they can oblige no other perfons or affemblies in the world, further than as the wifdom of the thing may induce 'em to follow a good example.

III. BUT as to points of Doctrine and perfuafion, decreeing Articles of Faith, or determining Controverfies about fuch (which is the proper bufinefs of the Churches in queftion) no body can be another's reprefentative or believe for him, no more than be fav'd or damn'd for him; every perfon being to ftand or fall by his own conviction, having his proper judgment of difcretion to determine for himfelf according to the light of his confcience. This is the voice of CHRIST; this is what we are frequently told in the New Teftament. There we are often commanded to examine the Scriptures, not by delegates, but with our own eyes. And PAUL, in his fecond Epiftle to TIMOTHY, affures us that (29) *the Scriptures are able to make*

us

(28) *Ch*. xiv. 40.
(29) *Ch*. iii. 15.

*us wise unto salvation, through the faith that
is in* CHRIST JESUS; which is to say, that
in the Scriptures we may. learn the Faith of
CHRIST, by which salvation is to be had.

IV. A S for them who sit in those Synods
or representative Churches, they must be sent
by the Clergy, or by the Laity, or by both.
If by the Clergy, they represent only them;
and if by the Laity only, so likewise of them.
But if they be sent by, or in the name of
both, surely he that sends may sit there as
well as he that is sent : or if none are qualify'd
to sit but such as are elected, they cannot determine but what their Principals approve. It
wou'd be very hard and absurd, if the sent
might exclude the senders. In the Assembly
of the Christians at Jerusalem, recorded in
the Acts (30) of the Apostles, to enquire whether their brethren of, the Gentiles were oblig'd to the Observation of the Jewish Cir-
cumcision and Ceremonies (because Christianity was. an improvement on the Law of
MOSES) and where it was determin'd to leave
the Gentiles to their former liberty, yet without expresly exempting the Jews ; nay and
PAUL did some time after (31) circumcise TI-
MOTHY, tho' his father was a Gentile, to
please the Jews, because his mother was of
their nation : I say, in this Assembly all sorts
of

(30) *Ch.* xv. 15 — 29.
(31) *Act.* xvi. 3.

of perfons equally debated and concluded, not only (32) *the Apoftles and Elders*, but likewife *the whole Church* or Congregation; and indeed it was but delivering their opinion, to which they did not fay that others were bound, but only wou'd do well (33) to conform.

V. MOREOVER, if thefe Synods be to decide the Controverfies that may arife among Chriftians, and that they fincerely defign to fearch for the truth without prejudice, and to act according to impartial juftice; then thofe of all fides ought to fit there with equal freedom and power, Greeks, Armenians, Proteftants, Papifts, Socinians, Arians, Quakers, and all other Sects, fince none may decide for others; and that for one Party to determine in their own favour, is to be Judges in their own cafe. But cuftom againft equity makes void the law. However, fuppofing that all Sects and perfons were freely admitted to feffion and fuffrage; yet it follows not that their final Judgment muft be neceffarily the truth, unlefs it be prov'd that truth muft be neceffarily of the ftronger fide ; whereas it has not been lefs frequently, and (perhaps as matters go in the world) it is moft commonly found on the weaker fide.

VI. 'TIS but too manifeft that moft of the antient Synods did not weigh reafons, but

3   number

(32) *Act.* xv. 22.
(33) *Ibid. v.* 29.

number voices. And to say that we ought to presume they always acted honestly, is to say nothing; unless it cou'd be prov'd that every body will always do his duty, that men will constantly perform what they profess, and execute the trust repos'd in them without being misled by ignorance, passion, interest, favor, or fear. Now just the contrary of all this appears in the antient Synods, as with very little labor may be prov'd from Ecclesiastical History. They generally came together to try their strength, and the smaller number seldom or never acquiesc'd in the Decisions of the greater; which made the breach wider than before, exasperated the parties, and, instead of healing Controversies, they occasion'd new heresies, schisms, libels, recriminations, tumults, and bloody murders. To gain their purposes of mastery or revenge, they have servilely flatter'd the higher powers, who had the means not only of corrupting them by gratifying their vanity and ambition; but also of getting always a majority of their own creatures sent there, and to condemn or approve what they pleas'd. Thus was the Council of Nice against ARIUS, and that of Ariminum for him; with a world of other examples. And really it is almost an argument against the reasonableness or integrity of human nature, to observe the perpetual jangling, clashing, and opposition of those Councils, one rejecting what the other establish'd, and others sub-
scribing

fcribing to neither; whence they proceeded to anathematize and damn one another without mercy, not feldom for mere trifles : and according as they were favour'd at Court, putting the Emperors and other Princes on perfecutions, banifhments, confifcations, and profcriptions; which inevitably produc'd a retaliation from thofe of the other fide, whenever they got an opportunity. Hence new Edicts, new Decrees, new Canons, new Articles of Faith; and all their refolutions as pofitively and peremptorily ratify'd as if God himfelf had directed their proceedings, which they moft blafphemoufly afferted, confidering their paffions, partiality, and infinite contradictions. Their elections were unfair and moftly feditious, their debates were manag'd without temper, their conclufions were form'd without reafons; and they never anfwer'd their end, nor ever procur'd any union but by force and feverity. In fo much that the Hiftory of antient Synods is a lively reprefentation of the ignorance, pride, and corruption of the Clergy of thofe times, from which vices the Laity were not free, and their failings were augmented by the contagious example of their guides and governors.

VII. B U T as men are always the fame unlefs amended by free Laws and a generous Education, and that from the like caufes the like effects will certainly follow; fo if we confider the canvaft elections, fierce debates, unseemly noise and rude behaviour, contradictory protestations, hasty and undigested Canons of some of our own Convocations, with the other Ecclesiastical Assemblies of Europe, we may perceive what virulence and factions reign in them, what tools they are made of by Princes and parties for and against one another; and how much more they seem concern'd for temporal Power and Dominion, for indifferent Rites and Ceremonies, or for avenging private piques, and indulging personal resentments, than for the true Faith, Reformation of Manners, or universal Peace, Toleration, and Charity. Tho' their practice is a proof that the Holy Ghost does not always preside in their meetings, yet I grant that they decree *what seems good to themselves*; wherefore if I look on what they determine as their own belief, 'tis more perhaps than I am strictly bound, but I shall never own it as the rule of my Faith. Happy, thrice happy had it been for Christianity, if there never had been any Synods or Councils to impose their arbitrary Dictates for Articles of Religion! This made GREGORY NAZIANZEN, and our late Archbishop TILLOTSON, with other excellent persons living and dead, mortally to hate such Assemblies, and to own that no good ever came of them. A bold and ungrateful, yet a noble truth! But to conclude my deduction that Synods are not the Church, I challenge that one Synod to be instanc'd, whether diocesan, provincial,

vincial, national, or œcumenical, to which all Chriftians fubmit, or which is in all things acknowledg'd by all parties, and which has not decreed many things held by the greateft number of Chriftians to be falfe and erroneous.

VIII. TAKING the Church therefore in what fenfe you pleafe, either for any promifcuous Affembly of Chriftians united for religious worfhip and inftruction, or for a feparate body of the Clergy for teaching and governing; yet the Church is as much as ever to feek under the notion of a form'd Society, which is to ferve for a ftanding and univerfal rule. The Members, in the firft place, of all Churches are individual perfons fubject to prejudice, weaknefs, and error. Secondly, no particular Church has any promife or privilege that it fhall not err for the future, no more than fuch as have done fo before. And, Thirdly, if all particular Churches may err, fo may likewife the univerfal and œcumenical Councils, fince they confift only of the Delegates fent from thefe, and differ but in number; nor does their coming together in general take away what they were in particular, but rather makes their error the greater. The variety of their own Creeds is a fufficient Argument againft them. Experience fhews that they are not lefs obnoxious to corruptions of perfuafion and practice than other affemblies. And they are the principal parents

rents of all the errors in Religion, which the people without them, or without some of the particular Clergymen whereof they were compos'd, wou'd never have thought of or imagin'd; besides that no general Council properly so call'd has ever existed. It is a mere chimera; not only because Deputies never did nor cou'd come to represent all concern'd, but likewise because all parties were never admitted.

IX. A Universal Church or Society, cemented by Letters of Communion, is as fantastical; since the particular Churches, whereof the Universal must consist, disagree in the most essential Articles of Faith, of Discipline, and Worship. The interests of civil Governments are so various, and places (where there may be good Christians) are sometimes so situated, as to make such a correspondence impracticable : and thousands of private Christians every where submit to the authority of no particular Churches. When those Letters were most in fashion, there was as little union, and as great impositions as ever: so that if the Bishops of Italy differ'd from those of Africa, and both from those of Asia, and Greece; or part of the Bishops of Italy oppos'd the Bishop of Rome, and the Bishop of Carthage accus'd the Bishop of Egypt (for the like cases not seldom happen'd) how cou'd any man discern from the Episcopal Character or Authority which of these were the true
Church?

Church? or if he was to examine the Controverſy not by dignities, places, or numbers, but by the touchſtone of Reaſon and the Bible, this is making every perſon his own judge, and granting all we deſire. Or if none of theſe expreſſions be forcible enough, I deſire to know what are the Terms of Communion on which a man is to be receiv'd in all particular Churches, as a member of the Catholick Church? Is it not undeniable in fact, that there are no fix'd terms, in agreeing to which you'll be admitted to Communion in all Chriſtian Churches? And as univerſals are made up of particulars, I wou'd likewiſe be inform'd where thoſe particular Churches are, or that one ſingle Church, with which the others are to conform as their exemplar? And if that Church can uſe any arguments to convince the reſt that it ſelf is the true Church of CHRIST, different from ſuch arguments as any private man can ſhew that he is a true Chriſtian (whether he lives in a Chriſtian Society, or with his Bible in a wilderneſs) I wou'd be glad to find 'em ſpecify'd? Thus the diſpute wou'd ſoon be ended. But if this cannot be done, I ſee not the uſe or neceſſity of ſuch a Church.

X. AS for one man to be the infallible judge of Controverſies, it is not only experimentally repugnant to human nature, and plainly unwarranted from Scripture; but that very Church which maintains this ſtrange

paradox

paradox has not determin'd whether the Pope be above a General Council or subject to it, that is, which of them is the Church ; whether they are both together the supreme Authority, or whether he can only utter oracles when he sits on his tripod; and this same chair, no less wonderful than the cap of FORTUNATUS, is to this day a Controversy undecided, what it is, or where. Nor is it conceivable to any that considers his own words, how a man that can err by himself, and a Council that can err by it self, shou'd both in conjunction become infallible. Or if reason were not to judge in the case, yet the numberless oppositions of Councils in the most fundamental points of Christianity, and the no fewer reversions of Papal Decrees by their successors, not to insist on the dubious titles and mutual excommunications of the Antipopes which divided Christendom, is an unanswerable demonstration against their pretences.

XI. LASTLY, be the Church which of all these you will, it cannot possibly be a standing Rule, since none of them is in constant being, and some of 'em wanting to the world for many score years : so that no controversy can be decided in the interval of the deaths of Popes, or the sittings of Councils, or during the intermitted correspondence of Bishops; there's no recourse to be had for resolutions of doubts to any tribunal of uni-

z   versal

verſal Authority. Thouſands therefore of private Chriſtians may die in their ſcruples or in their errors; nay whole ſocieties may be deſtroy'd before they can have the means of deciſion. Nor has any perſon a right all that while to pronounce another to be a Heretick, Schiſmatick, or Apoſtate, if he's to depend on ſuch an external authority, and not on the ſacred Scriptures alone, interpreted by his own Reaſon and Judgment. I conclude then, that people ſpeak very uncorrectly, or rather know not their own meaning, but precipitantly follow an habitual form of ſpeech, when they ſay that ſuch or ſuch a thing is the determination of the Church, and that they ſubmit to the Authority of the Church in all ages: phraſes I have ſometimes heard in the mouths of the Engliſh Diſſenters, generally from thoſe of the eſtabliſh'd Church, and always from Papiſts.

CHAP V.

Of the Marks of the True Church.

I. THE Chriſtian Religion, and figuratively the ſincere Profeſſors of it wherever diſperſt, but no form'd Society aſſuming to it ſelf the name of the Church, I grant to be (34) *the pillar and ſupport of the*
L 4 *Truth;*

(34) 1 *Tim.* iii. 15.

Truth; and I think I have alfo briefly made
out, that there is no fuch Church or fociety in
the world, to be deduc'd from the word *Ecclefia,* nor from Synods, Councils, Popes,
or Epifcopal Letters of Communion. Or if
fuch a Church or fociety there were, I prefume that none will be fo unreafonable as to
deny that it has certain Marks, whereby it
may be known and diftinguifh'd from falfe or
corrupt Churches, and from thofe that are
Heretical or Schifmatical, to fpeak in their
own confecrated language. Without thefe
it wou'd be perfectly the fame thing, whether
there was any fuch Church or not; and of
this the fticklers for a political affociated
Church are fo fenfible, that Marks of one
kind or another they have all affign'd. I fhall
examine them in order, omitting none that
ever came to my knowledge: for if I mifs-
the right Church, it is not for want of learning her peculiar properties, which fo many
pretend to teach. But in general this muft be
agreed, that the Marks ought to be better
and eafier known than the object they diftinguifh, and likewife be different from it in
the whole or in part; elfe they can be no
right tokens, nor poffibly ferve to fhew the
difference of one thing from another.

II. N O W the figns which the bulk of
Proteftants afcribe to the true Church, are
the preaching of pure Doctrine, the due adminiftration of the Sacraments, and exact
2   Difcipline.

Difcipline. I hope this is only a difpute of words, proceeding from want of accuracy in fome of the firft Reformers, who being in their old Syftems accuftom'd to treat apart of the Marks of the Church, wou'd needs make a diftinct head of it in their new Theology : for their Marks are fo far from being fuch, that they are the very things to be known, the effential points in debate ; fince the Doctrine, Sacraments, and Difcipline of all parties are to themfelves the beft ; and the Queftion is, by what fure Marks we fhall know which are fo in reality, and not merely in opinion. Befides, that there may be a true Church, that is a number of good Chriftians, where there is no preaching, nor any Ecclefiaftical Difcipline. PAUL affirms, that(35) *the Scriptures are able to make us wife unto falvation, thro' the faith that is in* JESUS CHRIST ; not to fpeak of the firft Proteftants, nor of the primitive Chriftians under perfecution, who had none other in the world with whom they wou'd communicate ; or, if there were, and it be faid that they communicated with them *in voto* (as the phrafe is) it fignifies no more than that they wifh'd to be in good company, and free from their prefent dangers or troubles.

III. FOR what is it, pray, to us here in England, who they be that are of the true Church in other parts of the world ? I do not
mean

(35) 2 *Tim.* iii. 15.

mean in a political fenfe, as nations may be to one another mutual fupports of liberty againft tyranny and fuperftition ; nor as we ought to tender the good and welfare of all mankind, as our brethren and the fellow citizens of this terraqueous globe; but I fpeak to the merits of the caufe : for we are never the worfe Chriftians if they fhou'd not be good, and if they be, we are not for that ever the better. 'Tis not the teftimony, correfpondence, equality, or fuperiority of others that can make us more to be Chriftians, than to be innocent or virtuous men, which we may actually be, and perfectly know it our felves, nay and are indifpenfably oblig'd to continue fuch, tho' all the world fhou'd confpire together to maintain the contrary. After the fame manner, if we are perfuaded of the Doctrines of CHRIST, and are confcious to our felves, that we fubmit to his laws, fulfilling his will, and taking his Gofpel for our Rule, we may be fully affur'd that we are good Chriftians ; and therefore Members of the Church of God, whofe true Union confifts in thefe things, and in having CHRIST for its head and author : but not in any form of external polity, which may be juftly alter'd according to the exigency of time and circumftances ; nor in the fucceffion of perfons, rites or offices, thefe being things with which the maintenance of truth has no relation or neceffary connection, and which (according to the ceaflefs viciffitudes

of

of human affairs) are impoſſible to be always preſerv'd the ſame.

IV. THE Romaniſts give us more Marks, but not more certainty. However I ſhall diſcuſs 'em all, becauſe as I write in favour of no particular Party, no more do I oppoſe any one as ſuch. In the firſt place, Catholicity is no mark, ſince I have prov'd already that there is no ſuch Catholick Church in their ſenſe, and that it is evidently begging the queſtion to make it a mark, if there were. A Catholick Society is nonſenſe, and Roman Catholick a contradiction. Secondly, Antiquity is no mark, ſince the Church muſt have been without it at the beginning; nor does it follow that the Doctrines never vary, tho' moſt of the names ſhou'd continue ſtill the ſame. Yet this is the ſtale and common cant of all Sects, as if Religion, like wood or wine, was ever the better for being old. The Papiſts do not only make this objection to the Proteſtants, but ſome of the latter are as apt as any to declaim moſt tragically againſt all changes or innovations; and the Heathens often alledg'd the venerable wrinkles of their Religion, how many nations, cities, and moſt flouriſhing empires, had for a long ſeries of time profeſs'd it with great ſucceſs, proſperity, and happineſs: *If Antiquity*, ſays SYMMACHUS to a Chriſtian (36) Emperor, *can add any Authority to Religions, we muſt adhere*

(36) *Orat. pro Ara Victor.*

here to the faith of so many ages, and herein imitate our fathers, who happily follow'd theirs. Thirdly, for the like reasons, Duration is no mark; besides, that the names and doctrines may not only frequently change (as they have done in effect, or there had been no disputes about them) but that several of 'em may quite decay and perish, as other institutions have done in course of time, which had persisted longer in the world than the Roman or any other Christian Church. Fourthly, a Promise of never failing is no mark; since it's in dispute to what Church that Promise was made, if ever it was to any, unless the word Church be rightly transfer'd from a Sacerdotal Society to the true Religion of CHRIST. Fifthly, The Multitude of Professors is no mark, because the Church wanted it at the beginning; and that the professors of other Religions may be, and often are, much more numerous: but tho' the purity of Religion depends not upon it, yet the authority and profit of the Church, I mean of the Clergy, is greatly concern'd in the multitudes that own them as their guides.

V. SIXTHLY, A Succession of Bishops is no mark, for it is not the Succession of persons, but the truth of the Doctrine that is to be known; besides that the Greek and Armenian Prelates pretend to retain their succession, no less than the Jews. Yet supposing it signify'd any thing, there's no uncontroverted

troverted Succeſſion in the world, the be-
ginnings being manifeſtly fabulous, diverſe
and long interruptions happening afterwards,
dubious and undecided titles not ſeldom advanc'd, nor the perſons agreeing either in
Doctrine or Diſcipline with thoſe that went
before them. Neverthelefs ſome who pretend to be Proteſtants, are ſo fond of this
Succeſſion, that they ſeem to make it the
ſole mark of their Chriſtianity ; for they allow no Chriſtianity that's good or ſound to
ſuch as are without it : and what's yet more
abſurd, they object as great Corruptions to
thoſe of whom they had it ; thus making
Epiſcopacy a real Charm, the very enchanted Caſtle that preſerves the Lady Religion ſafe,
when violated, loſt, or perſecuted every where
beſides. But more of this in other places of
the ſequel. Seventhly, Agreement with the
primitive Church is no mark ; for if this be
meant of the Apoſtles and their time, 'tis ſtill
the thing in queſtion : and if it be meant of
the following times, the primitive Chriſtians
differ'd among themſelves as much or more
than we do ; nor among the numberleſs
Churches, Altars, Sects, and Hereſies, which
they oppos'd to each other, is there one with
which the Roman or any other preſent Church
agrees. Eighthly, Union among themſelves
is no more a mark of truth than of error, and
their adverſaries are united as much as they ;
that is, all of them are ſplit into infinite parties and ſubdiviſions, each pretending to be

more

more perfect than the rest : no inftitution
that ever was, being rent into more Sects than
Chriftianity, nor any of thofe Sects having
a greater variety of opinions and practices, of
corrections and additions, than the Romanifts ;
notwithftanding the exquifite policy of their
Hierarchy, which was likewife feveral ages,
by various degrees and alterations, arriving
to that perfection. Ninthly, Sanctity of
Doctrine is begging the queftion, and the
thing that requires to be known. So is,
Tenthly, the Efficacy of the Doctrine, which
wants a mark inftead of being one.

VI. ELEVENTHLY, the Lives of
the Authors; Twelfthly, Miracles ; Thir-
teenthly, Martyrs; and Fourteenthly, Pro-
phecies are no marks : becaufe thefe things are
harder to be known themfelves from coun-
terfeits, than what they are faid to mark ;
and that all Religions and parties glory in a
large Catalogue of Saints, Miracles, Martyrs,
and Prophets, each maintaining theirs to be
the only true ones, and all others to be falfe
or fabulous, magical or delufory. Fifteenth-
ly, the Confeffion of Adverfaries is no mark,
fince they are not adverfaries but a party if
they come over to the Church ; and if they
continue adverfaries ftill, their confeffion
ought to go for nothing, who are fo unfin-
cere as to act againft their own conviction
and falvation. But in good earneft, what
fignifies the denial or confeffion of any one

to

to truth ? At this rate the truth of Chriſtianity it ſelf muſt yield to the obſtinacy of its adverſaries. Nor is, Sixteenthly, the ill Fortune of Adverſaries a better mark ; ſince this may be retorted on all Churches, nay on the primitive Martyrs, which affects the very Chriſtian Religion : and the ſucceſs of adverſaries is often greater than their misfortunes, witneſs againſt the Romaniſts, LUTHER, CALVIN, the Governments of Japan, Sweden, and other places where none is permitted to profeſs the Roman Church ; on the other ſide, the Duke of Alva, the Inquiſition, with ſo many Popes, Kings, Princes, and other perſons and places which thrive very well, tho' they perſecute Proteſtants with exile, fines, and priſons, with halters, fire, and ſword. And indeed the ſuffering of another may well ſerve for a witneſs of his own perſuaſion, but is no argument of conviction or rejection to me, ſince it makes equally for and againſt every thing. Seventeenthly, and laſtly, the Felicity of Profeſſors is fartheſt of any from being a mark ; for it excludes CHRIST from being the Head of his Church, it poſitively unchurches the poor Fiſhermen, the primitive Martyrs, and all Chriſtians almoſt for two or three hundred years ; not to mention the perſecuted, calamitous, and afflicted ever ſince, who yet are ſupported under their miſeries by finding themſelves ſtil'd *bleſs'd* when they ſuffer, and having a promiſe annex'd, that *of ſuch*

is

is the Kingdom of Heaven. But this, I grant, is the principal mark at which the Church aims; for the fake of this the external Policy was made to fignify the Church; thus the Church came by her riches and power; for thefe her fons will brawl, clamor, and perfecute, burn, and damn without mercy: thefe they wou'd monopolize to themfelves, and exclude as many from being fharers as they can; tho' it muft be own'd that no other Church has fo many means and methods, fo many dignities and preferments to make its profeffors happy as the Roman.

VII. HAVING thus gone carefully over all the Marks both of the Proteftants and the Papifts, we are fo far from finding out the true Church, that we have yet feen no reafons to believe there's any fuch thing, meaning it always of an affociated Body Politick in the fenfe of the Clergy: for if the word had been every where, as it is fometimes, tranflated Meeting, Affembly, Congregation, or the like, it had not become fuch a riddle, nor been the fubject of fo many and fo intricate Difputes. But the plaineft things in the world will be quickly perplex'd, by fuch as are like to get any power, or honor, or profit for fo doing; and the only reafon why the Axioms of Geometers are not contefted, is, becaufe on thefe fubjects it is neither dangerous nor unreputable to hold the truth, nor gainful or honourable to maintain the

the contrary. Where it is otherwife, things as plain as any in the Mathematicks are deny'd, even the teftimony of our very fenfes; as that what has the colour, and taft, and fmell of bread, and is no bigger than a fhilling, is perfect flefh and blood, nay an entire man, with the monftrous confequences of that Doctrine.

C H A P. VI.

Of Ordination, and the various Orders of Priefts.

I. IN the Argument of this Writing (37) I deny'd that there was inftituted in the Church a peculiar Order of Priefts (tho' Chriftian Priefts I do allow) no Priefts, I fay, whofe office it is to inftruct the people alone, and fucceffively to appoint thofe of their own function, whether by the hand of one prefiding Bifhop, or of feveral equal Presbyters. I proceed now to the proof of this Affertion. But here I expect to be told by fome people, that I may reafon as long and as plaufibly as I pleafe, without ever gaining their affent, tho' they fhould not be able to anfwer me in form; becaufe that for the fucceffive Ordination of Priefts, which conftitute the Church Reprefentative they find

(37) No. II.

exprefs paffages in the New Teftament. If it proves to be really as they pretend, I cannot blame them, and I wou'd do as much my felf; tho', by the way, this method of arguing from bare founds and feparate texts, is extremely fallacious, and may ferve as well to prove the contrary as the contents of any writing. Attention muft therefore be given to the fcope of the Author and the thread of his difcourfe, which muft always be reafonably interpreted according to this view, together with a diligent confideration of his particular expreffions, which muft not be underftood as they ftand by themfelves, but as they agree with the whole. How cou'd we prefer the New Teftament to the Alcoran, or believe that the one is true and the other falfe, if we did not after the ftricteft examination perceive the contents of the firft to be highly reafonable, ufeful, confiftent, and agreeable to the natural notions of God; whereas the latter is full of abfurdities, contradictions, ambiguities, and impoftures, which may well become a defigning and wicked man (as many fuch Inftitutions have by the like means long and often obtain'd in the world) but cou'd never have an honeft or a good Author, and leaft of all a divine original? But certain things cannot poffibly be defended, if the difcuffion of Reafon be admitted. Wherefore fuch as have an intereft to maintain them, will be fure to exclude Reafon from being a judge, and betake themfelves

felves for refuge to Authority, which is indeed to make ufe of force, and to reduce all at laft to implicit obedience. If the holy Scripture be the Authority they chufe, and that their Adverfaries accept of the conditions, as being perfuaded that the Writings of the Apoftles are the moft reafonable Books in the world; then they artfully cull out certain words and phrafes, which taken alone wou'd feem to countenance their opinions, when moft commonly the context is againft them : yet they have fuch paffages always in their mouths, and fo they eafily impofe on fuch as may truly reverence the Scriptures, but who will not be at the pains to fearch, to try, and examine them, as thofe divine oracles themfelves direct.

II. THUS they were hard put to it, who firft alledg'd in defence of Clerical Ordination thefe words of CHRIST in the Gofpel (38) of JOHN : *He that enters not by the door into the fheepfold, but climbs up fome other way, the fame is a thief and a robber.* Moft Sects and parties agree in their explanation of this place, as if it related to the due manner of admitting or authorizing Chriftian Priefts, Minifters, or Paftors ; for I fhall not difpute about the propriety of the words, when their meaning is fix'd. But there's odd charging, and mutual imputations, each making

M 2   ing

(38) *Ch.* x. 1.

ing thieves of moſt of the reſt : and for any juſtification to be expected from this text, they may be all alike guilty ; for it properly relates to the Perſon of CHRIST as the true MESSIAS, in oppoſition to all thoſe who pretended to be ſuch before him, if his own explication of this Parable may be prefer'd to that of the Clergy. And as he tells us that he himſelf (39) *is the Door* to the Sheepfold, ſo he has ſaid nothing of opening it to Prieſts of any ſort in particular ; but *by me,* ſays he, (40) *if any man enter he ſhall be ſav'd, and ſhall go in and out, and find paſture.* By the Fold he ſignify'd the Jews ; but lower (41) he ſays, *Other ſheep I have which are not of this Fold,* (meaning the Gentiles) *them alſo I muſt bring ; and they ſhall hear my voice, and there ſhall be one fold and one ſhepherd.* The Clergy being ordinarily call'd the Paſtors, and the People their Flocks, it was an eaſy thing for them to gloze this Parable to their own purpoſe, and to make ſimple perſons believe that they had the Door of the Church, and conſequently the Keys of Heaven in their keeping ; ſo that none cou'd enter either place, but by their means, without being guilty of burglary, nor purchaſe a little Chriſtianity from the Bible without being introduc'd by a maſter

(39) *V.* 7.
(40) *V.* 9.
(41) *V.* 16.

mafter of the ceremonies, and obtaining a licence from this fpiritual corporation.

III. THO' the place therefore regards the Evangelical Difpenfation, yet as the metaphors of Sheep and Shepherds are natural enough, and juftify'd in Scripture of the People and their Teachers, let us by way of accommodation (which yet is granting too much) underftand this Parable of the Clergy ; and even then it can only relate to the difpofitions that move a teacher to take that function upon him, but by no means to the way whereby he's call'd or admitted into his office. CHRIST himfelf being here call'd the Door, he fays, (42) that *whoever enters by him*, that is, according to his defign, *will* (as he did) *go in and out before the fheep*, provide them fhelter and pafture, and if it be neceffary, (43) *will give his life for them.* But he that breaks in any other way, that is, for other ends, as inriching or dignifying himfelf, does (44) *fteal, kill and deftroy : he that is a hireling flys, when he perceives the wolf a coming, becaufe he is a hireling, and cares not for the fheep* ; for they are not the fheep, but his wages that he loves, as the falfe deliverers, the hypocritical Scribes and Pharifees, and the fuperftitious domineering Priefts did before our Saviour. And he that is not a

M 3   Hireling

(42) *V.* 9.
(43) *V.* 11.
(44) *V.* 10, 13.

Hireling indeed, or, as bad, his flave, will grant that the Ordination in queftion can derive no Authority from this place. They are more concern'd to underftand it, who purchafe fuch offices by means no lefs indirect, than their purpofes are criminal; and who, uncall'd or unqualify'd, thruft themfelves into a bufinefs of fo great importance, both in the defign and execution of it; who (as in moft other preferments are wont to be done) make their court to great men, appear at their levees, flatter fuch as can befriend them, enter into private obligations with the patrons, and gain fome others by prefents, which is to corrupt them with bribes. Let them apply this place to themfelves, who to render the egregious effects of their Miniftry more diffufive, procure as many and as large Flocks as they can, or to be tranflated from fuch as are thin, and lean, and naked (and therefore want moft care) to the numerous, fat, and fleecy, which leaft need their help; nay who, rather than be no facred Shepherds, will difpenfe with the infpection of any flock, or living among their fheep, leaving them always the paftoral name and crook (whereof they feem mighty fond) and duly paying the falary, which, tho' deferving nothing for their pains, they gladly receive, as a reward (I fuppofe) of their good intentions, for we feldom fee any worthy fruits of their leifure. Let fuch, if they pleafe, found their practices on that text; unlefs they think it more

2

convenient

convenient *to* quit their right to the Ordain-ers, on condition that they admit none into the Sheepfold but men of their ftamp and complexion ; and then they are fure not to be told of their faults, which is a tender point, and what they cannot bear.

IV. ANOTHER Paffage produced for the Ordination of Priefts by Priefts (whether of their own or another degree) is in PAUL's (45) Epiftle to the Romans, viz. *How fhall they preach except they be fent ?* We grant that none may be a publick Teacher, no more than bear any other publick Office or Magiftracy, who is not duly call'd to his poft, and impower'd to execute it, according as the laws and cuftoms prefcribe in the place where he lives. But this text has no relation in the world to the matter, tho' all forts of Clergymen (at leaft the bulk of them) under-ftand it of Ordination : for it is not fpoken of the ordinary preaching of any doctrine, much lefs of the manner of authorizing any to do fo ; but it concerns the firft promulga-tion of certain matters of fact, as the abolifh-ing of the Mofaick Law, and the fucceed-ing of the Gofpel in its room. The Apoftle repeats an objection of the Jews againft their being condemn'd for not believing in CHRIST, whofe difpenfation no body cou'd difcover without fome extraordinary Revelation, with-

M 4 out

(45) *Ch.* x; 15.

Out exprefs notice from himfelf, or from fuch
as had feen and heard him. This, tho' PAUL
affirms the contrary, they deny to be their cafe
in the following words: (46) *How fhall they call
on him, in whom they have not believ'd? And
how fhall they believe in him of whom they
have not heard? And how fhall they hear
without a Preacher,* or one to tell it them?
And how fhall they preach except they be fent,
or that it be reveal'd to them? *But have they
not heard,* anfwers PAUL? (47) *Yes verily;
their found is gone over all the earth, and
their words to the end of the world.* Did not
Ifrael know, fays he? and then he quotes
MOSES and ISAIAH as prophefying of this very matter. Now what has all this to do
with Ordination? It might well be apply'd
to the firft Preaching of the Gofpel, but
with no appearance of reafon to the teaching, or inculcating, or preffing of the Chriftian Religion at this time, where it is already receiv'd and eftablifh'd, and when any
willing perfon in a Chriftian Country may
fufficiently learn it from his Bible * * * *

CHAP.

(46) *V.* 4, 15.
(47) *V.* 19, 20, 23.

C H A P. VII.

Of the Religious Teachers instituted by CHRIST.

I. THE Religious Teachers instituted by CHRIST were from their several provinces, as we have observ'd, call'd some Apostles, some Prophets, some Evangelists, some Pastors and Teachers, and some by more of these names as they were at certain times differently employ'd, or according to the several dialects of the countries where they preach'd. They were ty'd to no certain place nor constant residence, having generously undertaken, to the utmost of their power, to preach and diffuse the Christian Doctrine among all the nations of the earth, and to provide effectual means for the preservation of it wheresoever they planted it. Among other privileges peculiar to their body, they are sometimes term'd Ambassadors (which is but another word for Apostle) because they were immediately sent by CHRIST to offer his Doctrine to the world according to the instructions they receiv'd from him; so that this appellation belongs only to them, and is most improperly apply'd to the present Teachers, many of whom are nevertheless very ready to assume the title, and are not a

little

little proud of the fame. We read in other Hiftories (as well as in that of the New Teftament) of their journeys, their fuccefs, and their troubles, tho' mixt with many fabulous Narrations. But becaufe many pretend that TIMOTHY and TITUS were not admitted into the number of thefe extraordinary Teachers, befides the title of Evangelift exprefly given the firft, any one may in feveral paffages of the New Teftament acquaint himfelf with their labors, travels, and fellowfhip with the reft. Concerning TIMOTHY, confult the Acts of the Apoftles, the Epiftles to the Romans, Corinthians, Theffalonians, and the Hebrews. About TITUS, fee the Second Epiftle to the Corinthians, with that to the Galatians; and laftly, read the Epiftle infcrib'd to himfelf, where it is plain that he was left only for a while in Crete to finifh what remain'd imperfect, and to ordain Elders in every city there, which we'll prove by and by was a charge that belong'd to the extraordinary Minifters of Chriftianity, when perform'd by any fingle perfon. He went afterwards to Dalmatia; and PAUL may as well be reckon'd Bifhop of Corinth, Antioch, or Athens, becaufe he made fome ftay in thofe places, as that TITUS fhould be Bifhop of Crete. Nor can I difcover the reafon why TIMOTHY fhould not have as much right to the Bifhoprick of Theffalonica, whither he was fent by PAUL to confirm them in the Chriftian perfuafion, as to that of

Ephefus

Ephefus where he was defir'd by the fame Apoſtle to tarry for fome time, and fee that no falfe or ufelefs Doctrine might be taught there. It fignifies nothing to object here that they did not immediately receive their commiſſion from CHRIST, for fuch were not his only extraordinary Miniſters, but likewife all thofe able perfons that were willing to fpread Chriſtianity, and whom the Apoſtles chofe for their coadjutors either to do fo, or to travel and confirm it where it was already preach'd. Thefe were the Evangeliſts properly fo call'd, whereof PHILIP and STEPHEN were two as well as TIMOTHY and TITUS, to whom may be added the feventy Difciples: as alfo SOSTHENES, CLEMENS, BARNABAS, MARK, SILAS, and fome others.

II. But as it was not enough thus to fpread and fettle their Religion in the world, where it might foon be corrupted or forgotten, they always declar'd it a main duty of Chriſtians to inſtruct and exhort one another. Yet left thro' the wickednefs of fome, the negligence of others, and the peculiar occupations of all, this fhould not be fo exactly perform'd, they did, in every place, chufe out of their converts fit and able perfons to put people in mind of their Religion, and that as much by the example of their own lives, as by the reafonablenefs and evidence of their Difcourfes. Thefe ordinary Preachers of Chriſtianity were to refide with their own flocks.

flocks. They might not pretend to any new Doctrine, but were only oblig'd to publish and explain that already deliver'd; to the observation whereof they could not force any, but persuade all they could. They were not to fine, damn, or burn; but to exhort and convince gain-sayers. Nay, should they take upon them to trouble people with fabulous wonders, Traditions, or Genealogies; with Logomachys, philosophical Subtleties, or any thing not tending to the improvement of their understanding or practice, they were not to be heard or obey'd had they been Angels from Heaven. And however useful Miracles might be esteem'd to gain authority or credit to the first publishers of any Doctrine, especially among the Jews, yet this reaches not the ordinary Teachers: for when the question do's not concern persons, and that men are dispos'd to receive Truth from any hand, 'tis then the pure merit of the Doctrine, consider'd in its nature and consequences, that is to come under examination; without any fruitless disquisitions about its age or origin, which are the entangling pretences of designing heads, and proofs only to the weak or superstitious.

III. In all the ancient writings, as well the spurious as authentic, we find these ordinary Ministers of Christianity, call'd for the most part Presbyters or Elders, and sometimes Bishops, which Greek word should be tranflated

tranflated Overfeers. Now thefe two expreffions are but feveral defignations of the fame perfons. The name of Elder is taken from the gravity of their years, apteft to inculcate reverence and attention : for it was ever the policy of the beft Governments to make action the bufinefs of the young, as they did government and counfel the province of the old. The other Denomination of Overfeer imports the infpection committed to them over the information and conduct of the people ; they being the cenfors of their manners, and the monitors of their duty. This will undeniably appear from thofe places of the New Teftament, where Elders and Bifhops are promifcuoufly us'd for one another. When PAUL in his Epiftle (48) to TITUS enumerates the neceffary qualifications of an Elder, he fays among other things, *If any be blamelefs*, and prefently fubjoins, *becaufe a Bifhop muft be blamelefs* ; fo that Elder and Bifhop here fignify both one thing. And when the fame Apoftle fent for the Elders of Ephefus to Miletus, he exhorts them (49) in thefe terms : *Take heed to your felves, and to all the flock over which the Holy Spirit has made you Overfeers*. *Epifcopus*, every where befides a Bifhop, is here tranflated Overfeer not without a myftery ; for did they put in Bifhops, the people are not fo ftupid but

(48) *Tit.* i. 5, 6, 7.
(49) *Act.* xx. 17—28.

but they muſt conclude theſe two words to be ſynonymous: and according to the preſent ideas of theſe words, the paſſage wou'd ſound ridiculous, to tell the Presbyters that they were Biſhops. PETER exhorts (50) the *Elders to feed the flock of* CHRIST, *overſeeing it willingly, not by conſtraint ; not for baſe lucre, but out of a ready mind ; not as being Lords over God's inheritance, but as examples to the flock.* Now if the Elders were to overſee, ſurely they well might be, and for that reaſon, were ſtil'd Overſeers, that is, in terms of art, if they might biſhop the flock, they might be Biſhops of it. The qualifications and duties of Elders and Biſhops are the ſame in the Epiſtles to TIMOTHY to TITUS, and every where elſe. The ordination or appointment of both is the ſame, which muſt have been ſeparately confer'd, and different in form, were the perſons ſo in their capacities. The Apoſtles write to Biſhops and Deacons (51) at Philippi, where there cou'd not be plural Biſhops in the ſenſe of the word ; and ſpeak of Biſhops, or Elders and Deacons indifferently ; but not a word of Biſhops, Presbyters, and Deacons, as three diſtinct orders or offices. When there aroſe a difference among the Chriſtians about the obſervation of certain legal rites, we meet with the Elders call'd to conſult with the
Apoſtles

(50) 1 *Pet.* v. 12.
(51) *Phil.* i. 1.

Apoftles about that matter, and their Letters of refolution fent to the Chriftians of other Countries, without any mention made of another rank of ordinary Teachers. And fo it is all over the New Teftament, notwith-ftanding it is afferted by fome, that *'tis evident to all men diligently reading the Holy Scriptures and ancient Authors, that from the Apoftles time there have been thefe three orders in Chrift's Church, Bifhops, Priefts, and Deacons.* About the three words in Scripture there is no difpute; but that they fignify there fo many orders, I think the contrary is now made very plain.

IV. We meet with another fet of men, not more peculiar to Chriftians than to Jews or Heathens; I mean the Deacons, which fhould be properly tranflated Minifters or Servants. They were public fpirited (52) perfons of eminent probity (and not a particular fet of Ecclefiaftics) appointed to collect and diftribute what charitable people beftow'd upon the needy, in the faithful difcharge of which duty they did much approve themfelves to the community. The Chriftians then were fo far from having hofpitals or phyficians at command, as by frequent perfecutions to be perpetually expos'd to all the inconveni-encies of imprifonment, ficknefs, wearinefs, hunger, and cold: and becaufe women in thefe

(52) *Act*. vi.

thefe cafes are generally more ferviceable than men, there were pious and charitable widows (but none under fixty) appointed for that attendance. It was likewife a part of the duty of thefe to inftruct the younger fort of their own fex in Religion and Virtue; neither decency, nor the cuftoms of thofe times allowing the ordinary Teachers (who are no more exempted from certain paffions than other men) to be familiar with them out of the publick Affemblies. Some will tell you that after Chriftianity degenerated into fuperftition, and as a part of that corruption, religious Celibacy grew in fafhion, the Priefts got thofe Deaconeffes abolifh'd, that they might have a plaufible occafion of entertaining the young women in private. But letting that pafs, the Deacons were principally employ'd in ferving or miniftring to the fick, to the poor, and at tables in their feafts of charity; as the Elders or Overfeers had the charge of reforming manners, and propagating virtue. It behov'd fuch as imprint a fpiritual character upon the Deaconfhip, and make it a neceffary ftep to the Priefthood, to tranflate the Deaconefs Phæbe, a Servant of the Church at Cenchrea; for otherwife women might claim the Priefthood, and fo Epifcopacy, which would make a female Pope neither wonderful nor infrequent, confidering the intereft of the fair. But if the perfons were permitted to retain their original office of looking after the poor, there had

2   been

been no need of fhuffling thus with words to throw duft in the eyes of the people, who are not aware that *Servant* is but the tranflation of *Deaconefs.* I gave an inftance before of fuch fair dealing, and, to fpeak nothing of acknowledg'd difficulties, I have obferv'd fome hundreds of places in the New Teftament and other ancient writings, not only thus cunningly, but even faltly rendred; which is to be fear'd, could not proceed from any ignorance of the tongues in fome of the Tranflators, but either to maintain certain opinions and cuftoms already eftablifh'd, or to countenance the introduction of more. But to return to the Deacons, it is objected that PHILIP and STEPHEN preach'd; as if I had deny'd that men of parts, approving themfelves in the Diaconat, might not as well as all other Chriftians be tranflated to another office, as PHILIP was promoted to be an Evangelift. Befides, it is the undoubted right of every perfon in difcourfe or writing to maintain the truth, and upon proper occafions to teach it others; tho', for avoiding confufion, none but thofe allow'd may do it in publick Affemblies.

V. We are now to enquire by whom thefe perfons, thus fet apart for the common good of the Society, were and ought to be appointed or ordain'd. We have feen before that the extraordinary Preachers of Chriftianity did always nominate Elders, wherefoever

N they

they planted their Religion. For, to pass by their Authority, and the care of all the Churches being upon them, none doubtless, better knew the abilities of their own Proselytes. But no other particular persons can with more right succeed them in this privilege, than in their power of discerning spirits. As soon as the Christians became pretty numerous, the Elders were chosen by the votes of the People : and without these, the Apostles themselves did nothing of common concern. MATTHIAS was elected into the Apostleship against the other candidate JOSEPH the Just by the Ballot, or as we translate it, by the lots of about one hundred and twenty, which were all the Christians of the place. TIMOTHY, an Evangelist, was ordain'd by PAUL in conjunction with the Elders. The Deacons were appointed by the People, who are the best judges of such among 'em as deserve that office. And to add another instance, PAUL tells us that BARNABAS was, together with himself, tho' an Apostle, chosen by all the Assemblies to travel. It cannot be contested but that Apostles and Evangelists might be apppointed by those of the same order without the joint consent or approbation of others ; for it is highly reasonable, that the author or immediate publishers of a Doctrine (as well as of any new invention) should have the choice and nomination of the first managers. But if even upon such occasions, the Apostles thought fit to desire the concurrence

rence of their profelytes, what, pray, can incapacitate the People now from chufing the ordinary Minifters, fo immediately relating to themfelves? efpecially, feeing there are no perfons at this time in the world, to whom any deference ought to be paid upon the fcore of extraordinary gifts or power : and, equivocally to fay, that none can give but what they have, proves as ftrongly that the citizens of London cannot chufe their Sheriffs, nor the nobility of Poland their King, fince every elector is not himfelf a King or a Sheriff.

VI. In this cafe therefore, as in all other publick affairs of the People, the right of Election is theirs; or, which is the fame thing, of fuch a fufficient number, anfwerable to them, upon whom they fhall devolve it, when they cannot all conveniently meet in one place. If they be allow'd not only to chufe their Mayors and Aldermen, but alfo their Lawyers or Phyficians, of whofe profeflions they are fuch incompetent judges, with much greater reafon may they elect their Ecclefiaftick Teachers, in whom no effential quality is requir'd, that every Chriftian is not bound to poffefs. All men are frequently commanded by the voice of CHRIST and Reafon, not only to be well exercis'd in piety and the knowledge of the truth, but alfo to inftruct their families and neighbours, to admonifh and reprove, to comfort and edify one another.

So

So that the only difference between the People and their Teachers confifts, as I remark'd before, in this; namely, that left thefe duties fhould thro' vice, neglect, or bufinefs, be generally omitted, certain perfons are fet apart by all to preach them, which exempts no body from particular obligations. I affirm therefore that any Society of Chriftians may out of their own number, or any other body of people, pitch upon willing perfons, with the neceffary qualifications to be their Overfeers. This is the moft divine and regular Miffion upon earth, as agreeable to original practice, and the light of reafon which is the candle of the Lord. But that the Overfeers fhould exclufively of the People chufe one another, much lefs be ordain'd by one, is both unreafonable and unfafe, as I fhall make it appear e're I have done. Whoever affents to thefe truths, muft likewife grant that he's no longer an Overfeer that is depos'd for juft caufes, as being ignorant, debauch'd, or an enemy to the Government. No more is he that has no charge at prefent, tho' formerly the Paftor of an affembly : for 'tis the relation between the affembly and him that gave him this denomination, which perifhes as foon as that is diffolv'd. The diftinction therefore between a Minifter and the exercife of his Miniftry, is quite as ridiculous, as when in other words they fay, that he is a Minifter in habit who is not one in act, which is to be actually none at all. For my own part, I

don't

don't look upon any in the nation, however dignify'd or diftinguifh'd, that is not fome-where an actual Teacher, and as fuch receiv'd by the People, to be more a Bifhop, Elder, or Paftor (term it as you pleafe) than I think him this year Lord Mayor, that was fo the laft; or that a fhepherd remains one, after the flock is all fold to the butchers or de-vour'd by the wolves. And when I call thofe perfons by any of the aforefaid or equivalent names, I'm then forc'd to ufe the language of cuftom and not of reafon, which in many other points is the misfortune of more be-fides my felf. All they can claim is a capa-city of being Teachers, when any fociety pleafes to authorize 'em; to which every will-ing and qualify'd Chriftian may pretend as well as they: for this only amounts to poffibi-lity and fitnefs: nor will any body deny but that a man who has already approv'd himfelf in teaching, is preferable to another, of whofe abilities the world has had no experience, nor that fuch a perfon is deferving of honor and refpect wherever he comes, if he has worthi-ly executed his office; but the fame is as true of all other callings important to the com-mon-wealth.

VII. Moft of thofe who make Bifhops a fu-perior order to other Priefts or Minifters, teach a very different doctrine from this. For, according to them, the Bifhop only may ordain; and let the People be never fo unani-

mous

mous, or let their Teachers be unexceptionable in their lives, learning, and doctrine, yet if they receive not their power from a Bishop they have no Christian Church or Assemblies, nor can they reap any benefit from the practice of religious Duties. This is one of the most extravagant and uncharitable positions that was ever heard. It's absolutely as wild and contradictory to common sense, as Transubstantiation ; and excludes as many from Heaven, as this renders Idolaters. For to assert that such as are firmly persuaded of the doctrine of CHRIST, and conscientiously practise his precepts, are no Christians without this Clerical Hierarchy, is evidently as absurd as believing that to be no bread which I saw made and sold, wherein I find the usual colour, taste, and all other properties, because it was not bak'd in some oven appointed by Authority ; or as if I thought nothing could quench my thirst but what I drank out of silver. But if the effects of liquor remain the same, be the vessel of earth or of glass ; so they are good Christians, let their Mission (as they speak) be what it will, who believe and practise the Doctrine of CHRIST. Nor shall I make any distinction how they came by their Religion, whether under the discipline of masters, or by their own private industry and study.

VIII. Some are likewise so strangely blinded by Education, but more by Interest, as to imagine he ceases not being a Teacher that

was

was once lawfully ordain'd, tho' he becomes deaf, or dumb, or any other way incapable to exercise his office; a privilege never claim'd or pretended by any fort of Magiftrates, except of late by fome Kings, fince the Creation. This wonder is perform'd by virtue of a certain facred, unknown, invifible, yet indelible Character, as unintelligibly ftampt on the foul at the impofition of the Bifhops hands in Ordination, as a fmall crumb of bread is transform'd into the body of CHRIST by four words of a Mafs-prieft. *Chirotonia*, or the elevation of hands, was in moft Commonwealths (particularly thofe of Greece and Afia, where the Apoftles travell'd) the way of giving Suffrages at Elections, as it is now in the Guild-hall of London; whence the very act of appointing a Magiftrate, or giving of votes, tho' after another manner, is fometimes figuratively fo call'd, as none will deny that has read the new Teftament or prophane Authors in the original Greek. *Chirothefia*, or the impofition of hands, was a ceremony peculiarly us'd by the Jews, not always to denote an internal change or character, as fome ridiculoufly maintain (which I cannot perfuade my felf they believe) but, when there was nothing extraordinary, as a folemn defignation of the perfon appointed to any office in the Government; whereby the ratification of his Election was declar'd, himfelf fhewn to the people, and recommended to their love and refpect. Upon all occafions of this na-

ture

ture some sign must unavoidably be employ'd, whether it be by proclamation, the imposition of others hands, stretching out of his own; the delivering of a sword, a book, a staff; the putting on a crown, a cap, a robe, or any other way. But all these are in themselves indifferent, and depend entirely upon custom. Now most of the Christian Clergy have constantly retain'd every where the ceremony of ordaining Magistrates us'd in Judea, where the first of their order were appointed; while the people of other places observing their own national rites, and changing fashions sometimes in this as in other matters, are apt to imagine the Clergy would not depart from the common forms, if something more than a bare designation was not meant by their peculiar custom: particularly when they read that the first who were so ordain'd could perform extraordinary things; tho' daily experience may convince them, that nothing unusual follows upon the mere laying on of a Bishop or Presbyter's hands. Let such therefore as pretend the contrary, convince us by miracles; and let those, who are not so extravagant, acknowledge the use of this ceremony to be no more essential to theirs, than the ordination of any civil officers, and so let them indifferently use or forbear it according to the various Customs of different places, but never affect or press it as a necessary Rite of divine Institution.

A PRO-

A
PROJECT
OF A
JOURNAL
Intended to be publiſhed weekly.

Jan. 1. 1704-5.

I HAVE throughly conſider'd, Sir, the Subject of our laſt Diſcourſe, and I am not only perfectly convinc'd of the uſefulneſs of what you propoſed, but likewiſe fully determin'd to begin the Correſpondence you deſire ; which I hope will be agreeable to your ſelf, as I ſhall conſtantly endeavour it may neither be unprofitable nor ungrateful to the Publick. 'Tis very ſurprizing that ſomething of this nature has not been thought of in our country before, or, if any had form'd ſuch a deſign, that it was never yet executed. Perhaps they thought that the Law and the

Goſpel

Gospel were sufficient. Our Laws, it's true, enforce the observation of moral and social Duties, and 'tis acknowledg'd, even beyond the seas, that our Divines are the best Preachers in the world. But as all Duties come not directly under the cognizance of the Laws, nor all the different circumstances of any Duty whatsoever; so the Magistrate is but half obey'd by those, who can elude the intention of the Legislators, either in point of time or place, or in any other particular not foreseen at the beginning: and he's often not at all obey'd, by such as know no other reason of the Law, but only the authority that has given it a sanction, which they regard as a meer force, that might as well have appointed the contrary; a power that acts with no regard to the good of private persons, farther than they contribute to encrease the grandeur, wealth, and security of the Government. But when these very men perceive the beauty, harmony, and reasonableness of Virtue in it self; how much it is their own outward interest and inward satisfaction to practise it, (supposing there had been neither praise nor rewards to encourage it, nor any punishments or disgrace to prevent the contrary,) and when they see that the good of all persons indifferently is the scope of the Laws, whence the Government is wealthy, wise, or powerful, only as the wealth, and wisdom, and power of the Nation make it so: then a more chearful and sincere obedience will be
yielded

yielded by them to the Laws, and the Magistrate be better imploy'd in diftributing honor than inflicting of fhame. This is likewife as true of the Divines, becaufe the intrinfick worth and rational evidence of religious Duties, will naturally confirm what they preach to the people, viz. that fuch things are commanded by God, and acceptable to him, fince their being both intelligible and practicable make them truly worthy of God, who could not fhew his beneficence more, than in giving man a rule fo much for his advantage, which could not therefore be invented by thofe that teach it, for their own credit, gain, or authority.

2. But not to detain you longer upon a fubject you underftand fo well, I fhall rather convince you that I took your meaning right, by fhewing you in what manner I defign to execute your Project : for as to the juftifying of a private man for concerning himfelf with the publick, or proving that this is one of the propereft ways wherein I could ferve my Country, I fhall touch upon it in another Letter, which will be upon the Publick Good, or the common Intereft of the Society.

3. Once a Week then you may expect to receive a Letter from me, containing a Sheet of paper, upon fome fubject of general ufe, and which you are permitted for that reafon to publifh to the world. This is the whole

defign

defign in two words. But to make it plain beyond all fufpicion of faying one thing and meaning another, I take a Week's time for every Letter, not only to give my felf leifure enough without interrupting my other affairs, and not to overburthen the attention, or to pall the curiofity of the Reader: but alfo to leave no excufe for an ill performance, and to keep a juft medium between fuch Papers as come abroad too often or too feldom; which laft therefore are fometimes quite forgot, as the former muft exhauft the moft fruitful invention. The day of publication fhall be Wednefday, becaufe moft people are then in Town, and that thofe who come from their Country-houfes may receive this lecture frefh before them for their inftruction or entertainment; as they may lay it by, if the hurry of their bufinefs requires it, till they are gone again.

4. A Sheet of Paper is the leaft that can be taken for handling a fubject of any importance with the care it deferves, and perhaps in moft fubjects, that come under our confideration, it is paper enough too: for if Authors did not generally propofe, not fo much to clear the matter, as to write a volume of a certain bulk, their reafonings and facts might often be reduc'd within a very fmall compafs; and we fee fometimes, that the Abridgment of a folio by an able hand into half a fheet, is ab etter Treatife on the fubject than than the

2 Original,

Original, and more efteem'd by good judges. But however, when I chance to light on any Argument that cannot be fufficiently clear'd in one fheet, it fhall be continu'd in the next, or in more, as there may be a neceffity for it; tho' I am of opinion, that fuch cafes will very rarely happen.

5. As for the Subject of our Letters, it fhall be any thing that may be ufeful and acceptable to the publick; but chiefly the moral Virtues, remarkable paffages of Hiftory, philofophical Difquifitions, and the detection of popular Errors. The thread and body of the Letter will always confift of the main fubject, capable of fuch embellifhments and examples as may divert, as well as of fuch grave and folid reafonings as may inftruct. Any fubject in the world, and, what at firft fight would feem the unlikelieft to do it, may give a natural occafion for refolving important doubts in Learning, for making new Difcoveries in Nature or Art, for critical Remarks, and for quoting verfes, epigrams, fragments, and paffages of Authors, fuch as are not in the hands of every body, and that even the moft knowing would be fomething puzzl'd to find, or that indeed they never obferv'd. Not that I promife you all this, Sir: but that if now and then you meet with things of this nature, you may not think it foreign to the Subject; unlefs you find that there's no connection between them, nor any chain of thought

or

or expreffion, whereby the one gave occafion for mentioning the other.

6. The whole World is the ftorehoufe of
the Materials I fhall ufe; antient and modern,
foreign and domeftick Books; the Letters
and Converfation of other perfons; the face
of Nature and my own particular Thoughts.
So that 'tis impoffible I fhould ever be at a
lofs for a fubject, but rather in fufpence which
to prefer, and how with the exacteft judgment to chufe properly among fo many. But
one indifpenfable law I propofe to my felf,
is, that the fubject be fomething which may
be generally entertaining, for which reafon
I fhall always treat of it in a ftile and method intelligible to every body. The Quotations out of other Languages fhall be expreft in our own, with the original in the
margin ; excepting Verfes now and then,
which often lofe their grace and beauty tranflated, the whole turn perhaps depending on
the dialect wherein they were written. Let
no man therefore imagine that this will be a
work above his fphere or capacity : for 'tis
in the moral part of it equally intended for
the good of all, and the learn'd part of it
is particularly defign'd for thofe, who have
not the leifure, nor ever had the opportunity
to turn over many Books. And 'tis efpecially hop'd that the Ladies, who neither do nor
ought to undergo fuch drudgery, will in
thefe Letters find fomething that may pleafe
them,

them, tho' not worth their while to make a painful search for it in bulky volumes. 'Tis the duty of us men to ease and serve them in this, as in any thing besides.

7. This Miscellany therefore being design'd to be of universal benefit, the sheets are printed all on the same Paper and Letter with this Specimen, and the number of the Pages are continued in the order of other books: so that every person may preserve his sheets clean till a Volume be finish'd, which then he may cause to be bound after his own fancy. The heads, or Paragraphs, of every Letter are likewise number'd; that any thing may be the easier found or referr'd to, and for the more perfect framing of the Index, which will be at the end of every volume. Now one word to my self, and another to my Readers. As for me, I thus write a Book at my own leisure, and 'tis the same thing as if I publish'd it under some general Title, though the Pieces be entirely independent of one another; as some have done under the names of Collections, Various Readings, Memorable Things, Storehouses, Nosegays, Treasuries, Gleanings, or such other serious or whimsical Titles, denoting variety of Matter. And as for others, the method I take is infinitely preferable, because they have no trouble in reading the Book by parts, which would deter them in one volume. They have abundantly more time to digest
the

the contents, than if they came on their hands all together. The expence will be no more than if they bought the whole Book, nor fo much ; befides that 'tis perfectly infenfible to moft, and eafy to all manner of perfons.

8. Now, Sir, I'll tell you, and, in telling it to you, I declare to the Publick what I am refolv'd not to do ; and whenever I tranfgrefs thofe Rules, my labour, no doubt, will find a fuitable reception. There's no fear in the firft place, that the Reader fhould be difappointed as to the caufe of publication, the materials of thefe Papers not depending on the wind or weather, on dangerous or dirty ways, on private correfpondence or publick permiffion ; and therefore not fubject to amufe any with falfe or fham intelligence, to tire him with naufeous repetitions, or to banter him with idle tattle at home for want of good ftories from abroad : which is not faid in derogation of News-papers (which in all good Governments are of fingular ufe, under a due regulation) but as things they cannot poffibly avoid, if they keep up the order of their Papers, and to which the prefent undertaking is no way lyable. Neither, as in fuch daily Papers, fhall any part of ours be taken up with Advertifements of any kind, which would not only be unfair, but alfo ridiculous, to make the Readers pay for what others have loft or found, or what the Bookfeller has to fell, inftead of the matter with which

we

we have promis'd to furnish him. But an Account of Books newly publish'd, shall always make up, at least, one third part of this Journal.

9. Next we shall above all things avoid going out of our way to meddle with any Factions or parties at home, with civil or religious professions, designing to hurt none, and to oblige all, to the utmost of our power. We shall not rake into private or family affairs; much less abuse any person by his name at length or abridg'd, nor under any colour, representation, or pretence whatsoever; this being inconsistent with all good manners, policy, or society, being a real assassination when committed by anonymous writers, against whom the injur'd person has no reparation. Our design leads us not to concern our selves with particular men, or, if it should, it must be to speak well and not ill of them; and when we produce any as examples of worth or baseness, they shall be commonly out of antient or foreign History: or, since our own Country abounds with instances of all kinds, having been for many ages so famous a theatre of action; I may well mention the living for the honor and countenance of virtue, but in disparaging of vice, the names I use shall be of persons long since dead, and in whom the families of the living are not concern'd.

10. Not

10. Nor is it to be fear'd that this **Paper** fhould ever incur the difpleafure of the Government, fince ferving the Publick and the Government is certainly one and the fame thing, efpecially in our happy Country (if our own happinefs we could but truly diftinguifh and value) where the intereft of the one and the other are infeparable. By ferving the Government therefore, I mean, not being the penfionary of a fecret Cabal, nor the trumpet of a defigning Minifter, nor the tool of an ambitious Prince : but every man ferves a good Government, who contributes (according to his power) to render the members of it wife and vertuous, which leads them of courfe to be peaceable and obedient ; to bottom their felicity on the publick welfare wherein their particular intereft is involv'd ; confequently to promote the glory, wealth and tranquillity of their Country, whereof they become proportionable fharers ; and readily to yield all honor, duty and reverence to the perfon and authority of the Magiftrate, who deferves it fo well for the dangers, pains and care which he undergoes for the whole and every part.

11. I need fay no more, either as a preface to my Book, or as an account of my defign ; but that whoever has any thing to intimate or communicate, any hint that he thinks to be feafonable, any favorite notion or peculiar difcovery, which can naturally enter into this

this work, let such Pacquets be addrest to the Bookseller, with a Letter containing the desires of the sender, and I shall comply, or give reasons for not doing it, if the subject be of any importance; as to any observations or exceptions that may be made relating to these Papers, such as have a mind to cavil, to shew their talent, or to make a noise about something, will be sure to print without consulting any body; and to such we have nothing to say, because we have no amendment to expect from them. But as for those who are really concern'd for truth, and who have any doubts to propose, or objections to make, who require a further explication of any thing, or that can point out any real mistakes, they shall receive a satisfactory answer, and thanks into the bargain : for as I have merely engag'd in this undertaking for the sake of truth; so the Reader may be satisfy'd that I shall not endeavour to support it by any falshood.

12. And now, to return to your self, Sir, go on as you have advis'd and encourag'd me, to cultivate your understanding, to encrease your knowledge, to instruct your neighbours, and to rectify their manners. Whoever does not make use of his Reason, is not only ungrateful to neglect so excellent a gift of God, but actually prefers the state of brutes to humanity. But whoever, on the contrary, has addicted himself to a serious con-

templation

templation of the works of God and Nature; to a diligent examination of times and places, and to an impartial enquiry into men and opinions (which is what we truly call Philosophy, and not any peculiar system of the Schools) whoever, I say, will thus employ his mind, must needs be pleased with this Undertaking, and break out with CICERO (1) into this divine Exclamation : " O vitae Philosophia dux ! O virtutis indagatrix expultrixque vitiorum! quid non modò nos, sed omnino vita hominum, sine te esse potuisset? Tu urbes peperisti, tu dissipatos homines in societatem vitae convocasti. Tu eos inter se, primum domiciliis, deinde conjugiis, tum literarum & vocum communione junxisti. Tu inventrix legum, tu magistra morum & disciplinae fuisti. Ad te confugimus, a te opem petimus, tibi nos penitus totosque tradimus. Est autem unus dies bene, & ex praeceptis tuis actus, peccanti immortalitati anteponendus. Cujus igitur potius opibus utamur quàm tuis, quæ & vitae tranquillitatem nobis largita es, & terrorem mortis sustulisti ". *O Philosophy! thou guide of life, thou discoverer of virtues, and expeller of vices! what manner of life should not only ours, but that of all men in general be without thee? By thee it was that cities were founded, and mankind assembled into society which lived dispersed before. Thou first didst join them in their*

(1) *Tusc. Disp. l. 5. c. 2.*

*their habitations, next in marriages, and then
by a mutual participation of languages and
letters. Thou we'rt the inventress of
laws, the mistress of learning and manners.
With thee we take sanctuary, from thee we
beg assistance, to thee we perfectly and wholly
resign our selves: for one day well spent, according to thy preceps, is preferable to an er-
ring eternity. What other helps therefore
should we use but thine, who hast bestowed upon us the tranquillity of life, and remov'd the
terror of death.*

13. Thus I have done with my Plan. But
this design of a weekly Paper puts me in
mind of that most true saying of King SOLO-
MON, that *there is nothing new under the
sun,* no not in the meanest trifles which we
think are but of yesterday's invention, as (to
give you a trivial instance) the illuminations
in windows, which of late years we have
substituted to our old rows of bone-fires: yet
if you look into JUVENAL, you find them
there exactly describ'd and practised on great
days, especially on the birth-days of Princes:

*Herodis venere dies, pinguesque fenestris
Ordine dispositæ flammam vomuêre lucernæ.*

And tho' I will not at this time affirm,
that there ever was such a weekly Paper as
mine, yet 'tis undeniable of *the Daily Cou-
rant,* seeing there was in Rome a Daily Journal of all that past in that city, compil'd

with

with the approbation and under the direction of the Magiftrate. Thefe were the *Acta diurna*, of which I fhall give you more particulars, and fome fragments at the end of my Letter next Tuefday, which, as I promifed you, fhall be concerning *the Publick Good*. I need not be fo formal as to tell you every time, what you know fo well; and therefore now once for all I fubfcribe my felf your moft faithful humble and obedient Servant.

A MEMO-

A
MEMORIAL
FOR
The Moſt Honourable
THE EARL OF *** *
CONTAINING
A Scheme of Coalition.

MY LORD,

FTER paying my acknowledgements for your laſt favor, I cannot but complain I have ſo ſeldom of late the honor of admittance to your Lordſhip; and when I obtain it, that no opportunity is given me to ſpeak of any thing to any purpoſe. I am ignorant, as I told you, whom you meant t'other day, by my particular friends that were

O 4   againſt

againſt the Peace: but of this I am ſure, that all my acquaintance are unanimous in their ſentiments. Particular friends in this caſe I have none, but thē Houſe of Hanover: and, tho' a good Peace be a good thing, we are perſuaded no peace can be good for their intereſt at this time; and much leſs a peace that gives up Spain and the Indies to a Prince of the Houſe of Bourbon, or to any French Prince whatſoever. This, MY LORD, but not the ſpirit of any party, nor partiality for any miniſtry, is the ground of our oppoſi‐ tion. I therefore conjure your Lordſhip, by all the friendſhip I entertain and profeſs for you, to conſider, whether it be adviſeable in any Miniſter to carry on a thing ſo perfectly diſguſting to the next Succeſſor? and I be‐ ſeech you to permit me (as your moſt ſincere wellwiſher) freely to tell you, that a clan‐ deſtine negociation with France ſounds very ill to Engliſh ears, even in times of the profound‐ eſt peace. I have been ſo much amaz'd, on the one hand, at the circumſtances of this tranſaction from the beginning: and I have had ſo much confidence in your Lordſhip, on the other hand, as looking upon you to be moſt true to the Succeſſion, that I made my ſelf and others too believe, that the whole was a trick upon the French King and the High‐Church; and that, as ſoon as the pub‐ lick money was all granted, you wou'd up‐ on very good pretexts break with both of them, and be the author of a happy Coali‐ tion

tion between the true friends of their Country, which are the moderate Whigs and the moderate Tories. Several of these denominations have, from time to time, made application to me to convey their thoughts on this matter to your Lordship; which I wholly declin'd, when I perceiv'd such difficulties both of access and speech, as judging my good offices of this kind were no longer agreeable. Among the rest a person of undoubted credit among the Whigs, and that undertook (without presumption) for the leaders, propos'd about two months ago this Scheme, which I took in writing upon the spot from his own mouth:

I. A Coalition, wherein the Earl of G * * * and the Earl of S * * * should be left for some small time unemploy'd by consent, the reason of which is self evident: that in this administration your own figure should not only be chief, but be continu'd so, as a security whereof the balance of the Parliament should be put into your hands.

II. Present dissolution of this Parliament, which might be time enough for the year's service, witness the last Parliament of King WILLIAM; that the qualifying Act past last sessions, wou'd throw out at least a hundred; besides, that the heats about SACHEVERELL being quite allay'd, and such a number of hotheads disappointed by this Ministry, there wou'd wou'd not be fo much money fpent now on that fide.

III. Pretexts for the diffolution various, efpecially that the mony'd people will never truft this Parliament.

IV. A certain number of moderate Tories nam'd, in conjunction with whom the Whigs were willing to act.

And fo he concluded, that, the prefent Miniftry mifcarrying, you muft be ruin'd of courfe, all being imputed to your Lordfhip, who will be made to pafs for a fingle Minifter : whereas, on the foot of this Scheme, others will be anfwerable as well as your felf for any meafures that fhall be taken.

This meffage I peremptorily refus'd to carry, for the reafons abovefaid; but told the perfon (whofe name fhall be mention'd, if you defire it, according to the permiffion he gave me) that, if your Lordfhip intended any fuch thing at all, I was of opinion the proper time wou'd be after this Parliament fhould grant the year's charge : for then their falling into heats about the Peace, or reviving the High-Church projects againft the Diffenters, a mifunderftanding upon any fcore between both houfes, or fomething elfe that may break out by chance or contrivance, wou'd ferve as better pretexts for a Diffolution, and beget a better difpofition in the

electors,

electors, who underſtand nothing, at leaſt very few of 'em, concerning credit, tho' in it ſelf a moſt eſſential point. *Sed illud quoque valeat quantum valere poteſt.* Many other repreſentations of no leſs importance I was entirely diſcourag'd from offering; and had you given me the hearing, the world ſhould never have ſeen his Electoral Highneſs's late Memorial. Don't you now find by experience, MY LORD, that what I wrote to you about that Court near a twelvemonth ſince, is exactly true? Inſtead then of your P * * * and your S * * * you ought to diſpatch me privately to Hanover this minute, where you'll find me as ſecret, as I hope to be ſucceſsful. In my judgment it imports you not a little, were it but for the Queen's ſervice, to clear up ſome things there. If you are of the ſame opinion, I know Holland ſo exactly as to engage my life for paſſing and repaſſing unobſerv'd; giving out here, that I am retir'd ſome where into the country. I need ſay no more, but that as my intereſt is inſeparable from that Family, ſo none upon earth wiſhes better to your particular perſon. But we muſt come to a nearer underſtanding. If you'll pleaſe to ſend me any letter or meſſage, let it be to the ſame houſe where I lodg'd, and where your chaplain ſucceeds me. Delays are dangerous.

> I am,
> MY LORD,
> *Your Lordſhip's moſt faithful*
> *humble Servant.*

Another

MEMORIAL

FOR

The Moſt Honourable

THE EARL OF ***

London, Dec. 17, 1711.

My Lord,

I AM ſo far from being trouble-ſome by frequent, affected, or officious viſits to the great men, with whom I have the honor of being acquainted, that the fear of offending this way, is rather more likely to argue me guilty of negligence or diſreſpect ; and to make me paſs for one that ei-ther clowniſhly knows not, or that ſullenly cares not to make his court. But as my cir-cumſtances muſt clear me from the laſt impu-tation ; ſo the company I have ever kept, and the good reception I have often had from

I   many

many Princes, in whofe Courts I have re-
fided, or with whom I had any bufinefs to
tranfact, will (I doubt not) fet me right as to
the firft. *Principibus placuiffe viris, non ul-
tima laus eft.* Your Lordfhip in particular
will acknowledge, that I am not wont to
interrupt my friends about trifles. But I am
very fenfibly mov'd (I own) at the unufual
difficulty of accefs I find of late to your
Lordfhip, when at the fame time, I have
fcarce ever fail'd of meeting thofe going up
your ftairs or coming down; who, not very
long fince, wou'd have been afraid to be
found in the fame houfe with you : men (as
I then thought) the moft oppofite to you in
principles, and men who were the moft bitter in their farcafms againft your reputation,
when I fuffer'd the reproaches of my beft
friends for adhering to your intereft; perfonal, I mean, and not always political.

But as, in the quality of a States-man and
Prime Minifter, you are to deal with all forts
of perfons; fo I don't complain of their good,
but of my own bad ufage. I need not mention how many years ago our familiarity
commenc'd, founded upon the fame love of
Letters and Liberty, which to generous fpirits
are ftronger ties, than even thofe of blood or
alliance. As little need I mention, how inviolably I have obferv'd the rights of friendfhip, both in the times of your profperity
and adverfity. My enemies never objected
the

the contrary to me: whereas a certain (1) couple, I often fee coming from you, and who are known to be high in your favor, are remarkable for nothing fo much as the one for his levity, the other for his ingratitude, and both for their infufficiency; which indeed does excellently qualify 'em for tools, if that be your defign. They have ambition enough to turn and return, to fay and do, to unfay and undo as they are bid: nor have you any thing to risk, when you ufe them as tools deferve. To you (I can fay it without vanity) I am juft the reverfe. I might be fometimes miftaken in men, but never was fo in things. My management abroad, my behavior at home, what I whifper'd in private, and what I printed to the world, all fpeak the fame language, all tend to the fame end. But of this point on fome other occafion: my bufinefs now is more particular. My adhering to your intereft, MY LORD, when it was not my own to do fo, made feveral people entertain an opinion of me, to which I can lay no manner of claim; as if I were no lefs engag'd in your Lordfhip's confidence and concerns, than you are in my refpect and efteem. This perfeverance of mine, and this only, is the foundation of that notion, which, tho' to me fo reputable, I was never induftrious to propagate: but rather infinuated quite the contrary to all thofe, who, led by this miftake, follicited my intereft for accefs to

your

(1) S * * * and P * * *.

your perfon, or interceffion in their behalf; conftantly refufing the moft tempting offers, and often when I had not many guineas left for fuperfluous expence.

I defy the whole world to produce an inftance to the contrary. I laid an honefter Scheme of ferving my Country, your Lordfhip, and my felf: for feeing it was neither convenient for you, nor a thing at all defir'd by me, that I fhould appear in any publick poft, I fincerely propos'd (as occafions fhould offer) to communicate to your Lordfhip my obfervations on the temper of the miniftry, the difpofitions of the people, the condition of our enemies or allies abroad, and what I might think moft expedient in every conjuncture; which advice you were to follow in whole, or in part, or not at all, as your own fuperior wifdom fhould direct. My general acquaintance, the feveral languages I fpeak, the experience I have acquir'd in foreign affairs, and being engag'd in no intereft at home, befides that of the publick, fhou'd (one wou'd think) qualify me in fome meafure for this province; wherein I am of the mind more than one ought to be neceffarily employ'd. All wife Minifters have ever had fuch private monitors. As much as I thought my felf fit, or was thought fo by others, for fuch general obfervations, fo much have I ever abhorred, MY LORD, thofe particular obfervers we call Spies; which afperfion neverthelefs on

your

your account, neither I, nor yet some other men, who as little deserv'd it, cou'd wholly escape from the malice of yours or our own ill-wishers : as if none cou'd approach a great man, without entring straight into his measures right or wrong. But I despise the calumny no less than I detest the thing : and as you, on your part, must own that I never injur'd any man or woman to you; so I'll do you the justice, on my part, that Your Lordship never thought so unworthily of me as to hint, much less to require any thing of this kind. Of such general observations then as I offer'd, you shou'd have perus'd a far greater number, than I thought fit to present hitherto, had I discover'd by due effects that they were acceptable from me : for they must unavoidably be receiv'd from some body, and, as I said, from more than one hand, unless a Minister were omniscient. Yet I soon had good reason to believe, I was not design'd for the man ; whatever the original sin cou'd be that made me incapable of such a trust, and which I now begin to suspect. Without direct answers to my proposals, how cou'd I know whether what I did here was a service or a disservice ? whether I help'd my friends elsewhere, or betray'd them contrary to my intentions ? and accordingly, I have for some time been very cautious and referv'd. But if Your Lordship will frankly please to enter into any measures with me on a fair and honourable foot, I shall not

only

only use all the faithfulness and diligence in my power to procure the good of my country; but be more ready to serve your Lordship, in this, or in some becoming capacity, than any other Minister. They who confided to my management affairs of a higher nature, have found me exact as well as secret. My impenetrable negotiation at Vienna (hid under the pretence of curiosity) was not only applauded by the Prince that employ'd me, but also proportionably rewarded. And here, MY LORD, give me leave to say, that I have found England miserably serv'd abroad since this change, as in some cases before: and our Ministers at home are sometimes as great strangers to the genius, as to the persons of those with whom they have to do. I foresee that a little time will convince you of this, especially in .... where you have placed the most unacceptable man in the world, one that liv'd in a scandalous misunderstanding with the Minister of the States at another Court, one that has been the laughing-stock of all courts for his senseless haughtiness and most ridiculous airs, and one that can never judge aright unless by accident in any thing.

Now what is it that should hinder your Lordship, after so long an acquaintance, from honoring me with your Patronage and Commands, but some disagreement to the conditions demanded by me, or in the principles on which we are both to proceed? To persuade

suade me of either of these, I fancy will be a harder task than most men can easily perform. The annual allowance I have proposed is so moderate, and the ways of securing it to me (without costing your Lordship any thing) are so many and so obvious, that it will admit of no other question, but whether you are still disposed to comply with it : for I had your promise for it the last time but one I had the honor to discourse with you, besides all the Letters and Promises of providing for me in general before. By declining a publick Post, not only out of prudence, but out of choice (which yet will scarce be credited) all pretences are remov'd of irritating any party or persons that should not approve my preferment, a thing unavoidable prefer who you will: and there are so many ways of accounting for my being easy, besides one relating to Learning I shall not name at present, that this point likewise admits of no difficulty. The work I mean will be no party-drudgery, nor wou'd the greatest Prince on earth think it below him to patronize it, whether he had the best, or the worst, or no Religion. But such will never like it, as are not hearty lovers of their Country.

As for the Principles on which we are both to act, I hope we are still more agreed. The special ones of usefully serving your Lordship, and securing a competent maintenance to my self, are supposed of course. But the

2   general

general ones which with me are unalterable and indifpenfable, are civil Liberty, religious Toleration, and the Proteftant Succeffion. Thefe are my conditions *fine qua nòn:* and he that will not agree with me on this foot, muft never employ me nor ever truft me. This I take to be plain-dealing, as I take honefty to be the beft policy. Sooner than recreantly efpoufe Prerogative, Perfecution, or the Pretender, let me be utterly difcarded, be expofed to all hazards, difficulties, and inconveniencies. To obviate any mifunderftanding, My Lord, I mean no more by Liberty than a government of Laws and not of will, particularly our own excellent conftitution of King, Lords, and Commons: yet without the Juredivinofhip of the Prince, or the Paffive-obedience of the Subject, the Laws being to both an equal rule. As the Whigs mean no other Commonwealth, contrary to the calumny of the furious and ill-affected part of the Tories; fo I am perfuaded many of the Tories are far from aiming at fetting up irrefiftible Power or indefeafible Succeffion, contrary to the fuggeftions of fome weak but well-meaning Whigs. The Papifts and Jacobites are common enemies to both, and againft thefe they muft both join at laft, or be ruin'd. Such a Common-wealth's-man I only approve, as your Lordfhip formerly was, when you encourag'd me to reprint *Harrington's Oceana,* tho' neither of us imagin'd the model it felf to be practicable. For my own

part,

part, as I have ever been, so I still declare my self to be a Whig: a Whig, I say, by denomination as well as by principle, in the sense that I have explain'd this word in a book I wrote by your Lordship's allowance and encouragement, *the Memorial of the State of England.* But I declare at the same time, that I am far from thinking the Prince, or even his chief Minister, should make himself the head of a party; which will not only render either or both of them contemptible, but likewise plunge 'em into inextricable difficulties. In this very respect I have often admir'd and applauded your Lordship, for so often in certain affairs recovering the oversetting vessel to its former steddy course: and it shall be my ardentest wish, that no provocation of what nature soever, no precipitate measures of your associates, neither superior influence, nor inferior phrenzy, may be able to force you into any of those extremes, the edge of whose fury you have sometimes blunted or retorted with such admirable address. So have I always understood your conduct, and so have I always explain'd it in the sincerity of my heart, as well as by my inclination to have it so: so I understand your Lordship now (whether I be mistaken or not) and may I prove as true a Prophet as ever to my special Friends! But my mind in this matter is fully understood by the Scheme I presum'd to lay before you not very long ago about a Coalition, towards the effecting of which, nevertheless, thelefs, the management of affairs fince gives me very fmall hopes, and feems to portend quite the contrary, which muft needs end in-confufion.

Now if your Lordfhip keeps as firm as ever to the glorious principle of Liberty, you muft by an inevitable confequence be entirely fixt in the next human and heavenly princi-ple of Toleration. So far am I from appre-hending you fhould, as fome daily infinuate, promote any of the High-Church defigns, thofe projects of APOLLYON, that I am per-fuaded (whatever ufe you may make of the Proteftant Jefuits of Chrift-Church) you can never favor thofe Priefts who fawcily ftrike at the Queen's Supremacy, by afferting the In-dependency of the Church upon the State; who openly endeavour to make the Sacrament of the Lord's Supper pafs for a proper Sacri-fice the very effence of the Mafs; who as boldly prefs the duty of private Confeffion to a Prieft, in order to introduce the neceffity of his lucrative Abfolution; and who, by other means more covert and difguis'd, labour at reconciling ours with the Church of Rome, or rather to make the Englifh Church as pompous, fuperftitious, and tyrannical as the Papal : the ultimate end of A***, S***, M***, and fuch other Preachers for Bifhop-ricks, being nothing elfe but advancing the pride and power of Priefts. This is their *Church of England*, and by this word is the mob deluded. How can I, that think I know

your Lordſhip ſo well, ever impoſe on my
ſelf ſo far, or ſuffer my friends to ſwallow
ſuch a monſtrous abſurdity, as that you
ſhould not ſtrenuouſly ſupport the legal Toleration, ay and the general Naturalization too,
in their utmoſt latitude? as being the main
ſprings and ſecrets of making any country
flouriſh in wealth and learning, in arts and
arms. Your Lordſhip knows that I neither
am, nor affect to be thought, a Bigot; and
that I abominate Licentiouſneſs as much as I
venerate Liberty. But let no body imagine
that we Free-thinkers (whom ſome of narrow views ignorantly confound with thought-
leſs Libertines) ſhould be leſs zealous or cou-
rageous, than the moſt wholeſale believer or
the preciſeſt profeſſor of 'em all, againſt the
return of Popery under whatever denomination. The converts in King JAMES's time
were moſt of 'em Eccleſiaſtics or their Lay-
bigotted Pupils, and not one of 'em a Free-
thinker, no nor a Diſſenter: nor are the Free-
thinkers (for which glorious name they are
oblig'd to their enemies) ſo eaſily put off
with words as ſome others, ſince there may
very well be ſuch a thing as Proteſtant Popery; for Popery is in reality nothing elſe, but
*the Clergy's aſſuming a right to think for the
Laity,* from which not only follows the
leading or driving of them at their pleaſure,
but every thing imaginable the Prieſts ſhall
find conducing to their peculiar profit or authority. Engliſh Catholic ſhocks common
ſenſe

senfe, as much as Roman Catholic. You may play your Priefts then (if that be all?) juft as you pleafe againft one another, I fhall cheerfully go on to ferve your Lordfhip for the Proteftant caufe in general, which, even in the leaft reform'd parts of it, muft be acknowledg'd to be a noble ftruggle for Liberty, and a mighty ftep towards the ruin of fpiritual Tyranny.

Having expreft my felf fo copioufly, My Lord, upon Liberty and Toleration, I may be the fhorter upon our third principle of the Houfe of Hanover, from which the other two are infeparable. Liberty and Property, Toleration and Union, have occafion'd that Succeffion. On thefe it is founded, by thefe it muft be maintain'd againft all oppofition. And, as a fure earneft of a glorious future profpect, thefe are the domeftic hereditary principles of that Houfe: for, whatever our fools or knaves may prate of arbitary Power there, the inhabitants are Syncretifts by profeffion (that is German Occafional Conformifts) and never were there Subjects on earth better ufed, or more content; the Barons having an appeal from the Prince to a higher Court, tho' they never have occafion given them to make ufe of this right. Your Lordfhip appeared for this caufe as early as any, and if to the fame you are not ftill as firm as any, what a wretched Politician am I? how greatly mifled my felf? and how great a mifleader of others,

efpecialespecially of that illuftrious Family? This, I cannot in duty forbear telling you, is the place in which your enemies now attack you with their utmoft vigor, and, from certain odd circumftances, they perfift in their accufation with the moft fanguine hopes of fuccefs. It is here therefore that I daily exert my greateft efforts in your defence, and where I have a better right to be credited than any of your new friends. To this Houfe, in a word, I am wholly devoted out of inclination and principle. I have no other intereft than this, which I take to be the common intereft of us all. Tho' changing of fides is become fo fafhionable a thing, yet neither fear nor favor, no advantage or temptation, tho' ever fo confiderable, not the byafs of acquaintance, nor even the force of friendfhip, can take me off (as the phrafe is) from this principle of the Hanover Succeffion, where I have from the beginning fixt my reft : and therefore I cannot but be honeftly of the mind, that I ought to be more trufted and more encouraged, than fuch as have been ever indifferent or ever enemies to it. There's a long lift of thofe I mean, and which I am ready to produce upon occafion. I do therefore moft earneftly wifh, that all ugly appearances (whereof I have fo frequently complain'd in other *Memorials*) were quite taken away, and that a better underftanding were cultivated with the moft difcerning Court in Europe. Your Lordfhip will find by experience that I don't flatter.   Since

Since then, MY LORD, the truth of the matter is, that I have been for many years, both at home and abroad, your unwavering friend and adherent; one, for whom you have expreſt the greateſt kindneſs; one, to whom, ſince your late advancement, you have made repeated promiſes of the continuance of your protection; and one, who on many accounts may be more ſerviceable to you for the future than ever before: I cannot, I ſay, from all theſe conſiderations, but, in the nature of a lover, complain of your preſent neglect, and be ſollicitous for your future care. There being none but your ſelf (which may never happen!) capable to convince me that we are not embark'd in the ſame bottom, have I not ſome reaſon to expect good entertainment in the ſhip, where I have not been altogether idle? eſpecially, when I neither take upon me to control the officers, nor to claim any ſhare in the government. As to the obſervations I did propoſe to make, I fancy thoſe I actually preſented, are ſufficient to anſwer for thoſe I ſhou'd have made, had I receiv'd befitting encouragement. I appeal particularly to my early application about the pretended Weſt-Meath Plot, and the too real affair of the Scots-Medal; both which (from wrong ſteps taken againſt my advice at firſt) have ſince occaſion'd ſo much noiſe, and, if I be not miſtaken, they'll occaſion much greater yet, tho' ſeemingly now forgot. No body is puniſh'd at all that libels

bels the succession, tho' I have shewn such libels to be numerous, and openly sold. We'll see what the house does with CR ** L: yet one wou'd think that certain others never expected those to succeed, against whose sentiments they act in so desperate a manner. But, in plain truth, what shall we say after the pardoning of some from the gallows, whose execution might be a service to the Ministers as well as to the Nation? after the not punishing of one mortal for the late Invasion, a mercy not to be parallel'd in all history? and after the dismissing of those that were taken in the fact on such easy bail? The advancement of certain persons in Scotland, seems prodigious unaccountable to the irreconcileable enemies of Popery and the Pretender. I shall not say however that this is inconsistent with her Majesty's Speech, at the opening of the present Parliament (where being hearty *for the House of Hanover* is made by her an exprest qualification for preferment) because in the first speech she ever made in Parliament, she bids the nation expect *to find her always a strict and religious observer of her word.* Nor must your Lordship take ill what is meant so well, if I prophecy that two incendiaries (2) in Ireland, if not timely prevented, will occasion you many a heart-ake: seeing the honest people of England now do make the same inferences from the proceedings about Corporations in Ireland,

(2) *P* *** and *H* ** *.

land, that they did from the Declarations for Indulgence in Scotland, and from the Quo Warranto's and Regulators in England, in King James's time. *Verbum sapienti :* for surely the reigns of King CHARLES and King JAMES should be no patterns to men of revolution principles ; by which I mean those that acted in the Revolution, and that approv'd of it. Nor are many less alarm'd at the late unprotestant and unpolitick Addresses of certain Irish Bishops, and their noble pupils in leading-strings. I hope, during the power of such a father's son, the honest Northern Dissenters may not be so barbarously us'd with relation to the pension of their Ministers, as a reward (or shall I say a punishment?) for securing London-Derry, and preventing thereby a descent into Great Britain of a very dubious issue. Must reprisals be thus taken upon them, for the villanous impostor LANGTON's being struck off the Establishment? I further hope, that you'll keep some body from medling a third time in that Kingdom with matters above his sphere.

But I am launch'd perhaps too far, where my advice is not ask'd : and I am afraid by this time, Your Lordship may imagine I would give my self airs of importance. I appeal to your own experience, whether of all that transact any thing with you, I be not the farthest from this sort of vanity? Neither am I a medler or busy body, beyond what justly comes to the share of every free subject.

subject.   Have I ever obtruded on Your Lordship's privacies? or importun'd you to tell
me, what you did not think fit to impart of
your own accord? for as to the affairs of the
present conjuncture, I content my self with
knowing as much of 'em, as any man in the
world that is not in the secret, of which I
have given, where it was necessary, a most
authentic demonstration; and even to your
self, when, in my last *Memorial*, I declar'd
against any Peace at all at this time, as believing it must be such a peace, as will not
only render useless all her Majesty's triumphs,
sully the honor of the nation, betray our
best and firmest allies, but effectually ruin
theirs, and ours, and the liberties of all Europe, besides the manifest breaches of word
and faith in persons, whose character ought
not to be lightly prostituted.   I wish from my
soul, inconsiderable as I am, that you had
vouchsaf'd to ask me a few questions, with
regard to some particulars.

As for writing in defence of your person
or politics (the neglect of which was lately
objected to me, by one of your relations)
how cou'd I possibly divine, without your
express instructions, that I shou'd not be all
the while unskilfully thwarting your designs?
Far from being ambitious of recommending
your Schemes to the publick, I wou'd gladly have employ'd my pen to convince the
world, that it was neither by your Lordship's
privity

privity nor approbation (as your enemies give out) that our faithful Allies, especially the Dutch, have been treated of late, in a manner too injurious and scurrilous to be permitted even towards declar'd enemies, in any civiliz'd country. Posterity will be asham'd, when they read such infamous pieces. With what alacrity should I obey, were I authoriz'd to shew how the not calling of the wretched Abel Roper to account for his treasonable paragraph against the Succession, and his abominable usage of all men of worth, abroad and at home (not to forget the Author of *the good old cause*, of the *Oath to an Invader*, the *Examiner*, and such other open opposers of the Protestant Line ;) how, I say, this unexampl'd lenity towards such criminals, is consistent with our care and concern for the House of Hannover, and for the Liberties that have cost so much blood and treasure to secure ; for, believe me or not, I had rather be enabl'd to shew the true reasons, than to receive a bank-bill of a thousand pounds. My best apology for the length of this Letter, My Lord, is that the nature of the thing requir'd it. I have before made use in it of the simile of a Lover, and, as such indeed, I thought fit once for all to come to a thorow explanation : looking upon uncertainty as one of the greatest misfortunes that can befall me, and being resolv'd, if my affection be not kill'd by your unkindness (I mean to your self as well as to me) to become

indisso-

indiſſolubly yours; for which the only ſecret is, that you do inſeparably become your
Country's. I am with the ſame dutifulneſs,
zeal, and reſpect as ever,

My Lord,

Your Lordſhip's

moſt faithful, obedient,

and devoted Servant.

A MEMO-

A
MEMORIAL

Prefented to a

MINISTER OF STATE,

Soon after his Majefty King George's acceffion to the Crown.

HE chief heads of this Memorial fhall be the Clergy and the Laity. And as for the firft of thefe, I take it for granted, as a thing of publick notoriety, that but too many of the Clergy of England have no regard for any thing but profit and power; that the more you enrich or advance them, the more haughty and mifchievous they will be; not valuing any fort of Religion or Virtue, further than

than it merely ferves their intereft. This, you'll fay, ought not to be fo, to which I add, that 'tis pity it fhould be fo. But neither of us can deny the fact: and I conceive the only way to manage thofe men, fo that they may neither hamper the Government nor difturb the Peace of the People (by their intrigues and importunities with relation to the firft; or their impofing upon and gaining the money of the laft, by wheedling, and efpecially by practifing upon fick people) is to make the ftatute of Mortmain in force as formerly. Their revenues are fufficient, and much more than are enjoy'd by any fecular Priefts in the world. Nay, had many of them lefs, their cures would be better taken care of: and it is apparent that nothing ever did or can keep them quiet, but a ftrict and fteddy hand over them. I mean, that they be not fuffer'd (much lefs encourag'd) to meddle with politicks or civil affairs; but that they be ftrictly kept to their fpiritual office, as fet forth in a Sermon preach'd by the late Archbifhop of York. They muft be difcountenanc'd in their rampant practices, and thofe be never preferr'd who tranfgrefs in the above-mentioned particulars. Thus the thing may be eafieft affected, by a good Magiftracy in every County: for thefe I am fpeaking of, are meanly born and bred, ignorant for the greateft part, and made equally proud and infolent at the Univerfities. Therefore when they perceive the civil Government re-

folv'd

folv'd and fteddy, they will court and comply with the Magiftrates; being naturally fearful, and perpetually undermining each other : whereas the more the Magiftrate gives way to them, the more they'll grow upon him. It is felf-evident, that their great power and intereft is principally deriv'd (not from the populace) but from thofe of the Nobility and Gentry, who govern the people, and who are themfelves govern'd by thefe Priefts. When very young they are commonly their Schoolmafters, and always their Tutors at the Univerfities; whereby they cannot only lead them all their lives in matters above their reach, but even fright and deceive them as they pleafe; governing their perfons, families, eftates and intereft. A remedy therefore fhould be found out for a better Education and better Inftructions at our Univerfities. Among other methods, I fancy if the Fellows and Mafters of Arts in all the Colleges were not oblig'd to go into Orders, that it would go a good way towards the cure. But of this more particularly hereafter.

Now as to the Laity, they are divided into Papifts, Tories, Whigs, and Trimmers. The firft of thefe, if confiftent with the flourifhing condition of any civil Government, is not I am fure with a Proteftant one : becaufe their Religion not only obliges them to own a foreign Superior, to whom they yield a fubmiffion incompatible with their Allegiance to their natural Sovereign; but to break all faith, morality, and humanity with those which the Pope shall denuonce to be Hereticks, in order to advance their own Doctrines, all calculated for the interest of that damnable, bloody, and destructive Faction they call the Church. These men ought to be crush'd and subdu'd to the utmost (not for mere opinions in Religion, which every man ought to enjoy) but as they are constantly endeavouring, with all possible industry and artifice, to destroy all other Religions, to subvert Liberty and Property, the better to introduce their own Superstition. The Pope and his Clergy abroad (who formerly possest the best part of this rich and happy Island) leave no stone unturn'd to regain those powers and riches they formerly had. To this end they send over their best heads, generally natives of this Kingdom, to make converts directly; and indirectly, under the notion of zealous churchmen, to increase mystery, superstition, and priestly power, to divide the establish'd Church, to encrease the Sectaries, to corrupt the Universities, to raise antipathies among the People by party-names and distinctions; to bribe, (in a word) to lie, defame, and murther, or if there be any other villany more heinous than these. On such accounts no proceeding can be thought too severe, since this evil is become hard to suppress, or indeed to be tolerably kept under, by reason of the byass the House of the STUARTS has had all along

in

in favour of Popery, and the incouragement it has constantly receiv'd, tho' in a more covert manner, from the aspiring or the ignorant part of the Church of England Clergy. King GEORGE, on the contrary, will not only more effectually secure himself at home, and become prodigious popular, by appearing (as he is) a thorough Protestant, as having the Reform'd Interest much at heart; but thus acquire authority, credit, and confidence abroad, as the real Head of the Protestant Religion every where, and in every circumstance.

To proceed from the Papist to the Tories, these are of two sorts. The first are Nonjurors, perfect Rosicrusians in Government, a stupid, illiterate, stubborn, positive, noisy and impudent Generation; yet not very dangerous, so long as they have ingenuity enough to continue their scruples about the Oaths: but once they get the better of their consciences in this respect (which, a few silly creatures excepted, they generally do) then no sort of men are more clamorous about the Church, or more importunate for Places. These ought not only to be kept under, and discouraged; but also to be ridicul'd and made contemptible both in print and conversation: for they are never to be chang'd, and consequently never to be trusted; as being incapable of reason, and insensible of favours. Besides that it is an establish'd

maxim

maxim with them, to fwear and creep into places, the better to ferve their young Mafter, as thefe Wittals term the Pretender. The fecond fort of Tories are, 'tis true, men fo devoted to the Church of England, that they are implacable towards all other opinions, tho' ever fo little differing in form or fub-ftance from their own; but yet they are neither fo furious, fenfelefs, or wicked as the firft : for they wou'd not give up their own Property or the Liberty of Europe, they wou'd not willingly lofe our Trade or aggrandize France to the ruin of their native Country; and they are withal good friends to the Prote-ftant Line, and as averfe as any to a Popifh Succeffor. Thefe men therefore ought to be mildly treated, and thofe of 'em to be pre-ferr'd to Places, who have virtue and merit; which are the beft qualifications in all kinds of men, for Magiftracy and offices. This impartiality will highly pleafe the People, leave the Tories in hope, even the worft of them, and give no ground for the clamours of any Party.

The Whigs (I mean thofe who practife what they profefs) are virtuous, wife, and induftrious Church of England men; yet brotherly indulgent towards other Protef-tants, and all for a general Naturalization. To thefe ought to be added the Sectaries, who heartily join with them on one common bottom, againft Popery and Slavery either in Church or State. The Whigs of all de-nomination s nominations (whatever may be their failings or differences in other respects) are immoveably staunch for Liberty civil and religious, for Trade and the Balance of Europe, in which things I take the true interest of Britain to consist. So far are they from being against Kingship (as their enemies foolishly calumniate them) that they are to a man most zealous for the Act of Succession, particularly faithful to King George (whom they admire almost to adoration) absolutely determin'd to support his progeny, and such, in short, as may be depended upon in all the particulars aforesaid. I still mean those that are true to their principles, such as have kept their integrity in times of danger, that have not chang'd for interest or favour, and who are known (as all men are best so) by their actions. These are the men who ought to fill all posts of trust in his Majesty's service, both at home, and in his Embassies abroad: giving some places of honor, and of profit also, to such Tories as are to be wean'd off from their Party, or who are to keep them in hope and dependance.

The Trimmers are timorous pusillanimous knaves, who (forsooth) would not provoke any party, but smile upon all, and ever leaning towards the prevailing side, or hovering between both till they see who gets the better. I conceive no other use ought to be made of these men, but as tools to serve the

present

present demands; but such time-servers are never to be confided with posts of trust, nor with any such great places, that will procure them credit and power, both which they will be as ready to employ against as for the King, according to the influence their fears or their avarice may have upon them in a perilous conjuncture.

If this be the true state of our case, the next enquiry must be after a proper cure; which that we may the more certainly discover, we ought to lay down such principles, as will support all we shall build upon them in the sequel of this Discourse. There is no question to be made, but that mankind by nature is of the sociable species of animals, herding together in communities for their common safety; and that they quarrel among themselves, or oppress each other, just upon the same motives and topicks with other animals: such as food, venery, sickness, old-age, and want of understanding; but to a far higher degree by the use of speech, and especially of hands, which manage weapons to their own destruction, as well as that of their fellow-creatures. I conceive therefore, that true Virtue, Religion, and understanding, ought to provide against these evils of Society, by good Education and wholesome Laws, whereby sufficient food may be provided without violence, venery without force, the sick and aged reliev'd, and madmen and idiots taken care of. The

The rules for Virtue and Religion ought to be plain and simple, or (as we commonly speak) the naked truth, unchangeable, void of craft, of gain, or of power; being part of the civil government, and wholly depending upon the same. The Clergy shou'd teach those rules, and deliver those precepts without adding, diminishing, glossing, or commenting; which is the ready way to make Humanity shine, Justice flourish, and Communities happy. But since England is not what we cou'd wish it, we must endeavour to alter and amend by degrees, as far as practicable: and I think it very reasonable, that present care shou'd be taken, to prevent the Clergy meddling with Politicks in their pulpits or elsewhere.

This evil may in a great measure be cur'd by the King, and by the Diocesans proceeding according to his Injunctions, both sending such orders to the inferior Clergy, as shall seem most convenient; the King acting as Head of the Church, and the Bishops as Governours of their several Diocesses under him. They must be strictly kept to that Law and Canon already in force, viz. that no persons be admitted to take Orders, but such as have a title, or are truly presented to livings; nor that they be permitted to act or concern themselves in any civil employment whatsoever.

Great

Great care fhould be taken to reform the Univerfities, which, if fettl'd on the foot of Virtue, wou'd in twenty years bring up a generation, that fhou'd retrieve the worth, underftanding, induftry, and honor of the nation, now fo low, and almoft deftroy'd by a late fet of men, who were there vicioufly and ignorantly educated. Smiles and frowns will go a great way at the Univerfity, preferring one before another, as they excell in probity and proper endowments. Other methods will have their due effects, as obliging the Tutors to read Lectures to their Pupils in a regular manner; but efpecially encouraging fuch Tutors, as teach ufeful knowledge: reftraining them from dabling in Politicks, and that youth be not permitted to be out of their Colleges, but at certain hours, without the leave of their Tutors; nor to frequent publick houfes, but fconc'd when found there at any time of the day: that common fire-rooms be provided in all Colleges, and that feveral fuperftitious cuftoms be abolifh'd, with that fervile one of Scholars capping Fellows, Mafters of Arts or fuch others, any more than they do other men in other places: that prizes be given by the King to fuch as excell in Literature, or even in any exercifes relating to Trade, no lefs than in Mathematicks, Mechanicks, Agriculture, Navigation, Planting, Fifhery, Mineing, and fo on.

As

As to particular Professions, care should be taken, that no persons be prefer'd but such as are bred up to that same way, or are well skill'd therein; but by no means to give the same person two employments in different professions; I mean, that Lawyers be kept to affairs of justice solely, Physicians to take care of health, Soldiers for offence or defence; as Gentlemen to the Belles Lettres, to travel, to the court, to embassies, and to country-offices: the Merchants to trade, the Citizens to their various crafts, the Shop-keepers to diligence in retail and the plain rules of buying and selling, Farmers to the management of their lands, and Labourers to industry, sobriety, cheap diet and cloathing. In short, not to encourage them to entrench upon or intermix with each other, in any thing different from that which they were severally bred; unless in case of some extraordinary genius and propensity. This will quiet and please vast numbers of people.

Also it will be granted (I suppose) at first sight, that a prudent Economy shou'd be us'd in disposing of Places, since for any one place there are so many Candidates. No person therefore should have pluralities. Rich men shou'd be rewarded by titles or places of Honor: middling men shou'd be rais'd purely on the score of their Merit: and poor men for industry, honesty, and other fitting qualifications. A special regard ought to be

had

had to the various defires and inclinations of men : for a fmall thing rightly apply'd, may pleafe more than one of twenty times the value. But men extremely profufe or covetous, ought not to be prefer'd at all, thefe extremes making them mercenary, cowardly, and perfidious.

Education is of the laft confequence, and care fhou'd not only be taken to adapt the profeffions to the genius or inclinations of the youth; but alfo to encreafe the numbers of each profeffion, as the emergencies of State may require. And I think nothing will prove more pernicious to the Publick than the new erections of Charity Schools, where the poor Children are bred up all pen-men (forfooth) and qualify'd for fuch employments where they are not wanting, but which are on the contrary more than overftock'd. This caufes a prodigious drain from the Manufacturers and Labourers, who are obferv'd to grow much fcarcer fince this mifchievous invention, and which of courfe encreafes the price of man's labour, makes commodities be wrought worfe, and fent dearer to the market. It does further give the greateft encouragement to idlenefs, the poor folks ufing all means and intereft to educate their Children book-learned and Schollards; which is a moft inconceivable damage to the Nation : as to this fame Nation, I take the great number of Country Latin Schools to be a real lofs

and

and injury, fince four or five years of their childrens labor are loft and mifpent, by moft that can pay a fmall matter for their teaching ; tho' not one in five hundred makes any future ufe of it to their advantage, but rather to their ruin, and fo much of their beft time irrecoverably loft from learning other matters, infinitely more ferviceable to themfelves and the Publick. This fame Latin-monging fpoils their hand-writing, figuring, and true Englifh, the only accomplifhments requifite for the Populace.

Another matter highly injurious to the Publick, as it particularly reflects on the Prince, is that the Difcipline of the Army fhould be fo neglected as it is in England, that commands fhou'd be difpos'd of for money, not merit ; that falfe mufters and unfit men fhould be conniv'd at ; that advantage fhould be taken of the Soldiers cloathing and fubfiftence ; that they are not kept to eafy labour for the publick good in time of Peace, and care taken to employ them when disbanded. But the moft fhameful evil is, the Collonels, and others making their children of two or three years old, Captains, Lieutenants, and Enfigns. I have been credibly inform'd that girls have been lifted officers, nay, that children unborn were fo. Nothing can be a greater cheat, nor more difgufting to all forts of people, than to fee this practice ; and to pay the money (which fome want for neceffaries) to uphold this wicked-

wickedness: nor is it to be doubted but our good and wise King will forthwith redress this evil, for the fact is undoubtedly true ; besides that, he will have the more places to dispose of, to men devoted to his service, and greater numbers of officers and effective men to serve in his wars. Care should also be taken, that the Soldiers in their quarters should not meddle with the Magistracy, nor invade any man's property ; that they be kept to virtue and morals, and not to be suffer'd to destroy the Game, which is a great offence to the Country Gentlemen, tho' they even give their consent to the officers.

England is now so vicious and wicked, that it is of absolute necessity to put the several Laws strictly in execution, the doing of which tho' a seeming severity, yet is real charity : and no people will ever obey a Government that do not pay a ready obedience to the Laws. The declaration of pardoning none, will save the blood and punishment of thousands. Magistrates, in a word, must be oblig'd to do their duties, whereas they are at this time so complying, and so negligent to the last degree, that vice has got the better of almost all of them. Riots therefore, and Factions, and Tumults, particularly the disturbers of the Worship of such as are tolerated by law to exercise their Religion, shou'd be as severely punish'd as the law allows, and the abettors of such disturbers of the Peace
remarkably

remarkably difcourag'd : for in a good Government, all men ought to have free liberty to fpeak and write upon any fubject whatfoever, not inconfiftent with virtue, morality, or the civil adminiftration.

It's highly neceffary, that the Revenue and publick Money be put into a good method and frugal management, both as to the receipts and iffues, as well as in all parts of the application to proper ufes; correcting the finifter practices of under-officers, and preventing the lavifhing of great fums by bribery, or trades-men's cheating and omiffions, the flow execution of bufinefs both civil and military, efpecially going to market upon tick, the advancing of money upon loans or intereft, and ufing of extortion in returns. Times ought to be fet for undertakers, and no great contracts made privately or underhand, but publifh'd in the Gazette, and by other proper methods, to the view and confideration of all the world. But I am grown lefs follicitous about this moft effential article, fince his Majefty has fhewn his wifdom, by putting the Earl of HALIFAX at the head of the Treafury.

There's nothing the Nation labours fo much under at prefent, as the heavy load of publick Debts (tho' numbers of particular men be rich and opulent) and therefore its hop'd his Majefty will apply his great wifdom to this
work ;

work; and manage his own Revenue fo well, as to fpare (if poffible) fome part of it to the publick-fervice. This will gain him millions in time, and endear him to the People above all things: for nothing can pleafe them fo much after their late great payments, as fome fuch act, tho' a fmall infignificant matter. What acceffion of power and her people's love, did Queen ELIZABETH acquire by returning fome taxes, for which there appear'd no occafion? and by her frugal management of the purfe, were not all the purfes of the Nation at her devotion? Nor, give me leave to fay it, will any thing more difpleafe the people at this juncture, than the asking of an additional Revenue, as fome out of officioufnefs fhew themfelves ready to offer, and others on purpofe to make his Majefty odious, to entangle his affairs, and that the Hanover Succeffion may feem a national burthen: whereas it's humbly conceiv'd, that the prefent Revenue will anfwer all the demands of the Royal Family, till the neceffity of publick affairs requires the raifing of more money.

But that thefe main points, and capital articles, may not put fmaller matters out of our memory, which yet deferve our care, I am of opinion that Gypfies, Vagabonds, and Beggarly Strangers, ought to be taken up and feverely handl'd, if they cannot give a good account of themfelves: for they com-
monly

monly difperfe lyes and fcandal, they teach the people tricks and knavifh fhifts, they are examples of idlenefs and thieving, and have an opportunity (which I wou'd have underftood likewife of Hawkers and Pedlars) to carry about any treafonable defign, correfpondence, or libels, on which they may be put by crafty, difcontented, or ill-affected perfons; who rather than fail of their purpofe, will gain 'em with money.

The beft way to prevent this, and many the like mifchiefs, is to have Gentlemen of virtue, underftanding, and induftry made Magiftrates; men who know their bufinefs, and that will be fure to execute the Laws; men that will be zealous to retrieve the morals and manners of the people, who are diffolute and vicious to the higheft degree. But no Clergymen (as I faid more than once before) ought to be in the civil Magiftracy, and as few Lawyers, at leaft Attorneys and Pettyfoggers, as may be. And if any of thefe Magiftrates be remifs and negligent, or fhew others the worft example by tranfgreffing the Laws in their own perfons, let fuch be immediately turn'd out, and others put in their room without favour or affection. I had like to forget that all Fees ought to be afcertain'd by Act of Parliament, with a great penalty on thofe that will prefume to take more.

The

The preſent practice of the Courts of Law is extremely corrupt, dilatory, and expenſive; the Counſel abominably mercenary, and guilty of extravagant extortion in their fees; the Attorneys are arbitary in their bills, treacherous to their clients, the greateſt encouragers of cheats and falſhoods, ay and of perjury too; commonly beggars, poyſoning the peoples morals, ever ſetting 'em together by the ears, and awing them to that degree, that they perpetually live in fear, being little better than their ſlaves: ſo that the Law, which was ſpecially ordain'd for the relief of the poor and ignorant, is become their higheſt bane and oppreſſion.

I further preſume to hint whether (now that we have got a King who delights in hunting, the princely exerciſe of his Saxon Anceſtors) it may not be of ſervice, to enforce the Laws againſt Poachers, eſpecially as to ſhooting. Theſe being very numerous, and encreaſing every day, the miſchief is not only the almoſt intire deſtruction of the Game, even in his Majeſty's foreſts; but it makes the common people negligent of their callings, idle, lewd, inſolent, and beggarly. To prevent theſe or worſe effects, care ſhould be taken to revive and encourage by prizes or otherwiſe, ſuch other Sports and Paſtimes as were anciently in uſe for the publick exerciſe of the people; ſuch as Wreſtling, Cudgel-playing,

ing, throwing the barr, and the like recreations serving to increase strength and agility of body, no less than to procure or to preserve health. Among others it is more to be desir'd than hop'd (considering our more than Jewish superstition) that there shou'd be a reasonable exercise of the Militia after evening service on Sundays, particularly in summer, as it is practis'd in some Protestant countries abroad; which wou'd be useful to the State, and pleasing to the People: provided always, that their fire-arms be kept in a room for that purpose, excepting only when they are thus to be employ'd.

But why shou'd I longer insist on these particulars, when I consider that never before did Britain possess a King endu'd with so many glorious qualities; as true piety, fortitude, temperance, prudence, justice, knowledge, industry, frugality, and every other virtue, all supported by an active and even temper, by uninterrupted health and application: so that (thanks be to heaven) we may all rest assur'd that this greatest and best of Princes will encourage virtue and truth, that he will employ and countenance such men as will in time (under his benign influence) make these Islands the most happy, flourishing and potent Empire of the whole world; especially, by the destruction of Superstition and Vice, the highest and most glorious conquest.

A
MEMORIAL
Concerning the
STATE OF AFFAIRS
IN
ENGLAND
In the latter part of the Year **1714.** *

H E happineſs of the Nation, and the wellfare of Europe, as well as his Majeſty's quiet, does in a great meaſure depend upon the conduct that is to be obſerv'd in the preſent juncture ; and nothing but a Prince of ſo great wiſdom, experience, and ſteadi-

3
neſs

* **This Memorial was not drawn up by Mr. ToLAND, but found among his Papers ; and therefore properly belongs to the** *Appendix* **: but it was thought fit to inſert it here, as relating to the ſame ſubject with the foregoing Piece.**

ness can extricate us out of our present difficulties.

That the State of Affairs, upon his Majesty's coming to the Crown, may be the better understood, it's necessary that some short account should be given of the two Parties which so unhappily divide the Nation, their interest, views, and designs.

It's notorious that a great many of the Clergy in Queen ELIZABETH's reign came very unwillingly into the Reformation ; and that it cut them to the heart to part with the gainful Doctrines of Popery : the Pope's Supremacy they were willing to quit, but 'twas in hopes of gaining that Supremacy to themselves.

These men, who saw how fond JAMES I. was of arbitrary power, thought they had no way of making themselves absolute in ecclesiastical matters, but by allowing him to be so in temporal : and in order to it, they preached up the Divine Right of Kings, and that Obedience was due to them in all things, tho' never so contrary to the Law of the Land, if not contrary to the Law of God; and that Subjects on pain of damnation were obliged never to resist, tho' to save their Liberties and Lives, and that the descent of the Crown was unalterable by any human Laws.

These

These Doctrines did not spread much during King JAMES's reign, and serv'd only to create jealousies in the minds of his People, which had very fatal effects in the reign of his Son, who was intirely govern'd by these principles, and the party which embrac'd them, who went under the name of *Cavaliers*, as those that oppos'd them did under that of *Round-heads*.

CHARLES II. prefer'd none in Church or State, but who embrac'd those arbitrary principles; and the Universities made it their business to instill them into the youth: and then it was, that the parties were distinguished by the names of *Whig* and *Tory*; the latter joining with the King, hindred the passing a Law for excluding the Duke of York from the Crown, contrary to the bent of the generality of the Nation, who then dreaded nothing so much as a Popish Successor.

JAMES II. when he came to the crown, was so weak as to imagine the Clergy and Tories wou'd be tied down by their own Doctrines; and therefore courted the Dissenters, sufficiently exasperated against the Church by a long and severe persecution: this made the Church quickly renounce their former doctrines of Non-resistance, &c. and promise the Dissenters (who saw what King JAMES
meant

meant by defigning to divide the Proteftants)
to treat them for the future as their brethren;
but when they had opportunity of doing it,
then they fhew'd that they thought Faith was
no more to be kept with Schifmaticks, than
the Papifts do with Hereticks. And when
the Parliament, in fpite of all their oppofition, paffed the Toleration Act, they revi-
ved their old principles, and ever fince taught
thofe Doctrines in the Univerfities, by which
means moft of the Gentry have been poifon-
ed: whereas if King WILLIAM had reform'd
the Univerfities, and employ'd none but men
of revolution principles, Torifm had been
rooted out.

He, or rather his Minifter, to whom he
weakly intrufted the whole adminiftration,
induftrioufly nurs'd up the Parties, which
being pretty equal, the Court cou'd turn the
ballance on what fide they pleafed. This
oblig'd the Party they headed to come into
their meafures; fince otherwife they faw
they muft be oblig'd to give up their preferments and penfions to the other party. It
was this, and not any difaffection, which
made the Whigs act fo fcandalous a part with
relation to the coming over of one of the
illuftrious Houfe of Hanover. They had no
other way to preferve their leaders, and confequently themfelves, in their pofts; and
that the Tories put thefe difficulties on them,
not with any defign to ferve the Houfe of

Hanover,

Hanover, their conduct ever since has made very plain.

This dextrous management of the Parties brought things to that pass, that neither of them scrupl'd at any thing that wou'd serve their own side; and they seldom consider'd whether a man was rightly elected, but whether he was of the right side: and if one party propos'd any thing which was for the publick good, the other party, for that only reason, wou'd oppose it. And as one party was for humbling of France, supporting of the Allies, preserving the Toleration, hindring the Clergy from assuming more power than the constitution allow'd them; the other party (tho' their principles did not influence them) wou'd in opposition have taken the contrary side, by being in the interest of France, and the Pretender, and favouring the Papists both at home and abroad, and for persecuting the Dissenters.

And the Tories, tho' they were frequently courted by King WILLIAM, yet he cou'd never make them really his friends, or to join with the Whigs in the common interest. When they were out of favour, they clog'd the wheels of affairs, by providing deficient Funds, &c; and when employ'd, they favoured as much as they durst the designs of France: and King WILLIAM being in their hands, when the Spanish King died, they made him

own

own the Duke of Anjou, and fit ftill till the French were poffefs'd of the Spanish Monarchies; and acted fuch a part, that the King at laft cou'd not avoid feeing that all his careffes were in vain, and that his own, and the Nation's fafety, required the removing them from all places of truft, or profit. And how they acted fince, I need no more mention, than how they acted during CHARLES II. reign.

Though the greateft part of the Gentry, by reafon of their Univerfity Education, have been debauch'd into anti-revolution Principles; yet the Populace, who had no fuch education, and efpecially the better fort of them, in whom lies the greateft part of the riches of the Nation, and who have votes in choofing Parliament-men, were for the moft part true to the principles of the Revolution, and to the common Proteftant intereft; and when we had any tolerable Parliaments, it was owing to the little intereft the Clergy and Gentry had then over them.'

But thefe well meaning men were at laft impofed on by the perpetual noife the Clergy made about *the Danger of the Church*, and by being perfuaded by the Tories, that the Whigs, for the fake of their private intereft, wou'd never put an end to the War; which, they faid, had given them an opportunity of cheating the Nation of more than thirty

millions:

millions; but that if they wou'd be so much in their own interest, as to vote for the Tories, they wou'd force the Whigs to refund, and ease them of all their Taxes, and give them a glorious Peace, and a most flourishing Trade. These, and such like stories, made them desert their old friends, and vote for the Tories.

The High-Church Clergy, who since Sacheverell's Trial imagine they can rule the People as they please, will rather than endure a Whig Ministry have recourse to their usual arts, and cry out as much as ever of the Danger of the Church, in order to make the People choose such a Parliament as they hope will distress the King, and force him to put the administration into Tory hands.

And it can't be expected but that the Tories, who are now such a majority in Parliament, will do their utmost to be chosen again; and for which now they are in the Country making their utmost efforts, while the Whigs stay in Town, solliciting for places.

And the late Ministry, who know an honest Parliament must call them to account, are oblig'd to be at all possible expence to get one for their turn.

And

And confidering all the French King's hopes now depend on fuch a Parliament, it is to be prefum'd, that French Money will not be wanting to bribe the electors.

His Majefty's reputation abroad, his quiet at home, and the intereft of Europe, depending in a great meafure upon the temper of the next Parliament, all efforts ought to be made for obtaining a good Parliament.

And moft of the better fort of People, who now feel the effects of a bad Peace, and plainly fee that they were grofly deluded by the Tories, and that they neither made out any one charge againft the Whigs, or perform'd the leaft tittle of all their promifes, may eafily be brought over to join again with the Whigs, efpecially if due care be taken to have them rightly inform'd of all their late tranfactions, and Pamphlets writ to that purpofe be well difpers'd.

The late Miniftry, knowing how much it was for their intereft, bribed thofe who cry'd Pamphlets and Papers about the ftreets, to cry none but thofe of their fide; and were at no fmall expence to difperfe them into every corner of the Kindgom; and fince the paper war is like to continue, the Government fhou'd not fcruple fome fmall expence, to have that which is writ in its defence as effectually difpers'd. Nothing

Nothing would have a greater influence over the People, than if the King in his declaration for diſſolving of the Parliament expreſt himſelf fully as to the Danger the nation was in, both as to their religious and civil Rights. This wou'd make them perceive, that thoſe who cry'd out moſt of the danger of the Church, were the only perſons that brought the Church in danger.

It will be highly convenient that one, if not of the chief Traytors, yet of their moſt criminal Inſtruments, ſhou'd be convicted before the chooſing of a new Parliament; for then the Tories cou'd not take the advantage of the King's peaceably coming to the Crown, to deny all that was acted in favour of France, the Pretender, and Popery, nor ask why the Whigs have ſo little regard to the wellfare of their country, as not to puniſh, when it is in their power, at leaſt ſome one of the notorious Conſpirators : and I can't think that any one will oppoſe this proceeding, except he has been tampering with France himſelf.

That the eyes of the People begin to be open it's evident from the late election in the City, where a Whig Sheriff carry'd it by a majority of more than a thouſand : and becauſe there can be no doubt, but that they will carry the election for Parliament men in the City, by at leaſt as great a number,

it

it ought to be so contriv'd, since other Corporations are influenc'd by the example of
London, that the first choice of Parliament
men shou'd be made there.

And since there is a division among the
Tories, and some of them have distinguish'd
themselves from the Jacobites, by several
Votes in favour of the House of Hanover,
and in being against that destructive treaty
with France; there can be no reason, why
they ought not to enjoy his Majesty's favour;
provided in the elections they will oppose
the Jacobite Tories, and in Parliament come
into proper measures for punishing the be-
trayers of their country. This method will
very much increase the number of his Majesty's friends, and enlarge the true British
interest.

As for those, who according to their usual
custom, hope by a majority in Parliament
to force the King to discharge his faithful
servants, and to employ none but themselves,
they are his worst enemies; especially the Leaders amongst them, who slight his Majesty's
favour, and wou'd not accept the most beneficial employs, if not at the head of their
own party; many of which Party, tho' preferr'd by or got into the Parliament by means
of the late Treasurer, yet because he (tho'
as black as any other) wou'd not take such
hasty unadvis'd steps in favour of the Pretender,

as

as a late Secretary, they went over to him as acting more agreeable to their violent tempers.

And if there be any great men about the King, who either recommend Jacobite Tories, or make an interest for them in elections, it's plain they intend not his Majesty's service, but design upon the first opportunity to set themselves at the head of the Tory party.

In order therefore to the getting of an honest Parliament, it's necessary since the late Ministry pick'd out the most violent Jacobites for Deputy-Lieutenants, Justices of the Peace, and Magistrates, that they should be chang'd, and that such Whigs or Hanoverian Tories as are men of probity and courage, and of the best estates, shou'd be put into their places. In order to this, his Majesty ought to have a list of the best men in every county; and since the Lord Lieutenants, and other great men, will in their choice have more regard to their own creatures than his Majesty's service, it might be proper that those they recommend, be consider'd by some private disinterested persons.

The Collectors of the Duties, especially of the Excise, who can influence the Ale-house-keepers as they please, and who being a set of profligate men, have almost as much debauch'd the People, as the Clergy have the

Gentry,

Gentry, ought to be chang'd, or oblig'd on loſs of their places in the elections, to do their utmoſt for his Majeſty's ſervice.

If theſe and all other methods whatſoever, which are neceſſary for procuring a new Parliament, ſhould be ſtrictly obſerv'd, yet the Tories can have no manner of reaſon to complain, ſince they deſtroy'd the freedom of elections by mobbing the electors, and by bribing the returning officers, and by uſing all other indirect methods: and conſidering the Court may be ſecure almoſt to a man of the members from Scotland, and there are near one hundred and fifty, who by reaſon of their places depend on the Court, there can be no danger, if vigorous methods are taken, of not carrying a majority.

When the Clergy ſee a ſteady conduct obſerv'd by the Government, and that they have no way of getting preferments but by coming into its meaſures, they, who mean nothing by Church and Religion, but themſelves and their own intereſt, wou'd not long ſtand out; and in the mean time there may be ſuch diviſions ſown among them, and one Univerſity ſet againſt another, as they may be diſabled from doing much miſchief.

The Tories want courage as well as ſenſe, and may be us'd by a reſolute Prince as he

z

thinks

thinks fit : but if a Prince is so abject, as to court them, they grow most insolent in power, and no Exchequer is sufficient to satisfy their unreasonable demands ; and so mercenary are they, that there's scarce one amongst them but may be easily brib'd to betray his own party. Sir C * * * M * * * is a remarkable instance of this, who, tho' at their head for many years till his death, was by agreement against the Court in little matters, the better to serve it in greater.

CROMWELL by acting a steady part, and employing none but such as were hearty in his interest, tho' he had in a manner the whole Nation against him, yet govern'd as he thought fit ; whereas the STUARTS, tho' they had the whole Nation for them, yet by not observing such a conduct, but giving themselves up to be govern'd by a few worthless men (who as long as they enjoy'd their favour heap'd what preferments they pleas'd on themselves and their creatures) met with a great many difficulties, and their affairs were continually embarrass'd.

A Prince who only sees with his Favourites eyes, and hears with their ears, can be no better than their tool, to execute those designs that their ambition, their covetousness, their revenge, and their other passions will inspire them with ; and the more a King is a stranger, the more will they be tempted to

to endeavour to impofe on him, efpecially
if before they have govern'd other Princes as
they pleas'd : fuch men will take the merit
of all the good which is done to themfelves,
and lay the blame of all ill on him. A Prince
thus befieg'd by his Favourites, tho' his underftanding be never fo good, yet it will caufe
his own fubjects to have but a very mean
opinion of his parts. Whereas a King who
has a mind to govern, and not to be govern'd
by his Minifters, ought upon all occafions, to
receive information from fuch private perfons without doors, as are men of good underftanding, and have fhew'd themfelves in
the worft of times zealous of his intereft, and
who by being made eafy in their private circumftances, have nothing to do but to attend
to his Majefty's fervice.

These Men, tho' with the utmoft privacy,
may be permitted humbly to offer their o-
pinion, and with the like privacy receive his
Majefty's command. This wou'd give him an
opportunity to fee whether his Minifters acted
fincerely with him, and make them as well
as others have a juft opinion of his great penetration ; fo that none would dare ever to
impofe on him ; and the advantage his Majefty may receive (not to mention any others)
as to the management of his Revenue either
at home or in the Plantations (which laft is
under the worft regulation) would be very
confiderable. And the Trade of the Nation
has

has been so little the business of the Ministry, that no other use has been made of the Board of Trade, which cost the Government every year such considerable sums, than to skreen the miscarriages of the Ministry; and the filling up that Commission with Merchants, and such as understand Trade, wou'd be a great satisfaction to all the trading part of the Nation.

PHYSICK

PHYSIC
WITHOUT
PHYSICIANS:
In a
LETTER
TO
B *** G ***, *Esq;*

Non Rem antiqui damnabant sed Artem.
PLIN. Nat. Hist. xxix. 1.

O mention your Friendship, Generosity, or any other of your
good qualities to your self, is no
more improper, than doing it to
your acquaintance, or to those
whom your name has any way reach'd; that
is, telling them what they know already:

VOL. II.   S   but

but as thefe will be always well-pleafed, to find their experience or their opinion confirm'd by frefh inftances; fo you, SIR, ought never to be offended, at the grateful expreffions of thofe you have oblig'd, tho' praife be not what you either like or feek. I take the liberty therefore to repeat the ineffaceable fenfe I have of the concern you fhew'd, for my late indifpofition at London; and my thanks for fo feafonably affifting me even in perfon, to fly from the foggy, fmoaky, fteamy, and putrid air of that vaft City: which, in fo weak a condition, wou'd have naturally kill'd me in lefs than a fortnight, without needing the help of art to do it fooner. I am not ignorant, that certain men of vitiated palates, yet mighty pretenders to nice breeding, declare a difrelifh of all fuch perfonal acknowledgments, efpecially if public: but they are fuch as your favorite Author, the younger PLINY, has long fince defcrib'd, (1) *men who doing nothing themfelves deferving commendation, think it impertinent that any fhould be commended.* The difapprobation of fuch delicates I fhall ftudioufly court, by never failing to applaud merit.

As for my prefent ftate, I am recovering indeed, tho' very flowly: for having as yet little appetite, I can have no great ftrength;

nor

(1) Poftquam defiimus facere laudanda, laudari quoque ineptum putamus. *Lib.* 8. *Ep.* 21.

nor have I been once out of doors, fince laft abroad with your felf.   This is the effect of Phyfic, taken againft judgment, and given without any.   Had I obey'd the call of Nature, to which I am not wont to be difobedient, and retir'd from London when my Lungs and Stomach begun to fail me (which I per-ceiv'd both to do by degrees for four winters paft, tho' in the thickeft fogs breathing and eating freely in the Country) this fick-nefs had not in all probability happen'd : and when it happen'd, had I then quitted the Town with the fooneft, had I kept to Mr. LA MARQUE's fimple and intelligible manner of treatment, which fucceeded likewife to admiration (for I fhall never excufe my own blameable eafinefs in this matter) I had e'er now been in perfect health.   That honeft man, who's well worth your acquaintance, is a good Botanift, a dextrous Surgeon, and prepares his own Medicines ; joining all the three functions together, as of right they were united originally : and folely trufting to his own eyes, experience, and judgment.   But I muft needs be fafhionable, and perfuaded to put my felf under the care of a collegiate Phyfician by a noble Lord, the beft of Patriots and kindeft of Friends; who himfelf, the more's the pity, is fure to fall one day by the hands of the Doctors : men, who, the greateft part of them, ruin Nature by Art ; and who, by endeavouring to be always very cun-ning for others, by making every thing a myf-

tery, are frequently too cunning for themfelves.

This has been the point in regard to me,
fince my Phyfician (willing enough I believe
to do me good) plainly miftook both my
Cafe and Conftitution. It wou'd be tedious,
to give you an account of the particulars.
Thus much only I now tell you, that what
was given me for a gentle aperitive, to difpofe my body for ftronger operations, vomited and purg'd me for the beft part of
three days; brought on a loofenefs, that
cou'd hardly be ftopt in a week; and, befides
the continuance of the vomiting, threw me
into fainting and fwooning fits. Many material obfervations, that I made from time
to time on other people, flightly indifpos'd,
but difabled or difpatch'd by their Phyficians,
prefented themfelves on this occafion frefh
to my mind. On this you may therefore
depend, that, happen what will, I fhall never
more put my felf under the management
of fuch, whofe art is founded in darknefs,
and improv'd by Murther. Even this Gentleman, after my telling him how much and
how violently his Lenitive had vomited
me, which he own'd was contrary to his expectation, feem'd no otherwife concern'd
than gravely to fay, *That it was very remarkable.* Was it fo Doctor? I promife you
then, it fhall be the laft Remark, that any
Phyfician fhall ever make upon me; and the

reafon very good : (2) *They learn their Art* *at the hazard of our lives, and make expe-* *riments by our deaths*; which is the infallible fentence of one who was a thorough judge, and who'll tell you more truths prefently. From this cenfure however ought to be ex-empted thofe few gallant fpirits (far exalted above the herd of their profeffion) who, by their Learning, Integrity, and Application, deferve to be ftil'd the *Benefactors* and *De-livers* of mankind, in this like God him-felf : only it were to be wifh'd that they fol-low'd the example farther, and made the charge of their affiftance fo eafy; as barely to ferve for an exception from him, who be-ftows all his benefits freely. A diftinction (in fhort) ought to be made, be the number on one fide ever fo fmall.

But the whole myftery, with the number-lefs mifchiefs, of Quackery, (for, the caufe of the Difeafe being once known, all Phyfic, except manual Operations, a regular Diet, moderate Exercifes, and the proper ufe of Simples, is fuch) all Quackery, I fay, you'll find divinely laid open by the elder PLINY, in the 1ft Chapter of the 29th Book of his *Natural Hiftory :* a work little read by the Phyficians, and lefs underftood; fince even the delirious fables, charms, and other magi-

S 3   cal

---

(2) Difcunt periculis noftris, & experimenta per mortes agunt. PLIN. *Nat. Hift. lib.* 29. *cap.* 1.

cal vanities he so judiciously explodes, are by many of them grosly confounded with his approv'd remedies and most solid remarks. It is literally an unparallel'd performance, the like having never been accomplish'd before or after him: and the character his Nephew gives of it, is no more than just; that it is not only (3) *a work full of Learning, but likewise as diffuse and diversify'd as Nature it self.* Certain passages out of him, instead of a more modish New-year's Gift, I hereby send you; being sure they'll please, if they do not convince you.

After having given a historical account of the many changes, some of 'em from white to black as we say, that the Art has undergone (which is an insuperable objection against it) he proceeds (4) thus: *There is no doubt but all those Physicians, in hunting after fame by some novelty, make an assur'd traffick of our lives. Hence those miserable diversities of opinion*

---

(3) Naturae Historiarum xxxvii. opus diffusum, eruditum, nec minùs varium quàm ipsa Natura. PLIN. *lib.* 3. *Ep.* 5.

(4) Nec dubium est, omnes istos, famam novitate aliquâ aucupantes, animas statim nostras negotiari. Hinc illae circa aegros miserae sententiarum concertationes, nullo idem censente, ne videatur accessio alterius: hinc illa infelicis monumenti inscriptio, TURBA SE MEDICORUM PERIISSE. Mutatur Ars quotidie, toties interpolis, & ingeniorum Graeciae flatu impellimur; palamque est, ut quisque inter istos loquendo polleat, Imperatorem illico vitae necisque fieri. Ceu verò non millia gentium sine Medicis degant, nec tamen sine Medicinâ: sicut populus Romanus ultra sexcentesimum annum, nec ipse in accipiendis Artibus lentus; Medicinae etiam avidus, donec expertam damnavit. PLIN. *Hist. Nat. lib.* 29. *cap.* 1.

opinion in Consultations about the sick, not one of 'em declaring himself of another's Judgment, lest he should seem to approve his Sentiments: hence that Inscription order'd by a wretched patient to be put on his Tomb, THAT THE MULTITUDE OF HIS DOCTORS HAD KILL'D HIM. *The Art is chang'd every day, being as often patch'd up, and we are driven whithersoever the breath of the Grecian wits [who in-*vented this mystery] *will blow us. 'Tis moreover evident, that the greater tongue-pad any among 'em is, he straight becomes the soveraign disposer of Life and Death; as if thousands of Nations had not liv'd, and still do so, without Physicians, tho' not without Physic. Thus did the People of Rome for above six hundred years, whereas they were not backward in receiving the Arts; and even fond of Physic, till after trial, they condemn'd and banish'd it.* Here's our first passage.

Now, he that in these daily, these endless changes and contradictory methods, does not see the absolute uncertainty of the Art, must needs be either senseless, or prejudic'd, or interested: and it is as evidently observable in ours as in all ages before us, that those Nations, which have no Physicians, are troubl'd with few diseases; and these easily cur'd by Diet, Exercise, or Simples, whose effects have been long and generally known, many of them Specifics. Thus it is likewise with particular persons, who make little use of

Physi-

Phyſicians where they abound, of which
I could give many examples; my ſelf among
the reſt, till I became infected with this de-
plorable habitude of ſome of my beſt friends,
it ſelf the greateſt of Diſtempers.   But ſhall
we have recourſe to no ſort of Phyſicians? I
anſwer, that if there be any choice, 'tis the
hardeſt of all things to be made: for the
Doctors have almoſt as many jarring Sects and
incompatible Factions among 'em as the
Prieſts, and come little ſhort of hating each
other as heartily; that is, like Devils, according to a general (5) maxim. They broach no-
vel opinions viſibly for the ſake of thwarting
their Adverſaries, there being nothing ſo ridiculous or extravagant, which many of 'em
do not hold: generally founding their con-
ceits, upon ſome looſe ſcrap of one antient
Sage or other, which ſeems to countenance
what they maintain ſtanding thus alone ; but,
read with what goes before or after in the
ſame place, it ſignifies quite the contrary,
or ſomething as different as a Cock and an
Elephant.

Nor is this the worſt. They reduce all
Diſeaſes, with their Cures, right or wrong
to certain precarious Syſtems, or Hypo-
theſes, according to which he that expreſ-
ſes himſelf the moſt volubly or plauſibly,
ſets up immediately for an able Phyſi-
cian,

(5) Odium Theologorum eſt odium Diabolorum. *Conſenſ.*
Univerſ.

cian, and is by others fo deem'd : tho' he knows nothing of Anatomy, Botany, or any fuch requifite qualifications; and wou'd fooner kill a man according to the Doctrine he has efpous'd, than cure him by following any other method. PLINY does not exceed bounds a jot, in affirming (6) *with wonder and indignation, that their Art has been heretofore more inconftant, and is now more frequently alter'd, than any other, tho' none be more amply rewarded ;* the eafieft means, one would think, for acquiring of certainty and ftability. I fhall not infift on fuch flight crimes, compared to others, as their willfully protracting many times the cure of Difeafes; or their turning of fmall diforders into perillous fymptoms, in order to fqueeze the purfe of an opulent patient : nor yet am I prone to credit thofe Phyficians, who accufe fome of their faculty of willfully fending a patient out of the world; left another fhould have the credit of a cure, which they cou'd not effect. This fuggeftion may be owing to their mutual envy, which is long fince grown into more than one (7) Proverb.

But

---

(6) Mirumque & indignum protinus fubit, nullam Artium inconftantiorem fuifle, & etiamnum faepiùs mutari, cum fit fructuofior nulla. *Hift. Nat. lib.* 29. *cap.* 1.

(7) Medicorum Invidia :
Medicus Invidiae Pelagus :
Medicus Invidiae perforata Clepfydra.
Confenf. Univerf.

But not to quit such an entertaining and instructive companion as PLINY, a good way lower in the same Chapter I have quoted, there's another curious passage; which, tho' the matter of every body's observation, was never so happily express'd. He begins with the sottish credulity of the Patients, and goes on with the stupendous imposture of their Doctors; who, (to speak of the thing as modestly as may be) are departed almost as far from ESCULAPIUS and HIPPOCRATES, as the Christian Priests are from JESUS CHRIST and his APOSTLES. Thus run his (8) words: *Whoever treats of Physic, otherwise than in Greek terms, has no authority; no not with the ignorant vulgar, or such as understand not a word of the language: and they believe those things the less, which concern their health and preservation, if they are made intelligible to them. Thus (by HERCULES) it comes to pass in this alone of all Arts, that credit is presently given to any body, who professes himself a Physician, tho' a lye be not so dangerous*

in

(8) Imò verò auctoritas, aliter quàm Græcè eam tractantibus (Medicinam scilicet) etiam apud imperitos expertesque linguæ, non est: ac minùs credunt, quæ ad salutem suam pertinent, si intelligunt. Ita (Hercules) in hac Artium solâ evenit ut cuicunque, Medicum se professo, statim credatur, cùm sit periculum in nullo mendacio majus: non tamen illud intuemur, adeo blanda est sperandi pro se cuique dulcedo. Nulla praeterea Lex, quæ puniant inscitiam capitalem; nullum exemplum vindictæ. Discunt periculis nostris, & experimenta per mortes agunt, medicoque tantùm hominem occidisse impunitas summa est: quinimò transit in convitium, & intemperantia culpatur; ultroque, qui periere, arguuntur. *Hist. Nat. ubi supra.*

in any other regard : but this we do not see or consider, so flattering and agreeable is the hope, that every one conceives in his own behalf. Let it be *also consider'd that there is no Law, for punishing with death the ignorance that causes it ; nor so much as an example of any being call'd to account on such a score. They learn their Art at the hazard of our Lives, and make experiments by our Deaths : besides, that none, but only Physicians, may murder men with all security and impunity ; nay, and affront their memory afterwards, reproaching them with intemperance, and reviling the dead without provocation.* If you believe them, in a word, none ever perish'd by a Physician, nor recover'd without one. How disingenuous ! how barbarous ! first to torture and kill us, and then to give out, we did it our selves ; that we wou'd not be govern'd, and ate, or drunk, or did something else the Doctor forbad : whereas on the other hand, if a Patient's happy Constitution gets the better of an improper prescription, and the person mends ; then the Doctor has wrought a signal Cure, and the Medicine is cry'd up to the destruction of thousands. But all that Chapter, of which I only give a few choice sketches, ought to be carefully read over and over by every one, who values such near concerns as health and life.

Now, Sir, since I have so frankly declar'd against those Empirics, tho' not against Medicine,

cine, (which is the gift of God and Nature) I shall, when my health is confirm'd, and leisure permits, send you my thoughts more particularly, about the method how we may acquire the knowledge of those things, wherein this Medicine truly consists; and at the same time give you some necessary cautions against the intolerable cheats of the Apothecaries, who impose on the Physicians, as much as these on the Patients: for, to do every body justice, the latter have not done half the hurt to mankind as the former; and they wou'd do still less, did they prepare their own Medicines, and avoid those monstrous mixtures, which are the source of infinite mischiefs, and wherein a systematical conjecture has more place than reasonable or experimental knowledge. They were deceitfully invented to bereave people of their money and their senses. The poor Patients must never know what they take, nor ever pay enough for what they do not know. Besides that the several ingredients of those Compositions (by our Author prettily term'd *inexplicable*, or if you will *inextricable*) thus intangl'd and imbarrass'd, fermented, coagulated, or any other way alter'd, do often produce quite other effects than what were expected from their proportionable adjustment: whereas perhaps any one of them, at least some other Simple for certain, wou'd succeed as intended.

The

The genuine Books of HIPPOCRATES, with a few other pieces in that collection call'd *his Works*, are the beft guides and helps to him, that wou'd ftudy Medicine in the way of nature and experience. Such a perfon neither prepoffefs'd by any hypothefis, nor fervilely tying himfelf down to any fyftem, ought to pick what's rational, good and experienc'd, wherever he finds them; as well from an old woman or a favage Indian, as from Dr. MEAD, or Profeffor BOERHAVE: nor fhou'd he flight every thing that even Quacks and Mountebanks vend, who often light one way or other on an excellent remedy, by the credit of which they difpofe of numberlefs poyfons. Finally, he muft not be a THESSALUS, one *who in the reign of* NERO (as (9) PLINY acquaints us) *rav'd and foam'd againft the Phyficians of all ages before him, rejecting indifcriminately whatever they had invented or approv'd*: and this, not out of love to truth, or for the good of mankind; but to bring the whole grift of Rome and Italy (if not of the Empire) to his own mill, pardon fo vulgar an expreffion. The candor, judicious obfervations, and incredible diligence of HIPPOCRATES, will give us a nobler idea of things. That admirable perfon, whom for fome years paft I have efteem'd, as I do ftill, for one of the

(9) Eadem aetas, Neronis principatu, ad Theffalum tranftulit; delentem cuncta majorum placita, & rabie quâdam in omnis aevi Medicos perorantem, &c. *Plin. Ibid.*

the moſt accurate Philoſophers; and whoſe writings I have perus'd more than once on that account (for at the Univerſity I never look'd into him, then groveling under the prejudice of thinking him fit only for Phyſicians) HIPPOCRATES, I ſay, who has preſerved in part the ſalutiferous remedies of Eſculapius, ſhall be the champion of the next Letter: well aſſur'd, that we may as ſucceſsfully batter Quackery by his authority, as we do Superſtition by that of the Bible.

In the mean time PLINY ſhall hold his rank in this Letter, and entertain us now with a ſhort parallel between the no leſs eaſily than cheaply procur'd Simples of the Fields or Gardens, and thoſe expenſive far-fetch'd pernicious mixtures of the Apothecaries, equally ruining men's bodies and eſtates. Hear him, and be wiſer. *It (10) has pleaſed Nature to make theſe the only Remedies, things that may be prepar'd by every body, eaſy to be found without expence, and ſome of 'em our daily food. But the frauds of men, and ſharpers with baited hooks, have invented thoſe ſhops, wherein every man's own Life is*
publickly

---

(10) Haec ſola Naturae placuerat eſſe Remedia, parata vulgo, inventu facilia, ac ſine impendio, & ex quibus vivimus. Poſtea fraudes hominum, & ingeniorum capturae, officinas invenêre iſtas, in quibus ſua cuique homini venalis promittitur vita. Statim compoſitiones & mixturae inexplicabiles decantantur, Arabia atque India in medio aeſtimantur, ulcerique parvo Medicina a Rubro Mari imputatur; cùm Remedia vera quotidie pauperrimus quiſque coenet: nam ſi ex horto petantur, aut herba vel frutex quaerâtur, nulla artium vilior fiet. *Hiſt. Nat. lib.* 24. *cap.* 1.

publickly expofed to fale to him. There, compofitions and inexplicable mixtures are immediately cry'd up ; Arabia and India are rated on the counter, and a cure from the Red-Sea is apply'd to an inconfiderable bile ; whereas the pooreft man has, every day, the true Remedies for a fallet : but if fuch be brought out of the garden, or fome herb or fhrub be fought in the fields, the Apothecaries will of all arts become the moft contemptible. The paffage is in the firft Chapter of the 24th Book, and is too plain to need any comment.

I wou'd only here obferve, how many, how great cures we continually read and hear perform'd in the Eaft and Weft-Indies, by flowers, roots, leaves, juices, barks and the like. But, without going to foreign Countries, wonders are daily wrought by Simples in the Highlands of Scotland, in the Hebrides or Weftern Ifles, and in fome parts of Ireland, whither the plague of fyftematical Phyfic has not yet penetrated : and, what is ftill more obfervable, when, by the information of Travellers or otherwife, any Remedy of this kind is communicated to a collegiate Phyfician (as it fometimes happens) prefently this man of myftery, who fcorns to learn of any one, fo alters and difguifes his difcovery, by preparing it more artificially than the Natives, or incorporating it with a multitude of other things, that it either lofes all its virtue, or produces a dif-

ferent,

ferent, if not a contrary effect. In the mean time a noble Medicine, perhaps a Specific, is cry'd down and grows into difufe, thro' the credulity of thofe that implicitly hearken to a pretending Coxcomb. Thus even the Peruvian bark, and Ipecacuana root, are often render'd noxious or infignificant by pharmaceutic preparations.

We muft not ungratefully forget on this occafion thofe wife and worthy Ladies, who, confidering, or it may be fadly experiencing, the dangerous and often fatal compofitions, the clogging and naufeating flops of the Phyficians (to fay nothing of their imperious dictating oracular declarations, or infolent behaviour) take care not only of their own healths and that of their Families; but are alfo a common blefling in this refpect to all around them, whether in town or country: particularly to the lower fort of people, glad to live by cheap and obvious means; while the Great chufe to perifh by rules of Art, and to make a parade of their wealth, by the fums they lavifh on exotic drugs, not content with enriching one domeftic poyfoner. Among fuch beneficent Ladies, I had the happinefs to be for feveral years acquainted with one, who was wife to the beft and braveft Citizen that ever lived; whom, tho' by conftitution valetudinary, fhe skillfully nurs'd to a good old age: till at laft this excellent woman was feiz'd fo violently by a fever, that,

not

not being in a condition to order thofe helps for her felf, fhe was always fo ready to afford others, a Phyfician was call'd, and fhe dy'd univerfally lamented, nor did the truly deftitute Sir ROBERT CLAYTON, for this was the man, long furvive his faithful companion and preferver. That at prefent, SIR, I entertain ftrong hopes of a perfect recovery, that I am able to fend you this long Letter (written indeed by fits and ftarts in my intervals of up-fitting) is for the greateft part owing to the proper things, and directions for ufing them, fent me by a Lady, exemplarily tender of an infirm husband: and who, as in beauty and modefty fhe's inferior to none of her own Sex; fo, in a clear underftanding and an agreeable converfation, fhe furpaffes moft of ours. I am likewife inform'd by very good hands, that the Dutchefs of MARLBOROUGH (which I record to her Grace's honor, and will not be reckon'd the leaft of her virtues) contributes more to the eafe and relief of the never fame-dying Hero, her illuftrious confort, than all the aids of collegiate art; which, in fuch mighty circumftances, cou'd not poffibly fail of being procur'd, were there in reality any thing of this kind effectual or certain. I wifh fome of this great Lady's family had never feen a Phyfician. So much of this fubject for the prefent.

If any of the faculty fhould chance to fee my Letter, I know they would firft make an arrogant grimace, as difdaining one unfkill'd in their profeffion; and then pretend to anfwer it with an infipid Jeft, faying, that tho' I complain'd of being immoderately purg'd and vomited, I had not yet got rid of all my Bile. That is true: to let 'em fee I know fomething of the animal economy, tho' little of their juggling. Neverthelefs, I do affure you, my old friend, that I never wrote any thing with more phlegm in my whole life; which thofe facetious Gentlemen may be ready enough to allow, tho' in a different fenfe from you. But I care as little what they fay, as they do what becomes of their Patients: and if they provoke me (as CICERO faid of the Petty-foggers of Rome, who reproach'd him with not underftanding the quirks and chicanery of the Law) I fhall in three days become no lefs mafter of their legerdemain and jargon, than the beft of themfelves. This, however, would be throwing away too much time by any, that fcorn'd to make ufe of it to the fame vile purpofes. A nobler task attends me: for I fhall ftudy Nature hereafter with regard to the body of man, in her own way and for my own prefervation, as the beft Philofophers were antiently wont: there being nothing more pleafant than fo ufeful an amufement, very confiftent with other occupations. This I was always inclin'd to do, having early affifted at

two

two courfes of Anatomy, after being tolerably initiated into Botany : but I was diverted from fo good a refolution, I know not how. The Craft I abhorr'd, the Skill I admired ; herein precifely of my Author's mind, who fays, that *the antients did not condemn the thing, but the trade.*

While I am comforting my felf with thefe fage ideas, you are bufily retrieving your loffes by the villanous execution of a late execrable Scheme. Long may you enjoy health for your own fake, and that of your lovely family. But as I heartily intereft my felf in whatever concerns you, fo I particularly wifh, you may never become the prey of thofe mercilefs fharks, I have been hitherto defcribing : for were your purfe as large as your foul, it wou'd not fuffice both for Doctors and Directors ; and believe me, your body is as little to be trufted with the one, as your money with the other. By thefe you have loft part of your wealth, and I part of my health by thofe : wherefore let the caution be mutual, and be perfuaded that I am, Dear SIR, your moft faithful friend, your moft oblig'd and obedient Servant.

Putney, January
1721-2.

T 3   LET

LETTERS.

To * * *

Oxford, *Jan.* 1694.

SIR,

 Got safe to Oxford, tho' not without frequent apprehensions of being set upon by highway men; and indeed we narrowly escap'd, for the Coaches that came in next after us, and they say those of Monday before us, were all robb'd. I was so far from making any observations upon the country as I came along, that, as if I were never to know my way back again, I could not once look out, the weather was so tempestuous. One of the Fellows of New College, a violent partisan of the Clergy, happen'd to be my fellow traveller, of whom in that small time, as occasional discourses favour'd me, I inform'd my self of the abilities, genius, and disposition of the Doctors. The place is very pleasant, the Colleges are exceeding fine, and

I must

I muſt confeſs I never ſaw ſo much of the air of an Univerſity before. I ly under great obligations to the Gentlemen who recommended me, both for the advantageous Character they were pleas'd to beſtow upon me, and the ſuitable reception I met with : Mr. CREECH in particular has been extraordinary civil to me, and did me the honor to recommend three or four of the moſt ingenious men in the Univerſity to my acquaintance, who accordingly viſited me. The like did Dr. MILL and Mr. KENNET. This I look upon as very obliging, and ſo I take it, but it is very troubleſome, and ſomewhat à la mode de France : for I am put into as great agonies as Sir LIONEL JENKINS to anſwer the expectations of thoſe grand Virtuoſos; eſpecially ſome of their Antiquaries, and Linguiſts who ſaluted me with peals of barbarous ſounds and obſolete words, and I in return ſpent upon them all my Anglo-Saxon and old Britiſh Etymologies; which I hope gave them abundant ſatisfaction : Hebrew and Iriſh, I hope, will bear me out for ſome weeks, and then I'll be pretty well furniſh'd from the Library, into which I was ſworn and admitted yeſterday only : for it was not to be done, without being firſt propos'd in Congregation. This is the reaſon, SIR, that I have not ſooner written to you, having no account to give of my ſelf. For the future, I'll endeavour frequently to acquaint you with ſomething more entertaining than what concerns my ſelf; tho' if I

cou'd

cou'd underſtand what it is you moſt eſteem, I ſhou'd particularly ſtudy to give you ſatisfaction : with whatever elſe I can think may convince you, that I am not a little proud of the honor my friends did me, in making me known to ſo conſiderable and ingenious a perſon ; and that I am very ſenſible of your goodneſs in contributing to make my life more eaſy, and my ſtudies more free. I beg you, SIR, to acquaint Mr. FREKE as ſoon as you ſee him with the contents, whoſe care and favour I ſhall always endeavour to deſerve : looking upon him as the primum mobile of my happineſs. I forgot to tell you that Mr. CREECH is publiſhing *Lucretius* in Latin, with a Paraphraſe and Commentary, and *Manilius* in Engliſh Verſe, which will be nothing inferior to Lucretius. Dr. MILL has already communicated his Teſtament to me, and others ſent me ſeveral Books, I only inquir'd after, without any deſign of making bold ſo ſoon to borrow ; all which I attribute to the reſpect they owe their friends. I am conveniently and pretty reaſonably lodg'd at Mr. Bodington's over againſt all Souls College, to which place all my Letters and Pacquets are to be directed.

FOR

FOR

Mr. TOLAND.

Oxford, May 4, 1694.

Mr. TOLAND,

THE Character you bear in Oxford is this; that you are a man of fine parts, great learning, and little religion.

Whither or no this be your juft Character, I cannot fay; but this I can fay, and am affur'd of, that if it be, 'tis your higheft intereft to reflect ferioufly upon the matter, and to endeavour betimes to deferve a better. This is the whole occafion of my writing to you; and I entreat you to receive it as it is meant.

'Tis the conftant voice of the Holy Scriptures; and there is nothing more agreeable to our common reafon, than that much fhould be requir'd of him to whom much is committed: you are fenfible (I believe) that you have receiv'd a great deal; it lies at your door to employ it fo, as to be able to give up a good accompt to him, from whom you receiv'd it, at the laft day.

'Twould be a very grievous and bitter thought, when you lay upon your death-bed (and thither one day you muft come; God only knows how foon) to confider that your

parts,

parts, and your knowledge, which, if employ'd in the fervice of your maker, and to the benefit of mankind, might have entitled you to a nobler fhare of happinefs and glory; fhall not only be of no advantage to you, but fhall infinitely enhanfe and augment your condemnation.

Popular efteem, the applaufes of a Coffee-houfe, or of a Club of prophane Wits, are mean, unworthy ends; and which a man of underftanding is afham'd to ftoop for: they are too flender to fatisfy at the prefent; and 'tis certain they can yield us no comfort when we fhall have moft need of it.

But the difcharge of our duty, and a good confcience, are a never-failing fpring of pleafure : and what mighty advances may a man make in virtue, if fuch abilities as God hath been pleafed to blefs you with, were directed into a right channel?

Think not, Sir, that I fpeak thus to draw you over to a party; as though Religion either feared an ingenious adverfary, or needed a learned advocate : no, (bleffed be God) fhe ftands firm upon a rock, and 'tis not within the power of the eager malice of Devils, much lefs of the vain tongues of wicked men, to overthrow her : neither doth God need the fervice of any man; he, who ordains ftrength *ex ore infantum,* can work his ends, and

and maintain his own cauſe, without the concurrence of human wiſdom or policy.

No. Believe me, I am concern'd for your ſake: methinks, 'tis ten thouſand pities that any one ſhould freely chooſe to be eternally wretched, or but moderately happy, into whoſe hands God hath put the means of purchaſing an exceeding weight of Glory; and whom he ſeems to have deſigned to be a veſſel of honour.

All that I can do to you, is to entreat you by the love you bear your own Soul, to weigh impartially the evidences, and the conſequences of the Chriſtian Religion: if its evidences convince you not of its reality, I muſt pity your blindneſs; but if they do, then I am ſure its conſequences are ſuch as muſt either allure or frighten him that is not either very diſingenuous, or very ſtupid. The genuine iſſue of this reflection, will be an hearty reſolution of embracing the plain eaſy duties enjoined in the Goſpel: which, as it is the only ſure grounds upon which we may expect Salvation hereafter, ſo is it the true foundation of peace and ſatisfaction in this world: every ſtep we tread, before we have, in ſome meaſure, ſecur'd our peace with Heaven, is infinitely hazardous, and ſuch as fleſh and blood could not bear the proſpect of, were our eyes open. God who made you, and hath ſo richly bleſſed you,

of

of his great mercy, bleſs you yet farther, and make you become an happy inſtrument of his Glory. Amen.

Dear SIR, I remain your hearty well-wiſher and real (though unknown) friend and ſervant,

A— A—

FOR

Mr. TOLAND.

Oxford, May 7, 1694.

Dear Mr. TOLAND,

I Hear that you have received a Note of the 4th inſtant, which was ordered to be left for you at Nan's Coffee-houſe : I hear alſo with what acceptance you entertain it ; you ſay, the Letter has nothing in it immodeſt or uncivil ; but you cannot believe that he who wrote it intended you any kindneſs by it, becauſe he ſent it unſeal'd and to a publick houſe.

Now to this, I ſay, that ſuppoſing the Letter to be modeſt and civil ; it ſeems more equitable to impute any miſcarriage or accidental indecency in its delivery, to indiſcretion, rather than lack of kindneſs.

For

For, alas! had he intended to defame you, how eafy had it been to have pitch'd upon a more natural and likely means of procuring it, than the directing a Letter to your own hand? it being highly improbable that, if any thing were found there tending to your difparagement, you your felf fhould have divulged it.

No, affure your felf, Dear SIR, he who wrote it, meant you no harm, but rather the contrary; and if, through any accident, the matter went farther than his own, and your breaft, 'tis quite befide his intention.

That excellent fweet-tempered Religion, which he entreats you to look towards, and embrace; as it obliges its followers to love all men, fo it forbids them to defame or upbraid any: and I am fure, that he who fent you that Letter, would willingly put his hands under your feet, to do you any real fervice.

The true reafon of his fending it to the Coffee-houfe, was becaufe he knew not your lodgings; and to have enquired for them might occafionally have difcovered, what he defigns to conceal.

The caufe of his fending it unfealed, was a dependance upon the general integrity of mankind in this particular; arifing from the

odium

odium which attends bufy-bodies; and chief-ly thofe who examine other mens papers.

In fhort, whether you believe him your friend or your enemy; he paffionately defires you to lay to heart what he has faid. If he be an enemy, you will fufficiently revenge your felf upon him, by difappointing him of all occafion of reproaching you: if he be a friend, you will abundantly gratify him, by letting him fee the good effects of the travel of his foul: but, above all, by that means you will be a true friend to your felf. Dear Sir, farewell, and may the bleffing of God always attend you.

Dear Sir, I muft beg one favour of you. The ftory runs thus; that a Letter was left at the Coffee-houfe with this Superfcription, *For Mr.* Toland's *perufal.* Now, I confefs, this infcription feems to promife fomewhat fcurrilous and reflective: but you who know that this is falfe, may do me thus much juftice, as to fatisfy thofe you may fpeak with concerning it, that 'twas infcribed otherwife.

Mr. TO-

Mr. TOLAND's
ANSWER.

SIR,

IF I knew your person as much as I honour your merit, the stile of my Letter should, it may be, better suit your quality and station: but I am persuaded by the extraordinary temper of yours, that a sincere Answer is the greatest respect I can pay you. The grave and serious advice you condescend to give me, with this fair opportunity of vindicating my self from all indecent aspersions, cannot but oblige me to the highest pitch of gratitude. I bless God, that in this loose and sceptical age, there remains so much of the truly primitive spirit as the genuine fruits of it express in you. Indeed, your close and perspicuous arguments, so candidly manag'd, and so properly apply'd, could not well miss their effect upon any ingenuous man, under my suppos'd circumstances; but I heartily wish I could as justly claim the first two parts of the character, you say, I bear in Oxford, as I really abhor the last. You seem, SIR, to speak more of me from the discourses of others than any personal knowledge, and you are not ignorant how cautiously we should receive the informations of any, till we learn the interests and inclinations of both the parties. Had I the happiness of your acquaintance, which I passionately desire, I

could

could quickly convince you that the irreli-
gion laid to my charge, is as much owing to
the malice of my enemies, as the reputation
of parts and learning to the goodness of my
friends. Neither have I receiv'd so much as
you think, tho' more than I deserve, and
enough to render every neglect of my duty
inexcusable.

I am sensible all my actions should be calculated for the glory of God, and the good
of my country. To become more capable
of answering these ends, is the true reason
of the stay I make for some time in this
famous University. And further than they
contribute towards this design, neither the
exceeding agreeableness of the place, nor the
improving conversation of the members
should be to me any attractives. But to
what purpose should I study here or elsewhere, were I an Atheist or Deist, for one
of the two you take me to be? What a contradiction to mention Virtue if I believ'd there
was no God, or one so impotent that could
not, or so malicious that would not reveal
himself? Nay, tho' I granted a Deity, yet if
nothing of me subsisted after death, what
laws could bind, what incentives could move
me to common honesty? Annihilation would
be a sanctuary for all my sins, and put an
end to my crimes with my self. Believe me,
I am not so indifferent to the evils of the present life; but, without the expectation of a

better,

better, I fhould foon fufpend the mechanifm
of my body, and refolve into inconfcious
atoms. Now if I am perfuaded our Souls
are immortal and refponfible for their actions,
to be eternally happy or miferable in a future ftate, I muft be neceffarily of fome Religion : and I prefume you will readily acknowledge it to be the Chriftian, when I
affure you, that

" I. I firmly believe the exiftence of an
" infinitely good, wife and powerful Being,
" which in our language we call GOD, fub-
" ftantially different from the Univerfe he
" created, and continues to govern by his
" Providence ; of whom, through whom,
" and to whom are all things.

" II. Concerning CHRIST in particular,
" I believe that he is God manifeft in the
" flefh, or true God and Man, perfectly united
" without contrariety of will, or confufion of
" effence. As to his human nature, that
" according to the Prophets, he was born
" of a pure Virgin, conceived by virtue of
" the divine Spirit, and therefore ever free
" from all the finful diforders of fallen man.
" That he rofe from the dead the third
" day after he was crucify'd by the Jews, and
" forty days after afcended into Heaven,
" from whence I expect his coming at the laft
" day to judge me and all the world : and
" that when he was on earth he not only by

his

" his life gave us a perfect example, and by
" his Doctrine an infallible rule of all that
" we are to do, suffer and hope; but also
" by the sacrifice of his death, reconcil'd to
" mercy all such as do the will of his Father,
" particularly those that believe his word,
" imitate his works, and accept his inter-
" cession. That as well the holy adult de-
" ceased before his passion, as children dy-
" ing before the use of reason, are deliver'd
" from death by his merits, so that none
" can be sav'd without a Mediator. And
" lastly, that he is the only Ruler and Legisla-
" tor of the Church.

" III. I believe we are sanctify'd by the
" divine Spirit, who worketh in us, and with
" us, who directs and perfects us. I acknow-
" ledge the purity, excellence and obliga-
" tion of all the evangelical precepts, as they
" are comprehended under these three heads,
" to live temperately, justly, and piously ; to
" love God above all things, and my neigh-
" bour as my self. This is the sum of my
" assurance of eternal life, in hopes where-
" of I am now writing this unfeign'd Con-
" fession of my Faith.

Whoever consents to these Articles, and
receives the Scriptures for the word of God,
is my brother in CHRIST, let him think of
me or denominate himself as he pleases. I
will not contend with any about dubious or
obscure

obfcure points, and I do not fo much regard
frivolous matters, how fuperftitioufly foever
cry'd up by fome, as to erect them into terms
of Communion. I dare not confine the
Church to the narrow limits of a peculiar
Sect, or her Doctrines to the affected phrafes
of a Party; and becaufe the Gofpel teacheth
us mutual forbearance and the love of our
enemies, I would not be fufpected to favour
thofe I cannot abufe with unfeemly heat,
much lefs queftion the truth of what I hold
unlawful to impofe. No man can believe as
he lifts, and 'tis not juft any fhould fay what he
thinks not. All that we have to do is cha-
ritably to inftruct, and if we can, convince
the erroneous. We may pray for the obfti-
nate, and perfift in our endeavours, but further we have no commiffion. They have as
great an intereft to fave their own Souls, as we
to encourage them to it: and if they flight
our exhortations, we muft leave them to God.
The civil Society cannot be injur'd by this
Toleration, whilft all irregular practices are
punifhable by the Magiftrate; nor would I
defend it, did I fee the fin or the danger: fo
far am I from making it a fhelter to Athe-
ifm and indifference, as my ill-wifhers give
out.

Sir, I hope by this time I have fatisfy'd
your pious concern about my everlafting
happinefs, and the evidence of that Religion,
whereof, tho' I cannot pretend to be an in-

Vol. II. U genious,

genious, or a learned advocate, I shall always, according to my poor abilities, prove a faithful and a zealous one. I give you a thousand thanks for the pains you have taken about me in your two excellent Letters, which I shall still preserve and value. I am certain you intended me no hurt by them, which I may not say of those who suggested the unworthy thought. 'Tis true I was surpriz'd with the circumstances; yet never suspected your good intentions.

Things reflecting upon yours and my integrity were discoursed about the first Letter, which made me communicate it to several but in vain; for the malice of some Jacobites, who envy me common charity, proclaims my self the Author. This honor I'm sure is undesign'd, as the palpable absurdity that I should purchase a few commendations of course, at the expence of what is most laudable among men. But this is not the only time I have been grosly misrepresented by these Gentlemen, tho' ordinarily their efforts have contrary effects. At my first coming, they thought to frighten me with that terrible thing of a Commonwealth, an artifice I look'd upon despis'd, and forgotten as the incense of arbitrary power which they offer'd to the late Kings. But when they perceiv'd I was nothing shy of owning the true Constitution of the English Government, however basely nick-nam'd

by

by fome of its degenerate fubjects, they made a mighty noife about the Church, and falfly reported that I did not frequent the public worfhip from which they voluntarily feparate themfelves. Now they make my affiduity a fault for reafons as groundlefs as pitiful, fo implacable is their fpirit! But thefe miferable tricks not taking with the learned and the wife, they fhifted fcenes, and made me next an accomplifh'd Conjurer for ridiculing Necromancy, and the fecond Sight. A fimple ftory was whifper'd of the amazing feats I had done, which a worthy friend gave me occafion to expofe to the diverfion of the company, and the relator's difgrace. Well, if Magic won't do, Herefy muft. I am a dangerous Anti-Trinitarian, for having often publickly declared that I could as foon digeft a wooden, or breaden Deity, as adore a created fpirit or a dignified man. This Socinianifm and Arianifm are, one would think, very orthodox.

SIR, thefe are few of the numerous inftances I can produce of my adverfaries unchriftian hatred, which I pray God to forgive, as I do. Did they but mind their own bufinefs as much as I flight what they fay of me, they would afford the Coffee-houfe better entertainment. 'Tis to undeceive you and the reft of my honored friends, whofe favours I thankfully acknowledge, that I have writ this Anfwer. I was a while fomewhat back-

ward

ward to do it, left any fhould imagine I mind-
ed our State Enthufiafts, but at length their
clamours extorted it. I'm confident you'll do
me that juftice I expect, and becomes you,
tho' I dare not flatter my felf with the hopes
of your more defireable acquaintance. Had
you given me any Direction, you fhould have
feen this Anfwer before I receiv'd your fecond
obliging Letter; wherefore I entreat you, if
this comes to your hand, not to forget this
point the next time. I am, SIR, your much
oblig'd, and moft humble Servant.

F O R

Mr. T O L A N D.

Oxford, *May* 30, 1694.

SIR,

SOME time laft week, I got the fight of
a Letter which you left at the Coffee-
houfe for your Friend A. A. and it being
intended for a vindication of your Character, from the falfe and malicious afperfions
of your ill-wifhers, I am glad that I never
found means of getting it into my hands fe-
curely, before it was open'd : for I fhould
never have been able to have done you half
the juftice, which the timely appearance of
this Paper in publick hath done.

I am forry that you fhould think, that I
miftook you for an Atheift or a Deift: by
the

the character of *little Religion*, I meant no more than this : that you were one who dealt somewhat too freely with it, a man of an aspiring and uncontrouled reason, a great contemner of Credulity, and particularly an undervaluer of the two extraordinary Cures, wrought lately at London : these do not immediately prove a man an Atheist ; though, I confess, I was always apt to think, that they generally proceed from some degree of infidelity in the heart, which by a little indulgence may easily grow into an hatred and contempt of Religion ; and thence insensibly dispose the mind for Socinianism, Deism, Atheism, or any thing : but however, I am concern'd at it the less, since you acknowledge some have been endeavouring to fasten a bad Character on you ; and you have hence taken occasion to refute all Calumnies.

In the Letter you load me with much honor, much more than I expected, or deserve ; in those who never saw my Letters, this raises an opinion that something is in them very extraordinary ; but to those who have seen them, and to my self, 'tis an argument of great candour in you, who can love truth in so plain a dress : the abhorrence you express for Atheism, and your descanting upon it, even to the awakening the Civil power against it, give me grounds to believe that you have no real kindness for it : your concern for the looseness and

scepticism

ſcepticiſm of this age, inclines me to hope that you are neither prophanely nor ſceptically given; your ſo free declaration of your Faith, makes me think you an Orthodox believer; and your ſenſe of the obligation of the Chriſtian duties, and your reſolves of appearing in the behalf of Religion, confirm me, that you are, and deſign to continue a very good Chriſtian.

For, why ſhould I not acquieſce in theſe tokens of ſincerity? I confeſs, I hate a diſtruſtful narrow temper, which is jealous and ſuſpicious of all mankind; 'tis, methinks, a diſparagement to our common nature, when we refuſe to think well of another, till it's impoſſible to think otherwiſe, and is the very ſcepticiſm we condemn. No, I truſt, SIR, you are in good earneſt, and would not play with your ſoul's happineſs: and I doubt not, but you will ſoon make many be of my mind; for Religion is no lifeleſs thing, but when once it hath taken root in the heart, (which is its proper ſoil) as a tree planted in the fertile valley, or (as the Pſalmiſt ſpeaks) by the water-ſide, it cannot fail to bring forth its fruits, its genuine, undoubted, diſtinguiſhing fruits, in due ſeaſon.

And though God, who diſpoſes and cultivates the heart, alone knows the time of its harveſt, yet in man's judgment, no ſeaſon
can

can be more proper for its producing a plentiful crop, than while the underſtanding is mature, and in its full ſtrength, the mind freſh and impregnated with the dews and ſhowers of God's grace, and moreover adorn'd with all outward accompliſhments; than while the body is healthy and ſtrong, and in a vigorous capacity of miniſtring unto the ſoul. This is the ſeaſon, in which men expeȼt that a noble ſoil ſhould yield much fruit to be treaſur'd up in ſtore againſt a day of calamity, againſt the day of ſickneſs, old-age, and death : and I am fully perſuaded, that if a few generous ſpirits would ſtedfaſtly reſolve to employ their rich endowments in the ſervice of the donor, but eſpecially praiſe him with the tongues which he hath given them ; to ſtem the flood of impiety, and appear boldly in the behalf of virtue ; ſhewing as well the lovelineſs of being vertuous, as the baſeneſs and raſcality of being wicked; and ſtudy ſeriouſly to engage all they converſe with in that reaſonable courſe, which alone, can render them happy here, and glorious hereafter ; we ſhould ſoon ſee a bleſſed change upon the earth, ſin being by degrees extirpated, we might make ſome approach to our former Paradiſaical ſtate ; in the language of the Prophet, inſtead of the Thorn, would come up the Firr-tree, and inſtead of the Brier, would come up the Myrtle-tree : millions of ſouls (each of them better than the whole periſhing world) might

U 4

be

be refcu'd from deftruction, and entitl'd to glory ; and the happy undertakers themfelves; be affur'd of fhining as the brightnefs in the firmament, as the ftars for ever and ever : and oh! that God would touch the hearts of fome, who are fitted for this work, with the alone truly laudable ambition of becoming exceedingly beneficial to this world, and exceedingly happy in the next !

Dear Sir, I run out into this fubject, as well, becaufe my hopes of the good fuccefs of fuch an attempt (through God's blefling) are very ftrong and lively, (for I know that in reality, nothing is fo arrant a coward as vice, and nothing is fo forcible as reafon and love) as likewife, becaufe 'tis commonly reported, that you are at prefent upon a work, which I fear will not prove half fo advantageous to yourfelf or others : 'tis faid, that you are now publifhing a piece with intent to fhew, that there is no fuch thing as a *Myftery* in our Religion ; but that every thing in it is fubjicible to our underftandings. I confefs, I do not forefee what good influence it would derive upon our practice, if all the deep and hidden things of God lay open to the meaneft capacities (and there is no better argument with me, that the knowledge of them would be of no great ufe unto us, than that they lye fo very deep) but that ever they fhould be thus laid open to men in thefe bodies, I freely own, I think

next

next to impoſſible. Myſteries, 'tis true, are reveal'd to the meek, and it may be the pecu-
'liar reward of ſome very humble perſons, to
be admitted to behold ſome things within
the veil : but then I am perſuaded, that whatever they ſee there, is of the ſame nature with
St. PAUL's Αῤῥητα ; it cannot, it need not be
utter'd unto others. If you are really engag'd
in ſuch a work, 'twould be folly in me to
think of diverting you from it, by any
thing which I can ſay ; let me only beg
you to run over a book, entitl'd, *The Cauſes
of the Decay of Chriſtian Piety*, a piece of
the ſame lineage and integrity with the *Whole
Duty of Man*, in which, among other melancholy truths, the great miſchief of ingenious
perſons applying the choiceſt abilities to ſuch
ſort of purpoſes, is pathetically lamented.

Dear SIR, pardon, I beſeech you, the great
freedom I uſe with you, I am unknown to
you, and therefore am the freer; though I
confeſs, I think that ſome degree of this freedom would do no great harm in common
converſation. I earneſtly deſire of you to
let no man ſee this. You gave ſome reaſons
which oblig'd you to impart my other, I ſee
no ends which you can ſerve by diſcloſing
this ; let me entreat you therefore, by the
kindneſs which you ſay you bear me, not to
let this go any farther than your ſelf. As to
the perſonal knowledge, which you ſay, you
could wiſh ; I aſſure you it can be of no uſe

to you, and it may be very prejudicial to my felf, upon divers accounts; otherwise you may imagine I fhould not eafily decline your fo valuable an offerture: 'tis not any feeming modefty, but, indeed, real and neceffary prudence which makes me ftudy to be concealed.

Dear SIR, excufe all the trouble I have created you, and particularly that of this wearifome Letter: the matter, I hear, has made fome noife, and I am forry for it; all my comfort is, that I never intended it. Dear SIR, adieu.

I am
your real friend and fervant.

T O

THE REVEREND Mr. ***.

London, Sept. 12, 1695.

Reverend SIR,

I Can fend you no news foreign or domeftick this poft; and, which is the greater wonder, your Champions of the Commonwealth of Learning feem to have retir'd into winter-quarters too, for we never enjoy'd a more profound peace in this refpect: either no enemy appears at all, or, if now and then one makes an incurfion, he meets with
little

little or no oppofition; except a Captain ANTONIO ventures abroad fometimes to pick up his ftraglers, and curfe him afar off, as SHIMEI did good King DAVID. So, you know, *the Reafonablenefs of Chriftianity* was lately ferv'd.

However, I can be no fufferer by this filence of the Learned, as long as you are pleafed to honor me with your correfpondence. You are the oracle I confult about all my difficulties, and from which I never mifs of fatisfaction. What employs my thoughts at prefent may feem a great Paradox; but, unlefs your anfwer can make it in good earneft appear one to me, the world is like to have it one time or other for found Divinity.

The Subject is the *Book of Job.* After proving it, with others, more antient than the writings of MOSES, and fhewing it to be a real Hiftory and no Parable, contrary to the fentiments of the Jews and a modern author; I difcover the true Quality and Country of JOB, the nobleft pattern on record of a mind truly divine, endu'd with the moft finifh'd wifdom and refolution. So far, you'll fay, all goes very well. But further, I endeavour to make it appear in particular (for none before me, as I know, ever dreamt of any fuch thing) that only the Dialogue between JOB and his three Friends is the genuine Book,

3   beginning

beginning at verfe the fecond, of chapter the third, and ending at the laft verfe of chapter the thirty firft, according to our common divifion. Then I prove the Relation preceding this Dialogue, as an Argument to the Piece, wherein fuch odd, if not impoffible, paffages are told of Satan and the Sons of God, of Job himfelf, his wife, his children and friends, to be a meer Fable made by fome idle Jew ; who, finding the Hero of this excellent Poem labouring under the greateft afflictions, thought pity the particulars fhou'd be unknown : and fo by a liberty ordinary to the Rabbins, invented that monftrous Story, tho' without any fufficient ground for it, from Job's complaint and defence, or the reproaches and arguments of his Friends. I make the fame account not only of the latter part of the laft chapter, but alfo of the foregoing chapters, from the xxxii inclufively. And that fame Elihu the fon of Barachel, who takes fo much upon him in thofe chapters, I fhall demonftrate to be the undoubted Author of all the Additions.

But tho' it be not my intention to give you the detail of my reafons for this Paradox, yet I would have you confider, that the moft part of what I call in queftion, is penn'd in very dull and negligent profe ; whereas the native beauties of the Dialogue appear even through the verfion, which is all rimed verfe, according to the genius of the Eaftern Poetry.

The

The Dialogue too is full of Arabifms, which help us to difcover the original; but no fuch thing appears in the additions of the Hebrew Tranflator.

And to compleat all, I fhew by the beft Memoirs that any perfon can defire, what was JOB's true ftate, or the occafion of thofe Complaints, fo pathetically exprefs'd in this admirable piece.

All that I requeft of you, SIR, is, by the ftrongeft reafons you can think on, to fhew me any impoffibility in fuch a performance; and if no better occur to you, let me have all the negative difficulties you can make.

SIR,

I am

your unalterable friend and fervant.

A CON-

A

CONSOLATORY LETTER

To the honorable

Sir *ROBERT CLAYTON*, Kt.

*Formerly Sheriff, afterwards Lord-Mayor, and
still Alderman of London.*

London Decemb. 4, 1698.

Sir,

THE paffions are fuch an effential part of
our conftitution, and fo infeparably
united to our underftanding, that on this account they are commonly term'd *natural affections;* nor is there any part of our fabrick
wherein the effects of divine wifdom are
more vifible and obvious; feeing that to
have all our members fo wonderfully accom-
modated to their feveral ufes would fignify
little, if we wanted the paffions of joy and
grief, or the fenfations of pain and pleafure,
which are the primary fprings and motives
of all our defires and actions. Herein therefore the excellence or depravation of our
mind appears, according as reafon governs
our paffions, or we fuffer the paffions to corrupt our reafon. An inclination to eating
and drinking (for example) is very natural,
and

and abfolutely neceffary for our prefervation; but he, that confiders no further
than the pleafing and inviting taft of the
meat or liquor, acts unnaturally: while another, who meafures his appetite by a fufficient nourifhment and fupport for his body,
anfwers the defign of God in planting thefe
defires within him. In like manner, to
grieve or be afflicted for the lofs of any
thing which in it felf we count amiable
and worthy, or pleafing and profitable to us
in particular, is natural and juft; for without this affection we fhould not fufficiently
value thefe bleffings, or be enough follicitous.
to cultivate and preferve them: but on the
other hand, fo to let loofe our paffions on fuch
doleful occafions as to fet no bounds to our
forrow, and to defpair of all other comforts
at once, becaufe we have loft any fimple object of our felicity, is both unreafonable and
defencelefs.

Now, confidering that the firft motions of
our paffions are generally too violent to hear
advice; and that indeed this impetuous tor-
rent of the fpirits is nothing fo dangerous to
our bodily health or intellectual faculties, as
the melancholy and folitary thoughts that
fucceed (thefe being of a longer continuance
and of a more pineing nature) I thought fit,
SIR, to fpeak very little to you at the beginning concerning the early death of your moft
hopeful Nephew, and to write nothing at
all

all on this fubject (which I count not fo much your private lofs, as that of the publick in a ufeful Citizen) till your mind fhould be lefs difturb'd, or your firft tranfports well allay'd. And I muft acknowledge that I was greatly pleafed to perceive with how much decency and true manlinefs you behav'd your felf on this occafion; tho', for preventing the fatal confequences of future penfivenefs, I take the liberty at this time of laying a few confiderations before you. I knew the young Gentleman well when we ftudied at Oxford together, and valu'd him both for his perfonal merit and the hope I conceiv'd of his ability to ferve his Country in fome eminent ftation.

This makes, not me alone, but all his other acquaintance to be deeply fenfible of our lofs in him; and therefore to be companions with you (tho' not on equal terms) in forrow. But permit me to tell you, SIR, that of all others you have in my opinion the leaft reafon to torment your felf. That men are born mortal, every body knows, how few foever feem to confider it; for by many of their actions one would think they were certain of immortality here on earth. Nor are they lefs convinc'd that the whole courfe of life is fubject to infinite changes and accidents, which by their fudden or unforefeen effects always confound the weak and vitious,
but

but never catch the honeſt and wiſe unpre-
par'd; for a virtuous man of good underſtanding is placed above all the chances of
fortune; becauſe he conſtantly expects them,
and is never diſpleaſed but with the ill of
others or his own frailties, which he labors
to conquer and reform. Moſt people will
agree likewiſe that we ſhould not bear thoſe
things heavily, which we can by no means
avoid; and the experience of all ages muſt
perſuade us that we can neither by poverty
or pain, by ſlavery or diſgrace, nor even by
death it ſelf, ſuffer any thing new or unuſual;
which reflection alone ſhould teach us to live
content with that condition wherein we are
born.

But theſe arguments of Conſolation, tho'
very good and ſolid in themſelves, are yet
common to you, Sir ROBERT, with the reſt
of mankind. You have little reaſon in
particular to impair your health, or to leſſen
the tranquillity of your mind by abandoning
your ſelf to fruitleſs mourning, when you
ſeriouſly conſider that after having rais'd your
fortune ſolely by your own merit and indu-
ſtry (without loſing your honor or reputation by any indirect and criminal methods of
growing rich) you had the happineſs of ſer-
ving your country in the moſt publick capacity, as well in this City, as in the honourable
Houſe of Commons; and that in the moſt
dangerous times, but yet with the greateſt ap-

plaufe : that you ftill affift in the government of the greateft, freeft, and moft powerful City in the world, where you are univerfally efteem'd, particularly dear to the beft perfons, and that without your advice the moft eminent of your fellow citizens will not adminifter their own fhare of the magiftracy : that by publick and private charities, as well as by a generous and hofpitable manner of living, you have fhower'd the bleffings of a plentiful eftate the moft agreeably to the will of heaven, the exigences of the needy, and the approbation of the beft men : and that with all this you have neither neglected your own kindred, nor the relations of your excellent Lady, who all tenderly love and reverence you living, and will adore and blefs your memory when dead : I fay, when you confider all this you ought to entertain a becoming fatisfaction in your mind, and to contemn all the crofs accidents of the world.

When you further think on what you have done for that incomparable youth for whom you particularly deftin'd a large fhare of your eftate, and in whofe laudable actions your country might promife it felf as it were a continuation of your own life; how you gave him the liberal education of a Gentleman, and taught him the principles of true virtue, illuftrated by your own example and that of other good men ; you ought to be
greatly

greatly pleafed that nothing was wanting of your fide. And when on the other hand, you remember how well he anfwer'd all your care and hopes, how temperate, how learn'd, and how judicious he was; how prudent in his travels, and how pious in rendering his foul to God who gave it, you have the higheft reafon to rejoice that fo liv'd and died a perfon of the beft accomplifhments attain'd thro' your beneficence and direction. Thus irreproachably to lead his life, defervedly belov'd of every body; and thus to finifh his courfe agreeable to the utmoft perfection of nature, would certainly be hereafter, and has, no doubt, hitherto been the refult of your defires.

The only apology therefore left for your grief, muft be, that he died fooner than was good, for you or himfelf. But I have too great an opinion of your underftanding to imagine you fhould harbour any thought, which is not the lefs unreafonable for being fo common. A paffage to immortality, and a perpetual union with the fupreme Being cannot be reckon'd for his difadvantage; and were there no fenfation after death, he could not be reputed more miferable than before he was born: nor would this argument for forrow be lefs cogent from the firft moment of his nativity, fince you might be fure he muft inevitably die fome time or other. And as for you, I will not appear fo diffi-

dent

dent of your accuftom'd wifdom and gravity, as to fuppofe you fhould now be wanting to your felf in making good the character you have hitherto obtain'd of conftancy
and firmnefs; or that you will expect that
cure from length of time, which you ought
fpeedily to perform by your own reafon.
You have ftill many opportunities of bene-
fiting the world, you have the fame means
of doing good, and the fame difcernment to
chufe the propereft objects of your charity
or care. Inftead of one family you may
raife feveral, or prevent others from falling
to decay; and by what you defign'd to give
that lovely young Gentleman alone, you can
make the fortunes of many, who may prove
to be the ornaments of their country, and
will be the moft glorious monuments of
your piety, wifdom, juftice, liberality. But
to one who fo much exceeds me in age and underftanding, to hint thefe things is fufficient.

I fhall be extremely pleafed to learn that
thefe lines have afforded you any pleafure or
confolation; and if they fhould not have all
the effect I intended, yet I am fatisfy'd that
I did not fail of my Duty to ferve a perfon
whom all good men love, whom I particularly honor, and to whom I have fo great obligations.

T O

TO THE SAME.

London Decem. 7, 1698.

SIR,

As thofe who have not perform'd any worthy actions themfelves, think it impertinent that others fhould be commended ; fo the panegyrics, which fear or favor draws from fervile fpirits on undeferving perfons in corrupt times, occafion all juft praife to pafs for flattery. But in thofe ages and places where liberty and learning equally flourifh'd, every man's virtue had full juftice done to it ; nor were the moft glorious rewards propos'd to merit half fo effectual, as the diftinguifhing examples of brave or good men, to animate others with an emulation of their laudable actions. This manifeftly appears in all the writings of the old Romans, particularly in the divine volumes of CICERO, where we meet with fuch noble characters, and fuch lovely pictures of his friends and cotemporaries, as may enflame the moft infenfible to glory or applaufe.

In imitation therefore of thefe perfect models, I wrote the Letter which I lately fent to you, and wherein the chiefeft topic of comfort was the confideration of your own virtues. I fend you now, as a juftification of

this

this uncommon way of writing, and as an additional argument or example, the Tranflation of a Letter written upon the like occafion to CICERO after the Death of his belov'd Daughter TULLIA, a Lady of extraordinary learning and merits. CICERO, tho' the moft eminent philofopher, politician, and orator in the world, was not proof againft the firft impreffions of this misfortune: wherefore all the men of parts and quality that knew him, either came or fent to comfort him. MARCUS BRUTUS fent him a confolatory Letter, which CICERO himfelf frequently commends; but it is fince unhappily loft. LUCIUS LUCCEIUS wrote another to him; JULIUS CÆSAR one, and at laft he wrote a Confolation to himfelf: but the only one remaining is that of SERVIUS SULPITIUS, which I here fubjoin for your perufal, wishing you long life and an uninterrupted happinefs.

S E R V I U S   S U L P I T I U S

T O

MARCUS TULLIUS CICERO.

WHEN I was inform'd of your Daughter TULLIA's Death, I took it, as I ought, moft grievoufly and heavily, efteeming

ing it a common calamity. And if I had been there at that time, I had neither been wanting to you, nor yet have forborn to expreſs my grief in your preſence. Tho' this kind of Conſolation be miſerable and difficult, becauſe the relations and acquaintance, who ought to afford it, are themſelves afflicted with the ſame ſorrow, and cannot endeavour to do it without many tears; inſomuch that they may ſeem rather to want being comforted by others, than to be able to perform this good office to any elſe: notwithſtanding, what things offer themſelves at preſent to my mind I determin'd to write to you briefly; not that I think you ignorant of them, but that being hindred by your grief you may perhaps obſerve 'em the leſs.

Wherefore then ſhould you be mov'd at that rate by your private ſorrow? Conſider how fortune has dealt with us hitherto: and how all thoſe things are taken away from us, which ought not to be leſs dear to men than their children; I mean our Country, our Reputation, our Dignity, and all our Honors? What could be added then to our affliction by this one misfortune? or how can a mind diſquieted with theſe things not grow callous, and ſet a lower value on all other matters? But if (as I ſuppoſe) you lament her caſe, how often muſt you have hit on this thought, and I have not ſeldom done it, that in theſe times their fate is not the worſt,

who

who may without much pain exchange their
life for death ? Now, what was it that could
so greatly invite her to live at this time?
what thing? what expectation? what pleasure of mind ? Is it that she might spend her
days in marriage with any of the principal
youth ? as I believe a person of your figure
may pick and chuse a son-in-law among our
young men, to whose care you might safely commit your daughter. Or is it that she
might bear children, whom she would rejoice
to see in their prime ? who could wisely preserve the estate receiv'd from their parents ?
who should in their turns stand candidates
for honorable posts in the government ? who
should make use of their liberty in the service of their friends ? Now, which of all
these was not taken away before it was given ?

But you'll say it is a misfortune to lose our
Children. A misfortune indeed, if it be not
worst to be always afflicted and suffering on
this account. What afforded me no small
consolation I shall impart to you ; for perhaps the same thing may contribute to diminish your grief. In my return from Asia,
as I sail'd from Ægina towards Megara I begun to view all the regions on every hand
of me; behind me was Ægina, Megara before me, on my right hand Piræus, and
Corinth on my left ; which cities were once
in a most flourishing state, tho' now they lye
scatter'd, and mangl'd in ruins before you.
Thus

Thus I begun therefore to meditate with my self: *Alas! why should we poor men be displeas'd that any of our number dyes or is kill'd, whose life is naturally short; when the carcasses of so many cities lye expos'd in one place! Do thou therefore refrain thy self, O Servius, and remember thou art born a man.* Believe me, I was not a little confirm'd by this thought. Do you likewise, if it seems good, set the same thing before your eyes. Lately so many famous persons were destroy'd at once; besides our Empire is so greatly diminish'd; all the Provinces are shaken, and are you so vehemently disturb'd at the death of one woman, who, if she had not departed now, must have dy'd notwithstanding within a few years, seeing she was born of human race?

Recall therefore your mind from these things to the knowledge of your self, and rather remember those matters that are becoming your person; namely, that she liv'd as long as it was needful for her, and expir'd together with the Commonwealth: that she saw you her father, a Prætor, a Consul, an Augur: that she was marry'd to a couple of our hopefullest young Gentlemen: that she had enjoy'd almost every good thing in the world: and left this life when our government was destroy'd. What is it then wherein you or she can in this respect complain of fortune? Finally, do not forget that you

are

are CICERO, and he that was wont to comfort and advise others : nor imitate bad Physicians, who profess great skill in the diseases of others, and cannot cure themselves ; but rather call to your mind and propose to your self, what you are accustom'd in the like cases to prescribe other people.

There is no grief but length of time diminishes and softens; but for you to expect such a time, and not rather find a remedy for this matter from your own prudence, is unworthy. But if the very dead have any sense of our condition, such was the love she bore you, and her piety towards all her relations, that she requires none of your tears. Be rul'd then by your dead child ; by the rest of your friends and acquaintance, who are griev'd for your sake ; grant this favour to your country, that if there be any occasion, it may use thy assistance and advice : and lastly, since our hard fortune is such, and that we must act this complying part, do not suffer that any should suspect it is not so much your Daughter, as the bad times of the Commonwealth, and the victory of the opposite faction, that afflicts you.

I'm asham'd to write any more to you on this subject, lest I should seem to distrust your wisdom : wherefore, after offering you this one particular, I shall make an end of writing. We saw you sometimes bear your

prosperous

profperous fortune excellently well, which procur'd you great commendations: let us now then be convinc'd that you can equally bear adverfity, and that it feems no heavier burden to you than it ought; leaft of all virtues you fhould appear to want this fingle one. As for my felf, when I know that you enjoy more tranquillity of mind, I fhall acquaint you with the tranfactions of this place, and the condition of our Province.

Farewell.

ANTHONIO VAN DALE

S. P. D.

JO. TOLANDUS.

NON poffum, vir celeberrime, non poffum non te etiam atque etiam monere quanti ingenium & ftudia tua femper fecerim, nec quidem, ut frequenter evenire affolet, minuit præfentia famam : nam quæ in te fummopere elucent virtutes; mira fcilicet comitas, exquifitiffima doctrina, veritatis indagandæ defiderium cum libertatis tuendæ ftudio conjunctum, te mihi (quod vix poffibile credebam fieri) chariorem adhuc multo reddiderunt. Pergas ergo, Archæologorum quot funt quotvè erunt doctiffime, iifdem tibi
conciliare

conciliare modis omnes ingenuos, bonòs, & cordatos : herculeo nitaris labore horrenda superstitionis in lucem pertrahere monstra, & non ferendum excutere sacerdotale jugum : demonstres non ovum ovo similius esse, quam se invicem referunt sacratæ recentium & antiquorum, quibus popello illudunt & imperitant, artes, fraudes, strophæ : fac videant ipsi hebetioris acuminis homines nullo pacto in mirandis fabulis, horrendis ambagibus, vel reconditis mysteriis, sed in vera virtute & solida scientia, situm esse summum mortalium bonum :

Hi mores, hæc duri immota Catonis
Secta fuit, servare modum, finemque tueri,
Naturamque sequi, patriæque impendere
  vitam,
Nec sibi, sed toti genitum se credere mundo.

Ut breviter dicam, fruatur quam cito literatus orbis aureis illis, quos de Romanorum & Græcorum Sacerdotiis elaborasti tractatibus : nec longius, quam par est, expectentur secundæ melioresque de Oraculis curæ, quibus evulgandis non magis tibi aliàs conterraneos meos devincire poteris.

Altero meo hospiti, viro dignissimo Domino Drostio, grates ago innumeras ob tot in me favores congestos, & quos ut bene sentio non mereri me potuisse, sic doleo. Commendatum me habeas, quæso, tam forma quam ingenio præstantissimæ virgini, Domi-
næ

næ meæ COLARTIÆ, maximo Harlemi simul
& naturæ miraculo. Inter pretiosissima repo-
nam cimelia, quibus beare me dignata est mu-
nuscula; etsi adhuc vix mihi persuadere pos-
sum de veritate rerum earum quas tamen in
dubio mihi revocare non licet, quarum-
que propriis auribus & oculis experimentum
accepi.

Per literas quas hic ex Anglia accepi, intelligo Comitem PORTLANDIÆ huc certissimè
venturum, Regem manere domi hac æstate, nu-
merosam parari classem, Gallos nequaquam
timendos, & Parliamentum nostrum in proxi-
mum annum esse prorogatum ut nostri lo-
quuntur. Vale.

Nobilissimo Domino
JO. TOLANDO
A. VAN DALE S. P. D.

ME tibi percharum esse maximè guadeo.
At suffundis me tantis elogiis, quibus
me minime dignum sentio, maximo pudore.
Sumo tamen illa pro humanissima admoni-
tione; ut coner talia, per quæ, si non laude,
certe venia doctis ac cordatis viris dignus
videar. O si liceret cum talibus, qualis tu
nobilissime vir es, transigere mihi vitam!
Nunc vivo, ubi dum bene facere studeo,

3   male

male tamen audio, unius ob noxam & faci-
nus Ajacis Oilei. BEKKERUS nempe mihi
amicus fuit. Certè ſi jam non ſenex eſſem,
ac non uxoratus, mihiq; ſatis honeſta ac
qua ſatis commode ſubſiſtere queam, oblata
eſſet in Anglia conditio, ibi vobiſcum vivere ac mori libéret. Hic nullus eruditis
honos: aut ſi aliquis adhuc ſit, ſolis illis ob-
tigit, qui ſumma cum patientia (licet ſimul
ſummo cum tædio) ſervitutis pignus ferre de-
dicerunt, adulationiq; illorum, qui ipſis longe pejores ſunt ſe bene aſſueſcere valent.

Novellæ, quas mihi ſcripſiſti, pergratæ ſunt.
At hic Harpocrati litandum; niſi apud tales,
qualis tu nobiliſſ. vir, ac DROSTIUS noſter.
Reperies tamen & Amſtelodami Nicodemi-
tas. Ejuſmodi moribus quippe hic nobis vi-
vendum; niſi quibus ita vivere licet, ut aliis
non indigeant. Ego interim, dum adulari
neſcio, tacitus fata mea fero; mihiq; magis
magiſq; circa talia impero. Verum plura de
hiſce coram, cùm per diem unum aut alterum
adhuc ſimul vivere licebit.

Perilluſtri GRÆVIO, ut commendes me
ſicut deſidero, ita nullus dubito.

Vale interim optime virorum: atq; ut jam
cœpiſti, me amare pergas.

Harlemi 23 *Maii* 1699.

Peril-

Perilluftri eruditione viro

Georgio Joanni Grævio

S. P. D.

A. VAN DALE M. D.

QUOD dudum volueram, fed vix tandem aufus fum, id jam occafione hac captata facere inftituo; ut te fcilicet fuper ftudiis meis confulam. Cum itaque vellet ad te tranfvolare nobiliffimus Anglus Jo. Tolandus, oneravi ipfum meis nugis ad te fic perferendis. Non ipfum, celeberrime vir, tibi commendo; quod neminis commendatione indigeat: ipfe enim fibi eft optima ac maxima commendatio; at volo me per ipfum tibi commendari.

Verum ut ad rem accedam, eft mihi nunc, poft facra Taurobolia, fub manibus tractatus illis fubnectendus de Sacerdotiis, aliifque muneribus ἐπωνύμοις apud Græcos: qua occafione mihi plufquam centum Infcriptiones Græcæ partim explicandæ, partim illuftrandæ, partim confulendæ aut perpendendæ veniunt; circa quas ut mihi plures occurrunt difficultates, fic tu mihi, celeber. vir, fuper una atque altera confulendus es.

3   Ad

Ad te igitur, ut ad commune eruditorum oraculum confugio : nec tam λόξια atque obscura, quam illa fuerunt quæ ex Apollinis opertis prodibant, expecto. In ista igitur Inscriptione apud SPONIUM *p.* 356. *n.* 99. occurrit nobis primum ἀρχιερεὺς τριϛαπολέων, quod fateor me non intelligere : unde ad Hierapolim mihi confugiendum hic videtur; atque ita reponere velim ἱεραπολίτων, quod videre mihi videar, si non ex STRABONE atque STEPHANO, VITRUVIO ac PLINO, certe ex hac Inscriptione illam ad Sardianos pertinuisse, cum idem L. J. BONNATUS, de quo hic mentio, simul Ἀρχιερεὺς τ͂ Ἀσίας τ͂ ἐν λυδία Σαρδιανῶν, fuerit. Secundò, mihi molestias creat ille ἀγωνοθέτης διαρίων, quem quoque non capio, nisi ad Gladiatores Diarios referendus sit. Nosti, optime vir, quam multa vocabula Latina nobis in Græcis inscriptionibus occurrant, ut πραιφεκ͖ο͗ς, ϛαβελάρι☧, φράτηρ ἀρϛαλις, & nescio quæ non alia. Sic ergo crediderim τὸς διαρίὸς fuisse Gladiatores ipsos, qui certo die a Cæsaribus dato depugnabant : atque eo respicere non solùm eam inscriptionem quæ a LIPSIO *l.* 1. Saturnal. producitur; sed & illam quæ a GRUTERO *p.* 475. *n.* 3. exhibetur. Familias autem Gladiatorum suos procuratores, & minerarios, & ἐπιϛάΊας, adeoque & ἀγωνοθέτας habuisse, æque fere atque athletas, mihi ex inscriptionibus persuadeo.

Plura essent mihi quidem proponenda super aliis; at nauseam meis nugis tibi creare non

non audeo. Si videro hæc non nimis ingrata fuisse, proponam quoque quæ, cum super aliis, tum super *Archibucolo Dei Liberi*, tum super *Sacerdote Cereris Græca*, tum denique quæ super pluribus aliis concepi. Vellem namque cum minimo meo dedecore talia, nec nimis cruda, in orbem literarium protrudere. Atque, utinam mihi præsenti te consulere liceret! verum hic mihi subsistendum, ne tibi nimis ob nugas meas tædio fiam. Hoc tamen addam, *Oracula* mea nunc iterum sub Bomii prælo, non sudare, sed frigere, ac quidem ὕϛερον πρῴτερον : prior enim Dissertatio agit de origine ac progressu, seu potius de auctoribus Oraculorum ; posterior vero de ipsorum duratione atque interitu. Vale interim, celeberrime vir ; atque hoc temporis tui dispendium mihi, quæso, benignè condones, dum tuus ex animo sicuti semper permaneo.

Dabam Harlemi, 24 *Maii*, 1699.

T O

Mr. * * *

London, *June* 26, 1705.

S I R,

BY the discourse we had together last week, I find you have lain under the same mistake with many others in relation to my circumstances ; for I do no less positively

Y   sitively

fitively than fincerely affure you, that in my whole life, I had no relation whatfoever to my Lord Somers or my Lord Halifax, that I have no perfonal obligations to either of them, nor ever enter'd into any manner of tranfactions with themfelves or on their behalf, either here at home, or any where abroad. As to my Politics, I ever was and will be for a free Government againft what is arbitrary and defpotic; which is to fay, that I prefer ftanding and indifferent Laws to the uncertain and byaft will of any Prince. But concerning the feveral forms of free Government (which are all good in their kinds, tho' not all equally fo) I juftly think our own mixt Conftitution to be the beft that is now extant any where. With thefe fentiments I came abroad into the world; but as no body's born infpir'd, fo I am not afham'd to own, that I had not fo much wifdom and difcretion, as I had fincerity and zeal, in the management of my opinions. I thought every body meant what they faid as well as my felf; and therefore in the moft public manner I promoted the party I had efpous'd, without once confidering that their adverfaries wou'd all very naturally become my enemies; nor did I take any care to ballance that oppofition by procuring potent friends elfewhere. Befides what I wrote my felf, I likewife publifh'd the Lives and Works of Harrington and Milton, with fome other Authors; and tho' I profeft not to agree with

them

them in every thing (efpecially in their Democratical Schemes of Government) yet in general they greatly contributed to beget in the minds of men, as the effect has fhewn, an ardent love of liberty, and an extreme averfion to arbitrary power. This was reckon'd a public fervice, but rewarded only with the public applaufes of fuch as approv'd the undertaking ; while the other fide had the moft fpecious pretext imaginable to reprefent me, what yet in their fenfe I was not, a moft violent Republican.

But, SIR, you'll fcarce conceive my furprize, when by degrees I begun to difcover, that certain perfons, of whom I hitherto entertain'd a high opinion, meant nothing by the Public but themfelves ; and my wonder was yet greater when I perceiv'd fo many others, wifer and abler than thefe, contentedly become the mean tools of their avarice or ambition, being their exchange or coffee-houfe heralds, and the trumpeters of their praifes in all public meetings. This made me quickly diftinguifh between men and things, between profeffions and performances ; and it remain'd no longer a myftery to me, why they were fonder of imploying and preferring footmen, bankrupts, poets, players, and pettyfoggers, than men of family, learning, ability, or virtue : becaufe the firft wou'd not fcruple to do unexamin'd, what the laft might reject with deteftation or contempt, and ne-

Y 2   ver

ver come under such engagements as the others wou'd be sure both to promise and to perform; besides that they cou'd not bear any rivals to their reputed capacity, which made 'em discountenance the best spirits of their own party. Three or four Bills in Parliament did quite take the scales from my eyes. And who, I pray, cou'd endure to hear any Whigs oppose the Judge's Bill, the Triennial Bill, the Bill for regulating Tryals in cases of High Treason, and such like? when in the preceding Reigns they loudly call'd for these, as the very Laws of Nature, wherein they were most certainly in the right. Their reasons against these excellent Statutes were worse than even their opposition, as if the Whigs only ought to enjoy the benefit of wholesome regulations, and as if the Tories might reasonably suffer under brib'd Judges and perpetual Parliaments. As a judgment of God, the Tories might justly come under these punishments for promoting them formerly against others, without considering how another time (as it happen'd) it might be their own turn to feel the smart of such severities; but this partiality was strangely unbecoming the Whigs, who by their constant principles ought to be patrons of the Liberty of mankind. I was not a little scandaliz'd to find 'em, when all other colours fail'd, pretend they were against these Laws, because the Tories were for 'em, to serve their own purposes: for 'tis no matter who is for a good thing,

thing, nor for what ends, provided the thing it self be truly useful and necessary; tho' no excuse is to be made for men of good principles to appear for a bad thing; especially if they clearly perceive the ill of it, and have so declar'd it themselves before.

The business of the standing Army finish'd all, tho' I am far from being against an Army whenever our circumstances indispensably require it. By that time I understood so much of men and things, as most plainly to foresee that the endeavouring to gain that dangerous and invidious point, wou'd in the minds of the people quite ruin the credit of the Whig-Ministry. For this, I own, I was not sorry; but I was afraid that thro' their sides the cause of Liberty wou'd suffer, as very manifestly it did. Nevertheless those persons, in order to make their own court and fortunes, did violently insist on that matter, so displeasing to the nation, and so directly opposite to their own declar'd principles and profession. It became the very test (as they wou'd have it) of Whig and Tory, when they were all Whigs that wrote against it, tho' I will not say, they all had the same views, no more than all the Tories in opposing it in Parliament; but, as others are convinc'd that this controversy serv'd more truly for a test to discover the inside of those quack Ministers, and their worthless Tools, and to undeceive those who before this time had more favou-

rable

rable thoughts of both, but now call'd their ability in queſtion no leſs than their integrity. What changes, what Parliaments, what meaſures enſu'd, you well know, and all thinking men did expeĉt. Yet ſo enrag'd were theſe undertakers at their ſurprizing diſappointment, that they never forgave thoſe Whigs, who had the honeſty and firmneſs to adhere to their old principles. Uncertain men they call'd ſuch as they durſt not irritate too much; and thoſe they had leſs reaſon to fear (among which I had the misforfortune to be one) they either branded for Tories among the credulous herd, or repreſented as men of none or unſettl'd principles, and all were unſettl'd that wou'd not go thro' ſtitch. Neither of theſe are to be ever pardon'd for rendring their hopeful projeĉts abortive. However I am ſorry they are ſuch bad Chriſtians as not to forgive real or imaginary offences againſt them; or ſuch bad Politicians as to think themſelves infallible, incapable of committing any errors or miſtakes, and not as liable as others to the reverſes of fortune, which may occaſion the want of uſeful friends. Yet to this hour they cannot diſcern their friends from their flatterers, but proſecute the former with all the contumely and ill offices they are capable. And, believe me, SIR, this perverſe diſpoſition makes hundreds of Whigs to deſire that, however theſe Gentlemen ſet up for Liberty (which they wiſh long to continue) yet they may

never

never be the guardians of it: and 'tis but natural that they fhou'd endeavour to keep the power out of thofe hands who have the will to hurt them; efpecially fince there are fo many fit and able perfons in the Nation, under all diftinctions, who never approved of their maxims or practices (fome of which are lately employ'd, as the Duke of NEWCASTLE and others,) men who were either never tainted with notions of arbitrary Power, or at leaft were never ingaged in arbitrary Proceedings; and who are moft unlikely to be feduc'd or corrupted hereafter by reafon of their great quality, plentiful fortunes, and honeft principles.

But, leaving fuch Affairs to her Majefty's wifdom, I proceed to tell you, SIR, that the perfevering Whigs on the other hand, were always ready to prefer the public good to their private refentments; nay, they were content to wink at thofe needy Minifter's indirect methods of fcraping for eftates at home, fo long as to fecure them they wou'd be zealous and vigorous againft our enemies abroad: and therefore when the caufe of Whiggifm was thought to be attack'd in thofe Gentlemen's perfons, they cordially defended them againft the profecution of their enemies; which fervice they did 'em with more fuccefs, I am fure with a better grace than their fworn creatures and mercenary dependents. The thanks that I in particular had for my pains, was to be moft falfly reprefented by them not only at home but abroad; at the fame time that I was exhorted by my real friends to forget all perfonal injuries, and not to complain, if I fhould not think fit to commend. The Tories were againft me of courfe; and I cannot blame the Jacobites for being fo, if any reafons can be given to juftify the defence of a bad Caufe. But thofe who pafs for Tories, without being Jacobites, are perfectly mifinform'd about me, and if they knew how I reprefented them at Hanover, and in Holland, as being really for the Succeffion, and in what matters I was of opinion they deferv'd to be oblig'd, they wou'd undoubtedly believe me no enemy of theirs, how little I might thereby befriend my felf: for words are but wind (as they fay) and therefore names go for nothing with me, where men's actions demonftrate 'em to be true Englifhmen; fince healing of breaches, and enlarging the foundation, ought to be only a good Countryman's defign. But fuch a temper in any man is what certain great perfons deteft above all things, becaufe they can only hope to make a confiderable figure in fome narrow-bottom'd faction; whereas in a conjunction of all who agree in the Proteftant Religion and Succeffion (however they may difagree in fuch trivial matters as forms or ceremonies) their tinfel abilities wou'd be quickly obfcur'd by the fhining merit and fo-ld worth of very many Gentlemen in all parties.   From

From these several Considerations you may easily infer, that in the first year of her Majesty's reign, being a stranger abroad and friendless at home, I must needs have been in a very uncertain condition, were not the highborn persons, under whose protection I then liv'd, proof against all misrepresentations, and that they judg'd of things from their own knowledge and not by the passions of others, to which they are not so great strangers as they are thought or wou'd seem. 'Twas happy for me, they had this generous disposition: for at one and the same time I had a Tory Secretary of State writing Letters against me to foreign Courts as Agent to the Whigs, if not obnoxious to the Laws; and certain leading Whigs were persuading the same Princes that I was Mr. HARLEY'S Creature, which was a higher crime by far than being a Tory. But I protest to you, SIR, by all that's awful, that I have not spoke one word to Mr. HARLEY, nor receiv'd one Letter or Message from him, nor sent any to him, since King WILLIAM died. And in this particular I frankly confess, that from prudential considerations I acted by constraint against my own judgment; I mean in breaking off conversation and correspondence with a person of signal abilities, and excellent learning, by whom a man in my circumstances cou'd mightily improve, as before I freely acknowledge to have done. But this affected strangeness was merely

ly

ly to prevent the vile afperfions of others either againft him or my felf, which yet I was not able to accomplifh: tho' I did as little approve as any whatfoever fuch things, if any there were, as I thought in Mr. HAR-LEY might proceed from private refent-ments to the detriment of the public Good. Yet I wholly did and do approve the fenfe he then had of our corrupt Miniftry, and thank him for the ftrenuous efforts he made to diffolve it. But, in the mean while, I find my condition to be like that of your coquet Ladies, who taft all the bitter of the fcandal without enjoying any of the fweets of the fin. I paft for Mr. HARLEY's friend, when he was oppofed by the Court, and now that he's in power I'm inform'd that by the fuggef-tion of certain Scots and a Dutchman, he takes me for his enemy; tho' his real un-forgiving enemies will have me ftill to be his favorite, and oppofe me now on that very fcore.

With relation to another very great man, the Duke of MARLBOROUGH; I own that having known nothing of him but by the report of others, and being mifled by ap-pearances of a conjunction between him and the moft violent Tories, from whence I rea-fonably apprehended danger to the Succef-fion in the beginning of this reign, I gave my felf in Holland, at Berlin and elfewhere fome liberties in fpeech, for which upon
better

better information I have amply aton'd, doing him all the juſtice poſſible wherever I had injur'd him. And ſince his Grace has perform'd ſuch extraordinary ſervices for his Country (which have contributed not only to reconcile and endear him to all true patriots, but alſo to undeceive all well-meaning, tho' miſtaken perſons; and that his actions are an effectual demonſtration of his good intentions to the Succeſſion, whereof the Court of Hanover it ſelf never doubted) he has the means in his power of diſcerning the ſincerity of all who pretend to honor his worth; conſidering eſpecially the open enmity and ſcurrilous uſage he meets at preſent from many, who were his Flatterers and paſt for his Admirers before. The very ground of their careſſes (as their behaviour undeniably proves) was a preſum'd averſion in his Grace to the Proteſtant Succeſſion of the Houſe of Hanover, which they were far from making a ſecret till this laſt year, when their faireſt hopes were ſo happily and ſo gloriouſly defeated.

As for my Lords N * * * and R * * * (for I am reſolv'd to be ſo plain and particular, as not to trouble you with a ſecond Letter on this ſubject) the firſt had a perſonal pique againſt me, the Miniſtry of the ſecond was dreaded abroad yet more than at home, and I am ſo averſe to the Deſigns of both the men, that there was no friendſhip or favour to be

3   expected

expected from that quarter, and so none was
ever desir'd. To say it then in a word, my
support has been owing to the generosity
and esteem of the Earl of SHAFTSBURY, and
certain other worthy persons at home, together with some help from Germany; and
not in whole or in part deriv'd from my
Lord SOMERS, Lord HALIFAX, or any other
Ministers. The Duke of NEWCASTLE has
been my true friend; and, since I had the
honor to be known to his Grace, he has been
constantly infusing into me sentiments of
peace and moderation, the profoundest respect for the Queen's Majesty and Government, and a largeness of soul towards all
denominations of Englishmen, that wou'd
agree in the support of her Title and the
legal Succession; notwithstanding any difference of opinion in other matters, whether
of Church or State. To this disposition experience had already brought me without his
honest advice, and if enabl'd, I shall make it
plainly appear in the whole conduct of my
life.

Thus I have given you, SIR, the true reasons why I have not been hitherto put into
any Employment, nor ever yet su'd for one
to any Party. Whether it be a vanity to
own it, I know not, but it wou'd certainly
be a false modesty to conceal it from you,
that I thought my self neglected and ill-used
by the Whig-Ministers (as they were call'd)
which

which without all queſtion has begot ſuitable reſentments againſt their perſons, but no diſlike of the Cauſe in which they pretend to be ingag'd, which is the cauſe of human nature, and conſequently mine as well as theirs. You need not wonder therefore any longer that I made no application (ſince they ſay I was never deny'd) where the terms imported to become a tool at leaſt, and what the moſt is I forbear now to mention. But I was once ſo ſenſible of their unworthy treatment, that I digeſted the heads of a Paper, which I intended to call *Advice to the Whigs againſt the time they are next in power*, wherein I wou'd ſhew the true Whigs the ſeveral ſlights and failings of thoſe Gentlemen, what a diſcredit they brought thereby on the Party and danger to Liberty ; that they were the occaſion of any diſaffected perſon's getting into the Adminiſtration, and that they were by no means fit to head a Party, tho' they might be proper enough to promote or undermine one : in the ſervice I think they ought always to be kept, and therefore to be always fed in hopes. But I made no progreſs to reduce that Paper into method, and God knows if ever I do : for all I have repeated and much more I cou'd forgive, tho' not be able to forget, provided the peace of my Country requir'd it.

The preſent Lord Treaſurer is a perſon I never offended in word or writing, tho' in

3. *the*

the Art of governing by Parties, which I wrote fome years ago, I have fhortly but juftly characteriz'd all the other great men (with fome more) I have nam'd in this Letter, except Mr. HARLEY. This, you may be fure, cou'd not proceed from a forefight of his being one day, as he is at prefent, firft Minifter; but is a pure effect of his merit in the difcharge of his truft as a public perfon; for in all other refpects he's to me a perfect ftranger, tho' neither the name nor imputation of any Party cou'd prejudice me againft him, according to the part I have a good while acted, which is reckoned lukewarm by the pretended Whigs; and yet moft violent by the worft Tories, but in time, perhaps, may be *vice verfa.* Now, tho' I never yet did fo to any other, yet to him I find my felf moft readily difpos'd to apply in any manner, that he fhall think me fit to ferve the Queen or himfelf; for I am certain before hand, that it will be on fuch a foot as is agreeable to my principles, and for the particular benefit of the Succeffion. Tho' they have done whatever they cou'd to ruin me in all people's opinion, yet I commend the meafures his Lordfhip takes with thofe abdicated Minifters; but then let him always remember the late Lord SUNDERLAND, and confider whether they did not owe more to him, notwithftanding their ungrateful returns, for which, however, they have defervedly fmarted ever fince. Neither am I apprehenfive henſive that ſo wiſe a man ſhould receive haſty impreſſions againſt me as being too open, when I had no ſecrets to keep, or buſineſs to manage; nor as being too bookiſh, when I had no other employment for my thoughts or time, notwithſtanding the artful inſinuations of certain people in the world. 'Tis but putting me to the tryal. And might my own advice be heard in an affair that concerns me ſo nearly, I wou'd not deſire any public eſtabliſhment for ſome time, 'till my Patron had got experience of my fitneſs and ability, as well as that I might have an opportunity of curing certain prejudices in others which have done me much diſſervice, and which I never endeavour'd to prevent, becauſe it was never worth my while. You'll wonder all this time, that I have not mentioned the Church which is ſo much exaſperated againſt me; but as that is indeed the heavieſt article, and the leaſt excuſable, being matter of pure ſpeculation, yet 'tis undoubtedly the eaſieſt conquer'd, and I know the infallible method of doing it: but of this in particular among our ſelves.

I wou'd therefore go at preſent to Germany, as before I intended by encouragement from thence, and keep a conſtant weekly correſpondence with his Lordſhip, not only according to his Inſtructions, but likewiſe as to all Obſervations of my own, I ſhou'd think deſerving his curioſity or notice. I ſhou'd remain ſometimes at Berlin, or Caſſel, or Deſſau,

sau, that it might not be said I was more at
Hanover than elsewhere, or that I was sent
by any man or party thither; but my interest
there is so good, and they have such an opinion of my diligence and affection, that
when absent I shou'd know all that past there
and cou'd communicate what I thought fit
to them from other places, as well as when
I found it convenient to be upon the spot.
This I fancy wou'd be of some advantage
both for the Queen's service and theirs, and
the secret shall be kept by me inviolable, so
long as it shall be thought necessary so to do;
for I have pretences enough to go into that
Country on my own account, as to make
an ampler Description of it, or for any other
plausible intent. For my Appointment, I shall
be well content that it be paid me quarterly,
and that it be continued no longer than I
shall be judg'd to deserve the same or a better.

Whether such a person, SIR, who is neither Minister nor Spy, and as a lover of Learning will be welcome every where, may not
prove of extraordinary use to my Lord Treasurer as well as to his predecessor BURLEIGH
who employ'd such, I leave his Lordship and you
to consider. As for the service and gratitude I
shou'd owe to his family no less than to himself,
they are better understood than exprest; since it
is not words but deeds that must do the latter,
and that there can be no deeds without an opportunity. My friends on t'other side of the
Sea

Sea wish me impatiently there; and even in my Lord N * * *'s time, notwithstanding his Memorials, the Electress proferr'd to do something for me in a public manner, were I but recommended by any considerable persons, as I'll shew you by express Letters: for she believ'd (and I suppose not without reason) that I was strangely misreprefented to the Queen, with whom she justly desir'd, as she ever will do, to be upon the best terms she cou'd, and so durst do nothing openly in my behalf. Nevertheless, her Royal Highness knew better than any body that it was impossible I should not be most hearty for her Majesty's Title and Government, or be perfectly inconsistent and the falsest creature in the world to my own principles, and regardless of that Succession for which I profess so much zeal, and which I had publish'd to the world as the greatest happiness, not only to England, but to the liberty of Europe in general. I can make no other apology for the length of this Letter, but that it saves you the trouble of many more, and that in a narrower compass I cou'd not give a full and satisfactory answer to all your Questions, which yet may be all reduc'd to these two, why I was not employ'd before, and how I wou'd be employ'd at present?

I am, SIR,

your most oblig'd and humble servant.

T O

Mr. * * *

SIR,

ALL this time I have been a filent but not an idle Spectator. Publick matters go exactly according to my wifhes, and not otherwife than I expected from this Miniftry, which (I hope) in the principal fupports and fprings of it is inviolably united: and then the ornamental or fubfervient parts may be alter'd or amended at leifure. It is no fmall fatisfaction to me, that the judgment of the Queen, the Parliament, and the Miniftry, do fo unanimoufly concur with the Book, which (under your protection) I have publifh'd for their fervice; and which has met with all the fuccefs and reputation that any Author cou'd wifh, tho' he had declar'd his name, as I have been far from doing even to thofe I have oblig'd. It had the honour to be attributed by good judges to feveral eminent perfons, and among the reft to you; where it had moft certainly fix'd, were it not for the Character given therein of your felf, in which particular, the world believ'd that you wou'd be lefs juft and more referv'd, than any of your fervants, friends, or admirers. Among perfons of an inferior rank I have been nam'd (as I underftand) by many; but,

3

for

for want of good information, 'twas always with some doubting, wherein I am still determin'd to leave 'em. As for any thing in the Book not juft according to your fentiments, which perhaps may happen in a point or two, you'll have the goodnefs to confider that I wanted opportunity to confult you perfonally, for doubtlefs your fpecial Directions, or the honour of your Converfation at leifure hours, wou'd have made it another guefs piece; I having finifh'd it in a very few days, without any to advife me but Mr. P * * *, being in the country, and not mafter of time enough to polifh the very language.

Now, Sir, I have form'd another Defign, which may be as feafonable, ufeful, and neceffary as the firft; and therefore as well for that, as for fome other reafons, I humbly and earneftly beg the favour of one half hour's Difcourfe with you, wherever or in what manner you pleafe to appoint; for I can come by water, or at any time in the night. I wou'd not give you any trouble of this kind, while my friend Mr. P * * * was abfent, that I might not be oblig'd to make ufe of any other name. There's no time to be loft, and I am ambitious to have the next Piece without a fault; which I fhall judge it to be, if it has but your concurrence or approbation. Having fent one of the firft (under the feign'd name of Mr. FREEMAN) to Mr. SHOWER the Diffent-

ing

ing Minifter, I receiv'd the Anfwer which I fend you inclos'd, and more fuch from other hands: all affuring me that *The Memorial of the State of England* was the true ftate of the cafe, had lefs trifling, and more impartiality than any Book that had yet appear'd on the fubject. I flatter my felf you'll not wholly impute it to vanity, that I give you this account of a work, which in fome fenfe may be call'd your own, as in every fenfe I am, SIR, with the greateft fincerity and zeal,

Your moft faithful, humble, and
obedient Servant.

Mr. SHOWER's Letter *on receiving the* Memorial of the State of England, *as a Prefent from the unknown Author.*

Clerkenwell, Oct. 24, 1705.

SIR,

THE kind Prefent I receiv'd on Monday night, viz. *The Memorial of the State of England,* appears to me to be the moft judicious and feafonable of any thing lately printed. 'Tis the real ftate of our cafe fet in a true light, with excellent judgment and eloquence ; very likely to open the eyes, and calm the minds of many. I fhall moft gladly do what I can to promote the fpreading of

it ;

it; and accordingly desire twenty five may be sent me per first, and shall pay the porter the Bookseller's price, and so dispose of 'em, as to occasion the buying and reading of a much greater number. If the other Ministers nam'd have read it, I doubt not but their sentiments are the same with mine, tho' I have not had the opportunity to see either of 'em. SIR, I reckon it an honour to have been thought worthy of such a present; and 'twill be an additional one to kiss the hands of him who sent it, and express my thanks and esteem and un-feign'd respect, of which I hereby assure him, who am, SIR, his most oblig'd humble Servant,

JOHN SHOWER.

My Aversion and Inclination:

IN A LETTER

To Mrs. D * * *.

YOU send me news indeed, MADAM, that Dame SCRAG that unparallel'd o-riginal, imagines I am deeply smitten with her; by reason of some expressions in a Letter of mine to the Reverend Doctor, our common acquaintance. But that Gentleman and I dealing wholly in mysteries of one kind or

another,

another, I'll then allow her to comprehend
my meaning, whenever she has a particular
revelation either from him or me. But you
say the same thing was confirm'd to her by
one, who has an unlucky talent at writing
merry Ballads and waggish Lampoons; nay,
that he insinuated much more than he thought
fit to say. Such a heroic accomplishment is
enough, I confess, to beget a terrible idea of
that wight, in the breasts of all those Ladies who
blush as soon as they hear him nam'd; which
are the foolish, the frail, and the fickle, the
tattlers, the dawbers, the modish, and the
coquets, to all which I know her Ladyship
to be a perfect stranger. These characters will
reach nevertheless to a world of other women; which makes me wonder, that the ad-
venturous Poet does not put all the timorous
fair under contribution; which wou'd be a
surer way of enriching himself, than by dab-
bling (as he does now) in Politics, or by drudging (as he did before) in Trade. I don't say,
and you won't think, that on any account
whatsoever, her Ladyship shou'd either pay
her quota to him in coin, or be frighted by
his Satyr to quit any of her humors, which
are dearer to some women than the most
precious of their jewels: but in the particular you mention, she's certainly more afraid
than hurt, or rather, not being hurt, is the
reason she's not afraid; since the scandal (if
any was intended) must be entirely meant to
me, which yet I easily forgive, because none
will

will believe it. But, in the name of averfion, what have I done to occasion this fuspicion? for what have I not left undone to prevent it? Yet if it muft needs be added to the punifhment of my other fins, let it be faid at leaft, that I fuffer for a fin of omiffion; fince in all probability I wou'd take care not to be over intimately concern'd, unlefs with fome of your fly Gypfies that can keep a fecret, fuch as rarely fhew their admirer's Letters, and that never boaft of the number of their conquefts. But I appeal to her Ladyfhip, if fetting afide fome roguifh expreffions, which I know to be one of her favourite diverfions, I be not the moft harmlefs thing in the world as to deeds; and I am ready to take my corporal oath, that fhe was never one moment the object of my thoughts.

However, left her Ladyfhip fhould be ever fo little difcompos'd at fo ungrounded a furmife, and that I may ruin my felf all at once with fome other Darlings of mine (meaning the venerable fociety of vain and wanton Widows; the honourable company of Virgins, that have large fortunes and fmall underftandings; with the faded skins, and cherry-cheeks of both forts) I need but tell them in one emphatical word, that I have engag'd my heart: or, to ufe a longer form, fince they love chat, that I fhall be conftant to merit in the perfon of one excellent creature; and then the very old Maids themfelves, will

cry

cry out upon me for an old fashion'd lover.
Truft me, MADAM, this is a more infallible
receipt to get rid of what's importunate or
impertinent, than ever was invented for driving away troublefome flyes. It will effectually lofe me the reputation of intriguing,
which I have ever carefully avoided; nor will
I gain a little by it in another way, I fhan't
be apt to tell you at this time. And now if
you wou'd either know my fure prefervative
againft all mean temptations, or how my inclinations ftand towards fome of your other
female acquaintance, be pleas'd to learn from
my own pen the Character of my real or imaginary Miftrefs; for as to the defign of this
Letter, 'tis no matter whether it be a prefent Miftrefs or a future.

I affure you therefore in the firft place, that
fhe ever thinks before fhe fpeaks, tho' fhe never fpeaks half fhe thinks; which you'll fay,
is very much in either man or woman. You
know already who fhe is not. But then, as
fhe betrays no folly by giggling laughter, nor
any malice by leering fmiles, fo fhe can be very brisk and chearful in converfation, without poorly leffening, or fcandaloufly abufing
her friends. Her prudent obfervations (join'd
to moderate reading) will never let her be
at a lofs, when 'tis her turn to entertain the
company; tho' fhe's far from being the monfter they call a Learned Lady, or from thinking her felf oblig'd to furnifh all the talk
and

and diverſion: for ſhe never becomes the
ſubject of diſcourſe to others, but as ſhe's the
admiration of the good, or the envy of the
bad; and even theſe laſt are ſometimes heard
to praiſe her, in order to paſs themſelves
the better with their neighbours for ſincere
or judicious perſons. She avoids ill company
as carefully as ſhe does their faults: but if
by accident or miſtake ſhe happens to be
engag'd in ſuch, (as who can always prevent
it) ſhe behaves her ſelf ſo cautiouſly, as neither to diſoblige them, nor to ſcandalize o-
thers; yet leaving them without any hopes
of receiving a ſecond viſit, and the reſt of the
world without any juſt cauſe of reflection.
She has wit and beauty to make her be paſ-
ſionately lov'd in youth, as ſhe has ſenſe and
virtue to make her be honourably eſteem'd
in old age: and ſhe deſpiſes as much the nau-
ſeous flatteries of pretending coxcombs, as
ſhe values the diſintereſted commendations of
the wiſe and good, whom ſhe ſtudiouſly
imitates. Her Religion lyes not in her tongue,
but in her heart: and the outward performances of it do no more conſiſt in preciſely
lifting up her eyes to heaven, at the ſame
time that ſhe curtſies to the rake or the fop
in the next pew; than the private duties of
it are reading looſe Poems, placing of paint
and patches, conſulting the oracle of the
bottle, or uſing certain other amuſements
in the cloſet, from which ſeveral come out
more boiſterous Devils, than they went in
demure

demure Hypocrites. But the inoffenſiveneſs of her manners, the evenneſs of her temper, the charitableneſs of her diſpoſition, and the clearneſs of her whole conduct, make her be bleſt and admir'd for her goodneſs whereſo-ever ſhe comes; ſo that the propereſt prayer for diſcreet Matrons, is to wiſh night and day, that their own Daughters may be like her. To be as ſhort as I can in a very long Letter, ſhe's genteel without affectation, gay without levi-ty, civil to ſtrangers without being free, and free with her acquaintance without being fa-miliar.

I am convinc'd that thoſe Ladies who judge of other's inclinations by their own, and who have reaſon to wiſh all women were like themſelves, wou'd be ready to ſay, (if they ſaw my Letter) that this is an imaginary Miſtreſs; tho' if I had but her per-miſſion, I cou'd with pleaſure tell you her name, and defy their worſt malice to find a tittle in the deſcription, which is not out-done by the original. Yes, MADAM, there is in reality ſuch a Lady ſomewhere; tho' I am ſo far from pretending to a return of mu-tual love, that I cannot even ſay I ever made her a poſitive declaration. Yet as to the mere Character, I'm ſure, for the honor of your ſex you'll make no ſcruple to believe it. But then, for the honor of ours, I expect you'll likewiſe believe, that ſecure of ſuch a one's perſon and affection, I wou'd rather
undergo

undergo poverty and difgrace, accept of the woods for my lodging with the old Knights-errant, and be content with roots for my daily food; than being coupl'd (like the living and the dead) with any of a different ftamp, to poffefs riches and favour, to feed continually on exquifite dainties with the modern heroes, and to pafs all my time in gilded palaces. And tho' I have no reafon to doubt but fhe has a handfome fortune (for this I'd fcorn to examine) yet I heartily rejoice that fhe's none of your vaft eftates; left fhe fhould imagine from the conduct of moft other men, that one fordid arrow tipt with her gold, had mingl'd with thofe purer rays which are fhot from her eyes. This you may take for romantic language, tho' of you in particular I have a better opinion : and others, whofe good opinion I fhou'd be forry to deferve, will call it a generous folly. But I, who know that true happinefs is inward tranquillity and not outward pageantry, contemn the judgment of the multitude when it comes in competition with my own experience: my pleafure and repofe by no means precarioufly depending on what others think, or fay, or do: but folidly confifting in what I my felf do feel, and relifh, and enjoy.

Now, that I may a little fhift the fcene, I'll fay that for Dame SCRAGG, fhe's wonderful fagacious to fmell out an Amour before it is conceiv'd,

conceiv'd, and at such a terrible distance too.
But since to clear my self to her Ladyship
from the imputation of being her admirer
(which I wou'd not do to any other woman
on earth) is the main design of this long Letter; I need not (I suppose) give you any further trouble, than only to tell you, that I am,
with as much gratitude for your information,
as esteem for your friendship,

MADAM,

Your most faithful and obedient servant.

TO THE SAME.

I Lately made you my confidente, MA-
DAM, so far as to own I have a Mistress:
and, tho' lovers are commonly liars, yet you
may safely take my word for it, when I say,
I am so well pleas'd with the choice, that
I continually bless the day, the hour, the
place, where so sweet and charming a creature had the secret (and 'twas no small one)
to make her self the sole object of all my
care and wishes. 'Twas no distrust of you,
but want of leave from her, that made me
shy of telling her name: but having communicated her Character to you then, I now send
you her Picture, to see whether you judge
as truly of the one as you did of the other.
When you know the Lady, you'll swear I
4   have

have not flatter'd her; but nevertheleſs, MA-DAM, I aſſure you the piece is ſurprizingly like, for the impreſſions ſhe has made, are too deep and lively ever to be forgot. Yet if the copy ſhould not reach the original (as indeed it cannot) my skill in drawing muſt not be blam'd, but her unparallel'd perfections, which are inimitable as they are innumerable.

To repreſent her therefore in miniature, her perſon is abſolutely unexceptionable, as being the golden mean between two very diſagreeable extremes; not approaching that monſtrous tallneſs which preſently begets averſion, and as far from that lowneſs of ſtature, which generally occaſions contempt. Her carriage is graceful without affectation, and eaſy without neglect, which makes an undreſs or any kind of dreſs equally becoming her: but ſo, that in whatever manner ſhe appears, it's always thought by others to be out of deſign, as finding it for that time and occaſion the moſt proper. Her ſhape is exactly proportion'd to her perſon, neither ridiculouſly molded into nothing with ſqueezing engines, nor yet in the leaſt over-grown for want of care: but juſt as it ſhou'd be, enough to convince a man that he embraces a delicate woman, and is not vainly graſping at an airy phantom. Her hair is incomparably fine, extremely thick, and of a light aſh-colour, which makes it the greateſt ornament in the world, as partaking at once of

whatever

whatever is enflaming in the brown and softening in the fair. Her teeth are as even and white, and her hands as taper and genteel, as one of the correcteft fancy cou'd wifh in his own miftrefs, and the niceft wou'd not expect to find more in any other. Her lips are the native feat of all the fmiles and the graces; infomuch that the Bee (which fhe gave me for a device) wou'd take 'em for the moft beautiful flower in nature, it wou'd gladly dwell in the pretty dimples of her cheeks, and fuck honey from her fweeteft mouth for ever. Her complection is, in my opinion, wholly divine, and what of all others I infinitely prefer; frefh as the glories of the fpring, and fair as the pride of autumn. Lilies and Rofes are but faint poetick refemblances of thofe colours in her lovely face, which fo admirably exprefs all the charms of blooming youth, all the fymptoms of perfect health, and all that mixture of fire and phlegm, without which Love were but a lazy dream, and life it felf a burthen. In her dear eyes fhine all that's ingenious, gay, or engaging. No magick is half fo enchanting. No magnetick power is near fo attractive. No fhafts can hit more fure or deeper; as at the fame time no art can bring a more ready cure, nothing but themfelves having the virtue to heal thofe wounds they occafion: nor does their colour put me lefs in mind of heaven than their glory. Her forehead, her chin, her eyebrows, and all the reft of her features, are

exactly

exactly regular; and fingly or united are capable to charm the whole world, making young men mad, old men fools, and all women envious. 'Tis better to fay nothing of her breaft than not to fay enough, or in fome proportion to the tranfporting fubject, thofe heaving adorable twins of the moft refin'd and unfpeakable delights. But this is much better expreffed by imagination, and is a blifs to be touch'd, but never to be thoroughly defcrib'd. Nor do I queftion the exceffive perfections of thofe other beauties, which the troublefome difguife of garments hide from my longing eyes; and which as I have not feen I cannot pretend to paint, nor wou'd if I were able, fince it is the higheft ambition of my heart, that thefe may be only feen, admir'd, and poffeft by my felf. This ineftimable bleffing wou'd quickly render me the happieft man alive; as fhe wou'd become the happieft of women, if a thorough knowledge of her worth, and the moft difinterefted affection for her perfon, cou'd poffibly make her fo.

Thefe, MADAM, are but the external lines, and only the cover of a yet fairer foul, whence (according to old obfervation) the valuablenefs of the jewel may be guefs'd by the richnefs of the cafe. Her good breeding, good humour, and good fenfe, I have already defcrib'd in her Character: and, where thefe are, no other good thing can be wanting.

Now

Now I hope you'll own, that in fending you this rough draught of my Miftrefs's Picture, I have fent you at the fame time a fufficient juftification of my own paffion; having inviolably refolv'd to love her only to my laft breath (which fhe alone can hinder) with all the ardor of the youngeft man, and with all the conftancy of the oldeft philofopher. In fhort, MADAM, that Miftrefs alone I wou'd make a wife, of whom I think in this manner; and fhe (I think) ought to make that Lover alone her husband, who thus thinks of her: for tho' other things may render Matrimony fplendid, 'tis only this can make it happy. I have nothing more to add, but that her name is A, B, C, D.

T O

Mr. * * *.

SIR,

IN anfwer to yours of Saturday laft, be pleas'd to know, that the Seven Provinces coming to a ftricter Union than that of Utrecht (the foundation of their Republic) it was unanimoufly agreed in the year 1583, that the exercife of the Proteftant Religion alone fhou'd be publickly eftablifh'd, while other Sects fhould be onely tolerated, and Popery conniv'd at. This is the only Law,

with

with relation to the religious qualification of Magiftrates, that ever was made in the Provinces from that time to this: and that *Reformata Religio* did fignify therein the Lutherans as well as the Calvinifts at the time of making this Law, and that it is underftood of the Arminians no lefs than of the Gomarifts fince that time, I fhall have no difficulty to convince you ; juft in the fenfe, I fay, that Reform'd Churches fignifies all thefe in one Liturgy. For, tho' Reform'd or Calvinift, is now us'd commonly abroad in contradiftinction to Evangelic or Lutheran ; yet, at the time of making the Law aforefaid, it comprehended the whole body of thofe who made the Bible their only rule of faith, and who join'd in rejecting the Idolatry and Superftitions of Popery, together with the Supremacy of the Pope. As a proof of this, among abundance of others, feveral of the leading men, men of the greateft authority, and who had their fhare in making this very Law, were profeft Lutherans : moft of the cities of the Provinces were then full of Lutherans, who were admitted to Magiftracy equally with the Calvinifts : and Lutheranifm, in fhort, was the prevailing profeffion of diverfe places for fome time after the enacting of this Law, particularly of the city of Worden ; whofe inhabitants came afterwards to change of their own accord, without any pofitive or negative difcouragements to influence them.

As for the Arminians, or Remonstrants, who truly account themselves, and are no less accounted by others, to be Reform'd or Protestants; 'tis certain that they are by no means excluded from Magistracy, neither by the Law of the year 1583, when this distinction was not known, nor by any Law since: and at this very time many of 'em partake of the most considerable posts, being the prevailing Party in several places, as they are reputed to be so in the supreme Government it self; and, whenever you require it, I shall acquaint you with their names, being also willing to give you particular proofs of every other thing which I have hitherto asserted. Indeed at certain junctures, as, for example, under the late glorious King WILLIAM, (to whom the Arminians were no friends, by reason of their aversion to any Stadtholder) they were prudently kept out of offices, but not excluded by any Law: as those of the Church of England, who are disaffected to the present Settlement, are very justly kept out of places, tho' otherwise qualifying themselves by the sacramental Test. This, and no other, has been precisely the case of the Arminians in Holland: and the Anabaptists (who are unquestionably Protestants) are no otherwise excluded, than as they exclude themselves by their notions of Magistracy and the use of the sword; several of 'em being employ'd where their Consciences will permit 'em to serve, and particularly in the

the city of Amsterdam.   I speak all this time
of civil offices, for all the public Churches
are to be only serv'd by Ministers who sub-
scribe the Synod of Dort; with liberty, as I
said, to others, who pay their own Ministers.

To His Grace

My Lord Archbishop

O F

CANTERBURY.

May it please Your Grace,

MOnsieur DUBOURDIEU gave me an account how favourably your Grace was
pleas'd to receive the Book I took the liberty to send you; which I esteem not only
as an extraordinary obligation; but (considering my character in the world, which is not
what at present I deserve) I look upon it as a
demonstration of that Christian goodness and
greatness of spirit, with which you are acknowledg'd by all good men, to support and
adorn your high Station in the Church.   The
same reverend person, who was not wanting to me at several times in his friendly and
charitable admonitions, has further acquainted me with what he promis'd on my behalf
to your Grace, and which I shall always,

by the help of God, endeavour to make good; being firmly refolv'd in this laudable purpofe both by principle and engagement. He has been a witnefs for two years paft of my ordinary converfation, which he'll own to be very different from what it has former-ly been, and is ftill reprefented to be by thofe who do not know me, or are not willing I fhou'd make a better ufe of my reafon and experience: for I am forry to fay what I cou'd not chufe but obferve, that fome people wou'd rather fee a man, who is averfe to their enflaving Politics, run the risk of work-ing his own damnation and endangering the fouls of others, than to be exempt from their cenfure or revenge on the fcore of Religion, when they cannot otherwife attack him. Whoever is loyal and orthodox in the State, is with them a Heretick or a Traitor in the Church, let his life and doctrine be ever fo unblameable.

But if I can be fo happy, My Lord, as to approve my felf to the beft, I fhall reckon it no misfortune to meet with reproaches from the worft, which is a part of my duty no lefs to bear than to forgive. As I was born nei-ther infpir'd nor infallible, fo I fhall be far from juftifying any thing I may have hitherto done amifs: but this is no argument that I have never perform'd any thing worthy of com-mendation. And therefore, fince the bounds of this Letter cannot contain what I have to

fay

say on either of these heads, I humbly beg
the favour of you to permit me to wait on
Your Grace, to offer that further satisfaction
I am prepar'd to give, as well as to receive
your paternal advice and directions, which,
next to the sacred precepts of the Gospel, I
shall esteem the most obligatory rules whereby to frame the future conduct of my life.
I am, with all the sincerity and veneration
imaginable,

> MY LORD,
>
> *Your Grace's most faithful, duti-*
> *ful, and obedient Servant.*

March the 6th,
1706-7.

T O

THE REVEREND Mr. ***

Reverend SIR,

TO hear of scandal, quarrels, and defa-
mation, I am sorry, is no new thing;
the world did always abound with them, and
will continue to do so as long as envy, pride,
or avarice deprave human nature. Notwithstanding there be a sovereign light plac'd
by the Almighty in every man's heart as
well to moderate his passions as to guide his
actions; yet left we shou'd be too partial in

affairs

affairs which concern our own perfons, and fo be apt to miftake our felfifh inclinations for the dictates of unbyaffed reafon; we have public monitors and judges divinely eftablifh'd among us, both to inform us of our duty, and to regulate our behaviour. Tho' it be a moft wicked thing in any body to mifreprefent another, yet the fin is more notorious in that man whofe peculiar function obliges him to preach charity, peace, and forgivenefs to others: for nothing he can ever fay will have any great influence while his ill example feems to be fo ftrong an argument that he believes not his own Doctrine.

'Tis but too well known in how many particulars I might apply this with relation to my felf; but I'm fo much accuftom'd to the hard and undeferv'd ufage of fome men, that now it moves me not in the leaft; yet I was ftrangely furpriz'd to hear you cenfur'd by fome of your brethren in the country, as if you had receiv'd a bribe to give me the Sacrament, which fhews at once their ignorance and their malice: their ignorance in imagining you cou'd deny it me, and their malice in belying you after fo bafe a manner. My charity wou'd never let me fufpect that you were capable of being corrupted to commit any wilful iniquity, much lefs that you wou'd for a little money proftitute the moft facred ordinance of the Chriftian Religion. I wifh my circumftances wou'd allow me to

make

make the poor acknowledgment, I yearly pay the Minister, a great deal more : you know it was but one Guinea to you last year, and given a long while before you publish'd your intentions of administring the Sacrament. As for my participating of it, there needed no other known qualification (I hope) than being dispos'd as the Rubric directs ; and the bare act of receiving it ought to convince all charitable persons of my veneration for it : since I look upon it to be the public sign whereby we commemorate the death of JESUS CHRIST, the founder of our Religion, engage our selves to obey his Laws, and declare our hopes to enjoy the benefits of the same. Indeed I differ from you and others who think the Sacrament to be a means of conveying grace : which, if it be an error, has been profest to the world by many eminent Divines of our Church, and was never thought a sufficient bar to Communion.

It is a maxim with me never to believe a story which reflects upon any man's honor, till I have it from an unquestionable author : nor is it enough that it be one I esteem, if he knows no more of it than only by report ; and therefore I need not tell you with what tenderness we ought to handle reputation, since the injury is commonly irreparable. I am a true well-wisher to all mankind, but I particularly desire the conversion of my enemies. I doubt not

your

your juftice when occafion requires it, and you will not fcruple my fincerity when I pro-fefs my felf to be, Reverend SIR, your moft humble fervant.

T O

Mr. * * *.

SIR,

WHAT you heard from your Coufin about the Book of which he tells you I am mafter, is actually true; and no ftory of his making (as you fuppofe) to fet Doctor MORELLI's mouth a watering, nor any fcheme of my contrivance to vent my own notions under fuch a difguife. The Volume carries in it felf undeniable argu-ments of its age and authority: and, fince you fay your curiofity is fo great and pref-fing, you fhall by no means lofe your long-ing; for I'll tell you the hiftory of this piece in as few words as I can, yet omitting at this time all that I know concerning the per-fon and circumftances of the Author.

In the Court of Queen ELIZABETH 'tis generally acknowledg'd, even by her enemies, that there was a fet of very extraordinary men, and among them fome, who underftood every thing elfe as well as the Art of Govern-ment, and who faw further than any fince

(or

(or perhaps before) into the mysteries of Priestcraft and the extravagancies of Superstition. This knowledge of the follies of some men, and the frauds of others, did not a little serve to make them such exquisite Politicians, enabling them to take every thing by the right handle, what safely to abolish, what necessarily to retain, how to govern all men by the springs of their own passions, and to manage the whole machine by the chains and weights of prevailing opinions. Private Conferences they usually had, wherein they talk'd of every thing freely and without a veil, being secure from the censure or mistakes of the prophane vulgar, and in those things true to one another, tho' not seldom at variance on other occasions.

The most remarkable instance of their liberty in thinking, and of their prudence in concealing their notions is this Book, which was written with the privity of a certain number among them, who had the few copies that were printed, and the work was particularly dedicated to Sir PHILIP SIDNEY, of whom the Author has given an excellent character, as he has done of the French Ambassador Monsieur de MAUVISSIER DE CASTELNAU, and of FULK GREVILL, afterwards Lord BROOK, three principal men in this learned Club of Courtiers: the rest being a mixture of young and old persons, as Sir CHRISTOPHER HATTON, Sir THOMAS SMITH, Sir WALTER RALEIGH, Sir AMBROSE PHILLIPS, the Earl of LEICESTER,

z and

and some others: but the Encomium of Queen ELIZABETH, for the justice of fact, delicacy of thought, and eloquence of expression, seems to ingage the Author's affections, wherever he has occasion to mention her.

In the Book is represented a Council of the Gods, owning, rehearsing, and exposing their ancient worship, or the Religion of the Heathens, in a most learned, long, and elegant Oration made to them by JUPITER, on the Festival in commemoration of their Victory over the Giants. But the Gods are no less scandaliz'd and offended at the present condition of things, which they conclude to be yet far worse than in the Pagan times, both in respect of private Virtue and of public Government Having resolv'd therefore to make amends for their own past tricks and offences, and to destroy the succeeding impostures of others, they agree to act fairly for once, and to set up the intelligible, useful, necessary, and unalterable Law of Nature, against the mysterious, speculative, unpracticable, and changeable Institutions of all other kinds. But in order to this, finding no Letters so clear, universal, and durable, as the eternal fires of the Stars, they abolish the antient names of the Constellations: which, when understood, are but the histories of the tyranny, luxury, brutality, whimsicalness, and other defects of antient Princes or great men; or, where

not

not underſtood, many of them are fabulous, moſtly obſcure, and all unprofitable. Wherefore inſtead of theſe poetical fictions, they give the Conſtellations the names of the ſo long forgot and neglected moral Virtues, carefully marking, examining, confuting, and rejecting the oppoſite vices. All the antient Conſtellations, about forty eight in number, are ſucceſſively arraign'd ; and in exploding the Heathen ſtory (as that of *Orion*, or the *Bear*, or *Aquarius*, for example) there is commonly a parallel or alluſion made to ſome later Superſtition, which is ironically handled, and admirably turn'd into ridicule, in a method peculiar to our Author. Immediately after this, the contrary Virtue is ſet off to full advantage, being propoſed by ſome of the Gods, and decreed by JUPITER, to take up the room of the Heathen Fable ; but in ſo grave and ſolid a ſtile, that one is tempted to believe, it is not always the ſame hand that writes. The counterfeit of every Virtue, and all the falſe pretenders to that name, are patiently heard in making their ſeveral pleas to obtain the honor of a Conſtellation ; but are at laſt detected, condemn'd, and diſcarded, as the real Virtue is plac'd on its true foundation, and worthily preſented with a becoming Seat in the Heavens. The Law of Nature being thus methodically reduc'd to certain heads, and the Conſtellations bearing the titles of ſo many Virtues, as of Truth, Prudence, Temperance,

rance, Juſtice, Fortitude, and the like; this they call'd *the Book of Nature,* being equally legible and open, at all times and to all perſons.

The project was pretty enough; for in leſs than the ſpace of a fortnight, any body may become maſter of the celeſtial Sphere; ſo that even boys at ſchool might be taught this part of Aſtronomy with no ſmall pleaſure; and by giving ſuch names to the Conſtellations, they wou'd become the beſt monitors and moſt obvious memorials of their duty to all manner of people. It ſerv'd this purpoſe for Religion among the Heathens, which ſhews the thing is not impracticable another way. But our Author never dreamt of publickly eſtabliſhing it, but choſe it for a plan that ſerv'd at once to expoſe the Prieſt-craft of the Heathens and other people. However, this part of the Book is eaſily conceiv'd; and what is moſt ſingular in the whole, is the manner of exploding Superſtition. In a word, it was a very uncommon thought, and incomparably perform'd: for tho' this Volume exceeds not 261 pages in Octavo, ſmall print, beſides the explicatory Dedication containing about a ſheet; yet in one continu'd thread and contexture it contains the whole doctrine of the Sphere, the Learning and Hiſtory of antient Superſtition, the confutation of modern Impoſture, and a compleat Syſtem of Ethicks;

beſides

befides various incidents and digreffions.
How the fecret was kept, and this Book
(which was probably the Queen's own) came
to my hands, you fhall be told another time,
for this Letter is but too long already.

I am,

SIR,

your, &c.

To   *   *   *

Prague, January 1708.

SIR,

I HAVE nothing to add to what I did my
felf the honor to write to your Excellency per poft, but that the Countefs of
STERNBERG is not the only perfon at Prague
to whom I am particularly oblig'd : for the
very reverend Father Guardian, and the reft
of the worthy members of the Irifh Con-
vent, were not more difpofed to do me all
the good offices of humanity, than they were
forward to fhew me the moft zealous affection of Country-men. Yet I did not receive half that fatisfaction from their many
civilities to my own perfon, as I was charm'd
with their putting round the Queen's health
in full Refectory, where a great many ftrangers
were prefent, and of feveral Nations as well
as different Religions. Nor did I find 'em
lefs

less easy and well-bred upon this last article, than in other things; tho' I frankly told 'em my sentiments, and, perhaps, that I might sometimes, to improve by the discourse of ingenious persons, carry matters further than Reason or the Reformation will allow. But I must do that justice to the bearer of this Letter, Father FRANCIS ô DEULIN, Lector of Divinity, as to own my self not a little pleased with his courteous behavior and good literature. The least I cou'd therefore do in return of so much kindness and friendship, was to recommend him, according to his own desire, to a person of your Excellency's extraordinary candor and capacity, not doubting by my own experience, but that during his stay at Vienna, you'll not only favor him with your protection (he being a good Imperialist, without which I wou'd not espouse him) and be ready to forward or countenance him in all lawful occasions. But I am confident his own merit will prevail farther than any thing I can say in his behalf.

I am &c.

A

A
Mr. TOLAND.

Hanover, ce 30 d'Avril 1709.

MONSIEUR,

J'AY receu à mon retour le prefent de vôtre Livre avec l'honneur de votre Lettre,
& je vous en remercie. Mon abfence a été
longue ; autrement je vous aurois répondu
pluftôt.

Il y a plufieurs bonnes remarques dans tous
vos ouvrages, & je vous avouë facilement,
que TITE LIVE n'etoit rien moins que fu-
perftiticux. Monfieur HUET en appliquant
les Fables des Payens à MOYSE, a voulu pluftôt
faire paroitre fon erudition que fon exactitude,
dont il a pourtant donné de bonnes preuves
ailleurs ; & fon Livre des *Demonftrations
Evangeliques* ne laiffe pas d'eftre tres inftruc-
tif, nonobftant qu'il s'y donne carriere, en
fe jouant des Mythologies. Vous avez fort
raifon, Monfieur, de donner des grands elo-
ges à HERODOTE. STRABON eft un auteur grave, mais lors qu'il parle de MOYSE, il paroift
qu'il prend les actions & les fentimens de ce Le-
giflateur felon les preventions & les chimeres
des Grecs. Il n'en avoit apparemment que des
notices confufes, & il fe trompe manifefte-
ment

ment en croyant que le Temple de Jerusalem a été l'ouvrage de MOYSE, que les voisins des Hebreux avoient des coûtumes semblables aux leurs, & que la circoncision & la defense de certaines viandes auprès des Iuifs a été posterieure à MOYSE.

Je ne say, si vous avez trouvé, Monsieur, dans la Langue des Coptes ou Egyptiens qu'elle convient avec celle des Pheniciens & des Arabes, comme vous dites p. 145. Feu M. ACOLUTHUS de Breslau la croyoit convenir avec celle des Armeniens: mais ses preuves ne me satisfaisoient point. C'est une Langue fort differente des autres, que nous connoissons.

Pour ce qui est de vôtre but, j'avoüe qu'on ne sauroit assez foudroyer la Superstition; pourveu qu'on donne en même temps les moyens de la distinguer de la veritable Religion; autrement on court risque d'enveloper l'une dans la ruine de l'autre auprès des hommes, qui vont aisement aux extremités; comme il est arrivé en France, où la bigoterie a rendu la devotion même suspecte: car une distinction verbale ne suffit pas. Ainsi j'espere que vous serez porté à éclaircir la verité, comme vous avez travaillé à rejetter le mensonge.

Vous faites souvent mention, Monsieur, de l'opinion de ceux qui croyent qu'il n'y a point d'autre Dieu, ou d'autre estre eternel,

que

que le Monde, c'est à dire, la matiere & sa connexion (comme vous l'expliquez p. 75.) sans que cet estre eternel soit intelligent (p. 156.); sentiment que STRABON attribuë à MOYSE selon vous (p. 156.), & que vous même attribuez aux Philosophes de l'Orient, & particulierement à ceux de la Chine (p. 118.). Et vous dites même (p. 115.) qu'on y peut appliquer (mais par equivoque) l'Estre parfait, l'Alpha & l'Omega, ce qui a esté, qui est, & qui sera; ce qui est tout en tous, dans lequel nous sommes, nous nous remuons, & nous vivons, formules de la Sainte Ecriture. Mais comme cette opinion (que vous marquez rejetter vous même) est aussi pernicieuse, qu'elle est mal fondée; il eut été à souhaiter, Monsieur, que vous ne l'eussiez rapportée qu'avec une refutation convenable, que vous donnerez peut-être ailleurs. Mais il seroit tousjours mieux de ne pas differer l'antidote aprez le venin. Et pour dire la verité, il ne paroist pas que la pluspart de ceux des anciens & des modernes, qui ont parlé du Monde comme d'un Dieu, ayent crû ce Dieu destitué de connoissance. Vous savés qu'ANAXAGORE joignoit l'Intelligence avec la Matiere. Les Platoniciens ont conçû une Ame du Monde, & il paroit que la doctrine des Stoiciens y revenoit aussi : de sorte que le Monde selon eux étoit une maniere d'Animal ou d'Estre vivant le plus parfait qui se puisse, & dont les corps particuliers n'estoient que les membres. Il semble que STRABON aussi l'entend ainſi dans le paſſage que vous cités. Les Chinois mêmes, & autres Orientaux conçoivent certains Eſprits du Ciel & de la Terre, & peut-être même, qu'il y en a parmy eux, qui conçoivent un Eſprit ſupreme de l'Univers. De ſorte que la difference entre tous ces Philoſophes (ſur tout les anciens) & entre le veritable Theologien, conſiſteroit en ce que ſelon nous & ſelon la verité, Dieu eſt au deſſus de l'Univers corporel, & en eſt l'auteur & le maiſtre (*intelligentia ſupramundana*) ; au lieu que le Dieu de ces Philoſophes n'eſt que l'Ame du monde, ou même l'Animal, qui en reſulte. Cependant leur Tout (πᾶν) n'eſtoit pas ſans intelligence, non plus que nôtre Eſtre ſuprême. Madame l'Electrice a couſtume de citer & de louer particulierement ce paſſage de l'Ecriture, qui demande s'il eſt raiſonnable que l'auteur de l'œuil ne voye pas, & que l'auteur de l'oreille n'entende pas ; c'eſt à dire, qu'il n'y ait point de connoiſſance dans le premier Eſtre, dont vient la connoiſſance dans les autres.

Et à proprement parler, s'il n'y a point d'Intelligence univerſelle dans le monde, on ne pourra point le concevoir comme une Subſtance veritablement une : ce ne ſera qu'un *aggregatum,* un aſſemblage, comme ſeroit un troupeau de moutons, ou bien un étang plein de poiſſons. Ainſi en faire une Subſtance eternelle, qui meritât le nom de Dieu, ce feroit ſe jouer des mots, & ne rien dire ſous

de

de belles paroles. Les erreurs diſparoiſſent, lors qu'on conſidere aſſés les ſuites un peu negligées de ce grand Principe, qui porte qu'il n'y a rien, dont il n'y ait une raiſon qui determine pourquoy cela eſt ainſi pluſtôt qu'autrement : ce qui nous oblige d'aller au delà de tout ce qui eſt materiel, parce que la raiſon des determinations ne s'y ſauroit trouver.

Les deux ouvrages l'un en Latin l'autre en Italien que GIORDANO BRUNO a publié *de l'univers* & *de l'infini*, & que j'ay lûs autre-fois, font voir que cet auteur ne manquoit pas de penetration. Mais malheureuſement il eſt allé au delà des juſtes bornes de la rai-ſon. Il donnoit auſſi dans les Chimeres de l'Art de RAYMOND LULLE. Je n'ay jamais lû ſon *ſpaccio della Beſtia triomfante* : il me ſemble, qu'on m'en a parlé un jour en France, mais je ne le ſaurois aſſeurer : il y a trop long temps. Ne faudroit il point dire *ſpec-chio* au lieu de *ſpaccio?* M. DE LA CROSE m'a dit, que vous luy avez monſtré ce Livre.

Madame l'Electrice ſe porte encore bien, graces à Dieu. Elle vient de perdre ſa ſoeur Abbeſſe de Maubuiſſon bien plus agée qu'elle, & qui s'eſt aſſez bien portée juſqu'à ſa derniere année. Je crois que Monſeigneur le Prince Electoral ira encore faire la campagne.

Au reſte je ſuis avec zele,

Votre tres humble & tres
obeiſſant ſerviteur.

LEIBNIZ.

P. S. Mes amis m'ont preſſé de faire meˑ
tre au net mes conſiderations ſur la Liberté
de l'Homme & la Juſtice de Dieu par rapport à
l'Origine du Mal : dont une bonne partie
avoit été autresfois couchée ſur le papier pour
faire lire à la Reine de Pruſſe qui le deſiroit.
J'y examine toutes les difficultez de M. BAYLE
& tache de les reſoudre, pendant que je
rends juſtice à ſon merite. Car je n'aime pas
d'accuſer les gens ſur des ſimples ſoupçons.

TO

Mr. LEIBNIZ.

Feb. 14, 1710. N. S.

SIR,

I Lately did my ſelf the honour to ſend
you the *Letter* I publiſh'd that very day,
as an antidote againſt Dr. SACHEVERELL's
ſeditious Sermon ; and the Articles ſince ex-
hibited againſt that Incendiary by the Commons, ſhew that I did not only rightly ap-
prehend the ſcope of his writings, but that
I no where ſtretch'd his meaning, and that
his principal view has been the defeating of the
Succeſſion in the Houſe of Hanover. I ſhou'd
have ſent you freely the Articles at large,
whereof I have an authentick copy ; but
that I ſuppoſe your Envoy at our Court
wou'd not leave the Elector to the blunder-
ing

ing abstracts of Gazettes, in a matter that so nearly and essentially concerns himself and his Posterity.

I then promis'd by the following post to send a larger pacquet concerning your self: but your Bookseller TROYEL, who offer'd me his service in this particular, was not prepar'd enough till now, that he has some sheets of yours to send. Some time ago, he told me he was printing your *Considerations upon the Liberty of Man, and the Justice of God, with relation to the Origin of Evil*; and that you were making some addition to it, upon the account of what Dr. KING, the Archbishop of Dublin, has written upon the argument. Tho' TROYEL, without your permission, would not let me read your Considerations, yet I was easily persuaded, that the most solid and accurate Monsieur LEIBNIZ wou'd reconcile those points infinitely better than that Prelate, who, since the publication of the other Book, has printed a *Sermon* likewise (which I may term his *curae secundae*) upon this very subject. But a friend of mine in England, a Lay-man like your self, and a Gentleman of a good estate, has just now publish'd a notable censure of this Sermon, which he has sent me with some other things, and which I thought wou'd not only be proper, but likewise agreeable to you at this juncture. I have therefore deliver'd them this morning to your Bookseller for

this

this purpofe. A word now to your former Letter.

My *Adeifidaemon* will be reprinted at the Hague, as foon as I tranfmit thither an additional Differtation, tho' upon a different fubject. I fhan't make the leaft alteration either in *Adeifidaemon* or the *Origines Judaicae*: fince the attempts to anfwer or cenfure them appear to be as impotent as they were malicious, and therefore have confirm'd others no lefs than my felf in the truth of my allegations; for their invidious confequences I utterly difclaim as illogical and falfe. The epiftolar animadverfions of my true friends, I take as kindly, as I have treated thofe of my envyers with contempt: but none of thofe whom I juftly admire and revere, have been more pertinent and candid than your felf, which indeed is your moft laudable behaviour towards all mankind.

You frankly acknowledge that LIVY was nothing lefs than fuperftitious, tho' certain Journalifts would foolifhly endeavour, out of mere oppofition, to produce the contrary; wherein they only fhew the littlenefs of their fpite, and the greatnefs of their ignorance, from which character I muft needs exempt the Gentlemen of Leipfick, who have done me juftice to my fatisfaction.

I wholly

I wholly agree to what you ſay about carefully diſtinguiſhing Religion from Superſtition, left the one be unwarily involv'd in
our cenſure of the other: and 'tis to your
zeal for keeping inviolably to this rule, that
I muſt attribute a few miſtakes, that have ſlipt
you in relation to the *Origines Judaicae.*
After beſtowing a juſt commendation upon
Strabo, you add, that he repreſented the
Actions and Doctrines of Moses according
to the prejudices and chimeras of the Greeks:
whereas in almoſt every particular he gives
a quite different account of him, from what
the Greeks, or their Latin copiers, have left
upon record; and the deciſion of this point
depending upon fact, I need ſay no more
about it, till the paſſages be produc'd that I
have overlook'd or miſunderſtood. Where
he had his materials is another queſtion, of
which, I have yet ſaid nothing, but only
ſhewn how fraudulently Monſieur Huet had
miſrepreſented him. Neither does Strabo,
Sir, (as you charge him) any where ſay that
Moses built the Temple of Jeruſalem, but
only that he conducted the Jews to the place
where that Fabrick ſtood in our Author's
time, και απηγαγον επι τον τοπον τȣτον, οπȣ νυν εςι
το εν τοις Ιεροσολυμοις κτισμα; and he afterwards
very plainly aſcribes the erecting of it, as
a real Cittadel, tho' under the pretence of a
Temple, to thoſe Tyrants who had preverted
the Moſaick Inſtitutions. The Queſtion is not

all

all this while how much STRABO was in the right, but what he precisely thought, whether in the wrong or not. As to the Rites he affirms were introduc'd after the time of MOSES, perhaps he's mistaken in those you specify : but in the *Respublica Mosaica* I shall unanswerably prove that many things, both rites and precepts in that abridgment we call the *Pentateuch*, are long posterior to MOSES; and this will I do after quite another manner, than SPINOSA cou'd, or LE CLERC wou'd have done. You add, that STRABO's manifestly mistaken, when he says that the neighbours of the Jews had many ceremonies and customs like to theirs. This he no where says, tho' I do; nor can any man doubt of it that reads their MAIMONIDES, or our SPENCER. From these and more antient Authorities I shall demonstrate this thing in the foresaid work, and not from the passage of STRABO, where διὰ τὴν ὁμιλίαν ought to have been translated *by reason of acquaintance or commerce* (propter confuetudinem aut commercium) and not *of rites or manners*, as it is there. This is the only place where thro' inadvertence I have left him wrong translated; for from the third word μιγάδων I have corrected the version even to the end.

You own that Monsieur HUET, in applying the Pagan Fables to the Person or Doctrine of MOSES, intended rather to shew his learning than his exactness; and I agree
with

with you, that in other things he has shewn himself exact enough. But this subject, methinks, requir'd more exactness than Romances either in Love or Philosophy; and his very title of *Demonstration* ought to have remov'd afar off every thing that was not of the utmost accuracy. But the truth of it is, that, whatever I may with you ascribe to his learning, there runs a large vein of Priest-craft throughout that tedious work, which has not charms enough to make any Infidel read it; and you, who have no superior in the Mathematical sciences, well know, that the very arrangement of his Propositions (to say nothing of what he alledges for proof of 'em) is far from being exact. This, as I understand from France, I shall be soon oblig'd to prove, which will cost me neither time nor pains, as having it ready cut and dry'd; and, in the mean while, I send you the character of his work from a very able man in Germany, and one you intimately know.

You doubt whether I have found any affinity between the Coptick Language, and that of the Phœnicians and Arabians. But I have neither in page 141, to which you refer, nor any where else, mention'd the Coptick Language; as believing that Jargon so call'd at this day, to have very few genuine remains of the ancient Egyptian Language: and so for ought I know, Monsieur Acoluthus of Breslau

Breflau might have been in the right in comparing it with Armenian, which I don't understand. Yet, if your curiofity will require it, I am ready to fhew you, that the Egyptian words preferved in the Bible, and thofe in other old writings (except fome introduc'd under the great Kings) were as much of the fame origin and conftruction with the Hebrew, as Arabick or Cadean ; and as Swedifh or Iflandifh are with the prefent German, and any other Dialect of that with the old Gothick.

As to what you faid with regard to two other points, the one of JORDANO BRUNO and his writings, efpecially his *Spaccio de la Beftia triomfante* ; and the other of the Pantheiftick opinion of thofe who believe no other eternal Being but the Univerfe, I fhall do my felf the favor to write you in my next. Pray, let me have your thoughts of my printed Letter, with the liberty of reading what's printed of your work ; and be pleas'd to direct your anfwer to be left for me at TROYEL's. After my duty and fervice, where juftly due, I am *&c.*

TO

T O

Mr. LEIBNIZ.

SIR,

LAST poft day I gave a Letter for you, and two fmall Books, to your Bookfeller TROYEL; who promis'd to fend them, with other things of his own, without delay. But that Letter was too long already to add any more to it, and therefore I fhall do my felf the honor at prefent to anfwer another point in your former Letter, concerning JORDANO BRUNO NOLANO, and his writings. Several befides you had a curiofity to fee the *Spaccio della Beftia trionfante (Beftiae triumphantis expulfio)* and at laft I found my felf oblig'd to fend as far as Vienna, a kind of Differtation upon this fubject, which is all that feems neceffary in general, and which I enclofe herein for your perufal. My Copier is indeed a very young Lad, but in reading over his tranfcript, I have corrected all his miftakes. I confefs fomething more particular ought to have been faid concerning the *Spaccio,* which of a printed Book, is I believe the rareft in the world. But on the other hand, 'tis not a fecret to be communicated to every body. Yet as very few are mafters of fo much judgment and difcretion

as

as Monſieur LEIBNIZ, 'twou'd be a derogation to both, as well as a breach of the honor and friendſhip I profeſs for him, if I did not impart what I have written to another excellent perſon on this ſame argument; which is firſt, a moſt circumſtantial account of the Book it ſelf, and ſecondly, a ſpecimen of it, containing three articles out of forty eight. This you may depend upon receiving per next, and in the mean while, permit me to have recourſe to you, as an Oracle in Hiſtory, for the ſolution of a doubt that has long puzzl'd me about the Chineſe Language, and which the late publication of ſome Books in Italy has ſtrongly reviv'd.

I need not quote any particular Authors for what you have read in ſo many, I mean the extreme and almoſt inſuperable difficulty of a foreigner's ever learning, to any tolerable degree, that Language, or even of a native Chineſe to be perfect maſter of it under many years application. This proceeds in part (ſay they) from the hieroglyphical forms of their Letters, vary'd into numberleſs figures, but not ſo expreſſive of what they repreſent, as to make 'em eaſily intelligible; partly from the multifarious accentuating or different pronunciations of one and the ſame word or character, which reſpectively vary the ſignifications thereof; and laſtly from the infinite number of words, as well as from the moſt frequent uſe of
figura-

figurative expreſſions. The Jeſuits urge this
difficulty at preſent more eagerly than ever
in their famous Diſpute againſt the Dominicans, and in certain *Reflections,* printed by
them laſt year at Rome I have among others noted this paſſage in the 11th Reflection.
*La lingua Cineſe é coſi difficile e oſcura, che
per quanto ſtudio ci ponga un Europeo, ſe in eſſa
non ſi iſi allevato da teneri anni, & non vi abbia con oſtinato ſtudio di molti luſtri, & per
vero deſiderio di convertire quell' anime, tutta
impiegata la forza d'un grand ingegno, non può
giugnere a ſaperne quanto ne ſappia il minimo
de' Dottori Cineſi.* Thirty years ſtudy is the
ſpace they commonly allow an European,
to be able to judge or decide any controverſy ariſing from the genius of the Language.
The contrary of all this, you may remember,
was affirm'd to you, and by an Italian Auguſtine Friar, about three years ago at Wolfembuttle, who afterwards repeated the ſame
thing to me at Berlin; nor did I ſee any
reaſon to queſtion his veracity in this point,
tho' I vehemently ſuſpected what he ſaid of
the Compaſs. But I am yet more than ever
perplex'd, by an *Anſwer* that has been lately
publiſh'd to the ſaid *Reflections* at Turin by a
learned Dominican, who produces no contemptible teſtimonies againſt the aſſertion of
the Jeſuits, of which I ſhall here tranſcribe
a couple. The firſt is cited out of the fourth
part of Dr. FRANCESCO GEMELLI CARERI'S
Giro del mondo, Book the ſecond, and Chapter

ter the 9th; this Author having travell'd over all China, was a great favorer of the Jesuits, and his words are these: *la lingua Cinese al parere de Missionari (Gesuiti) é la più facile di tutte l'altre Orientali. Se per apprendere una lingua principalmente fa d'uopo memoria, quella lingua sarà più facile che averà minor copia di parole; perche sempre é più agevole ritenerne una picciola quantita, che molte: ora, la lingua Cinese é composta di sole 320 monosillable, quando la Greca & la Latina hanno una infinità di parole, di tempi differenti, nomi, & persone: adunque essa devo essere assai più facile. Si aggiugne à ciò che non fa di mestieri altra memoria che degli accenti, iquali sono come la forma, da cui si distingue la significazione delle parole. Il popolo però pronuncia bene il tutto con somma facilità, senza sapere che cosa sieno tuoni ò accenti, che non sono conosciuti che dà Letterati. Non potrà di ciò dubbitarsi, quante volte si voglia por mente che li Padri Missionari, che vanno in Cina, con l'applicazione di due anni predicano, confessano, e compongono in quella lingua, come se fosse la loro propria; quantunque vadano in quelle parti già auvanzati in età, onde hanno composti e stampati moltissimi libri, che sono ammirati e stimati dà medemi Cinesi.* But left the Jesuits shou'd cavil against the Authority of GEMELLI, as being a Lay man, my Author produces an unexceptionable witnefs; namely father GABRIEL MAGALLIANS, a Portuguefe Jefuit, moft converfant in the

I

Chinefe

Chinese language, who lived thirty seven years in China, and twenty five of these in the capital city of Pekin. This Missionary in the 96th page of his *Relation* has this passage : *La lingue Cinese é più facile della Greca, della Latina, e di tutte l'altre d' Europa. E certo che uno, ilquale studi con applicazione e buono metodo, può in un' anno molto ben' intendere e parlare in idioma Cinese. Ed in fatti vediamo che tutti li nostri padri, che presentemente faticano in questa missione, in capa a due anni sanno così bene questa lingua, che confessano, catechizano, predicano, e compongono con tanto facilità, come se fosse la lor lingua naturale.* This is a plain contradiction to what the Jesuits have pretended ever since the Papal Decree appear'd likely to go against them; alledging that the other Missionaries had not sufficient knowldge of the Chinese Language, to determine whether the controverted Rites and expressions were atheistical and idolatrous or not. But the Franciscan and Augustine, as well as the Dominican Missionaries, very justly reply, that supposing the Chinese Tongue so difficult to them as is pretended, it must needs be as difficult likewise to the Jesuits ; or else on the contrary, as easy to them as to the Jesuits. This is certainly true, and therefore the inquiry between you and me, is not how the several disputes or interests of these Gentlemen are or may be determin'd, but what is true in fact concerning the difficulty or facility of the Chinese Language,

guage, wherein by the concordant confeſſion of both, there are contain'd ſuch vaſt numbers of excellent Books, and containing a Philoſophy eſpecially very different from what obtains in our parts of the world. Wherefore I deſire the favor of you, not only to communicate your thoughts to me on this ſubject, and ſuch obſervations as I'm ſure in a long tract of reading you have moſt judiciouſly collected, but to refer me likewiſe to ſuch Books, as you ſhall think the moſt proper to give me due light and ſatisfaction.

After preſenting my duty and ſervice as before, I remain,

> S I R,
>> *Your moſt obſervant and devoted admirer.*

A

Mr. TOLAND.

Hanover ce 1. de Mars 1710.

MONSIEUR,

J'Ay receu ce que vous m'avez envoyé contre le Docteur SACHEVEREL, auſſi bien que le Sermon de M. l'Archevêque de Dublin, avec la refutation, dont je vous remercie. J'ay trouvé de bonnes choſes dans

3   le

le Livre de ce Prelat fur *l'origine du mal*; mais
je ne faurois goûter fon fentiment, qui tend
à nous faire croire, qu'il y a dans les fubftances libres une volonté ou election, qui n'eft
point fondée dans la reprefentation du bi-
en ou du mal des objects, mais dans je ne
fay quel pouvoir arbitraire de choifir fans
fujet. Son *Sermon* auffi ne me fatisfait pas,
lors qu'il femble nier, que nous ayons de
veritables notions des attributs de Dieu.

Il eft vray, que Strabon eft un bon Auteur : mais je crois pourtant, qu'on peut dire
qu'il fe trompe fort en parlant des Juifs. Il ne
paroit point fondé d'avancer les points fuivans :
1, que des Edomites chaffez de l'Arabie, fe
font joints aux Juifs & ont pris leur loix : 2,
que les Juifs font Egyptiens d'origine : 3,
que Moyse a été un Prétre Egyptien : 4, que
Moyse a crû, que Dieu eft le Monde : 5,
que Moyse a occupé les environs de Jerufa-
falem : 6, qu'il a obtenu ce pays fans combat :
7, que le pays des Juifs eftoit peu digne d'étre
matiere de combats : 8, qu'au lieu d'armes
Moyse a employé les ceremonies de la Religion : 9, que les peuples voifins fe font joints
à luy : 10, que fes fucceffeurs ont introduit
la circumcifion, & l'abftinence de certaines
viandes. Je ne veux point éplucher le refte,
mais je ne faurois diffimuler la faute qu'il a
faite dans un fait voifin de fon temps, en croyant qu'Herode a été un des Prétres ou Pon-
tifes des Juifs. M. Casaubon a remarqué

encore, que STRABON trompé par d'autres auteurs, a confondu le Lac de Sirbone avec le Lac Asphaltite, où le Jordan se perd.

La Langue Cophte garde beaucoup de l'ancien Egyptien, & des personnes y versées le croyent bien different de l'Arabe.

M. HUET étant, sans doute, un des plus savans hommes de nôtre temps, merite qu'on parle de luy avec moderation.

Quant aux Chinois, je crois qu'il faut distinguer entre leur Caracteres & leur Langue. Les Caracteres en font difficiles à apprendre, & les Jesuites ont raison de soutenir, qu'il faut beaucoup de temps pour qu'on soit en état de bien entendre les livres de cette nation; mais la Langue n'est pas fort difficile, quand on en a attrappé la prononciation : aussi est elle fort imparfaite ; les savans ne la cultivant point, parce qu'ils s'attachent aux Caracteres. Le Pere GRIMALDI m'a dit, qu'il arrive quelque fois aux Chinois dans la conversation de tracer les caracteres en l'air ou autrement, pour se mieux expliquer.

Au reste je suis

MONSIEUR,
votre tres humble
& tres obeissant serviteur,
LEIBNIZ.

TO

Mr. * * *.

York-buildings, *Feb.* 9, 1710-11.

SIR,

SOmething I was to finish for Prince EU-GENE, with whom I hold a literary cor-respondence, and which I have transmitted to his Highness last post, is the reason I have so seldom apply'd to you in person or paper (if I may so speak) since my arrival. But tho' I intend to do my self the honor of wait-ing on you to morrow, yet my duty obliges me to send you this Letter to day. I have, indeed, been very busy hitherto (which hur-ry is now over) yet I have been at times in all places and with all people. My long ab-sence has given me a good pretext for an unaffected reserve, as seeming ignorant of every thing at home, which makes all men desirous to inform me on the foot of their own schemes and principles, being God knows sometimes extremely different, and frequently inconsistent.

That I never admir'd the late Ministry, to whom I was under no tie of affection or gratitude, you remember as well as any man; and you know, that by the Ministry,

I don't

I don't mean every man that was then in Employment: but that I neither difparage nor commend them now, any more than over-flatter the prefent Miniftry, which I am likewife far from under-rating, is what you'll be doubtlefs inform'd of from the Coffee-houfes, where you great men (be of what fide you will) need have no fpies in pay; fince there are fo many officious expectants in each of them ready to perform that fer-vice. I therefore hear and fee every thing. I have the pleafure very often by crofs quef-tions, or a feeming compliance, to draw that out of fome people, for which they wou'd be ready to hang themfelves, if they thought I rightly underftood them; tho', after ftar-ting their defigns, to the beft of my ability, their perfons for me fhall be always fafe. Bantering and fooling, indifference and doubt-fulnefs, are fuccefsful engines in this art of disburthening, which you know the French call *tirer les vers du nez,* and we Englifh *pumping.* In fhort, I fet up not pretendedly, but in downright earneft, for converfing with all men and about all things; which conduct I have exactly obferv'd ever fince my going laft abroad, and fhall ever continue it.

Let this ferve as a preface, SIR, to what-ever I may have occafion to write or fay to you for the future, and in particular to what I am now going to tell you; which is, that a violent fufpicion is ftrongly rooted in the

minds

minds of many, and indirectly affecting all, as if I know not what long-winded meafures were concerted in favour of the Pretender's more eafy accefs to the Britifh Empire ; and confequently againft the rightful and lawful claim of the Houfe of Hanover. Believe me, this notion alone does the Court more harm, than all the artifices of all the men that are difoblig'd in the nation. I will not difpute but that the late Minifters and their creatures would gladly clog the wheels ; as fome ill-affected, ignorant, or difcontented Tories wou'd drive 'em much too faft. But other Whigs and Tories wou'd not be willinger to get more money than they have at prefent, than to improve by any hands the money they have got already, cou'd they entirely truft the Government. Nay, tho' I fhou'd agree with your Projectors, that fome keep up their money out of fullennefs, and others in expectation of greater advantages when the Court is in greater diftrefs ; let me take the liberty neverthelefs to affure you, that there are a third fort, and thofe not the leaft wealthy or numerous, who for the reafon given before (well or ill grounded) dare not at this juncture part with their money on any terms, tho' ever fo inviting. Such people have with the greateft earneftnefs and fincerity beg'd me for a reafon to fet them at eafe.

C c 3

Now

Now since by conquering this same point of Money, you conquer all other difficulties, I think it behoves the Court by some un-affected method (yet as much for their own honor as possible) to settle the minds of the subjects; and to act in respect to the House of Hanover with more openness and hearti-ness than they are hitherto observ'd to have done either there or elsewhere. Dry and general expressions will not do: friends must be confirm'd, and enemies put out of hope. I cou'd tell you the answers that men have ready in their mouths to that part of the Queen's Speech which relates to the Succes-sion, and which (by the way) seems even to me not to be over-punctually follow'd by the countenance and preferment given since to certain persons whereof I saw a list, with whose former conduct and characters I am throughly acquainted, and who I have reason to believe are not chang'd by an oath, what-ever they may be by a place. They cannot at least be said to be *zealous* for the Protestant Succession.

I am not a stranger to the principles and practices of certain Scots I can meet every day about Westminster, no more than to the peculiar construction they put on the Oath of Abjuration. I know what is further said in the world concerning the affected stile, or rather incoherent jargon of the late Ad-dresses dreffes; nor want I explanations from fome of the Addreffers themfelves. I am glad however on other accounts that fuch Addreffes there were. But to pafs over a thoufand things of this nature and tendency, I muft not forget that fome of the Writers that wou'd diftinguifh themfelves by their zeal for the prefent Miniftry (as the *Examiner,* for example) have given but too much ground for thefe furmifes by very odd and imprudent , if not difaffected and villanous expreffions.

'Tis likewife prodigious to think, that LESLY, who deferves to be hang'd, was not as much punifht at leaft for his *Good old Caufe,* as Sir ROWLAND GWYN for his *Letter,* or GILDON for publifhing and defending it. Tho' I don't mention 'em, I am not ignorant of other fuch Books that have pafs'd uncenfur'd, to the no fmall amazement of every body. There are fo many fcatter'd particulars of this kind, which tho' fingly perhaps unheeded, yet collected and fet fairly in one view, wou'd (I durft wager) bring down ftocks lower than ever.

Certain informations now before the Attorney General againft two Scots Officers, as alfo againft a man from Exeter (to name no more) and the fham-plot of thofe two rampant St. German Priefts LANGTON and HIGGINS, againft fome honeft Gentlemen in Ireland,

land, whereof I have a very particular account, from one of the Gentlemen themselves, cannot but make people remember and dread the days of King CHARLES and King JAMES. 'Tis ever an ill fign when Informers are encourag'd.

I will not infift on the choice of Minifters to the Court of Hanover, almoft from the beginning : nor on certain, I was going to fay childifh, ways of treating them, of which they'll be the laft themfelves to tell you; and I own that I am far from being commiffion'd to do fo, or any thing like it. I am however afraid, and I wifh I may never have occafion to fhew, that you have all of you a wrong notion of that place, where you may depend upon it that there are neither Whigs nor Tories; and where as Mr. H *** (if he has any faith in me) is the higheft in their efteem for a Politician, fo he may be the firft in their confidence as a friend, without forfeiting any of his duty to his prefent Royal Miftrefs, whofe true intereft and theirs are, in their opinion, infeparable. Never, I am fure, were heirs apparent or prefumptive lefs difpos'd to make the poffeffor uneafy, or lefs in haft to leap at a Crown, being already fo eafy themfelves. Yet this is far from rendring them indifferent, as fome fhallow monfters have mifconftrued their difcretion ; the Elector's language being unvariably this, that he'll always do by the Queen, as he wou'd

have

have his fon do by him. The late Minifters, we may naturally imagine will not be wanting (if poffible) to ruffle this their tranquillity, as well as improve the miftruftful difpofitions, and, I hope, ill-grounded jealoufies of the people.

As to Credit (which is the main point at prefent) the very perfons in the City, who abhor the thoughts of any defign for the Pretender in Court or Parliament, yet finding thofe that believe fuch defigns keep up their money, will likewife keep up theirs for fear of the worft : fince the leaft confufions on this account muft ruin a world of men. 'Tis in your will, I am perfuaded, and for God's fake let it be in your power, to obviate the malicious defigns of your own and the Nation's enemies.   A method may be eafily found out : tho' I have known a boat overfet, becaufe the skipper wou'd not flacken his fail at the defire of a paffenger. Our Britifh Court muft often condefcend to fatisfy the doubts or defires of the People, nor does even the French King always neglect it.

Pray, SIR, miftake me not ; as if I had the Englifh fpleen or a German penfion.   I own it is impoffible for any man to be more in the interefts of that moft illuftrious Family than I am ; and as I hope to out-live every man alive that's older than my felf but you, fo I have a real and hearty concern for what's to come. But for all that, you may safely rely upon it, that this Memorial is deliver'd out of perfect good will to you, most sincerely intended for your service, and I doubt not but so you'll understand it. I am in my self entirely secure as to the event. Tho' time and things have taught me to be cautious of every body, yet I am convinc'd that too much jealously is as bad, if not worse, than none at all. Were I sure, as I am certain of the contrary, that every man and woman they suspect was imbark'd in such a Plot, yet I shou'd not much fear for the Succession's blowing up or sinking their ship. Nay were the Pretender landed at Leith or in the Downs (which is believ'd to be the meaning of the hieroglyphical Almanack from Christ-Church, where the allegorical health is *Confusion to Philosophy*, that is to Sophia and her *friends*) should this happen, I say, I shou'd not despair of his being quickly driven out again; and in this case foreigners, I fancy, wou'd inter-meddle whether we wou'd or no. But 'tis better he shou'd not come at all, lest you or I shou'd fall in the scuffle.

For the rest, I do assure you, Dear Sir, that what I have laid before you is not wholly pick'd from common fame, nor yet the language of tools or factious fellows; but that of entire trust in me from some of the most considerable men in the Nation and City,

City, the apprehensions of Tories as well as of Whigs, many of whom have ever despised those whom you may be apt to suspect of putting such notions in their heads, or such words in their mouths. But to conclude, I have besides a demonstration to my self that a majority of the nation does more or less believe the matter that has occasion'd this Letter. The Jacobites give out they are cocksure of it, the Whigs fear it may be too true, and many of the Tories know not what to think: but I know in such a case with whom some of them wou'd be most likely to join. The October Club, if rightly manag'd, will be rare stuff to work the ends of any party. I sent such an account of those wights to an old Gentlewoman of my acquaintance, as in the midst of fears will make her laugh. I am with my head, with my pen, and with my heart,

SIR,

Your most faithful
and obedient servant.

TO

T O

Mrs. * * *.

MADAM,

IF we corresponded in all things as punctually as we have done this week, in interchanging the good news, no pair in history cou'd exceed us. But by yours before the last (for both which I return my heartiest thanks) I find that a Lady of your acquaintance and my self, differ very much in our notions about Solitude, which I take to be quite another thing from Retirement. I am ready to own that without Retirement one is in a perpetual hurry: it reiterates all our enjoyments by recollection; and furnishes us with materials as well as desires for new pleasures, when we produce our selves again upon the theatre. Solitude, on the contrary, not only deprives us of both the past and the future, but always inclines the present hour to joyless melancholy, which sooner or later ends in something intractable, Timonean, (pardon the word) or perhaps more fatal. And if this be true of the meanest and most thoughtless peasants, tho' little differing from brutes in all they do; how much more must it be so of such elevated genius's, whose ready and just conceptions of things, whose

proper

proper but unaffected expreſſion, and whoſe engaging affability ever join'd to diſcretion, make them the only Angels, capable to render others happy, and to be ſo themſelves, in converſation, friendſhip, love, or affairs, or all together.

This is exactly the Character of the Lady, who pleads for Solitude; and who you tell me looks upon the Book of Nature, as ſufficient to employ and divert her. Pray acquaint her from me, that no man in the world admires that ſame Book, more than my ſelf, but that it is ſtill only in Retirement; and I fancy I ſhou'd underſtand it better, were ſhe there to tell me the names of the flowers, or I to tell her their virtues: beſides that, after all, we peruſe the Book very imperfectly, if we do not frequent the beau monde, pleaſe and be pleaſed, hear and relate; all which being natural, are ſo many agreeable pages of that infinite volume. I ſhould be very angry at what your acquaintance ſays of *her time of day*; were not their proper perſon the only thing, wherein Ladies of her ſenſe are allow'd to ſpeak by contraries. Perſuade her therefore to come to town, and aſſure her, that whoever looks upon her with my eyes, muſt allow the Picture I ſend you to reſemble her in every particular. I never read it, but I thought ſo, and conſequently thought of herſelf.

L

TO

TO

Mr. * * *.

SIR,

I Had the honor of receiving your Letter yesterday by the hands of Dr. F***. The Motto you sent, being one of five I had since collected for your choice, is already set in the frontispiece: for in subjects of this nature, I have as just a deference for your taste and judgment, as ever VIRGIL or HORACE had for VARUS. I likewise acknowledge your criticism, as to narration in general, to be right, where we ought to be very sparing of Epithets, except when they are absolutely requisite: for they only, and their cousin Adverbs, make all the distinction of things, nor can any writing be without them. But on the other hand, I admit not your French *Telemachus*, nor any other the most correct French Author for a Rule in Language: for their own is neither a good original, nor capable of imitating such. What Frenchman can say the *all-permeating Aether* or *swift-footed* ACHILLES? tho' words of this kind be as essential to Pastorals (whether in prose or verse) as to Tragic or Epic Poetry.

There

There may be however a vicious affectation of these in such Pieces as most require
them. Nor do we Authors (and 'tis only laziness or a more unpardonable modesty that
keeps you from being of our number) always
print every word we write in the first heat
of our imagination. This sort of pruning
is call'd by our friend HORACE *ambitiosa re-
cidere ornamenta*; and the Recitation of the
Antients to their judicious acquaintance (a
thing wholly neglected by the Moderns) was
principally design'd for this purpose. Mine
was so to you: but I had done it in vain,
if you had not used a liberty wherein nothing is to be blam'd, but the excuse you
make for it. If you don't send me word
that you have business or better company
to morrow, I shall have further discourses
with you on this subject. In the mean
time, believe me to be in the strictest sense,

SIR,

*Your most true
and faithful servant.*

T O

TO

Mr. * * *.

SIR,

SINCE you cannot read the *Memoirs* of Monſieur CASTELNAU in the original, I ſend you a tranſlation of his *Character of Queen* ELIZABETH, which, in my opinion, is a maſter-piece. He had long reſided Ambaſſador at her Court from France, and was very much in her favour, tho' in Religion Popiſh; and, as ſuch, hath often miſrepreſented the Proteſtants, eſpecially thoſe in France: which is an undeniable argument for not ſuſpecting his ſincerity when he ſpeaks well of them.

THE

CHARACTER

OF

QUEEN ELIZABETH.

" THO' this Princeſs was poſſeſt of all " the great qualities that are neceſ-" ſary for reigning a long while, which ſhe " likewiſe did; yet, however good her un-" derſtanding

" derftanding might be, fhe wou'd never
" either decide or undertake any thing of
" her own head, but always imparted every
" thing to her Council. What happen'd in
" the time of AUGUSTUS, when the Tem-
" ple of JANUS was fhut as a fign of the uni-
" verfal Peace of the Empire, might be as
" truly faid of her reign; for the Queen
" of England having avoided all wars, by
" ftudying to fix them upon her neighbours
" abroad, rather than to draw them upon
" her own Kingdom, and to feed them at
" home, fhe preferv'd her fubjects by this
" means in very great tranquillity. Nor was
" it with any juftice that fhe was taxt by fome
" with avarice, for not having made any confi-
" derable liberalities(forfooth) which not only
" load thofe with envy on whom they are
" conferr'd, when exceffive; but very often
" are the caufe of cenfure upon thofe who
" beftow them withont reafon, and unlefs the
" gift be a work of charity or neceffity.
" A further and fufficient defence againft this
" unjuft charge of being govern'd by avarice,
" is, that the faid Queen did entirely dif-
" charge all the debts of her Predeceffors,
" and put her finances into fo good order,
" that no Prince of her time did amafs fo
" great riches, and levy'd with fo much
" equity, as fhe did, without ever laying
" any extraordinary taxes or new-invented
" impofts to fqueeze her fubjects. This ma-
" nagement is the reafon that for the fpace of
VOL. II.   D d   " eight

" eight years she never demanded the ordi-
" nary subsidies and free gift, which the Eng-
" lish are accustom'd to grant their Princes
" from three years to three years: and, what
" is more, her subjects having offer'd her in
" the year 1570 the usual sum without her
" asking of it, she not only thank'd them
" without accepting thereof; but likewise
" assur'd them, that unless absolute necessity
" requir'd it, she wou'd never raise a crown
" upon them, but what wou'd be just
" necessary for supporting the government.
" This single action deserves the highest
" praise, and may well entitle her to the
" reputation of being extremely liberal.
" But yet further, she neither sold the of-
" fices of her Kingdom, nor made money
" of them any other way, tho' other Princes
" are wont to give them to the highest bid-
" der: a thing that ordinarily corrupts ju-
" stice and policy, with all humane and di-
" vine Laws. Besides her maintaining of
" her subjects in peace and tranquillity, she
" continually built a great number of Ships,
" which were the fortresses, the bastions,
" and the ramparts of her State, causing a
" new man of war to be launch'd once every
" two years; and such Ships they were, as
" made account to meet with nothing on
" the seas capable to resist them. These
" were the buildings, these were the Palaces
" that the Queen of England begun from
                                    ". her

" her very accession to the throne, and
" which she delighted to continue ever
" after. She exercis'd withal another sort
" of prudent Liberality, which is, to spare
" no expences in order to know the secrets
" of foreign Princes: and this was particu-
" lar to her, that she chose rather to lend
" without interest, than to borrow her self
" on any conditions, tho' ever so gainful.
" She has been indeed most basely calumni-
" ated with certain Love-Intrigues, which I
" can affirm with much sincerity to have
" been mere inventions, and stories not on-
" ly spread by malecontents at home, but
" likewise forg'd in the closets of Ambassa-
" dors, to make those Princes averse to her
" alliance, to whom her friendship might be
" of the greatest advantage. Had she had an
" inclination for the Earl of LEICESTER
" (as it was positively reported) and that she
" had preferr'd him not only to all her own
" subjects, but likewise to those foreign Prin-
" ces that courted her, what cou'd hinder
" her from marrying him? especially, seeing
" that the three estates of her Kingdom,
" and the neighbouring Kings and Princes,
" did often beg it of her with great earnest-
" ness, or to marry any other, even of her
" subjects that she might best like. But she
" was pleased to say to my self an infinite
" number of times, and long before I had
" the honor to reside in her Court, that were
" she ever disposed to marry, it shou'd only

D d 2   " be

" be to a Prince of a great and illuſtrious
" Family, and of Royal lineage, not inferior
" at leaſt to her own ; and this more for the
" good of her Kingdom, than for any parti-
" cular affection : nay, and that if ſhe thought
" any of her ſubjects were ſo preſumtuous
" as to deſire her for a wife, ſhe wou'd
" never admit him afterwards into her pre-
" ſence, but, contrary to her natural diſpo-
" ſition very oppoſite to cruelty, ſhe wou'd
" play him ſome ill turn ; ſo that there re-
" mains no reaſon to doubt, but that ſhe was
" always no leſs chaſte than prudent, as the
" effects do plainly demonſtrate. What ſerves
" for a further good proof of what I here
" allege, is, the curioſity ſhe had to learn
" ſo many Sciences and Languages, beſides
" her continual application to affairs of ſtate
" foreign and domeſtic, that ſhe cou'd ſcarce
" have any leiſure to think of amorous paſ-
" ſions, which are the offspring of Idleneſs
" but not of Letters : a thing well under-
" ſtood by the ancients, when they made
" PALLAS the Goddeſs of wiſdom, to be a
" virgin, and without a mother, and like-
" wiſe the nine Muſes to be ſo many chaſt
" virgins. For all this, I know the Courti-
" ers will ſay, that Honor conſiſts only in re-
" putation, and principally the honor of
" women, who are happy if they have but
" a good name. Now if I have been carried
" ſomewhat too far out of my road to de-
" ſcribe the praiſes of this Princeſs, the par-
" ticular

" ticular knowlege I had of her merits will
" ferve me for a lawful excufe; as the re-
" hearfal of them feem'd alfo neceffary, that
" the Queens, who fhall come after her,
" may take the example of her virtues for
" their looking-glafs.

Read now all the Hiftories that expreffly
or occafionally relate the Actions of this
incomparable Princefs, and you'll find that
this Character might well ferve for argument
to them all : fo judicioufly cou'd the French
Minifter croud immenfe matter into a very narrow room. When I write on that fubject, which
I hope to do e'er it be long, I am refolv'd to
take it for my text; and to enlarge on the
following heads, viz. That fhe was,

1. Bafely envied by the Scotch race, and
her day abolifh'd by King JAMES II.
2. Maintaining the ballance of power
abroad, and the head of the Proteftant intereft every where.
3. No fingle Miniftry, but the refults of
a wife Council.
4. Preferv'd peace at home by keeping the
war abroad (1), where fhe always entertained fufficient forces, both to affift her allies,
which fhe never abandon'd; and to maintain military Difcipline in her Kingdom.

(1) Bellum foris, pax domi.

5. Not

5. Not prodigal of the public money to worthless favourites. The Popish Libels on that subject against a time of need.

6. She did discharge the public debts in reality, and not in idea ; as the public credit was held up by effects and not by a vote.

7. When she forbore receiving the usual taxes, she was at the same time engag'd in foreign wars. This was liberality to her People.

8. Never rais'd money to enrich favourites, and supply the luxury of a Court.

9. No selling of offices after the basest manner ; that is, bestowing them as bribes to the turbulent or corrupt, and not as favours to men of merit ; and splitting them among many to make the more voices, or quartering those you dare not employ on those you do.

10. Her care of augmenting the Fleet, and how it dwindl'd under her Successor, the ships she built rotting in the Docks.

11. By paying well for the secrets of Princes, she was not at a loss what measures to take, nor ever shamefully forc'd to change her schemes with every wind.

12. Never borrow'd at excessive premiums, a sure sign of mismanagement.

13. Marry'd only to her Kingdom, and not changing her Ministers with her Lovers. Steddy, and not saying and unsaying, denying and affirming, as she was bid ; a sign that those who do so, either know not what is a doing at all, or no judges when they do know it.

14. Her

14. Her prodigious knowledge, her affability, her polite Literature, not mewing her self up, but filling all foreigners with admiration of her wit as well as her wisdom.

15. Scorn'd to misally her self with the sprouts of the Law or the Gospel.

16. Her example to be follow'd by Kings as well as Queens.

17. Sometimes changing Ministers, but never measures; so that her motto of *semper eadem*, her own choice and no imitation, was not a satyr but a panegyric upon her conduct.

CASTELNAU, who liv'd in England 23 years, was admirably well acquainted with her genius; and, knowing by our constitutions, that other Queens might probably reign here before time cou'd abolish his *Memoirs*, he drew up this Character for a guide, an encouragement to their good conduct.

TO

Mr. * * *.

SIR,

THE following abstract of a French Letter writ from Carolina, in the year 1688, being fall'n into my hands, I thought the account it gives of the honest Indians of that Country, would not be unacceptable to you.　　Dd4　　*An*

An Account of the Indians at Carolina.

I had but little knowledge of Mankind, whilft the only means I had of judging was from the Books of Morality, and the Conver-fation of thofe, amongft whom I then liv'd. All things are fo order'd and fo compos'd there, that 'tis very hard to make a found Judgment of what a Man is. The fubmif-fion one owes to Princes, to Juftice, and to Ecclefiaftical Power, do keep men fo ftrongly within the bounds of a certain duty, as well as the prevailing cuftom of yeilding obedience to fome perfons more powerful then themfelves, and more capa-ble of doing them harm; that it is almoft impoffible ever to fee Man in a ftate of pure nature: but in this Country, where he feems to be free from all thefe tyes and ob-ligations, one fees him in his true light, and without a mask. And truly one may fay, that the apparent exaggeration of the Pro-phets in the Old Teftament, did never carry farther the deformity of the Jews character, then can be made that of the Chriftians: fo far are they from having the marks of a Chriftian that hardly have they of a rational creature. One fees them daily exclaming againft one another, without zeal towards God, without piety or affection, not help-ing one another, having no other God but their riches, without confidence in divine

Providence,

Providence, murmuring always against him upon the most trifling vexation, as if God Almighty were ungrateful in giving so small
rewards and encouragements to those who
make profession of being Christians.

This is it that teacheth me to know what
Man is in his depraved state. But on the
other hand, God has been pleas'd to grant
me a sight of Man such as he ought to be,
and thereby has made me understand, that in
creating us, he has not left us unprovided of
natural abilites to avoid the evil for its
uglines, and to search after the good for
its beauty only; without the fear of punishment attending the one, or the hope of recompence to induce us to the practice of
the other. Would you imagine, Sir, that
the example should be seen and found a-
mongst these Indians, of whom you seem
so unwilling to believe any such matter? Yes,
Sir, it is these very Indians that have made
me blush for shame to be a Man, and yet so
little reasonable; and to carry the name of
a Christian, and yet so remote from the practice of an Evangelical life. We know our
Saviour's precepts without observing them,
and they observe them without knowing
him : were they to have all the Gospel word
by word by heart, they could not practice it
with more exactness and strictness then they
do it already.

One

One fees fo wonderful an union amongft this People, that you never hear of any difputes or quarrels among them. They are an induftrious and laborious Nation; fubmiffive to fuperior Powers, but without being their flaves; obeying without repining or grumbling their Sovereign's orders: never minding their own particular Interefts, when the Publick has need of their fervice or endeavors; never fuffering their neighbour to be in want, whilft they have where-withal to make them fharers with them; hofpitable, religious obfervers of their word and promife; never lying, never taking away from another what belongs to him; no ways diffolute, luxurious or debauched; the marry'd women being modeft and vertuous, as to every thing that looks like gallantry, as well as the unmarry'd; civil and obedient to their husbands, according to the advice of St. PAUL: all of them courteous, affable, and obliging towards ftrangers, no ways favage nor morofe, no ways ungrateful, and never forgetting a good office; valiant and proud in war, tractable and mild in peace, hating thieves, robbers, lyars, and all fuch as break their word. This is the true Character of the Indians, with whom I converfed moft. I muft needs own to you, SIR, that after having liv'd among them fome weeks, I could not but admire and be amaz'd at the lives of other men, and how

we

we toil and labor for superfluities that we may very easily be without. It was amongst them that I learn'd to seek after what is necessary, and to undervalue the great hurry of business of the world, in which, there is nothing but anguish and vexation of spirit. Good God! What sensible difference I found betwixt the happy quietness and repose I enjoy'd amongst them, and the trouble I meet with daily amongst people, a thousand times more savage then they. But, O Sir, if this People were Christians, what pleasure would there be never to part from them? 'Tis true they are not Christians, and 'tis to be fear'd will never be. When I discoursed them upon it, they gave me such an answer as made me hold my tongue for shame. " You would (say they) have us become " Christians? well, to what end and purpose? " Is it to make us better than really we are, " or is it not rather to make us as wicked " and vicious as your selves, to render us " Adulterers, Whore-masters, Lyars, Mur- " therers, Robbers, without faith, honor, or " honesty, minding nothing but how to de- " ceive one another, and to destroy you up- " on pretence of Justice? Is this a party to " choose, and to oblige us to renounce the " simplicity of our manner of life, and the " sweet tranquillity of mind we now en- " joy? " When I attempted to represent to them, that 'twas not our Religion that made us such as they painted us; since

3   it

it taught us to lead better lives: they reply'd, " that all the Indians that became
" Chriftians, were fallen into the fame vices
" and irregularities, that are practic'd amongft
" us ; and that therefore they would not
" run the hazzard of it.

To   * * *.

Dear SIR,

HAVING waited a fortnight after the
publication of my Book, and no Anfwer coming out in that time (as I fee not
what can be reply'd to fuch plain facts, befides railing, which will never pafs for reafon) I thought my felf bound to attend no
longer, and fo came down hither at the earneft requeft of a Gentleman, to whom I owe
very many obligations. In one word he's
neither King-ridden nor Prieft-ridden. I fhall
not however during my fmall ftay, wafte time
in merely feeing the country, or indulging
the pleafures it affords: but on the contrary,
I fpend an hour or two every morning on
a Piece that will make a much greater noife,
and raife a far nobler fpirit than *Dunkirk
or Dover*. I am perfuaded it will be reckon'd
a very acceptable fervice by all true lovers
of their Country.

But

But 'tis very hard on the other hand, that while I thus incur the odium of the French Party in power, I fhould be neglected by thofe whofe Englifh principles, and I may alfo fay whofe private interefts, I fo heartily promote. I do all this, its true, from the unalterable love I bear to Liberty ; but while they find their account in it, methinks, they fhould not be the lefs thankful. I hope at leaft they will now fee, how unjuft their Sufpicions were, that I had ftill a fecret underftanding with my Lord * * * whofe Spy they us'd approbrioufly to ftile me ; tho' I expoftulated with him more, and fpoke more plain truths to him, concerning the deftructive meafures I faw he was taking, than any one of them has done. I neither defire nor expect my word fhould be taken for this: for I have authentick Proofs of it in the copies of feveral Writings or *Memorials* on that fubject, to every one of which, the perfon who entertains me here is a witnefs, as having been privy to the fame ; and in particular to the laft Letter I wrote his Lordfhip about two years ago, wherein upon certain (as he thought) ambiguous words he let drop about the Houfe of Hanover, I utterly renounc'd his friendfhip, and confequently all the advantages one in my circumftances might hope from his Protection. Since that time I never fpoke nor wrote to him more : and thus while I behav'd my felf as if I had the

3   moft

moſt plentiful fortune to ſupport me againſt his reſentments, yet am I ſhamefully abandon'd as if I were his Creature in the worſt ſenſe.

I ſhould not have taken the liberty, SIR, to be ſo particular with you, if I were not thoroughly convinc'd that you are not onely upon the firmeſt Principles engag'd in the nobleſt cauſe in the world; but likewiſe becauſe I found you always inclin'd both to juſtify and favour me, as knowing well that I neither was, nor cou'd be any thing but a Whig. Indeed a perſon who has ſo nice a taſte of polite Literature himſelf, cannot but patronize a lover of Letters in a lower degree than I am : and hence therefore it is, that I throw my ſelf on your generous care, not doubting but you'll take ſome pains to ſet me right with thoſe who know me not ſo well, and ſo diſpoſe 'em to put me in a condition of writing as freely as I think. Being reſolv'd to ſet out for London next monday, there's no need of honouring me with an Anſwer, and in the mean time, I am, with the profoundeſt reſpect and ſincerity.

SIR,

Your, &c.

TO

TO

Mr. * * *.

Dear SIR,

THE Book I do my self the honor to send you by next munday's carrier will sufficiently inform you, how I have been spending my time for some weeks past at Epsom ; and the distance of that place from London, as well as my continual attention to a thread of ancient and modern facts, will excuse the interruption of Correspondence. Yet the loss to me has been in some measure made up by the assurance I receiv'd from time to time of both your healths and kind remembrance.

I flatter my self that in the foresaid Book you'll meet with more novelties, than in the ordinary course of postage I cou'd have sent in that time ; and I am sorry on the other hand, that you are too sure to find in it many things that will be no news to you. Discoursing of Liberty, nay, assertaining and maintaining it, I cou'd not but act with the greatest freedom, and indeed it wou'd not only be improper, but, in my opinion, in-

effectual

effectual to do otherwife : fince the principal
art of perfuafion is to appear perfuaded your
felf; and, to tell you the truth without dif-
guize, it is impoffible for a foul that's really
fir'd with the love of his Country, not to exprefs in the moft pathetic terms a deteftation
for Tyranny, a contempt for Slaves, an averfion to Traytors, and refentment of injur'd
Truft. But all this while I have not acted
without caution likewife, expecting little
affiftance from many of thofe that will be
the loudeft to applaud me : and therefore,
the coming out of the Book being fixt to
next Tuefday, I have provided my felf with
a privacy where I fancy I may be fafe enough
till the firft fury be overpaft, if they think
it advifeable to make any profecution. Clips-
ton is too far off, or it were the fecureft
place in the world.

But leaving the event to time, you are to
underftand, that, without any regard to thefe
things, I am in about three weeks time bound
for Germany ; tho' firft for Flanders, and next
for Holland. I believe I fhall be pretty well
accomodated for this Voyage, which upon
many accounts I expect will be very fhort.
Lord! how near was my old Woman being
a Queen! and your humble fervant being
at his eafe! All is not over yet, and fome
fymptoms are promifing enough. I have been
the bolder upon this prefumption, nor am I
alone, fince all the Princes in Europe take
their meafures on the fame foot.

You'll receive Mr. STEELE's *Crisis* by the same carrier that delivers you my *Art of Restoring*. I think it a very good Book, but it does not answer the expectation of many others, who are good friends to him and the Cause.

Our naval armament goes on very slowly: and whether design'd to reduce Barcelona, Copenhagen, or London, either of these, or all three in conjunction with the French, is yet a secret to the body of our People, but none to me, as per next I shall irresistibly convince you.

I am, SIR,

your &c.

TO

Mr. TOLAND.

Pau 23 July 1714. N. S.

Dear SIR,

IT is about five weeks since I came to this place, but was not settled till very lately in a house fit for my purpose, with Stable, Coach-house and Garden. The Town is but small, and full of Persons of Quality, which makes good houses so scarce, that I thought

VOL. II.   E e   I should

I ſhould have been forc'd to go ſomewhere elſe. I have taken one for a year at leaſt, and think I ſhall ſtay longer, finding the place very pleaſant and very healthy, as far as I am yet able to judge. The City is ſurrounded with very fine walks, either for coach, horſe, or foot, and the Country much the moſt fruitful of any part of France, thro' which I paſs'd. The people of condition are extremely civil, by whom we have been viſited univerſally, with promiſes of much friendſhip and ſervice. I have been viſited but once with the Gout ſince I left England, with a very moderate fit ſince I left Paris, which is more than has happen'd to me for ſeveral years paſt. It might poſſibly have been ſo, if I had ſtay'd in England, but I had rather impute it to the exerciſe of my journey, and the warmth and goodneſs of the air. I go out ſometimes on horſe-back, but for the moſt part in the coach, where I ſeldom fail of meeting twenty or thirty more belonging to this little Town. We got hither by eaſy journies without meeting any misfortune; and, tho' we paſs'd a great deal of bad way, my horſes perform'd ſo well, as to loſe no fleſh when they came hither, and are as good and freſh as at firſt.

The Country we paſs'd thro' is ſufficiently miſerable, wanting almoſt all neceſſaries for a comfortable ſubſiſtence; the peaſants ſcarcely may be ſaid to live, and thoſe they

z   call

call Gentlemen are proportionably in a worse condition. The fields are very much deserted, whole towns abandon'd, and the houses fallen down as if they had been visited with an earthquake; servants for manufactures are much wanting, and those that remain are very idle and avoiding labour, which together with the diminution of money, and the late universal plague amongst their sheep and cattel, makes their wool scarce, and their manufacturing dear. And yet they reckon'd this a blessed condition in comparison of what they felt in the time of war, and look upon the peace as no less than a restoration of their beings, which were reduc'd to their last gasp. It must needs be a long while before the country can recover the damage and desolation caus'd by the war, and in all likelyhood they will never be able to do it: and if the Bill of Commerce passes, I do not see how any Province will get by it, except such who deal in wines and brandies.

Every body here talks very confidently of an Invasion of England with a considerable force, but deny that their King is any way concern'd in it, disguising all under the Emperor's name: many stick not to affirm openly, that the Queen is expected shortly in France, and preparations are making for her reception. No doubt if she quits her Kingdom upon any account, she will find a welcome here. Ee 2 The

The ſtate of Learning in this Kingdom is very low, and ignorance and barbarity creeps infenſibly upon the people of all conditions: the Prieſthood being eas'd of their ſtudies and pains in confuting adverſaries, will be ſure to take care to keep the lay people as ignorant as they can. And we may expect if things continue in the preſent ſtate, to ſee this nation over-run with witchcrafts and apparitions, miracles, and all the barbarities of the 12th and 13th Centuries.

I am,
Dear SIR,
Your moſt affectionate humble ſervant,

T. RAULINS.

/ TO

Mr. THORESBY.

London Sep. 29, 1715.

SIR,

MR. DES MAIZEAUX, the Gentleman who publiſh'd Monſieur BAYLE's Letters, and who has oblig'd the learn'd world with ſeveral of his own Productions, was ſo taken with your Ducatus Leodienſis, (as all perſons of curioſity and judgment muſt neceſſarily be) that he ſent an account of it to a foreign Journaliſt, with whom he keeps a correſpon-

correſpondence. After having mention'd your Book, he adds, in relation to your ſelf (1) :

" M. Thoresby avoit été élevé pour le
" commerce, & il y faiſoit de fort bonnes
" affaires ; mais la paſſion violente qu'il
" avoit pour toute ſorte de Curioſitez & de
" Raretez lui fit abandonner cette profeſ-
" ſion pour ſuivre ſon inclination naturelle.
" Le Catalogue des Raretez de ſon Cabinet
" n'eſt pas moins curieux qu'inſtructif : il ſe-
" roit à ſouhaiter que tous ceux qui poſſedent
" de ſemblables treſors vouluſſent imiter
" Mr. Thoresby.

Of this I knew nothing till I ſaw the Journal, and then Mr. Des Maizeaux own'd he had tranſmitted that Paragraph, which will make the Book enquir'd after beyond the ſeas. In effect, a famous Bookſeller in Holland, has upon this notice ſent for ſome copies.

I thought my ſelf ſo much intereſted in what concerns the fame of an honeſt man, tho' not long happy in his acquaintance, that I cou'd not refrain ſending you this account. The juſtice done in it to your merit, ought to be imitated by all thoſe of your Countrymen, who do not envy you, for there are no parties in the Republic of Letters : and

(1) *Nouvelles Litteraires du Samedi* 28 Septembre 1715.

if

if foreigners are so highly pleas'd with peru-
sing your Antiquities of a place they never
saw ; I think the Town of Leeds, which you
have not only rendred illustrious, but even immortal, shou'd after their example (of which
I cou'd give many instances) in gratitude erect
your Statue, accompany'd with a most honorable Inscription.

You may remember, SIR, that Mr. DES
MAIZEAUX inserted his name in your *Album*
the day I took leave of you. He forgets not
his promise of furnishing you with some
hands. I shall likewise add others, to those
you have already been pleas'd to accept. In
the mean time, I beg the favour of you to
lend or procure me an account of such Traditions, concerning the *Druids*, as may possibly obtain in your northern parts: what
Monuments are ascrib'd to them there, or
that are likely to be theirs, tho' vulgarly taken otherwise : and what places (if any) are
evidently, or conjecturally, call'd after them.
Such an account, in whole or in part, will
lay a singular obligation upon,

SIR,

Your most faithful
obedient servant.

Mr.

Mr. THORESBY's

A N S W E R.

Leeds Octob. 12, 1715.

SIR,

I Take the opportunity of the very first post to acknowledge the favour of your most obliging Letter, with the inclos'd Paragraph out of the *Nouvelles Litteraires,* wherein I perceive that Mr. DES MAIZEAUX has done me the honor to mention the *Ducatus Leodienſis.* My humble ſervice and thanks to that learned Author: but his and your candor hath, I fear, been too extenſive as to any thing of my performance, who being bred a Merchant, want the advantage of an Academic Education; but *la paſſion violente* he juſtly obſerves in me, did me in that reſpect a kindneſs, and made me give over in time before the gentleman in Holland I was in partnerſhip with, run himſelf aground.

I am ſorry I cannot more effectually anſwer your requeſt as to the *Druids,* we not having any traditions, *&c.* relating to them in theſe parts. They ſeem to me to have retired with the Britains to Wales: whatever I have been able to procure relating to them,

E e 4   (mention'd

(mention'd p. 493.) being procured from thence. Only I have often thought that *Bard-ſay* near Wetherby in theſe parts receiv'd its name from the Bards their contemporaries; 'tis even yet a private retired place near the foreſt, proper for contemplation.

I am particularly pleaſed with one expreſſion in yours, that *there are no parties in the Republic of Letters*, for I am (as you kindly obſerve) an *honeſt man*, (let me add ſimple and plain hearted) and can converſe with great eaſe and ſatisfaction with both high and low, (tho' I cou'd wiſh all diſtinctions were laid aſide) and have correſpondents of both denominations. But you will pardon me for wiſhing that a Gentleman of ſo much humanity, learning, and curioſity, was, in one point, more of the ſentiments of the Catholick Church. Pardon, SIR, this ſingle expreſſion as proceeding from the affectionate deſires of a ſimple recluſe in his country cell, where he prays for peace and truth, and the welfare of all mankind. I ſhall not for the future diſturb you with any thing of this kind, but moſt readily ſerve you in any thing that lies in the power of,

SIR,

Your moſt faithful humble ſervant

RALPH THORESBY.

TO

Mr. TOLAND.

Bruſſels July 31, 1716.

SIR,

I Will not now make any excuſe for trou-
bling you with an account of what I
ſhall ſee abroad, ſince it is only in obedience
to your commands that I do it.

I ſet ſail from Dover to Calais about
twelve of the Clock on the the 12th of July
O. S. and arriv'd there five hours after,
which was the 23d N. S. (which you know
is uſed almoſt all over Europe). As ſoon as I
landed, the Soldiers of the Garriſon told me
I muſt go before the Governor, and the *In-
tendant de la Marine*, before I could go to
the Inn, which I accordingly did; there I
was ask'd my name, who I was, what I came
there for, and how long I intended to ſtay,
and as ſoon as I had anſwer'd their queſ-
tions they told me I might go.

Calais is but a ſmall town, much about the
bigneſs of Dover, but more compact; the harbour is well fortify'd, but that part of the
fortifications which is towards the land, is
old and out of order. You are not ignorant

norant that this Town belong'd formerly to the English, and it's the moſt part built by them, for the three principal Churches, and almoſt every thing that is ancient, had its origin from our fore-fathers. Here is a Garriſon of a thouſand men.

On the 25th I went for Dunkirk, which is eight leagues from Calais, I din'd in the way at Graveline, where there is a Garriſon of fifteen hundred men. This town lies upon the coaſt, and I was told the French King had once a deſign to make this a ſea-port, but Dunkirk was afterwards thought more convenient: it's juſt four leagues from Calais and three leagues from Mardyke, which laſt place is but one from Dunkirk. When I came by Mardyke I got out of the coach to go and view the Canal, which is a prodigious work and very large, for it's wide and deep enough to receive a firſt rate man of war, and capable now of containing even beyond the ſluice two hundred or two hundred and fifty ſhips; ſo that it may in time (that is whenever our enemies think there is occaſion) be as prejudicial to us as Dunkirk, or perhaps more, ſince it's ſo much nearer the ſtreights of Dover and Calais, as it's remov'd from Dunkirk, which laſt place, I think one of the prettieſt towns I ever yet ſaw. Though there is nothing very magnificent, yet there is nothing looks mean or poor: it's built moſt of brick, which upon

account

account of the colour refembles very much our ftone; the ftreets are large and well pav'd, which gives a good air to the place. I went to view the bafon and fortifications, which though ruin'd, yet the remains give a man an idea of the vaftnefs of the work, which I believe is the greateft the laft age has produc'd: there are two vaft moles which feem to rife like mountains a confiderable diftance in the fea, upon which forts were built, and form'd the mouth of the harbour. Whether it's fo far demolifh'd as that we may have nothing to fear from it, is of little confequence, fince Mardyke will as well ferve their turn.

On the 27th I left Dunkirk and travell'd on the fand of the fea almoft to Newport, which is five leagues and a half: it's a fmall but very clean town. This is the firft place out of the dominions of France: here is a Garrifon of feven hundred men paid by the Emperor. From hence to Bruges is fix leagues, which is a very large place and pretty well built, but prodigioufly crowded with Monafteries; and now upon the road one cannot travel in any common carriage but one is fure of the company of two or three fat Priefts. As I ftaid but one night at Bruges, fo I had little time to inform my felf of any thing remarkable here. From hence to Ghent is eight leagues, which I pravell'd by a boat drawn by horfes. Ghent is the capital of Flanders,

Flanders, and is very large and well built, but the walls take up a much greater circumference than what the houses fill up. I was here to see several of their Churches which were very fine, as indeed almost all the Churches in Flanders are. I was at a little Chappel, where they told me the Virgin MARY had cur'd a great many blind people, and the Pictures of them who had been cur'd were hung up in the Church; amongst the cur'd they shew'd me one who they said was an English Countess. But I could not learn her name. In the Town-house there are several very good Pictures containing the history of CHARLES the fifth, who you know was born here, and they shew the Chamber he was born in. On the 29th I left Ghent and came here: the road from Ghent to Bruffels is all pav'd with stone, and it's ten leagues or thirty English mile long; here on each side the way is as fine a Country as ever I saw in my life, and I never saw more plentiful crops of corn, or a finer soil. I observ'd they did not mow the Barley as we do, but reap'd it with a Sicle and set the corn up in Sheaves as we do wheat: I could not but wonder to see them plowing the lands before the corn was got off of the ground, which we never do in England, but a confiderable time after harvest. I din'd at a place call'd Aloft, just half way to Bruffels: it's upon the road from Ghent that you have the best view of Bruffels, which stands

upon

upon a hill that defcends gradually.   I fhall
fay no more of Bruffels now, but fhall conclude, SIR, your moft humble Servant.

T O

Mr. C * * *.

My Dear Friend,

THO' you well know my heart, yet I
cannot forbear putting you to a penny
charge, to receive my moft fincere acknowledgments for all your favours of all forts,
for which you fhall never want at leaft the
payment of gratitude.

As for the rich uncharitable company, in
which, you tell me you were t'other day,
I freely forgive them; looking upon men
of their difpofition, as much more requiring pity than my felf.   They are Lovers :
and all fuch, we know, have their judgments
no lefs blinded, than their tafte vitiated.
Money is the fole object of their affection,
and whatever is fo to any man, in that he
places his chiefeft happinefs : fo that 'tis natural for him not to confent any way to its
diminution, but to endeavour by all means
poffible the increafe of it; and in this purfuit he'll confequently perfevere, without reflecting

flecting on the uncertainty of the future, whether his treasure will ever descend to those for whom he destines it, or whether whoever enjoys it may not be both unthankful to him, and also in other respects unworthy of such a possession. I need not speak of those accidents in life, which are as common as unforeknown. But the man who can distinguish the use of mony from the abuse of it, who makes it is his servant and not his mistress, takes incomparably more pleasure in what he contributes to make easy his friends in distress, to relieve the poor and the needy, or to promote undertakings of public benefit, than in what he saves and hoards over and above the rules of prudent foresight. For I wou'd not be so understood, as if every man was not to look to the main chance, and to preserve his estate clear and intire : whatever any body does inconsistent with this, is neither generosity nor charity, but prodigality and profuseness. A man of sound understanding on whom Heaven has bestow'd a liberal mind, will easily perceive where the medium lyes, what he can spare, and what he ought to lay up.

Dear HARRY, a lecture of this kind wou'd be receiv'd as an affront, by the muck-worms you had lately in your company, and by their brethren every where ; as one, whose sins happen to be touch'd in a Sermon, thinks the preacher did particularly aim at him, tho'

he

he was not at all in his thoughts : but to
such as your self, that have done a thousand generous, kind, and charitable offices,
(which are far from being lost, tho' the re-
ceivers may prove unthankful or otherwise
undeserving ;) to such, I say, this Doctrine
sounds agreeably, and is truly relish'd by them,
being ever accompany'd with the inward satisfaction, that necessarily flows from all good
actions.

I can tell you however for your comfort, as
every thing rejoices in its like; that you are not
the only rich man, who knows how to do
handsom things : for, as I wrote to you not
long since, that we must ever thankfully
publish the beneficence of our friends ; so,
since the receipt of yours, Sir W * * *
S * * * (to whom I neither wrote nor sent
and who only accidentally heard of my in-
disposition) sent a servant to see how I did,
with a very affectionate Letter, and five
Guineas inclos'd in it. The manner of doing this has made a deeper impression upon
me, than if another had presented me with five
hundred Guineas in a disobliging way : as
most certainly the circumstances of giving
are sometimes no less disobliging, than those
of denying.

After my service to your brother and all
friends, I mean such as are truly so, were
they even poorer than my self, (for real

friend-

friendſhip knows no diſparity of conditions)
I am with all the faculties of my ſoul,
Honeſt Dear HARRY,

Your moſt oblig'd and moſt
faithful Servant.

TO

Mr. TOLAND.

Plymton, July 10, 1720.

SIR,

YOUR *Nazarenus* fell into my hands
but very lately, which muſt be my
apology, if I ſhould happen to anſwer the
two Problems you have propos'd, a little of
the lateſt.

The firſt Problem is thus:

" WHETHER, without having recourſe to
" miracles, or to promiſes drawn from the
" *Old Teſtament* (which is the ſame thing, if
" you don't take thoſe promiſes for wiſe
" foreſight) it can be demonſtrated by the
" intrinſic conſtitution of the Government
" or Religion of the Jews, how, after the
" total ſubverſion of their State for almoſt
" ſeventeen hundred years, and after the diſ-
" perſion of their nation over the whole
" habitable earth; being neither favour'd
                                        " nor

" not fupported by any potentate, but rather
" expos'd to the contempt and hatred of all
" the world: they have neverthelefs pre-
" ferv'd themfelves a diftinct people with all
" their ancient rites, excepting a very fmall
" number of ceremonies, they were neceffa-
" rily enjoin'd to practife within the bounds
" of Judea, and which they are no longer
" permitted to do? while that in the mean
" time the Inftitutions of the Egyptians, Ba-
" bylonians, Greeks, and Romans (nations
" that were much more powerful) are long
" ago entirely abolifh'd, and brought to no-
" thing: and that the names only of certain
" celebrated Religions fubfift yet in Hiftory;
" without even fo much as the names re-
" maining of fome other worfhips, that
" doubtlefs were neither lefs believ'd, nor
" lefs extended.

This Problem I find anfwer'd, as it feems
to me, to fatisfaction, in SPINOZA's *Tractatus Theologico-Politicus*, towards the end of
the third Chapter p. 61. of the octavo edition, printed 1674. Whofe argument I fhall
only enforce by faying, that it feems pretty
evident, when a man has once fuffer'd any
mark in his flefh, which cannot be defac'd
or repair'd, purely upon account of his Religion, he will not be inclin'd to be perfuaded out of it by any thing lefs than a de-
monftration; or elfe fome great temporal
advantages.

And that the Jews are not altogether impregnable to fair ufage, notwithſtanding Circumciſion it ſelf, we have an inſtance in the above cited page.

The ſecond Problem, you expreſs in this manner:

" WHETHER a fufficient reaſon can be af-
" ſign'd, drawn from the nature and frame of
" the Jewiſh Republic or Religion (without al-
" ledging miracles, or promiſes not account-
" ed miraculous, as aforeſaid) why, during
" the time that they were the independent
" Lords of their own country, and that their
" Government ſubſiſted in a flouriſhing con-
" dition ; they were perpetually inclin'd
" to the moſt groſs Idolatries, always in ſuf-
" penſe whether they ſhould follow BAAL or
" JEHOVAH, and having a ſtrong propenſity
" to mix or marry with the women of o-
" ther nations, contrary to their fundamen-
" tal Laws ? whereas, ſince their actual dif-
" perſion among theſe ſame nations, they
" are obſtinately careful to keep their race
" entire, without corruption or mixture :
" and that, notwithſtanding the moſt agree-
" able temptations or the moſt exquiſite tor-
" tures, they abhor beyond all expreſſion
" Idolatry of every kind ; but particularly
" the adoration of dead men (from which
" they are evidently exempt) as they are ſur-
" prizingly

" prizingly uniform in their worſhip and
" doctrine, which is not deny'd, by any body.

As to the firſt part of that Problem,
this too is in a great meaſure anſwer'd by
the ſame Author p. 293, and ſeveral of the
following pages.

To which I add, that as the mind of man,
eſpecially of the vulgar, ſeems of it ſelf to
be prone enough to Idolatry, that is, to worſhip the Deity under ſenſible Images, and
perhaps by degrees the Images themſelves,
they might eaſily in the time of the Judges,
ſlide into that Idolatry, partly thro' converſation with the idolatrous nations that were
intermix'd, and a fondneſs of being like their
neighbours, tho' enemies, who were probably
more polite than themſelves; and partly thro'
ignorance, which might be occaſion'd by want
of copies of the Law; which ignorance I gueſs
to be MICAH's caſe in the Appendix to the
Book of Judges : for MICAH ſeems to be
a perſon that meant well, Judges xvii. 13 :
and partly perhaps thro' lazineſs or an un-
willingneſs to go up to worſhip at the proper place. Judges xviii. 31.

As for the Kings, the ſame Author ſhews
that they had ſufficient reaſon not to be over
fond of the Levites. If ſo, I add, that 'twas
eaſy for the Kings to perſuade themſelves,
there was no great matter in ceremonies,

F f 2   that

that God might be worſhip'd in one place, as well as another, either with or without repreſentations: on the ſame principles as JEROBOAM did, thro' another motive. See JOSEPHUS p. 506 of L'ESTRANGE's oct. edit. and as eaſy to perſuade the people thro' the ſcarcity of copies of the Law. Which Law was found in JOSIAH's time after it had been long loſt.

As to the ſecond part of the ſecond Problem; I anſwer: 1. All that are in a ſtate of perſecution, are induſtrious to fortify themſelves and their children in the principles of their Religion, and more careful than at other times, in the practice of it.

2. Add to this, that if any one trangreſſes amongſt his own brotherhood in a foreign country, he has neither numbers nor great men to keep him in countenance, as he might have had perhaps upon many occaſions in his own country. They are already ſhun'd by ſtrangers, to be ſhun'd too by their own fraternity would be abſolutely intolerable.

The foundation of the whole ſeems to be Circumciſion: without Circumciſion probably they would not have continued a diſtinct people, nor without being a diſtinct people, been ſo obnoxious to the hatred and contempt of others, nor conſequently have had

that

that temptation, or rather that provocation to adhere fo ftrictly to their ancient rites.

An anfwer to this will be a very great favour to

SIR,

Your admirer and unknown humble Servant.

S * * * R * * *

TO

Mr. * * *.

SIR,

THO' the laft *Independent Whig* (1) be an incomparable Paper; yet, as it fometimes happens to the moft accurate compofitions, there is a flip of memory at the conclufion of it.

The *Tribe of* LEVI had not an equal *fhare* of Land with the others, nor an equal *right*; but only certain Cities with their fuburbs, fcatter'd throughout all the Tribes, for their more convenient attendance every where. Yet the Tribes, with refpect to their poffef-

Ff 3

fions,

(1) Numb. ix. Wednefday, March 16, 1720.

fions, were ftill in number twelve; that of Joseph, having been divided into two, namely, thofe of Ephraim and Manasseh. The Tythes and Offerings were given the Tribe of Levi, inftead of their fhare of the Land. *The Lord fpoke unto Aaron* (Numb. xviii. 20.) *thou fhalt have no inheritance in their Land, neither fhalt thou have any part among them: I am thy part, and thine inheritance, among the children of Ifrael.* This is often repeated and inculcated elfewhere. Yet, for all this, the Tribe of Levi was far from being in a worfe condition than their brethren. There was, on the contrary, much better provifion made for them than the reft, and with little or no labor to themfelves.

1. Thus, all the fin-offerings of all kinds were theirs, except fuch as were made in their own name or that of the whole Congregation, with thofe particular portions, which were to be confum'd by fire. See the entire 4th and 6th Chapters of Leviticus.

2. They had the like right to the trefpafs-offerings, with the like exceptions, as may be feen, Levit. vii. and elfewhere.

3. The fame is as true of the peace-offerings, which were many and of various kinds, Levit. xxiii. *& alibi.*

4. Theirs was the oil, that was offer'd by perfons infected with the Leprofy, Levit. xiv. 12, 13.

5. Alfo

5. Alſo what remain'd of the ſheaves of the firſt-fruits, whereof Levit. xxiii. 10.

6. The two wave-loaves, with the good things accompanying them, Levit. xxiii. 17.

7. The twelve huge loaves of ſhew-bread, renew'd every week, Levit. xxiv 9.

8. The remainder of the meat-offerings, Levit. vi. 16.

9. The skins of all ſacrific'd beaſts (no ſmall income) except ſuch as were wholly conſum'd with fire, Levit. vii. 8.

10. The breaſt and right ſhoulder of all the peace-offerings, and the heave-offerings, Levit. vi. 30, &c.

11. The cakes and the loaves, offer'd with the ſacrifices of thankſgiving, Levit. vii. 12, &c.

12. The like things accompanying the ram, offer'd by the Nazarites, Numb. vi. 17——20.

13. The firſt-born of all clean beaſts, that is of all beaſts good for any thing, without redemption, Numb. xviii. 15.

14. The firſt-fruits of all manner of grain and fruits, Numb. xviii. 13.

15. All the beſt of the oil, and all the beſt of the wine, &c. in firſt-fruits, Numb. xviii. 12.

16. The tythe of the tythes, paid by the Levites to the Prieſts, Numb. xviii. 28.

17. A cake of the firſt dough from every family, Numb. xv. 20.

18. The firſt-fruits of wool, from every one that had ſheep, Deut. xviii. 4.

19. All

19. All devoted things living or dead, particularly fields or farms not redeem'd before the year of Jubilee, Lev. xxvii. 16, 20, 28, &c.

20. Every trefpafs, that had none to claim it, Numb. v. 8.

21. The fhoulder, the two cheeks, and the maw of all beafts kill'd for daily ufe, Deut. xviii. 3.

22. The mony given for the redemption of the firft-born of men, Numb. xviii. 15.

23. The like for the redemption of the firft-born of unclean beafts, Num. xviii. 15, 16.

24. The tythes of every kind, which alone were an immenfe Revenue, *Paffim.*

25. The forty eight Cities with their fuburbs or liberties, Numb. xxxv. 2, &c.

Now, if the particulars of thefe and fuch other heads be confider'd, as feveral fums of mony from all mafters of families, a general poll-tax, bullocks, heifers, rams, lambs, ewes, goats, kids, doves, fpices, oil, wine, corn, fruits, wool, skins, ftuffs, flower, loaves, cakes, firftlings, wood for the Altar, and diverfe other fpecies too tedious to enumerate (befides that mony was to be given in exchange for many of them) the revenues of the Priefts might be truly call'd Royal; and, in effect, by virtue of thefe, they feiz'd on the Royalty it felf at laft. But feveral unanfwerable reafons may be given, why no fet of men among Chriftians, can derive the leaft claim from the Priefts and Levites, who

who were peculiarly adapted to the Jewish Theocracy; and were the Ministers of JEHOVAH the King of Israel, attending in his Palace, &c: whereas there was no manner of Priesthood instituted by JESUS CHRIST or his Apostles, the Elders, whereof we read in the New Testament, having been all Lay-men; and either the proper Magistrates of the Jewish corporations and communities, or such others set up by the first Christians in imitation of these, for the management of their own private affairs. Nothing in the world can be more easily prov'd than this. Priest, Altar, Sacrifice, &c, are as contrary to original Christianity, as Idolatry, Immolation, Augury, &c. Wherefore, the writer of *the Independent Whig* did very well, in calling the Christian Clergy, the pretended successors of the Jewish Priests: but it was a mistake to say, that the Tribe of LEVI had a right to the twelfth part of the lands, and that the incomes of the Priests were moderate. However, he's safe enough in the ignorance of his adversaries. I am with grateful respect,

S I R,

Your most faithful obedient Servant.

T O

T O

The Right Honourable

THE LORD SOUTHWELL.

London April 27, 1720.

My Lord,

IF I am guilty of any fault in not doing my felf the honor to write to you before now, my Lord MOLESWORTH muft anfwer for it, who told me you waited for the coming of a yacht from Ireland: and I was of opinion my felf, that a Letter directed to Mr. SMITH at the Cuftom-houfe, before your Lordfhip's certain arrival, might occafion fome miftake, which is eafier prevented than excus'd. But this apprehenfion being now remov'd by advices from Chefter, I gladly make ufe of the liberty you were pleafed to allow me of writing to you, as I fhall regularly continue to do, till I underftand from your Lordfhip that you are weary of the correfpondence.

Before all things I earneftly intreat you to accept of my fincereft thanks (the only return my gratitude enables me to make) for the happinefs of your acquaintance; which

I

as

as well on account of the honor it reflects on me, as the real improvement I have receiv'd by it, I shall ever infinitely value. I thank you especially for making me known to so many of our Countrymen, to whom I was a greater stranger before, than to most Nations of Europe. Tho' I dare not say, that Philosophy has eradicated all prejudices in favour of my native soil, nor that indeed it ought to produce this effect (since one may be no less a citizen of the world, than of any particular place, by embellishing one quarter, and delighting in it, more than another) yet I can faithfully assure your Lordship, that in the small efforts whereby I have endeavored to serve Ireland, I was acted rather by those principles which teach me what is due to all mankind, than by any byass to that Kingdom, in which I have spent so little of my time. Those eternal notions of Liberty and Slavery, I imbib'd with the first milk I suck'd from the Muses; those notions, I say, which were fortify'd in me by the conversation and writings of the ablest men in England, and which were absolutely perfected by the same means in Holland, as they shall direct my actions during the whole course of my life: so I neither know by the impulses of nature, nor was taught by the precepts of my masters, to restrain the blessings of them to any time or place; much less to make Ireland a single exception, and still by a greater absurdity to make acquest to be a

conquest,

conqueft, or that the conquerors fhou'd be as ill treated, if not worfe, than the conquer'd. Wherefore you may depend upon it, that I fhall lofe no time, nor fpare any pains to go on with the Work, which your Lordfhip's defires and my own inclinations have encouraged me to undertake. Materials flow in on me as faft as I can wifh : but on this fubject I fhall have the honour to entertain you more particularly in my next.

I heartily congratulate you on the no lefs furprizing than agreeable revolution, that has happen'd here fince your departure : but as well for your fake as my own, I do not think it proper to enter on the particulars either of the motives or the means, the prefent effects or the conjectural confequences of this happy Reconciliation of the Royal Family, till I am certain that my Letters come fafe to your hands. The fame reafon muft hold as to all other news, public or private; and I hope you'll think it none, that, with the jufteft fentiments of obligation and refpect, I am,

MY LORD,

Your Lordfhip's

moft faithful obedient fervant.

TO

T O

Mr. T O L A N D.

Breckdenſton near Dublin
June the 25th, 1720.

S IR,

I Shou'd be glad that any thing my Lord CASTLETON met with in my Lord SHAFTSBURY'S *Letters* to me wou'd encourage him to try for heirs to his honours and eſtate. I think he owes ſo much to his family and country. I was always of your opinion that thoſe Letters were very valuable for the reaſons you give, and had it in my thoughts that it wou'd be a good thing to publiſh them. But upon farther conſideration that my Lord SHAFTSBURY'S relations might take it amiſs that I divulge family ſecrets, and that it wou'd be conſtrued a piece of vanity (now much in uſe) for me to print my own commendations, (as you know there are ſuch in ſeveral of thoſe Letters,) I concluded it better to have ſuch publication deferr'd till after my death. If you have any good reaſons to think otherwiſe let me know them. You may, if you think fitting, communicate them to Mr. COLLINS, and take his opinion of them, and what is beſt to be done with them. I own I am proud enough of having been not only

I ſo

ſo intimate with that great man, but to have had a hand in the firſt forming of his mind to virtue. There are other great Miniſters now living for whom I endeavoured as much, but as they have forgot it, ſo will I. The Lord SHAFTSBURY was of a different temper, and carried on his friendſhip to my ſons, the eldeſt of which did him ſignal ſervice in Italy, where (at Naples) he died.

I will conſult friends here before I determine any thing touching the reprinting the Iriſh Pamphlet which I ſent you : and if they think it proper I will ſend you word. You may believe it to be S***'s; for he was here with me to get me to uſe my intereſt that no hardſhip ſhou'd be put upon the Printer, and did in a manner own it. I believe it was writ in haſte, for perſons do not always write alike.

I am glad to hear your Book is likely to ſwell to the bulk you ſpeak of. In Sir JOHN DAVY's Hiſtory of Ireland, how it came to paſs that it was not thoroughly ſubdued till King JAMES the firſt's time (whoſe Attorney General here he was) you will plainly find that the Parliaments of England never intermedled in the leaſt with the affairs of Ireland from the firſt conqueſt to the time he wrote. I have that Book here, and if you find it difficult for you to meet with it there, I will contrive ſome way to ſend you mine.

In

In anfwer to the offer about ferving me in any of the Subfcriptions now on foot; I fhou'd be glad enough to make one among them, and get a little money, (which I need to pay off fome debts) in any honeft Project. The time, I fuppofe, is over in the South-Sea Company. Sir T * * * J * * * whofe judgment and honefty is to be relied on, is beft to be advifed with in this, and you may do it if you pleafe in my behalf. I have good credit, having never yet, I thank my ftars, forfeited it in any one inftance, and fhall be beholding to your good friend Sir T * * * (for fo he has fignally fhewn himfelf to my very great pleafure and fatisfaction) if he can put me into a like method.

And as to the Harburg Project, I do not underftand what it is; but if I cou'd do it and become one of the undertakers, without great risk (or fubfcribers), you may fpeak to Sir A * * * of it. I am defirous of having my fmall oar in the public boat, and not too obftinately to refufe profit. Since the Nation is a fharing, I have contefted long enough, and may now without imputation come in for my part of it; tho' I believe I am too late for any fignal gain. However, this matter I refer to my friends, being only fure of one thing, that I have endeavour'd to deferve well both from Britain and Ireland. Adieu.

I am,
Your moft faithful
friend and fervant
MOLESWORTH.

T O

The Right Honourable

THE LORD MOLESWORTH.

London, June 25, 1720.

My Lord,

THE laſt I had the honor to write to you was from the South-Sea houſe, where I never was before that time. Sir T *** has generouſly kept his word with me, adding a further promiſe, that on the next ſuch occaſion, about three months hence, he'll procure me the liberty of another Sub-ſcription, any body elſe laying down the money, and on that ſcore going halves for the profit, than which there is nothing more common. I wiſh in the next you'll do me the favour to write to me, you wou'd pleaſe to mention him in a manner that may ſhew his kindneſs to me has oblig'd your Lord-ſhip, as ſeveral of my other friends have already thank'd him.

This will come the more naturally from your hands, not only as you are generally known to be my trueſt Patron, but likewiſe as your very name (ever auſpicious to Liber-ty) has been made uſe of to ſecure this Sub-ſcription

ſcription to me : for the very day before, the Directors, by reaſon of the multitude that offer'd to ſubſcribe, made a private order that no one perſon ſhou'd be in two Liſts, and that none except a Parliament-man ſhou'd ſubſcribe for a thouſand pounds. Upon this, Sir T *** put in your name for mine, as being ſure you wou'd not take it ill, ſince there was no time for asking your leave ; and that moſt of the Lords and Commons, who had voted againſt them, did ſubſcribe, without being ſuppoſed by ſo doing to have in the leaſt alter'd their judgment. In a word, there was no way of ſecuring my Subſcription but by a Parliament-man's name, and I my ſelf wou'd not be ſhelter'd by any name but yours, had he conſulted me, for which he had not time.

I was offer'd a thouſand pounds advantage three hours after the thing was done, and thirteen hundred this very day : but my benefactor aſſures me that at the opening of the Books it will be worth a great deal more. You may eaſily gueſs I will be govern'd by him in this point. Another ſuch job will make me as eaſy and independent as I deſire, without ever Stockjobbing more : ſince I may buy an annuity of two or three hundred pounds, tho' the purchaſe of land is got up to thirty years, and, if things go on at this rate, will mount much higher.

All things are in the utmoſt tranquillity. Private news I have none, and the public are only ſuch as the papers contain.

I am, &c.

T O

Sir T *** J ***.

S I R,

WHENEVER any man profeſt himſelf my friend, or at any time did or de-ſign'd me a favour, I was always gratefully inclin'd to do him what ſervice lay in my power, unleſs he became an enemy to the Liberty of our Country, in which caſe I hold all ties to be diſſolv'd, and all obligations can-cell'd. As I have known you for many years, not only under as fair a character as any Mer-chant in London, but likewiſe a moſt zea-lous friend to the Britiſh Conſtitution: ſo I cou'd not be unconcern'd to ſee you involv'd of late in the ſame difficulties with the reſt of the South-Sea Directors, whom I cannot perſuade my ſelf to be all equally guilty. You in particular have frequently expreſt to me your diſlike of ſeveral meaſures, when the whole town madly applauded them. You condemn'd the too great power that was lodg'd in a few hands, and the arbitrary uſe

they

they made of it; acting as it were by infpi-
ration (thefe are your own words) and publifhing their Refolutions but a very fmall time
before they were to be put in execution.

I am not acquainted enough with the nature of mercantile Companies, to account
why fuch as difapprove the conduct of their
fellow Directors, do not enter their Protefts,
or fignify their difallowance in fome publick manner, fo as to be matter of record.
But obferving your uneafinefs at almoft every
thing from a little before the third Subfcrip-
tion, I have been urgent with you, ever fince
the Parliament took this affair in hand, to
clear your felf with the fooneft, as believing you rather imprudent than criminal :
for I fhall never think ill of any one, of whom
I once thought well, till matters of fact make
it impoffible for me to think otherwife. I
have follicited you to be fpeedy and frank in
confeffing all you knew, (to which I found
you well difpofed) as the moft certain
way to fhew a man's innocence, if he be
really excufable: and having the honor to
wait fometimes on the right honourable the
Lord Vifcount MOLESWORTH (whofe fole
view I am confident is doing juftice to the
Public, without the leaft prejudice againft
any particular perfon) I propos'd to you to
wait upon him, and to be as candid as his
integrity and your cafe requir'd. You readily agreed, provided his Lordfhip wou'd ad-

mit

mit of it: and upon my reporting this to him, he did not think it adviſeable to ſee you without ſome more of the Committee were preſent.

This, as far I can remember, was on Wedneſday the 18th of January; and accordingly you met ſome of the Committee at his Lordſhip's lodgings the next day. To what paſt there I am an utter ſtranger, for I cou'd not be ſo impertinent as to ask his Lordſhip, what I was ſure before hand he wou'd never tell me. All the diſcourſe I had with your ſelf that day was about your Treaſurer, whoſe flight you much lamented, becauſe he cou'd clear and prove what was in no other mortal's power, and that there wou'd be the utmoſt intricacy and confuſion without him. You added, that you little thought of Mr. KNIGHT's intention to withdraw himſelf, when that very Saturday on which he fled, you were earneſtly exhorting him (in conjunction, I think, with Sir ROBERT CHAPLIN) to give the Committee a full account of every thing; and that hereupon he ſaid, *I know the other Directors will lay all upon you of the Committee of the Treaſury, and that you'll charge me of courſe: but if it comes to that, and that I muſt be oblig'd to ſay all I know, I ſhall diſcover ſuch things as will amaze the world,* or words to this effect. This declaration, you ſaid, had taken from you all ſuſpicion of his deſigning an eſcape, and this is the ſubſtance of what I remember;

remember; and I repeat thefe things now, to the end that if ever my name fhou'd be mention'd on occafion of the fervice I heartily defign'd you, whether effectual or not, you may be fatisfy'd that I acted in all things according to the tenor of this Letter.

I wifh you a happy iffue out of all your troubles, and am, with the greateft fincerity,

S I R,

Your moft faithful
obedient fervant.

A Letter written in the name of a Member of the Houfe of Commons to another Member.

S I R,

I AM very forry I fhou'd be oblig'd to go into the country at this juncture, when the public credit, and a confiderable fhare of my private property, lie at ftake. But domeftic affairs indifpenfably require my abfence for near a month. I am not, however in any pain about the iffue, ·fince moft of the Members of our Houfe are fo deeply interefted themfelves, over and above their duty to the State, without whofe flourifhing condition, we muft needs all be miferable. **My**

G g 3 opinion

opinion concerning the Directors of the South-Sea Company, I'll give as frankly as you defire it, and the rather, becaufe your worthy relation, of whofe honour and ability I am equally convinc'd, is chofen one of the Committee to enquire into their conduct. Neither my gains nor loffes by the South-Sea are fo extraordinary, as to render me too fevere or indulgent. But as my concerns requir'd, and my education enabl'd me to examine into this affair with the utmoft application, both in juftice to my felf and my friends; fo I have taken all proper methods to gain the trueft information. Among other things, I have carefully read over the feveral Accounts and Papers which have been laid by the Directors before the Houfe of Commons, and made the ftricteft enquiry, that I cou'd poffibly, into the behaviour of thofe Gentlemen, efpecially with relation to the feveral fteps they took in the execution of the Scheme which was intrufted to their management. The refult I fhall briefly and impartially now lay before you.

In the firft place, it appears to me (and I believe will be fo found upon examination) that the Scheme was form'd, and carry'd on without being communicated to the Court of Directors, or even mention'd to them, till after it was open'd to the Houfe of Commons by the Chancellor of the Exchequer. About three millions of money were in this manner offer'd by the undertakers without their

knowledge

knowledge or confent; which you'll own to be a pretty affuming way of proceeding, but perfectly of a piece with their fubfequent management. In the fequel of this negotiation, the Bank intervening, and offering to take the Scheme, it was by fome people judg'd proper, in order to defeat the propofal of the Bank, to have a power lodg'd in the Sub-Governor and Deputy-Governor to offer whatever they fhould think fit : a power perhaps the greateft that ever was trufted to any two men, and for the confequences of which thofe only feem refponfible, who were fo forward to grant it, while others deem'd it unreafonable and dangerous. One of the many bad confequences was, that feven millions and a half of the Company's money, being very near two thirds of every man's property in that corporation, was given at once. If this be the cafe, as I have all the reafons in the world to believe it was, then I can not with any juftice think, that fuch of the Directors who had no hand in thefe tranfactions, who knew nothing of the Scheme till it was brought into the Houfe of Commons, and who probably diflik'd it as much as any others, when they underftood how dear they were to pay for it, can be faid to be the authors of the mifchiefs, which this unaccountable undertaking has brought upon the Nation. Mifchiefs they are with a witnefs, and which I am as far from extenuating, as in my ftation I fhall be from fcreening the guilty : but I am alfo perfuaded

that

that with me you will be for diſtinguiſhing
thoſe who may be innocent, and no leſs
ſufferers than the loudeſt accuſers.

I do not find in the general Account of
the Proceedings of the Directors, nor yet in
their Minutes, any orders given for ſelling
of Stock for the Company's account. If they
who peculiarly proſecuted the Scheme, gave
directions for the ſale of the five hundred and
odd thouſand pounds, which were diſpos'd of
about the time of the paſſing of the Bill,
without acquainting the other Directors with
it (a circumſtance that cannot eſcape the impartial attention of the Committee) how can
that crime be in any juſtice imputed to thoſe,
who were entirely ignorant of it? In God's
name let it reſt where it ought—— but, for reaſons you may eaſily gueſs, I ſhall not dwell
on this particular.

The Money Subſcriptions were taken (as
we all know) and hurry'd on in ſo incom-
prehenſible a manner, that this way of proceeding cou'd not, I dare ſay, be the reſult
of a number of men acting with cool and
deliberate thoughts. 'Tis highly probable
that the peculiar contrivers of the Scheme
did in their private meetings concert all things
beforehand, without the participation or
concurrence of their brethren; and ſo impos'd what they pleas'd upon the reſt of the
Court, which conjecture of mine, I fancy, will
prove

prove to be matter of fact, when the Directors are examin'd by the Committee. In a word, what thro' the defign of fome, the ftupidity of others, and the avarice of all, the fuccefs of the managers was fo great, and the applaufe they met with fo univerfal, that their authority became abfolutely incontrollable in the Court of Directors; nor had it been fcarce fafe to have oppos'd them, without the imputation of obftructing credit, even among thofe without doors, they were at that time fo much in favor with the inconfiderate people. Thus every Director was oblig'd to fubmit to a fmall proportion allow'd him for himfelf and friends. So the bulk of thefe Subfcriptions was left to the difpofal of the Sub and Deputy - Governors, to ferve perfons of diftinction, &c. This, I am credibly inform'd, occafion'd a great deal of murmuring among fome of the other Directors, but to no purpofe: for the pill muft be fwallow'd, and you are too well acquainted with the nature of fuch Courts in other Companies, to imagine that Protefts cou'd be either practicable or ufeful.

No fooner did a good Sum of Money arife by the Subfcriptions, but it naturally brought on the queftion, *what to do with it?* 'Tis rumour'd abroad, and has been privately told me with much affurance, that feveral of the Directors would have had this money apply'd to the paying off of *the Redeemables,*

deemables, and infifted hard upon it : but this fuited not the defigns of the Scheme, and fo it was carry'd for lending money on Stock and Subfcriptions. With what pernicious confequences this fatal refolution has been attended, too too many felt to their forrow : but I can never be of the mind, nor I prefume any of the Committee or the reft of the Houfe, that thofe Directors who oppos'd it, are in this refpect culpable, or ought any way to fuffer for it.

You know as well as I or any man, that when Stock begun to fall, great crowds, and among them perfons of the firft Quality, were daily at the South-Sea Houfe, preffing the Directors to buy. A Cabal is fufpected to have then fold a vaft quantity of Stock, which is a thing deferving the niceft enquiry. If they influenc'd counfels within, and the Company's money was made ufe of to buy their Stock, I take it to be a heinous crime in thofe who were the promoters of fuch a defign. But they, on the other hand, who innocently gave their confent to it, in order to fupport the price, and hinder the finking of the Stock, after Subfcriptions had been taken at a thoufand, and the Redeemables at eight hundred, do not, in my opinion, deferve any blame ; fince they did it with a good intent, and cou'd not forefee the fuddain and precipitate fall of the Stock.

Thus,

Thus, SIR, I have given you the beft information I cou'd about this matter. I have
learnt from my own and the experience of
paft times, not to be fway'd by popular ob-
loquy, no more than by popular favor.
There's always a mean in fuch cafes, tho'
the bent of the multitude is generally
to extremes, being naturally more addicted
to confound than to diftinguifh. Wherefore
I cannot but think people are too fevere in prejudging and condemning the Directors by the lump: for as I hope, and
fhou'd be very glad, to fee the real Authors of
our prefent uneafineffes brought to condign
Punifhment; fo I fhou'd be as forry, that any
honeft well-meaning Director fhou'd fuffer
for mifmanagement he cou'd not help, and
which 'tis very likely he difapprov'd. But
thefe are reflections that cannot efcape the
wifdom or juftice of the Committee, and I
hope to be with you my felf, before the matter is finally decided. I am, &c.

T O

TO

Mr. * * *.

May 21, 1721.

I Have juſt read over Dr. HARE's new Piece (1). I ſee he has learn'd from Dr. S * * * to write ſcandal in his *Title-page.* But I am apt to believe, that, in the drawing up of the Anſwer it ſelf, he ſtudy'd no pattern ; and, leaſt of all, his own. He has in my opinion condeſcended to the meaneſt of all abuſes ; and were I to draw up a charge againſt him, I wou'd do it in the words of SOCRATES, which PLATO (in his *Apology*) introduces him ſpeaking againſt MELITUS. Ἀδικεῖν φημὶ ἄρεον, ὅτι σπουδῇ χαριεντίζεται, ῥαδίως εἰς ἀγῶνας καθισὰς ἀνθρώπους, περὶ πραγμάτων προσποιούμενος σπουδάζειν καὶ κήδεσθαι, ὧν ουδὲν πώποτε τούτῳ ἐμέλησεν. It ſhews, I think, no great concern for truth to declare, as he does at his firſt ſetting out, that his (2) having promis'd to anſwer the Biſhop was the only motive for doing it. 'Tis a happy expedient he has found out, of mixing his obſervations on real or ſuppos'd Atheiſtical Books and

---

(1) *Scripture vindicated from the Miſinterpretations of the Lord Biſhop of Bangor : in his Anſwer to the Dean of Worceſter's Viſitation Sermon concerning Church-Authority.*

(2) *Pref. Page 1.*

and Persons, with confutations of the Bishop. This is such an ungenerous insinuation, that (if I cou'd not otherwise guess at the Dean's temper) I must think it owing to the most virulent malice: as if there were something so agreeing between them, that they cannot well be separated. But perhaps he thinks himself qualify'd to be a Drawcansir in controversy. If so, I don't question, but the Bishop will soon prove him mistaken: tho' he is resolv'd, it seems, not to heed whatever is advanc'd against him for the future. Sure no man had ever less reason to insult his adversary with a Q. E. D. at the conclusion of a Paragraph; in which, as far as I am able to judge, whatever he dwells on, either makes for the Bishop, instead of refuting him, or is inconclusive, or entirely false. One manifest contradiction in it, I cou'd not help taking notice of. We are told (in page 6) that Κύριοι, when given to civil Governors, is an honourable appellation only; and that *Dominus* is the rendring, not of Κύριος, but of Δεσπότης. This he himself refutes in page 9, where he says Κύριος is equivalent to Δεσπότης, and signifies *a property of the Governor in the persons govern'd.*

As to his Quotations for settling the sense of the word πείθεσθαι, I am not without some suspicion, that they will all recoil upon himself. ARISTOPHANES I am confident (to whom he chuses particularly to appeal, as writing

in

in the familiar ſtile) can't ſerve his purpoſe. This Author being a favorite of mine, I was eaſily induc'd to examine all the places, where he uſes this word : and I aſſure my ſelf it no where ſignifies *to obey*, in the ſtrict ſenſe of the word. It occurs three times in his PLUTUS :

Ἕτεροι δ᾽ ἐπλούτουν Ἱερόσυλοι Ῥήτορες,
Καὶ συκοφάνται, ἢ πονηροὶ· ΚΑΡ. πείθομαι. (3)
and again,

Ὃν ἐγὼ φιλῶ μάλιϛα μεῖὰ σέ. ΠΛ. πείθομαι. (4)
and again,

Τί ἂν ἂν, τὸ πρᾶγμ᾽ εἴη ; πόθεν καὶ τίνι τρόπῳ,
Χρεμύλ@ πεπλύ]ηκ᾽ ἐξαπίνης ; ὒ πείθομαι. (5)

And in his NUBES, where a ſtupid illiterate fellow is ſhewn a Map of the world,

Αὕ]η δὲ σοι γῆς περίοδ@ πάσης. Ὁρᾷς ;
Αἰδε]μὲν Ἀθῆναι. ΣΤΡ. τί σὺ λέγεις; ὒ πείθομαι. (6)

In all theſe places it is impoſſible the word ſhou'd mean any thing, but *I believe it is as you ſay*, or *I cannot be perſuaded it is ſo*. The ſame ſenſe is to be put upon it in this verſe of his ACHARNENSES :

Κάκιϛ᾽

(3) Ver. 30.
(4) Ver. 251.
(5) Ver. 335,
(6) Ver. 207.

Κάκιςʹἀπολοίμεν, εἴ τί τούʹͺων πείϑομαι. (7)

In the NUBES, where a father is endeavouring to prevail upon his ſon, to forſake a looſe way of living, by all the arts of a mild perſuaſion, we have the following words :

᾽Ω παῖ, πιϑῦ. ΦΕΙ. τὶ ἂν πιϑῦμαι δῆτά σοι (8) ;
ΣΤ. Ἐκςρεψον ὡς τάχιςα τοὺς σαυʹοῦ τρόπ‍ͺς,
Καί μάνϑανʹ ἐλϑὼν ἅʹγ ἐγώ παραινέσω.
ΦΕΙ. Λέγε δὴ τί κελεύεις ; ΣΤ. χϳ τὶ, πείσει ;
ΦΕΙ πείσομαι. (8)

After this, Juſtice is repreſented making uſe of ſeveral arguments to gain him over to her ſide : but Injuſtice ſhews him, to what reproach he will be expos'd, if he ſuffers himſelf to be perſuaded by the other :

Εἰ ταῦϑʹ, ὦ μειράκιον πείσει τύτῳ, &c. (9)

The inſtance out of the VESPAE, upon which the Dean lays ſo great a ſtreſs, is far from declaring in his favour. An old fool is there repreſented, reſolving to continue his practice of frequenting the Courts of Judicature :

(7) Ver. 151.
(8) Ver. 87.
(9) Ver. 996.

cature: and his fon endeavouring by feveral arguments to diffuade him from it, the *Chorus* advifes him to comply with his requeft:

Πιθοῦ, πιθοῦ λόγοισι, μήδ᾽ ἄφρων γένη. (10)

Can it be faid that the father (whofe power over the fon, according to the Dean, ought to be very great) is here bid to obey the fon? The father all this while continues filent. The *Chorus* tells the fon, this filence is owing to his being convinc'd of his miftake; and that he will now confent to do, what before he cou'd not be perfuaded to:

῎Α σοῦ παρακελεύοντος οὐκ ἐπείθετο, (11)
Νῦν οὖν ἴσως τοῖς σοῖς λόγοισι πείθεται,
Καὶ φρονεῖ μεθιςὰς ἐς τολοιπὸν τὸν τρόπον,
Πειθόμενος τε σοί᾽ ——

The fon continues to prefs him to a compliance,

῎Ιθ᾽, ὦ πατερ, πρὸς τῶν θεῶν ἐμοὶ πιθῶ. (12)

To which he replies, τί πείθομαι σοί; and upon his fon's telling him, not to concern himfelf with judicial proceffes, he anfwers,

(10) ver. 728.
(11) ver 744.
(12) ver. 757.

Τοῦτ᾽

—————————————————— Τοῦτο δὲ (13

'Αδης διακρινεῖ πρότερον, ἤ 'γὼ πείσομαι.

In all thefe paffages, which very unluckily
for fome body follow fo clofely in the fame
Scene, and which give light to each other, it is
manifeft that the word has not the fenfe the
Dean wou'd make it confefs ; but only *to be
or not to be perfuaded, to comply or difagree.*
In the AVES of the fame Poet, where a perfon has a propofal to make, which, if accepted, he thinks will be of great fervice to
the Republic of Birds, we meet with the following words :

῎Η μεγ' ἐνορῶ βούλευμ'ἐν 'Ορνίθων γένει, (14)
Καὶ δύναμιν, ἤ γένοιτ' ἀν, εἰ πείθεσθέ μοι.
ΕΠ. τί σοι πιθώμεθ'; ΠΕΙ. ὅ,τι πίθοισθε; Πρῶ-
τα μὲν, &c.

Here it can fignify nothing, but *to follow advice :* and afterwards, where the fame perfon
feconds the *Chorus,* in defiring an interview
with the Nightingale, it can't be faid any
obedience is demanded.

῎Ω τοῦτο μὲν νὴ Δί' αὐτοῖσιν πιθᾖ. (15)

(13) ver. 759.
(14) ver. 163.
(15) ver. 662.

Again we find this terrible word in his LY-
SISTRATA.

Κ𐅵δέποθ' ἑκουσα τ'ανδϱὶ τῷ μῷ πείσομαι. (16)

This is the paſſage in which the Dean ſeems
to triumph, when he obſerves, it is here us'd
of unwilling obedience. But he's ſtrangely
miſtaken in the meaning of it. The Athe-
nians are ſuppoſed by the Poet to declare
war againſt the Lacedemonians; and the
women, not knowing how to ſpare their
husbands, endeavour to oblige them to make
peace. Till this is accompliſh'd, they bind
themſelves by oath not to admit them to their
embraces. LYSISTRATA in the name of the
reſt reads the oath, declaring ſhe will ſuffer no man to careſs her; that ſhe will ſtay
at home, and adorn her ſelf as much as poſſible, to appear the more engaging in her
husband's eyes; and, that when ſhe has by
theſe arts enflam'd him, ſhe will refuſe to
ſatisfy his deſire.

Κ𐅵δέποθ' ἑκουσα τ'ανδϱὶ τῷ μῷ πείσομαι. (17)

'Tis ſtrange the Dean ſhou'd interpret a modeſt expreſſion for love-familiarity, to be
obedience. His Lady, I believe, is of another mind. I forbear to mention, that the
phraſe

(16) ver. 223.
(17) Ubi ſupra.

phrafe ἐκ ἐκων πείθεσθαι does not mean to be
unwilling to obey in any good author. In
PLATO efpecially, who often makes ufe of
it, it can fignify nothing but *not eafily to be
perfuaded.* Οὐκ ἐκων πείθεται, ἢ ῥαδίως ἐθέλει
πείθεσθαι, ου πάνυ ευθέως ἐθέλει πείθεσθαι, are
with him equivalent expreffions. Thofe I
have alledg'd are all or moft of the places
in ARISTOPHANES, where this fame word
πείθεσθαι is to be feen; in none of which, I
fancy, will it be found big with that authority the Dean contends for.

As to the more ferious part of the argument, where he does not refute himfelf
(which I think is often the cafe) I fee nothing but what the Bifhop has already anfwer'd. I fhou'd be glad to be inform'd, what
relation a confiderable part of his Book has
to the prefent Controverfy. He is very fond,
I obferve, of marginal notes; one of which
(I mean his emendation of HORACE) I fuppofe was introduc'd to fix to himfelf the reputation of a judicious Critic. I was the
more furpriz'd at this, becaufe, in the *Poft-
fcript* of his *Sermon,* he promifed the Bifhop,
that he wou'd not turn to any other fubject
to recover that character.

TO
Mr. TOLAND.

*Albemarle-ſtreet, January
the 5th, 1721-2.*

SAturday night about nine I received yours of that day, which gives me ſuch a diſmal account of your ill ſtate of health, that I was extremely concern'd at the condition I found you were in, I doubt for want of neceſſaries.

I cannot forbear wiſhing you were in town, for I doubt you cannot eaſily get ſuch broths and bits of eaſy digeſtion as I ſhou'd take care to procure for you. Your Landlady may be a very good woman, and have a great reſpect for you, but her poverty may prevent her from providing ſuch ſort of victuals and drinks, as are proper for a ſick man reduced to ſo weak a condition as I find you are. Indeed I expected you every day in town after the Letter I wrote to you laſt week, not imagining you had been ſo much out of order : tho' I ſaw by your looks that a fit of ſickneſs was growing upon you, which I hop'd your Vomits and Purges had prevented in a great meaſure.

I intend

I intend to follicite the Peer your old ftingy acquaintance and my neighbour, and fee whether a Letter, which I fhall fend him, will move him once in his life to be generous and charitable.

Your reflexions upon the Phyficians, and the Injuftice of the World are very right; but you muft not indulge melancholy thoughts at fuch a time. Let it fuffice you to know, that although my circumftances are narrow enough, you fhall never want neceffaries whilft I live. I am fenfible that bare neceffaries are but cold comfort to a man of your fpirit and defert; but 'tis all I dare promife. Tis an ungrateful age, and we muft bear with it the beft we may, till we can mend it. Adieu, be cheerful, and think of going with me for Ireland.

Yours fincerely,
MOLESWORTH.

TO THE SAME.

Munday night 9 a-Clock.

I AM forry to find you continue fo ill, and yet dare not prefcribe any thing for you: no forts of Quacks have credit with you, and I can recommend nothing to you but your own kitchen Phyfic. Veal broth with

H h 3

barley,

barley, or (if you be enclined to a loofenefs) with rice boiled in it, is very proper. 'Tis a very fickly time: there is a rot among our Lords, five or fix of them are dropt off within this week, yet little lofs to the Public.

I am glad you got the Madera, and wifh I had a ftock of my own to fend you more. I beg'd the bottle I fent you from Doctor WELWOOD, for the right fort is not to be bought. I writ the moft moving Letter I cou'd invent to your ftingy Peer, and he excufed his writing an anfwer; but by word of mouth told my man, that he had already fent you fomething, meaning, as I fuppofe, the chetif prefent my Lady H * * * mentions. 'Tis a fad monfter of a man, and not worthy of further notice to be taken of him.

I wonder your appetite does not mend in that fine air: 'tis a fign your diftemper has not done with you.

Adieu, let me hear from you now and then, fince I am not able to fee you.

Yours

MOLESWORTH.

T O

To * * *.

S IR,

A S I wou'd never serve my friends by halves, were I in a capacity to be useful to them; so I shall set no other bounds to my good wishes in their behalf, but what nature her self has irrevocably set : and therefore, that all the years of your life, and those of each in your hopeful family, may be attended with health and prosperity, is my very hearty and unfeign'd wish, this year and as long as I live.

The day after I had the honor to see you in London, I fell mighty ill, having been lingring before; and the Doctor that was call'd to me, made me twenty times worse, if possible. All acknowledge that he had like to kill me. I was brought hither the Saturday following (which was the next before Christmas) and have never since been able to go out of my Chamber, scarce to walk cross it for some time. From that day to this I never tasted a bit of meat, being solely confin'd to broths and other liquids; not by the Doctors, but my stomach, which refuses and throws out every thing else : *sit venia*. Had not my Lady H * * * flatter'd

H h 4   me

me more than once in her Letters, that you would be so kind as to call on me; I shou'd have given notice to you before, as to one of my best friends, of the condition I am in, tho' very perceptibly better than I was. I need say no more on this subject.

The last time I was at your house, seeing the young Ladies drudging at the longwinded and unweildy *Cleopatra*, I promis'd to accommodate them with entertainment of that kind, that should please them much more; and especially *Zayde*, the best understood of all Romances. I thought then to be the bearer my self, but since I cannot yet be so happy, I take the liberty to send it now; and, when they have done with this, I shall send 'em another.

I am,

S I R,

Your most faithful humble servant.

T O

TO

Mr. TOLAND.

Thurſday, Feb. 8, 1721-2.

Dear S I R,

I Began to be very uneaſy at not hearing from you for eight or ten days together, and had order'd my man to walk to Putney this morning, when I receiv'd your Letter laſt night.

The return of the ſpring, and your keeping to kitchen Phyſic, will reſtore you to health. I would not have you venture a-broad too early, altho' I long to ſee you. Among other things, I wou'd ſhew you the moſt noble Collection of Papers, and authentic Records for the writing a Hiſtory of the late Wars (from King WILLIAM's death to Queen ANNE's Peace) that you can poſſibly imagine. The Colonel L * * * and I would deſire your aſſiſtance, and wou'd endeavour to make you find your account in ſo doing, for ſo much of your time and pains as ſhould be employ'd that way. But 'tis time enough to talk of this, when you are reſtor'd to perfect health.

My Lady H * * * is a perſon very much be-yond the rank of our modern Ladies. I have

3 always

always efteem'd her as fuch, and fhe has as conftantly made good my opinion. You and I might give twenty inftances of this. But none pleafes me better at prefent than her kindnefs and charity for you.

I think'tis very wholefome for you not to be troubled with publick news, unlefs you were better. You will come into a new world when you get once abroad again, and every thing will be ftrange and diverting to you one way or other. Our weather is too good for the feafon of the year : but do you keep to a great fire fide till March be far advanc'd. Our Parliament will be up in a fortnight, and I intend to fit in no future one.

Adieu.

Yours,

MOLESWORTH.

T O

T O

The Right Honourable

THE LORD MOLESWORTH.

Putney, Friday-Noon.

MY LORD,

WHEN I feem'd to be in a fair way of mending, my old pains in my thighs, reins, and ftomach, feiz'd me violently two days ago ; with a total lofs of appetite, hourly reachings, and very high colour'd water. I take it for granted, that thefe are fymptoms of approaching Gravel, and therefore I comfort my felf with the thoughts, that when this Gravel comes, I fhall together with it be difcharg'd from my pains.

In my laft, I told your Lordfhip, that tho' your refolution of ferving in no future Parliament, might be beneficial to your felf, it wou'd be detrimental to your Country : but if I had not been in hafte to finifh a long Letter, I fhould have added, that upon fecret thoughts, even your Country wou'd be a gainer by a retirement from bufinefs at this age. My reafons and examples for fupporting this affertion are numerous. Yet

4   confi-

considering my prefent unfitnefs for writing, I fhall only trouble you with the example of CICERO, who during the feven year's fpace that he was forcibly kept out of bufinefs, wrote all thofe incomparable Books, which are much more ufeful to the world, than the whole courfe of his Employments. The great noife he made in the Forum has not contributed near fo much to his Immortality, as the fruits of his Retirement, whereof neverthelefs we have but the leaft part remaining. In like manner, MY LORD, that excellent work, wherein you have made fuch progrefs, and which feems to refemble fo nearly CICERO *de Republica,* will be a nobler task, and more ufeful to mankind, than any Senatorial efforts : *nec aliud fcribendi genus tam è dignitate veftra mihi videtur.*

I am, &c.

T O

TO

Mr. TOLAND.

March 1, 1721-2.

Dear TOLAND,

I Wonder I hear nothing from you or of you : you muſt needs be very ill, or careleſs ; I had much rather it were the laſt. I hope altho' I do not ſend you ſupplies (ſuch ſmall ones as I can afford) yet that you wou'd be ſo free as to ask me in caſe you wanted them, for I am one of thoſe who with a friend deſire freedom, and expect to be told when other reſources fail. Pray let me hear from you often. I am ſometimes very much indiſpoſed, ſometimes tolerably well in health ; now I am the latter, but that may not continue.

You will ſee that I am embark'd in a grand affair, no leſs than ſtanding for Weſtminſter. I have employ'd all my friends as ſollicitors and runners about, and great hopes are given me. I am ſorry you are not in a ſtate of health to do me ſervice. Believe me, when I tell you, you ſhall fare as I do,

and

and if that be not extraordinary well, blame not.

Your affectionate
friend and servant,

MOLESWORTH.

Mr. TOLAND's
A N S W E R.

Putney, March 2, 1721-2.

MY LORD,

I Was never a careless correspondent; or were I so to any, sure I am, it should not be of all mankind to your Lordship. Neither was it for not needing assistance of my friends, I have been so long silent; but by reason of almost incessant pains, and very extraordinary weakness. Two or three days before your servant call'd here last, I grew much worse than I was; and from a mending state (the vigour of my mind increasing, tho' with little influence on the infirmity of my body) I relaps'd again into all my former symptoms, more frequent and malignant than ever. This has oblig'd me to put my self into the hands of a Physician, who I believe to be an honest man, prepares his own medicines, and explains every thing he does to me. He
has

has already put me to feveral little expences, fome of them extremely ufeful to my poor corpufcle, as four dimitty waftcoats, which a vifit from Sir T *** J *** enabled me to pay. I need not defcend to more particuculars, ready pence going neceffarily out every day.

Since you will embark once more on that troublefome fea, I heartily wifh you all good luck, and wifh I had been able to run for you night and day, which with great ardor I wou'd. I am, with the utmoft truth and zeal,

MY LORD,

Your Lordfhip's

*moft humble and
moft obedient fervant,*

F I N I S.

AN

APPENDIX,

CONTAINING

SOME PIECES

FOUND AMONG

Mr. *TOLAND*'s

PAPERS.

OF THE
IMMATERIALITY
OF THE
S O U L,
AND ITS
DISTINCTION
FROM THE
B O D Y:
BY
Mr. BENJAMIN BAYLY, M.A.
Rector of St. JAMES's in Bristol.

IN A
LETTER TO ***.

SIR,

I T is with no small pleasure and in-struction that I have read those Papers, that lately pass'd between you and the learned and reverend Mr. CLARKE, concerning the *Immateriality of the Soul*; and although it would be too great presump-

tion

tion in me, to pretend to determine on which side the advantage in that Controverſy lay, yet certainly you engage me to you too powerly in ſome particulars, and if I may not ſay you demonſtrate againſt Mr. CLARKE, yet I and the whole world muſt ſay, you demonſtrate moſt evidently your own incomparable parts and underſtanding. So that if a man ſhould fancy you worſted in that diſpute, yet however it was not Mr. CLARKE that worſted you, tho a very learned and ingenious man; but that invincible thing, Truth, which at that time peradventure one might conceit your enemy. But let that be as it will, my intention is not to meddle in it, but rather to propoſe to you an Argument of ſomewhat a different kind, and which ſeems to me freer from exception. And as your great Candour and Ingenuity, and the general Reputation you have for a man of unſpotted virtue, as theſe make you highly deſerve any endeavours that can be uſed, to ſet you right in matters of an important nature; ſo the ſame virtues, I am ſure, muſt render any ſuch endeavours highly acceptable to you, from whomſoever they proceed, and how weak ſoever they ſhould prove. 'Tis true, you profeſs to believe the Soul immortal, from the authority of divine Revelation, and becauſe you profeſs to believe this grand principle of all Religion, it would be the utmoſt uncharitableneſs in any man to queſtion it; eſpecially, when no contradiction, but the higheſt agreeableneſs

ableneſs to this belief, is found in your life and converſation; but how to make this belief agreeable to your ſentiments about the Soul, is verily a difficulty with me; and if I could have reconciled this, or made you conſiſtent with yourſelf, I ſhould not have troubled you on this point, notwithſtanding you had held the Soul corporeal. I ſhall wave any farther introduction or ceremony to you, and lay before you the argument itſelf, which, if you pleaſe to conſider, and give your thoughts on it, you will both ſhew me an extraordinary civility, and perhaps give ſome farther light to the ſubject, upon which you have been lately employ'd.

THE Argument is in PLATO (1); and as his writings you know are, it proceeds by way of Dialogue, between SOCRATES and ALCIBIADES. The ſubſtance of it, I ſhall endeavour to tranſlate, and then make ſome remarks upon it.

" *Socra.* Who is he that diſcourſes
" with you? Is it not SOCRATES? And who
" is he that hears? Is it not ALCIBIADES?
" *Alcib.* Doubtleſs. *Socra.* And what is this
" buſineſs of diſcourſing? Is it any thing but
" a man's uſing ſpeech? Are not theſe the
" ſame? *Alcib.* It is not to be deny'd. *Socra.* Is not then he that uſes a thing, and

(1) PLAT. Alcib. 1ſt.

" the

" the thing used, different, distinct from one
" another? *Alcib.* How say you, SOCRATES?
" *Socra.* To the purpose. Consider any han-
" dy-craftsman. Is he not different from the
" tools and instruments that he uses in his
" work? The thing that cuts from the person
" that cuts with it? *Alcib.* Past question.
" *Socra.* What? in regard to any musical In-
" strument, is not the thing the same? Is
" not the Lute one thing, and he who plays
" on it another? *Alcib.* Confess'd. *Socra.*
" And this, ALCIBIADES, was the purpose of
" my question to you just now, whether he
" that uses a thing, and the thing used, do
" not always appear different, distinct, things?
" *Alcib.* They do so indeed. *Socra.* Very
" good! And pray what does one of these
" handy-craftsmen in exercise of his occupa-
" tion use? *Alcib.* He uses his instruments.
" *Socra.* Does he not use likewise his hands?
" *Alcib.* His hands likewise. *Socra.* And
" his eyes? *Alcib.* I grant ye. *Socra.* And
" was it not before granted, that he that uses
" a thing, and the thing used, are different?
" and consequently that the Musician, or any
" other artist is different, not only from his
" instruments, but from his hands and eyes,
" those parts of the Body that he uses? *Al-*
" *cib.* Very true. *Socra.* And does not a
" man use his whole Body? *Alcib.* I think
" so indeed. *Socra.* Carry this still along
" with you, That the thing used, and he who
" uses it, are different. *Alcib.* I remember it,
" SOCRA-

" SOCRATES. *Socra.* I therefore conclude,
" that what we call a Man is a thing entirely
" different from his Body. *Alcib.* I cannot
" deny it. *Socra.* What is it then in this
" compofition that we may moft properly
" call the Man ? *Alcib.* Nay, in that you
" muft excufe me, SOCRATES. *Socra.* What!
" know you not what it is that ufes the Bo-
" dy ? *Alcib.* Full well. *Socra.* Is it any
" thing but the Soul ? *Alcib.* No, certainly.
" *Socra.* And is not this what rules and go-
" verns the Body ? *Alcib.* No doubt."

THIS, in my opinion, will furnifh us with
idea's, at leaft lay a foundation of proving (I
had almoft faid demonftrating) the Soul's diftinction from the Body.

AND in order to it, I fhall firft premife a
few things, that my meaning may be the
more clearly apprehended; and next, confider
more exactly, the force of the preceding
Argument.

1ft, IT is not my intention from this argument, to conclude any thing immediately
touching the nature of the fubftance of the
Soul, not indeed whether it be perfectly immaterial, divefted of all the properties of matter, (as I take it *immaterial* fignifies) and confequently of extenfion, as well as others; although it be often retain'd by fome who conceive the Soul immaterial and goes into its

idea,

idea, which feems to me very difagreeable. For what is immaterial but a negation of all matter? And while men affert this of the Soul, they fhould ftill continue to it, the primeft property of matter, if not repugnant, yet for certain is extreamly incongruous, and the ground of endlefs difficulties and jargon. But with this, I have nothing to do here.   By the Body, we underftand this corruptible fyftem of matter, which is made up of divers parts, blood, animal fpirits, &c. and a particular difpofition and organization of thofe parts; and my intent is to prove the Soul none of thefe, no mode, quality, power or faculty of any of thefe feparately, neither the refult of the whole taken together; but that which thinks in us is a fubftance, and a diftinct fubftance from the Body.   And I rather chufe to call the Soul a diftinct fubftance from the Body, than call it immaterial; becaufe many men have taught the Soul to be a diftinct fubftance from the Body, and yet have difcours'd of it as material (as did, I conceive, TERTULLIAN) but then their idea of this matter, of which they thought the Soul to partake, was vaftly different from their idea of the Body: it was matter of a different kind, matter and matter differing in their language and idea's, almoft as much perhaps, as Spirit and Body does now according to the moderns.   With the rectitude of this way of thinking, I have nothing to do.

2dly,

2*dly*, WHAT we underftand here by the terms *fubftance, faculty, mode,* &c. By *fubftance*, we conceive fomething that fubfifts of itfelf, and that is the fubject of what we term *properties, powers, faculties, modes,* &c. Thefe latter cannot fubfift, nor act of themfelves, and this is what diftinguifhes between them : all powers and faculties muft be powers and faculties of fomething, as Mr. LOCKE fays fomewhere, *to conceive of a thing as capable of acting, is to conceive of it as a fubftance*; and therefore to conceive thus of any faculty, we depart from our idea of a faculty, and conceive of it as a fubftance; and if we can for certain demonftrate any thing to act of itfelf, we demonftrate it to be a fubftance; and if we can prove the Soul thus to act of itfelf, we prove it a diftinct fubftance from the Body.

3*dly*, BY the *Soul*, I underftand fomething that thinks within us. And this I fay, on purpofe to prevent any fufpicions in you, that I endeavour to impofe on myfelf or you, by taking that for granted, which ought to be proved; as poffibly might be imagin'd, when I fay, *the Soul acts upon the Body*, &c. by which I do not fuppofe the Soul and Body two diftinct fubftances, but Soul is equivalent with me to Thought, or the power of thinking, be it what it will.

4*thly*, WHAT I mean by *different* or *diftinct fubftances*. Now it is certain, we may
and

and are very apt to fancy differences and diftinctions as to things where there are really none. As for example; any fyftem of matter, any common ftone or pebble, is one diftinct thing or fubftance, but yet it is made up of feveral parts; but from this diftinction of parts, it would be a ftrange way of arguing, when the queftion is concerning any one Body or Syftem of Matter, hence to infer it feveral diftinct things or fubftances, becaufe the thing itfelf confifts of thefe feveral parts, in a peculiar way difpofed and united. So in confidering Man, I would not impofe fuch a grofs fallacy on myfelf, becaufe in this compofition, I can conceive it made up of feveral parts, hence to infer man compounded of feveral diftinct fubftances. It avails nothing therefore, unlefs thefe parts can be proved of a different diftinct kind. Thus you fee I labour to free myfelf from all ambiguity of expreffion; and if I am impos'd on, I am fure it is not with my own knowledge and confent.

TO return to the Argument of SOCRATES, in which two things are carefully to be confider'd:

I. WHETHER the Soul acts upon the Body, or ufes it as an inftrument or organ.

II. WHETHER this demonftrates a real and fubftantial diftinction between Soul and Body.   1ft,

1ft, WHETHER the Soul acts upon the Body, or ufes it as an inftrument or organ. That is, when the parts of the Body are found and rightly difpofed, whether Thought or this thinking power doth not communicate motion to them, influence, direct, govern them. This every man experiences, at leaft of many parts of the Body; my hands, eyes, &c. I move according to the direction or determination of my will. The only doubt that can be ftarted, is, whether Thought thus moves the whole body, or whether there are not fome invifible parts, viz. the Brain, and animal Spirits, from whence this motion or influence is derived. I undertake therefore to prove this propofition, *viz.*

THAT the motions of the Body, fuch as we term voluntary, proceed not ultimately from the Brain, or any other invifible parts of the Body, but from Thought, or the power of thinking.

FOR example, my hand is at reft; by the determination of my will, I move it. What is that that moves my hand? According to the common hypothefis, immediately I confefs it is the Mufcles, animal Spirits, &c. But then what moves, or at leaft differenly determines them? (for it muft be granted, the mufcles and animal fpirits that immediately move my hand, muft receive motion, or a different

deter-

determination of motion, when my hand moves, from what they were in, when my hand was at reſt) I ſay then, from whence proceeded this motion of the Nerves, animal Spirits, &c. that immediately mov'd my hand? We will ſay, from ſome parts or part of the brain. (And in this, we ſay no more than can be prov'd, what none that I know, deny.) But what moves, or at leaſt gives a different determination of motion to this part of the brain, from whence this motion in my hand is derived? (for it muſt be granted again, that this part of the brain, from whence this motion to my hand is derived, muſt be at that inſtant put into motion, or ſome different diſpoſition, or determination of motion, from what they were in when my hand was at reſt. Theſe parts of the brain cannot be in the ſame motion or diſpoſition, when my hand moves, as when my hand was at reſt.) Well! I ſay, what gives theſe parts of the brain this motion, or this different diſpoſition or determination of motion? Muſt it not be reſolved into thought or the power of thinking? for certainly here is nothing elſe to do it.

LET us examine 2dly, Whether this argues two diſtinct Subſtances in Man, whether this will infer that that thinks in us, to be a Subſtance different from the Brain, animal Spirits, &c. I think in truth, this is as demonſtrable.

FOR

FOR certainly, If a Body at reft, moves, fomething muft put it into motion; again, if a Body in motion, be differently determin'd in its motion, fomething muft alter, or differently determine its motion, or elfe the Mufician might be the fame thing with his Fiddle, the Horfe with his Rider, and the Tennis-ball with the Wall, that rebounds it. To be guilty of a little tautology. Here is a Body at reft. It is moved. Muft it not be fomething that moves it? Again, here is a body moving in a ftrait line, it inftantly changes from this to a circular one. Can this be without fomething that changes and guides its motion? The parts of the brain are at reft, or under fome peculiar motion, or difpofition; this thinking power gives thefe parts motion, or a different difpofition or determination of motion. Muft not this therefore be fome real fubfifting thing, different from the brain or the parts of it, that it moves or directs? I faw once a Phyfician by moving the nerves, at fome diftance from the hand, move the hands and the fingers in a Skeleton diverfe ways. Was not the Phyfician different from the Skeleton? What the Phyfician did, Thought did in the living man more compleatly. Why is not then that which thinks in us a different thing from the body, that it moves? I know not, how other men think, but it feems to me, I have hardly about any thing more clear Ideas. But yet to examine this matter the moft feverely.

I

I will therefore fancy to my self three Suppositions, whereby I will endeavour to solve this, without the affiftance of a diftinct Subftance from the body. ⁻

1ft, I will examine, whether fome part or parts of the brain cannot move, or differently determine themfelves.

2dly, WHETHER this may not arife from fome peculiar organization, &c.

3dly, WHETHER a power of felf-motion cannot be fuperadded by GOD to fome peculiar part or parts of the brain. As I have not met with any thing very different from thefe, fo I believe it is not eafy to form any very different hypothefis.

1. WHETHER fome parts of the brain, cannot move or differently determine themfelves. The parts of the brain are matter, and whatfoever a man may fancy about the powers of matter, one can never fancy matter, when once at reft, capable of giving it felf motion, or differently determining its own motion; no more than it can convert it felf from a fquare to a round figure: which, if it could do, I know not what it might not do, it might give it felf underftanding and wifdom as well, and all other attributes of the Deity. And this is not only the cafe of Matter, but of

any

any other thing; to talk of giving itself that, which it had not, is a plain contradiction, because giving suppofes the being already poffeffed of that, which is to be given, and yet the latter claufe fuppofes, that it has not, that which is to be given. So that if by matter's moving it felf, be underftood of matter's giving it felf motion, (and it muft give it felf motion, or another muft give it, for motion cannot arife out of nothing) nothing can be more evidently abfurd. But no body imagines fo abfurd a thing.

YES really, I think, he imagines the felf fame thing, who thinks, that matter at reft, be it the brain, or any other matter, can move itfelf, can ftop or differently determine its own motion. For while matter is at reft, motion is not in it; while it moves in a right line, it moves not in a circular one. When it moves therefore here is an addition of motion made to it; when it moves from a ftrait to a circular line, its motion is changed. Whence is this motion in the firft cafe, this alteration of motion in the fecond cafe? The force and interpofition of another being, is difown'd. If therefore this motion be derived from it felf, muft not itfelf give it? for certainly here is fomething added, when motion is added, here is fomething that was not before; which muft be derived from itfelf or fome other being. But may it not have a power

power of moving itself, although it doth not always actually move?

STILL we cheat our selves with terms. For what is this power of motion in matter? To me it is nothing but a capacity of being moved, and then still it will require some other thing to move it, as in many cases, a power in things, signifies nothing, but a capacity of being acted on; but in this case, I think it is clearly so. For if you take power here for something active in matter, I would ask you two things. First, when this power is brought into act, or influences the parts of matter, whether matter then is not passive, or receives not the influence of that power, (this it must surely do, or else matter would never move) and yet in regard this power of motion is a power of matter, I would ask you again, whether matter is not at the same time active. So that the same parts of matter, it seems, at the same time, are both active and passive. Can you reconcile this? that at the same time, matter should be both active and passive, or act and not act? To me again this has the face of a very gross contradiction. If you say, this power acts separately on matter, and so exerts itself on the parts of matter: I agree with you, but then this is evidently our Idea of a Substance distinct from matter.

2dly. SEEING in the present case of voluntary motions, this force that moves the brain,

brain, and upon which the motion in my hand depends, I fay, feeing this force is not actually exerted upon the parts of the brain, when I move not my hand (for if it were actually exerted, my hand would actually move) I would ask you what it is that actually exerts it, and again ftops it. We all feel, it is done by the mediation of our wills; but willing is nothing towards moving or determining any parts of matter, unlefs fome force or influence attends it. And the point is, to what belongs this force and influence : if you fay to matter, you make the thing to be moved, and that which moves it, all one ; and again you fuppofe, fuch a power in matter, that I dare fay, is your own and every body's idea of a fubftance ; and you prove to me that which thus acts upon matter, to be no fubftance, and I will prove to you, matter is no fubftance. But of this again hereafter. I fuppofe not this your opinion, that matter as fuch, can move it felf ; but rather the others remaining. I proceed therefore to examine,

II. In the 2d place, Whether this may not arife from fome peculiar difpofition of parts, organization, &c. Whether this way cannot be explain'd thefe voluntary motions. And I think, it is impoffible. By difpofition and organization of parts, I underftand a fort of clock-work or mechanifm, from whence we will fuppofe thinking to refult. What fort of mechanifm or difpofition of parts, this as you will not undertake to shew, so I shall not trouble you, nor my self about; whatsoever it be, I hope to prove clearly, voluntary motions can be the result of no such thing.

1. I suppose you will grant me that any mechanism whatsoever can produce nothing but necessary acts or effects, and if you suppose the Soul the result of any sort of organization or disposition of parts, in my present conceit I think my self able to maintain, this result, viz. the Soul, either a different substance from the mechanism, disposition of parts, or else man a necessary agent; for thinking here follows from this organization and disposition of parts, and consequently must not only be necessary in general, but in the several and particular acts of it; and choice and willing being particular ways or modes of thinking, these must be necessary, as necessary as striking in a clock. So that here will be an end of all sort of Liberty and freedom in man; and because I believe, we have demonstration for these, we have certainly demonstration against thinking's being any result of mechanism and disposition of parts, &c. I take it here it is impossible you can defend any sort of liberty in man, if thinking be nothing but the result of mechanism. For the cause that produces thinking, acts necessarily, and hence that thinking should be free, is a perfectly unintelligible thing. For thinking is the effect, and that the effect should

be

be free, when the caufe acted neceffarily, that produced it, is perfectly irreconcileable to it-felf; unlefs you take the effect, which the dif-pofition of parts, &c. which is nothing but the power of mechanifm, produced, for fome-thing difengaged from this mechanifm, for fomething free, and that depends not upon the mechanifm; then indeed you can defend freedom, but then this thinking power is no longer a power of the mechanifm, an effect that mechanifm produces, but a diftinct thing and fubftance. And I moft paffionately long to have you arguing on this point, denying Liberty in man, or defending it on your prin-ciples; making thinking the refult of me-chanifm or a difpofition of parts, altogether a neceffary effect, and yet a free thing. But what do I talk of a free thing? thinking is the refult of mechanifm of a certain organi-zation and difpofition of parts, doth not there-fore this certain organization, difpofition of parts, &c. produce thinking? And then what is thinking here but an effect? And to talk of an effect's acting, is ridiculous and contra-dictory, as if a man fhould talk of the ftri-king in a clock's acting, when ftriking is con-ceived as nothing but an effect produced by the difpofition of parts in the clock. 'Tis true, to fay there is a power in the clock to ftrike, is well, becaufe this is the caufe of it: but to confider ftriking as the refult of this power in a clock, as fomething arifing out of it, and actually produced, this is to

con-

confider it as an effect; and to talk of an effect's acting, is either to confider an effect, as fome real thing that can act of itfelf, or elfe is down right nonfenfe. And yet I have heard men difcourfe, that the power of thinking is the refult of mechanifm, of fome difpofition of parts, &c. of the brain, which, if this power be no real thing, is idly call'd a power, it is only a bare effect, and can no more act, than as I faid ftriking in a clock can act; and if the cafe be fo, if thinking flows from a difpofition of parts, mechanifm, power of the fyftem, (for thefe words fignify much the fame) to me, there hath not been a greater cheat, a greater folly in all ages, than this notion of the Liberty and freedom of man.

TO make this yet clearer if poffible. Thinking arifes from matter organized, or difpofed after fome peculiar manner, that we know not, into a fyftem. We muft therefore affirm, if there be nothing in man but matter, that matter thus difpofed, &c. thinks. I here ask you, whether it be not agreeable to your ideas, that if nothing guides matter thus difpofed, there could be no fuch thing as freedom; for freedom implies in fome cafes, a power of acting or not acting; but you can never deduce this from any being, that has nothing in it, but matter difpofed into a fyftem. For there being nothing to hinder its operations, it would always act or operate, where the caufe were fufficient; where the caufe were not
fufficient,

fufficient, no operation or effect would fucceed. And hence, if I miftake not, Mr. HOBBES was obliged, from this principle to deny all Liberty in man. But I am fenfible I tire you.

2dly, NEITHER is this fuppofition of thinking's refulting from matter organized, &c. lefs contradictory to the fenfe and experience of mankind, touching the force and energy that the Soul has upon the mechanifm or fyftem it felf. Certainly our idea of any thing, that arifes from the organization of matter, implies a neceffity in that which is fuppofed to refult from it, it is under a fort of fubjection, and is a flave to that mechanifm or organization, is made out of it. But now thinking is fuch a vigorous active thing, that it turns upon its very author, and lords over it, commands the fyftem or machine it felf, and how will you reconcile this to organization or mechanifm? There is ftriking in a clock (I ufe this boldly, becaufe it hath been your own illuftration) which is a quality or effect refulting from the difpofition of its parts; now fhould this ftriking be able to return upon the mechanifm, rectify, alter, fufpend its motions, would not this be a marvellous thing? Indeed it is fenfelefs to fuppofe it. Does not thinking do this? Is it not by this, we move the whole machine of the body from place to place, that we guide, fufpend, new determine many of its motions and operations? To me it is clear, if think-

ing

ing refulted from any difpofition of parts, quite the contrary would follow : thinking could do nothing on the body ; but here, a different difpofition or motion of the parts of the body is produced by thinking. This is ftrangely contrary to my ideas.

III. I proceed to the 3d fuppofition, Whether a power or faculty of felf motion, cannot be fuperadded by God to fome peculiar part or parts of the brain. This was originally Mr. LOCKE'S, and although no perfon has a higher efteem for that great man, yet I cannot but look on this notion as an error and flip in his writings.

THIS hypothefis differs from the former in this, viz. the former, fuppofes matter and motion under fome certain difpofition and organization of parts capable in it felf of producing thinking : this, fuppofes matter and motion in itfelf, howfoever difpofed and modify'd, entirely incapable of thinking ; elfe there had been no need of recurring to the power of God. So that if we fuppofe the body of man framed exactly, as now it is, yet if this faculty of thinking were not fuperadded by God, it would be a machine indeed, a fyftem, but would never think. I have two or three things to obferve to you upon this.

1. THIS however is as unlikely to be apprehended and entertained by fceptical men, as the old common hypothefis, of God's introducing and fuperadding to the fyftem of the body, an immaterial fubftance ; becaufe this as equally requires the immediate application of a divine power, to fuperadd this faculty as a diftinct fubftance : and I believe, it is much the fame with them, to fuppofe God fuperadding either faculties or fubftances; their hopes and expectations for certain, extending farther ; that thinking might arife from bare matter and motion, without any act of a fuperior caufe. But unqueftionably you being not of that crew, which is for juftling God out of the world ; I own, the obfervation idle and impertinent.

HOWEVER, it hath been thought an objection to the fuppofition of two diftinct fubftances in man, that it requires the conftant and immediate application of the Deity, perpetual creations towards the propagation of mankind; and this requires fomething like it, a conftant and perpetual fuperaddition of faculties to every individual man, nay if you allow (as I perceive you do) brutes to have fenfe, here muft be a fuperaddition of a faculty of fenfation to every one of them too, *to mice, and lice, and mites,* &c. which although not quite fo abfurd as the creation

of

of diſtinct ſubſtances, yet will I believe have ſuch a ſhare of it, as will not eaſily be digeſted. If you aſſert this ſuperadded faculty communicated from father to ſon, &c. if I not greatly miſtake, this will have likewiſe a plentiful ſhare of abſurdity.

2dly, ACCORDING to this doctrine of the ſupperaddition of faculties, as well as according to the foregoing, I intreat you to conſider, how to conceive the Soul of man immortal. You receive this principle from divine revelation. Granted. But yet you may ſo conceive of the ſoul, as to render that promiſe of immortality impoſſible to be fulfilled, as I believe, it is impoſſible, according to the preceeding Schemes. For immortal, I preſume, you apply to the ſoul itſelf, not the body; for every one ſees the body mortal and periſhing. The ſoul therefore this promiſe concerns, and by its immortality, I preſume, you underſtand that it exiſts, and acts, and thinks after the diſſolution of the body; that it doth not remain in an eſtate of inſenſibility, till the reſurrection. If this be your opinion of the immortality of the ſoul, which, I think muſt be of all ſuch, as hold it immortal, I would fain know how you can reconcile this to your principles. For it is clear, if thinking naturally ariſes from ſuch a diſpoſition of parts, &c. and death deſtroys this diſpoſition, it deſtroys the ſoul

and

and its thinking. One of thefe two things, muft be faid here. Firft, either that God preferves fome parts of the body from diffolving at death, to which thinking more efpecially belongs. To this many things might be oppofed, but all I fhall fay to it, is this : methinks it argues thofe parts fo very peculiar from the reft of the body, that it looks like a diftinct fubftance, and it feems extravagant for a man to deny the Soul a diftinct fubftance, when he allows between the parts of the body fuch a vaft diftinction. Or elfe, 2dly, fomething more abfurd muft be faid, viz. that God can preferve a meer mode of a body, without the body itfelf, without its fubject, which is worfe than *Tranfubftantiation.*

'TIS the fame, according to the fuppofition of the Soul's being a faculty of thinking's fuperadded by God. If you fay this power or faculty can be preferved without fome fubject, it is clearly to me a fubftance, it being entirely contrary to our idea's, that powers and faculties fhould exift of themfelves, or be fupported in being, even by the power of God. I muft imagine therefore, while the argument lies under this view, many things that Mr. DODWELL afferts to a man of your underftanding and clearnefs of conception, muft appear ftrange paradoxes, becaufe you feem to me to truft to Reafon, as the principle

that

that is to direct you in matters of belief; and I can never think you can reconcile the sub-sistence of Accidents and Modes, Powers and Faculties, whatsoever hard names are given to them, to your Reason. But this only by the by.

3dly, IT is suppos'd by this notion of thinking's being a faculty superadded to mat-ter by the power of God, as before premis'd, that matter in itself, howsoever disposed, moved, and organized, would not think; and it is quite two different things, so to dis-pose matter, that matter thinks, and to super-add a faculty of thinking to it. In the first case, matter is made to think; in the latter, this thinking faculty thinks in it. There is as much difference between these, as between the second and last hypothesis, which indeed are your own; for how often do you distin-guish to Mr. CLARKE, between thinking's be-ing a power of matter, under such or such a texture, motion, &c. and a superaddition of a faculty of thinking to it by God? which must suppose some distinction between them : and the distinction is this, matter may be so disposed and moved as to think, or else may have a faculty of thinking superadded by God. Now, I say, our idea of this latter case sup-poses matter not to think, but the faculty su-peradded to think in it; for before this think-ing faculty was superadded, although the

system

fyftem of the body were juft as it is, the body would not think: fo that if in thinking, this thinking faculty any ways depends upon the difpofition and motion of the parts of the body, or fyftem, it is owing to the divine appointment; and if God had fo appointed, this thinking faculty would have thought as well in a ftone, a clod of earth, as in an organized body, nay, without any body at all. As 'tis plain: for according to our prefent fuppofition, howfoever the divine power had modify'd or difpos'd matter, thinking would never have proceeded from it. How therefore doth the bare fyftem concur towards thinking? Nothing at all certainly in itfelf. And if it concurs nothing at all, (I mean any otherwife than God hath fo order'd it) this thinking faculty is a fubftance. Again, it may think as well in any other body, as a fyftem, or organized body. Laftly, as well without any body at all, as with it. All which confirms that this notion is the fame with that it pretends to differ from; and if fome underftand the fame by power as others do by fubftance, I have nothing to do to oppofe them, provided they do not think themfelves all the while far above others in point of knowledge and difcovery of truth.

THUS, Sir, I have freely reprefented to you what my thoughts fuggefted on this fubject,

ject, and have no other aim in the world, but a profound respect to you and truth, which you so constantly profess in your Writings. If I am under mistakes, it will be charity in you to point them out to me, and shall be ever most gratefully receiv'd and acknowledg'd by

Your very humble Servant.

CRITI-

CRITICAL REMARKS

UPON

Mr. TOLAND's BOOK,

ENTITLED,

Nazarenus, or Jewish, Gentile, and Mahometan Christianity :

CONCERNING

The Opinions of the Cerinthians, Carpocratians, Ebionites, and Nazarens.

NAZARENUS, *c. 6. p.* 17.

" THE Cerinthians before them, (i.e.
" the Basilidians) and the Carpocra-
" tians next, (to name no more of
" those who affirmed JESUS to have
" been a meer man) did believe the same
" thing, that it was not himself, but one of
" his followers very like him, that was cruci-
" fied."

THE

THE Author has not referred us to any ancient Writer for the confirmation of the account here given; and it is apparently different from that which IRENÆUS, and after him EPIPHANIUS, have given of CERINTHUS's opinions.

IRENÆUS's words are:

Cerinthus . . . . docuit . . . fuisse eum Joseph & Mariæ filium . . . & post Baptismum descendisse in eum Christum, ab ea principalitate, quæ est super omnia figura columbæ, & tunc annunciasse incognitum Patrem, & virtutes perfecisse; in fine autem revolasse iterum Christum de Jesu, & Jesum passum esse, & resurrexisse: Christum autem impassibilem perseverasse, existentem spiritalem. Adv. Haeres. lib. 1. c. 25.

Cerinthus taught that he (i. e. Jesus) was the Son of Joseph and Mary . . . and that after his Baptism Christ came down upon him from that principality which is above all things, in the figure of a Dove; and then gave an account of the unknown Father, and wrought Miracles; but that at last Christ flew back from Jesus: and that Jesus suffered, and rose again; but that Christ continued incapable of suffering, being of a spiritual nature.

EPIPHANIUS's words are:

Ὁυτος εχηρυτῖεν ... ανω-θεν ... εκ τʊ ανω Θεʊ

His Doctrine was . . . that after Jesus, who sprung

μετα το αδρυνθηναι τον Ιησυν τον εκ σπερματ⌾. Ιωσηφ ϗ Μαριας γεγεννημενον κατεληλυθεναι τον Χριστον εις αυτον, τυτεςι το Πνευμα το αγιον εν ειδει περιστερας εν τῷ Ιορδανη· και απεκαλυψαι αυτῷ, και δι αυτυ τοις μετ' αυτυ τον Αγνωςον Πατερα· Και δια τυτο, επειδη ηλθεν ἡ δυναμις εις αυτον ανωθεν, δυναμεις επιπετελικεναι· Και αυτυ πεπονθοτ⌾ το ελθον ανωθεν αναπτηναι απο τυ Ιησυ ανω, πεπονθοτα δε τον Ιησυν, και παλιν εγηγερμενον· Χριστον δε τον ανωθεν ελθοντα εις αυτον απαθη αναπταντα, οπερ εςι το κατελθον εν ειδει περιστερας· και υ τον Ιησυν ειναι Χριστον. *Haeref.* 28. *Edit. Hervag. Bafil. p. 53.*

fprung from the feed of Joſeph and Mary, was grown up to his full bigneſs, Chriſt came down upon him from above from the Father, i. e. the Holy Spirit, in the fhape of a Dove in Jordan, and made known to him, and by him to thofe that were with him, the unknown Father : and that therefore, after the power was come upon him from above, he wrought Miracles : and that when Jefus fuffered, that which came upon him from above left him, taking its flight upwards ; but that Jefus fuffered and rofe again : whereas Chriſt who came upon him from above, defcending in the form of a Dove, was not capable of fuffering, and fled back again ; and that Jefus was not the fame with Chriſt.

THUS

THUS far Epiphanius's account agrees with Irenæus's; but he afterwards gives a somewhat different account of his opinion, which contradicts the former, and seems highly improbable.

His words are:

Ὀυῖ@. δὲ ὁ Κηρινθος... φασκει παλιν τολμησας Χειϛον πεπονθεναι και ε- ϛαυρωσαι, μηπω δὲ ε- γηγερθαι, μελλειν δε ανιϛασθαι, οταν ἡ κα- θολυ γενηται νεκρων αναϛασις· ασυϛατα τοινυν ταυτα παρ᾽ εκεινοις τα- τε ρημαῖα και νοημαῖα· *ibid.* p. 54.

This same Cerinthus has the confidence to say, that Christ suffered and was crucified; but that he is not yet risen, but that he shall rise at the general Resurrection of the dead. Therefore these thoughts and ſpeeches among them are inconsistent.

BUT it seems clear that Epiphanius does not take care to speak exactly in his account of this matter, he using the word CHRIST several times where he ought to use the word JESUS, (which was by no means proper to be done, when he was relating the opinions of one, who so carefully distinguishes between JESUS and CHRIST) of which careleſsneſs of expreſsion, take the following instances:

Εξηγειῖαι και ἐῖ@. εκ Μαριας και εκ σπερ-

And this Cerinthus gives us to understand, that

μαῖ©. Ιωσηφ τον Χει-
σου γεγεννᾶσθαι. *ibid.* p.
53.

that Chriſt was born
of Mary and of the
ſeed of Joſeph.

WHEN he proceeds to confute CERIN-
THUS's opinions, he has theſe words :

Ουτε γδ εκ σπερμαῖ©.
Ιωσηφ ὁ Χειςος κ. τ.
λ. *ibid.* p. 55.

For neither was Chriſt
of the ſeed of Joſeph,
&c.

NOW it is certain from IRENÆUS, that
CERINTHUS did not ſay that CHRIST was de-
ſcended from JOSEPH ; and EPIPHANIUS himſelf knew it, and therefore unleſs we ſuppoſe
him to put the word CHRIST inſtead of JE-
SUS, he fights without an Adverſary in this
paſſage.

WHEREFORE it ſeems reaſonable to
me, to lay moſt ſtreſs upon IRENÆUS's account, which is more clear and conſiſtent
than EPIPHANIUS's, and which has ſo much
the advantage of it in point of antiquity ;
and conſequently there is no reaſon to think,
that CERINTHUS diſputed the matter of faſt,
that JESUS, who was crucified at Jeruſalem,
roſe again from the dead ; and that ground
of wonder is removed, which is ſuggeſted in
thoſe words of this learned Author, in p. 18.
" 'Tis a ſtrange thing, one would think, they
" ſhould differ about a faſt of this nature ſo
" early ; and that CERINTHUS, who was con-

VOL. II.   c   " tempo-

" temporary, a countryman, and a Chriftian,
" fhould, with all thofe of his fect, deny the
" Refurrection of Chrift from the dead." It
is remov'd (I fay) fo far as CERINTHUS is con-
cerned in it; as depending chiefly, if not only, on EPIPHANIUS's carelefs and confufed way
of expreffing himfelf, or his miftaken reprefentation of the matter. And this learned
Author himfelf, in the fame page, informs,
that EPIPHANIUS confounds every thing.
AUGUSTIN's words in this matter would
have been more to the purpofe, than the paffage our Author refers to in EPIPHANIUS,
had they had any good foundation. They
run thus :

Cerinthiani à Cerin-
tho . . . Jefum homi-
nem tantummodo fu-
iffe, nec refurrexiffe
fed refurrecturum af-
feverantes. lib. de Hæ-
ref. n° 8.

The Cerinthians from
Cerinthus . . . main-
tain, that Jefus was on-
ly a Man, and that he
has not already rifen,
but fhall rife again.

BUT AUGUSTIN probably borrow'd from
EPIPHANIUS; and his account is very imper-
fect, and in one part of it manifeftly falfe, if
IRENÆUS's be true.

FROM none of thefe accounts does it
appear, that CERINTHUS believed that it was
not JESUS himfelf, but one of his followers,
very

very like him, that was crucify'd; but the contrary.

AS to CARPOCRATES and his followers, IRENÆUS in his account of them, *Haeref. lib.* 1. *c.* 24. makes no mention of their denying that JESUS suffered, and saying that another suffered in his stead; but tells us, that they pretended to have an image of CHRIST made by PILATE, when JESUS was among men.

TERTULLIAN gives us this account of him:

Carpocrates . . . dicit Chriftum . . hominem tantummodo . . . hunc apud Judæos paffum: folam animam ipfius in cælo receptam, eo quod firmior & robuftior cæteris fuerit: ex quo colligeret, tentata animarum falute nullas corporis refurrectiones. Tertul de Præfcr. adv. Haeret. cap. 48.

Carpocrates . . . faith that Chrift . . was a meer man . . . that he suffered among the Jews: that his foul only was received into heaven, becaufe it was more firm and ftrong than others: from whence he inferred, that the falvation of Souls alone being attempted, there was no refurrection of the body.

EPIPHANIUS faith nothing in his account of the CARPOCRATIANS (*Hæref.* 27.) about their denying that JESUS suffered, or afferting that another suffered in his stead; but mentions

tions

tions their having images or pictures of CHRIST made by PONTIUS PILATE. AUGUSTIN tells us, that they deny'd the Resurrection of the Body, and worshipped the images of JESUS and others. *Lib. de Hæref.*

BUT in none of these accounts, nor in that given by EUSEBIUS, (*Hift. Eccl. lib.* 4. *c.* 7.) is there the least hint, that CARPOCRATES suppofed that JESUS did not fuffer, but another in his ftead. And TERTULLIAN afferts the contrary.

NAZARENUS, *c.* 6. *p.* 18.

" THE EBIONITES, according to EPIPHA-
" NIUS, had not the Genealogy in their Go-
" fpel, which makes it needlefs for him to
" fay elfewhere, that the CERINTHIANS re-
" jected it, whofe Gofpel was the fame.

EPIPHANIUS indeed tells us, that the EBIONITES and CERINTHIANS did both ufe the Gofpel according to MATTHEW, and that only : but he does alfo tell us, that they did not ufe that which was whole and compleat, but one that was imperfect and adulterated; and it does not appear, that MATTHEW's Gofpel, as ufed by them, was in all points the fame ; fo that one of thofe fects might expunge or admit fome paffages which the other did not, tho as to the main body of the Gofpel, it was the fame. Therefore tho the Genealogy were
want-

wanting in the MATTHEW of the EBIONITES,
yet it might be let ftand in that of the CE-
RINTHIANS; and then EPIPHANIUS, without
being guilty of confufion or inconfiftency in
this matter, might tell us, that CERINTHUS
made ufe of this Genealogy to prove that
JESUS was the fon of JOSEPH and MARY.
And that this was the cafe, according to
EPIPHANIUS's reprefentation of the matter,
may be inferred from the following paffages
compared together.

OF the MATTHEW of the EBIONITES, he
fays :

Εν τῷ γвν παρ' αυῖοις Ευαγγελιῳ κατα Μαῖθαιον ονομαζ:μενῳ, вχ' ἑλῳ δε πληρεςατῷ αλλα νενοθευμενω ϰ ηκεωπελασμενω· 'Εβεϊκον δε τвτο καλвσιν εμφερῖαι, κ. τ. λ. *Hæref.* 30. p. 64.	In their Gofpel, according to Matthew, which is not compleat and perfect, but adulterated and mutilated, (they call it the Hebrew Gofpel) it is found, &c.

OF the CERINTHIANS, he fays :

Χεωνῖαι τῷ κατα Μαῖθαιον Ευαγγελιῳ απο μαρвς ϰ вχ' ὁλῳ, αλλα δια την γενεαλογιαν την ε:ζαρϰον, ϰ ταυτην μαρτυριαν φερвσιν απο τв	They ufe the Gofpel according to Matthew in part, but not compleat (or not all of it) but becaufe of the Genealogy according to the

Ευαγγελιω, παλιν λε-
γοντις ὁτι αρκετον κ. τ.
λ. *Hæref.* 28. p. 54.

the flesh, and they (or
they also) bring this
Testimony from the
Gospel, again saying,
that it is enough, &c.

BUT in this place the construction is difficult, and our learned Author seems from
this very passage to infer, that the CERIN-
THIANS rejected the Genealogy; which does
not seem clear to me from the words of
the Author, which run as above, and should
(if they can) be interpreted so as to consist
with what he saith elsewhere of their making use of the Genealogy. See his words relating to that matter:

Ὁ μεν Κηρινθ&. ἠ
Καρποκρας τῷ αυτῷ
χρωμενοι δηθεν παρ'
αυτοις Ευαγγελιῳ, απο
τ̄ αρχης τε κατα Μἰ-
θαιον Ευαγγελιυ δια
της γενεαλογιας βυλον-
τα παριςαν εκ σπερμα-
7&. Ιωσηρ ἠ Μαριας
ειναι τον Χριςον· Ου-
τοι δε αλλα τινα δια-
νουνται, παραξαφαντις
γαρ τας παρα τω Μἰ-
θαιω γενεαλογιας αρ-
χονίαι την αρχην ποι-
ειαθαι ὡς προειπον, λε-

Cerinthus and Carpo-
cras using the same
Gospel with them (i.e.
the Ebionites) would
prove from the Ge-
nealogy in the begin-
ning of the Gospel
according to Matthew,
that Christ was of the
seed of Joseph and
Mary. But these (i.e.
the Ebionites) are of
another mind. For
they cut off the Ge-
nealogies in Matthew,
and begin *the Gospel,*
as

γοντες, ὅτι εγενετο εν | as I said before, at
Ταις ἡμεραις Ἡρωδε x. | those words (Matth. 2.
τ. λ. *Haref.* 30. p. | 1.) In the days of He-
65. | rod, &c.

FROM whence it is plain, that EPIPHA-
NIUS did not think that the Cerinthian and
the Ebionite Gospels were word for word
the same; tho they went under the same
name, and might in most things agree. And
this he might do consistently enough with
what he had said before of the Ebionite
Gospel, in those words :

Δεχονlαι μεν ἠ αυτοι | They also own the
το καlα Μαlθαιον Eu- | Gospel according to
αγγελιον· Τυτο γαρ | Matthew, for they, as
και αυτοι ὡς και ἑι κα- | also the Cerinthians
lα Κηρινθον και Μηριν- | and Merinthians, use
θον χρωνlαι μονω· *Ibid.* | this only.
p. 60.

BUT it is probable he never saw this Gospel according to the HEBREWS (which he
imagin'd to be the same with that according
to MATTHEW) as may be inferred from the
following words :

Εχυσι δε το καlα Μαl- | They (i. e. the Naza-
θαιον Ευαγγελιον πλη- | renes, of whom he is
ρεστατον Εβραΐσι..ουκ οιδα | there giving an ac-
δε ἑι ἠ τας γενεαλογιας | count) have the Gospel
τας απο τυ Αβρααμ | according to Matthew

in

αχει Χειςυ πεειαλον.
Idem. Hæref. 29. ad finem.

in Hebrew ... But I do not know whether they have taken away the Genealogies from Abraham to Chrift.

NAZARENUS, *cap. 9. p. 26.*

" EPIPHANIUS affirms, that the NAZARENS
" took this name to themfelves, but not that
" of JESSEANS after JESUS, nor of CHRISTI-
" ANS after CHRIST, and that all Chriftians
" whatfoever were ftiled NAZARENS."

THIS account leads one to imagine, that EPIPHANIUS derived the name JESSEANS from JESUS, which he did not. His words run thus :

Ὀυτοι γαρ ἑαυτοις ονομα επεθειτο, υχι Χειςυ, υτε αυτο το ονομα τυ Ινσυ, αλλα Ναζωεαιων· Και παντες δε Χειςιανοι Ναζωεαι ιτοτε ωσαυτως εκαλυντο· Γεγνε δε επ' ολιγω χενω καλειθαι αυτυς Ιεσσαιυς, πειν η επι της Αντιοχειας αρχην λαβωσιν οι Μαθηται καλειθαι Χειςιανοι· Εκα-

For thefe (the Nazarens) gave themfelves the name neither of Jefus nor of Chrift, but of Nazarens : and all Chriftians were then called Nazarens. But it came to pafs, that in a little time they were called Jeffeans, before the Difciples began to be called Chriftians at Antioch.

λ𝜀υτο δε Ιεσσαιοι δια τον Ιεσσαι οιμαι, επειδηπερ ὁ Δαβιδ εξ Ιεσσαι κ. τ. λ *Hæref.* 29. p. 55, 56.

tioch. They were called Jeffeans, I fuppofe, from Jeffe ; for as much as David defcended from Jeffe, &c.

THE perfons whom he, thro miftake, fuppofed to be called JESSÆANS, were the ESSÆANS mentioned by PHILO (*vid. ibid. apud Epiph. p.* 57.) who feem to me not to have been CHRISTIANS, nor does it appear, that they were, from PHILO's account of them, in his Book concerning the contemplative Life, but a fort of JEWS, who lived a Monaftic Life in Egypt.

NAZARENUS, *cap.* 9. *p.* 26.

" THEY were likewife call'd by way of
" contempt EBIONITES or Beggars.

I know none of the Fathers that fays EBIONITES was a name given to all Chriftians on account of the meannefs of their Condition.

OUR Author proceeds and fays (*ibid.*) this
" is very evident not only from the Silence
" of IRENÆUS, but alfo from the exprefs
" Teftimonies of ORIGEN and EUSEBIUS,
" that they were thus nicknamed becaufe of
" their mean condition : and even from the
" Hebrew word *Ebion* (אביון) itfelf, which fig-
" nifies

" nifies *poor*, and was a moſt proper Epi-
" thet for the firſt Chriſtians.

I do not ſee the force of this way of arguing ; viz. IRENÆUS ſpeaking of the Ebionites, whom he repreſents as a particular ſort
of Chriſtians, who held doctrines different
from other Chriſtians, for which he ranked
them among the Hereticks, does not mention
any man of the name of EBION as their lea-
der, nor indeed gives us any reaſon of their
name ; therefore not only they, but all Chriſtians whatſoever, were called Ebionites from
the meanneſs of their condition.

BUT it will be proper to conſider the expreſs teſtimonies of ORIGEN and EUSEBIUS,
to which we are referred, as delivered in their
own words.

ORIGEN's words in the firſt place referred to, run thus : (they being part of his
anſwer to CELSUS, who eſteem'd the Jews ridiculous for ſuffering themſelves to be ſo im-
poſed upon by JESUS, as to leave their country-
laws, &c.)

Μηδὲ τυτο κατανοησας,
ὅτι οἱ απο Ιεδαιων εις
τον Ιησυν πιστευοντες ᾧ
καταλελοιπασι τον πα-
τριον νομον· εισι γᾦ
κατ᾽ αυτον, επωνομρι

Not conſidering that
the Jews who believ-
ed in Chriſt did not
leave their country-
law. For they live
according to it, receiv-
ing

της κατα την εκδοχην
πλωχειας τυ νομυ γεγε-
νημειοι· Εβιωντι γδ ο
πλωχος παρα Ιυδαιοις
καλειται· Και Εβιωναι-
οι χρηματιζυσιν οι απο
Ιυδαιων τον Ιησυν ως
Χειςον παραδεξαμειοι·
Και ο Πέτρος δε μεχει
πολλυ φαινεται τα κα-
τα τον Μωϋσεως νομυν
Ιυδαικα εθη πετηρηκε-
ναι, ως μηδεπω απο
Ιησυ μαθων αναβαινειν
απο τυ κατα το γραμ-
μα νομυ επι τον κατα
το πνευμα οπερ απο
των Πραξεων των Απο-
ςολων μεμαθηκαμεν, κ.
τ. λ. *Contra Celsum*,
lib. 2. p. 56.

ing (or being call'd by) a name agreeable to the poverty of the Law, according to their way of understanding it. For E-bion among the Jews signifies poor ; and those of the Jews who received Jesus as Christ, are called E-bionites. And Peter for a good while appears to have observed the Jewish customs according to the law of Moses, as having not yet learned of Jesus to ascend from the letter to the spirit of the law, as we learn from the Acts of the Apostles (chap. 10. 9.) &c.

IN the other passage referred to, he having mention'd those words of our Saviour (in Matt. 15. 24.) I am not sent but unto the lost sheep of the house of Israel, goes on saying,

Ουκ ελαμβανομεν ταυ-
τα ως οι πλωχοι τη

We took not these words as those do,
who

διανοια Εβιωναιοι της
πλωχειας της διανοιας
επωνομοι· (Εξιω γαρ
ὁ πλωχος παρ᾽ Ἑβραι-
οις ονομαζεται·) ὡςε ὑπο-
λαβειν επι τες σαρκινους
Ισεαπλιλας προηγυμε-
νως τον Χειςον επι-
δεδημηκεναι· κ. τ. λ.
Idem Philocal. cap. 1.
p. 17.

who being of a poor
understanding, receive
the name of Ebionites
from the poverty of
their understanding;
(for a poor man is
called Ebion in He-
brew); so as to sup-
pose that Christ came
chiefly to the Israe-
lites according to the
flesh, &c.

IN both these passages there is nothing
said of the Ebionites being poor or beggars
as to their circumstances in the world, or
their being nick-named from those circumstances; but from their poor interpretation
of the Law, which, as it was understood by
them, answered the name which PAUL gave
it of beggarly elements (πλωχα ςοιχεια, Galat.
4. 9.) so that as far as appears from his own
account, the antient Fathers seem rather to
have taken an occasion from these words of
PAUL, to determine the name of Ebionites to
have been properly given them, than from
their outward poverty.

BUT let us see whether EUSEBIUS's words
are more to our Author's purpose:

Εβιωναιες τετες οικειωι
επεφημιζον οἱ πρωτοι

The ancients did pro-
perly call those Ebio-
nites,

πΊωχως ἡ ταπεινως τα
περι τȣ Χριςȣ δογμα-
τιζοντας ἐ δοξαζοντας·
Λιτον μεν γαρ αυτον
ἡ χοινον ἡγȣντι· κ. τ.
λ. Hift. Ecclef. lib. 3.
c. 27.

nites, who had a poor and mean opinion of Chrift; for they efteemed him to be a meer and common man, &c.

BUT he afterwards mentions one fort of Ebionites, who did not deny that our Lord fprung from the Virgin and the Holy Spirit; tho they did not own him to be God, the Word, and Wifdom; and did, as the firft, adhere to the law of MOSES, and keep the Jewifh as well as the Chriftian fabbath, rejecting PAUL's Epiftles; and goes on thus:

Ὁθεν παρα την τοιαυ-
την εγχειρησιν της τοιας
δε λελογχασι προσηγο-
ειας τȣ Εβιων ονομαΘ.
την διανοιας πϯωχειαν
αυτων ἀποφαινονΘ·
Ταυτη γαρ επικλην ὁ
πΊωχος παρ᾽ Ἑβραιοις
ονομαζεται. Ibid.

Wherefore upon this account they got the name of Ebion, denoting the poornefs of their underftanding; for by this name do the Hebrews call a poor man (or this word fignifies poor in Hebrew.)

FROM which words it feems plain, that EUSEBIUS thought they received their name, not from their circ·..mftances, but the nature of their opinions.

NOW

Now it appears hence, that whether this were the true reaſon of the name given the Ebionites or not, 'tis what ORIGEN and EUSEBIUS (as did alſo others of the antient Fathers who treat of this matter) give of it; and no proof of the contrary appears, unleſs you will take thoſe Ebionites own account of it, which is recited in EPIPHANIUS, to which our author refers us, p. 27. But ſo far as I have learn'd of the character of thoſe Ebionites in EPIPHANIUS, either from EPIPHANIUS himſelf or other ancient books, it does not appear clear enough to me, to induce me to lay much ſtreſs upon either their honeſty or their judgment.

NAZARENUS, *c.* 9. *p.* 27, 28.

" WHATEVER confuſion and diverſity
" may be obſerved concerning them in IRE-
" NÆUS, JUSTIN MARTYR, EUSEBIUS, EPI-
" PHANIUS, AUGUSTIN, THEODORET and others
" of thoſe they call the old Fathers, 'tis con-
" ſtantly agreed among them, that the Na-
" zarens and Ebionites affirmed JESUS to
" have been a meer man, as well by the Fa-
" ther's as the Mother's ſide, namely the ſon
" of JOSEPH and MARY, &c. &c.

I remember not where IRENÆUS, JUSTIN MARTYR and EUSEBIUS give this account of the NAZARENS, as holding all the opinions
here

here recited in common with the EBIONITES.
Nor fhall I believe it till fome plain paffages
be produced out of them to prove it. IRE-
NÆUS has not entred the NAZARENS into his
lift of Heretics; neither he, nor JUSTIN MAR-
TYR, make mention of them under that name.
EUSEBIUS, as far as I remember, is filent concerning them; his Hiftory furnifhes no paffage
to fupport this account. TERTULLIAN indeed mentions the NAZARENS; but does not
charge them with thefe opinions. I make it
a queftion whether any one of the Fathers
before the fourth Century mention the NA-
ZARENS as Heretics, and agreeing with the E-
BIONITES in their fentiments; and if they do
not, I fee no reafon for our Authors ufing the
words EBIONITES and NAZARENS promifcuoufly, as if they fignify'd precifely the fame
perfons.

EPIPHANIUS has put the NAZARENS into
his lift of Heretics. He tells us they obferved
the law, but does not pofitively fay that they
held CHRIST to be a meer man defcended from
man, as well by the father's as by the mother's
fide.

His words are:

Περι Χριϛ8 δε 8κ οι-
δα ειπειν, ει κJ αυτοι
τη των περειρημενων
περι Κηρινϑον καj Μηριν-

But as to Chrift I
cannot fay whether
they (i. e. the Naza-
rens) being led by the
wicked-

Ϩον μοχϑηριᾳ αχϑεντς, ψιλον ανθεωπον νομιζυσιν η κρϑως η αληϑεια εχει δια Πνευμαϊ Ὁ. Ἁγιυ γεγενῃαϑαι εκ Μαριας διαϐεϐα υνται. *Hæref.* 29. *p.* 58.

wickednefs of the Cerinthians and Merinthians hold him to be a meer man, or affert that he, as the truth is, was (born of) fprung from Mary by the Holy Spirit.

A S to that paffage relating to the reafon of JESUS's being own'd for the Son of God, 'tis not exprefly affign'd by IRENÆUS, ORIGEN, EUSEBIUS or TERTULLIAN in their account of the EBIONITES as theirs; (THEODORET I have not by me, and fo could not confult him,) and as far as I have yet been able to find, EPIPHANIUS is the chief, if not the only author, that has given us an account of the EBIONITES affigning that reafon; but it does not at all appear even from him, that the NAZARENS join'd with them in it. And according to his account, that was not the only reafon of his being call'd the Son of God affign'd by them.

His words are :

Ιησυν γεγενημενον εκ σπερμαϊ Ὁ. ανδρς λεγυσι ϗ επιλεχθεντα. ϗ ὕτω κατ᾽ εκλογην ὑον Θευ κληθεντα απο τυ ανωθεν εις αυτον ηκονϊ Ὁ.

They fay that Jefus was begotten of the feed of a man and chofen; and fo called the Son of God according to election from

Χειςυ εν ειδει περιςε-
ρας· υ φασκυσι δε εκ
Θευ Πα]ερς αυτον γε-
γεννηαθαι αλλα εκτισ-
θαι, κ. τ. λ. *Haeref.*
30. *p.* 66.

from Chrift's coming down upon him in the form of a Dove. But they do not fay that he was begotten but created by God the Father, &c.

Τον Χριςον λεγυσι Πρ-
φητην της αληθειας· Και
Χριςον ύον Θευ κατα
πρηοπην κ̀ κατα συνα-
φειαν αναγωγης της ανω-
θεν πρ̀ς αυτον γεγενη-
μενης· Τυς δε Περφητας
λεγυσι συνεσεως ειναι
Περφη]ας κ̀ υκ αληθει-
ας· αυτον δε μονον ει-
ναι Περφητην κ̀ ανθρω-
πον κ̀ ύον θευ κ̀ Χρι-
ςον κ̀ ψιλον ανθρωπον,
ως πρ̀ειπομεν, δια δε
την αρετην 6ιυ ήκον]α εις
το καλειαθαι ύον Θευ.
ibid. p. 67.

They fay that Chrift was a Prophet of truth, and Chrift the fon of God on account of his proficiency and intimate acquaintance with the fublime knowledge that came to him from above. But they fay the Prophets are Prophets of underftanding but not truth; and that he alone is a Prophet, and man, and fon of God, and Chrift, and a meer man as we faid before, but that by a virtuous life he came to be called the fon of God.

SO that if I underftand him right, EPIPHA-NIUS fuggefts three particulars upon account of which according to the Ebionites he was called the Son of God, viz. his being chosen and marked out by God by the descent of CHRIST in form of a Dove; his being favoured with a deep knowledge of divine mysteries, and his virtuous life; unless you rather suppose the two first to fall into one.

IN the Gospel according to the Hebrews which was used by the Ebionites, the Holy Spirit is called by our Saviour, his Mother, as appears from divers passages in ORIGEN and JEROM, as particularly that where ORIGEN has these words:

Εαν δε προσιεται τις το καθ' Ἑβραιυς Ευαγγελιον, ενθα αυτ⊙ ὁ Σωτηρ φησι· Αρτι ελαβε με ἡ μητηρ μυ, το ἁγιον πνευμα εν μια των τειχων μυ, ϗ απενεγκε μυ εις το ορος το μεγα Θαβορ κ. τ. λ. *Com. in Joann. Tom. 2. p. 58. D.*

But if any one admit the Gospel according to the Hebrews, where the Saviour himself saith, my Mother the Holy Spirit took me a little while ago by one of the hairs of my head, and carried me to the great mountain Tabor, &c.

BUT on what account the Holy Spirit was called his Mother, does not appear. By that descent he was endued with wisdom and knowledge, if JEROM's conjecture be right, in his Commentary on Esai. 11. 2. On occasion of those words, " the spirit of wisdom and " the spirit of understanding", he there cites a
fragment

fragment of the Hebrew Gospel of the Nazarens, which I shall add here because the Spirit calls him there his first begotten:

In Evangelio, cujus supra fecimus mentionem, hæc scripta reperimus: Factum est autem cum ascendisset Dominus de aqua, descendit fons omnis spiritus sancti, & requievit super eum & dixit illi: Fili mi, in omnibus Prophetis expectabam te ut venires & requiescerem in te. Tu es enim requies mea, tu es filius meus primogenitus, qui regnas in sempiternum.

In the Gospel above-mentioned (i. e. the Hebrew one) we find these things written: But it came to pass that when the Lord came up from the water, the whole fountain of the Holy Spirit came down, and rested upon him, and said to him, In all the Prophets I look'd for thee that thou mightest come, and I might rest upon thee. Thou art my rest, thou art my first born Son, who reignest for ever.

WHERE AUGUSTIN makes the Ebionites and Nazarens agree in all the particulars mentioned by our Author, I know not. In his Book of Heresies he mentions them as two sorts of Heretics, and tells us the Nazarens own CHRIST to be the Son of God, but does not say on what account; and that

d 2

the

the Ebionites fay Christ was only a man.

AS to the paſſage referred to in Eusebius by our Author, to prove that he made the Nazarens and Ebionites agree in all the particulars here recited, I find mention only of the Ebionites there; and he does not tell us that they affirmed that Jesus merited to be peculiarly call'd the Son of God, by reaſon of his moſt virtuous life, but only that he was juſtify'd on the account of it.

His words are :

Λιτον αυτον ϰ ϰοινον ηγευντο, ϰατα προϰοπην ηθυς αυτον μονον ανθεωπον δεδιϰαιωμενον. *Hiſt. Ecclef. lib.* 3. *c.* 27.	They were of opinion that he was a meer and common man, but that being only a man he was juſtify'd upon account of the excellency of his morals.

OUR Author himſelf obſerves, that in Eusebius's time the Ebionites were divided in their opinion about the parents of Christ.

Nazarenus, *cap.* 9. *p.* 28.

" Eusebius faith that ſome few of them (the Author had been ſpeaking of the Ebionites and Nazarens, whom he calls
Jewiſh

Jewiſh Chriſtians) " in his time, that is, the
" fourth Century, believed like the Gentile
" Chriſtians, the mother of CHRIST to have
" been a Virgin ; and that he was conceived
" by virtue of the Spirit of God, tho' ſtill but
" a meer man, &c.

THE placing thoſe words, *believed like
the Gentile Chriſtians*, after this manner in
this ſentence, might induce one to believe
that they were made uſe of by EUSEBIUS
himſelf, which they are not ; for

His words are :

Αλλοι δε παρα τυτυς
της αυτης οντες περοη-
γοειας την μεν των ει-
ρημενων εκτοπον διεδι-
δρασκον ατοπιαν, εκ
παρθενυ κ̈ τυ αγιυ
Πνευμαῖ℗. μη αρνυμε-
νοι γεγονεναι τον Κυ-
ριον· υ μεν εϑ' ομοι-
ως κ̈ υτοι περϋπαρχειν
αυτον Θεον λογον οντα
κ̈ Σοφιαν ομολογυντες
τη των περπεων περι-
ειρεπονῖο δυασεβεια. *Hiſt.
Eccleſ. lib. 3. cap. 27.*

There were others be-
ſides theſe who went
under the ſame name,
who quitted the ab-
ſurdity of thoſe be-
fore-mentioned , not
denying the Lord to
be ſprung from the
Virgin and the Holy
Spirit. But theſe like
the others not own-
ing that he had any
exiſtence before, as be-
ing God, the Word,
and Wiſdom, were in-
volved in the impiety
of the firſt.

WHERE

WHERE it is proper to obſerve, that he ſpeaks not here of the Nazarens but the Ebionites; that he does not ſay whether there were ſome few or many of this party of the Ebionites, nor makes any mention of the Gentile Chriſtians; nor ſo much as hint to us any thing that ſhould perſuade us that it was an opinion peculiar to Gentile Chriſtians before his time, to think that the mother of our Lord was a Virgin.

ADD to this, that theſe two different ſorts of Ebionites were obſerved before Eu-SEBIUS's time by ORIGEN;

whoſe words are :

Ουτοι δ'εισιν οι διτλοι Εβιωναιοι· οι, η τοι εκ παρθενυ ομολογυντες ομοιως ημιν τον Ιησυν, η υχ ετω γεγεννωθαι αλλ' ως τυς λοιπυς ανθρωπυς. *lib.* 5. *contra Celſ. p.* 272.

Theſe are the two ſorts of Ebionites, being either ſuch as with us acknowledge Jeſus to be born of a Virgin, or ſuch as pretend, that he was not born ſo, but as other men.

THESE things conſidered, it muſt be own'd, that the account of our Author would have been more ſatisfactory, it he had diſtinctly told us which of the Fathers aſſerted one part and which the other, of thoſe things he has put together in page 27, at the end of the page, and at the beginning of 28: it not appearing from the paſſages he refers to, that all thoſe he mentions agreed in all the particulars.

NAZARENUS, *c.* 12. *p.* 40, 41.

" NO other ſcheme can reconcile Chri-
" ſtianity and the promiſes of everlaſting du-
" ration made in favour of the Jewiſh Law:
" which are poorly, I will not ſay ſophiſtical-
" ly, evaded by making the words *eternal,*
" *everlaſting, for ever, perpetual,* and *through-*
" *out all generations,* to mean only a great
" while; that the way of CHRIST's *accom-*
" *pliſhing the law,* was to aboliſh it; and that
" *till heaven and earth ſhall paſs,* ſignify'd till
" the reign of TIBERIUS CÆSAR.

WITH reſpect to this paſſage one can hardly forbear obſerving that our Author's ſcheme may be reaſon'd againſt, by arguments drawn from theſe phraſes, as well as that of thoſe whom he oppoſes. For according to the Ebionite ſcheme JESUS came into the world to aboliſh ſacrifices, and conſequently that part of the Levitical Law relating to them is not now to be obſerved, as appears from a paſſage cited by EPIPHANIUS, out of the Goſpel according to the Hebrews, which was in uſe among the Ebionites.

His

His words are :

Ελθοντα κỳ ύφηγησαμε- | *But they say that* he
νον ώς το παρ' αυτοις | came and declared, as
Ευαγγελιον καλυμενον | it is said, in what is
περιεχει, ότι ηλθον κα- | called the Gospel by
ταλυσαι τας θυσιας· κỳ | them, that I came to
εαν μη παυσησθε τε θυ- | abolish sacrifices, and
ειν, ε παυσεται αφ' ύ- | if you cease not from
μων ή οργη· *Hæres.* | sacrificing, wrath shall
30. *p.* 66. | not cease from you.

S O that one part of the business of JESUS upon earth was to declare those who continued to sacrifice to be under wrath. What then is become of the statutes made in favour of the eternal duration of the Jewish laws about Sacrifices ? With respect to the orders given about the Paschal Lamb, the law says, " ye shall observe this thing for an or-" dinance to thee and to thy sons for ever", *Exod.* 12. 24. And again some parts of the sacrifices of the peace-offerings are given to AARON the Priest and to his sons by a statute for ever, *Levit.* 7. 34. So with respect to what the High-priest should do on the day of atonement, 'tis said " this shall be an everlasting " statute unto you", *Levit.* 16. 34. and divers other such passages there are. For those phrases cited by our Author as favouring the perpetual duration of MOSES's law, are as commonly made use of in reference to sacrifices as to
                                                            any

any ordinances whatfoever in the law; when yet our Author owns the law to be changed with refpect to thefe. Vid. *Nazaren.* p. 63, 64.

NAZARENUS, *cap.* 16. *p.* 62.

" *Works* there (i. e. in JAMES's Epiftle)
" fignify the Levitical Law, as *Faith* is put for
" Chriftianity;" and afterwards " *Works* are
" interpreted to fignify the Levitical rites.

OUR Author's fenfe of the word *Works* is not countenanced by the examples here made ufe of to prove JAMES's doctrine. " Was not (faith " JAMES) ABRAHAM juftify'd by Works? cap. 2. " 21. and was not RAHAB juftify'd by Works?" ver. 25 : when yet ABRAHAM was dead fome hundreds of years before the Eftablifhment of the Levitical Law, and RAHAB was a Canaanitefs, and not obliged to the obfervation of it. And the *Works* by which they were faid to be juftify'd, were neither of them fuch as were bound upon them by that Law. So that according to this interpretation, JAMES infifts upon it, that the Jews were to be juftify'd by the Works of the Levitical Law, becaufe their Father ABRAHAM and another perfon were juftify'd without them.

WHEN I confider the titles given by JAMES to the Law, the obfervance of which is recommended as fo neceffary, which is called " the ingrafted word which is able to fave
" fouls

" fouls in cap. 1. 21; and the perfect law of
" liberty ver. 25; and the inftances of obedience
mention'd in cap. 2. as alfo the examples of
obedience before mentioned, I cannot perfuade my felf that by *Works* he only means
the Levitical rites, if he do at all directly mean
them. It feems more agreeable to the tenor
of his difcourfe to fuppofe that he means by
Faith a firm and well grounded perfuafion
of the certainty of any truth made known
to us by God, and particularly of the principles of the Chriftian Religion; and by *Works*
fuch kind of actions as thofe principles are
defign'd and fitted to put us upon. And his
defign is plainly to teach us that if we entertain in our minds the beft principles in
the world; as particularly thofe which the
doctrine of Chrift teaches us, yet if we do
not act up to them we muft expect to be
condemned. And that of Chriftians he and
he only who acts according·to thefe his principles fhall be accepted, acquitted, and pro-
nounced righteous by God when his cafe comes
to be try'd.

NAZARENUS, cap. 16. p. 63.

" THAT *the Law was our fchoolmafter*
" *to bring us unto Chrift* .... is a phrafe to
" be underftood only of us Gentiles.

THIS I can by no means grant, when I
confider the words immediately preceding
and

and following thofe here cited. The words preceding (Gal. 3. 23.) are, *Before Faith (or the Faith) came, we were kept under the Law fhut up unto the Faith, which fhould afterwards be revealed.* So that the law was the Schoolmafter only of thofe that were under it, which very perfons were freed from this Schoolmafter by the coming of the Faith; as the words following inform us, ver. 25. *But after that* (the) *Faith is come, we are no longer under a fchoolmafter.* Unlefs therefore we will fuppofe the Gentiles to have been under the Levitical Law before the Gofpel was publifhed, the words ver. 24. cannot reafonably be apply'd to them, efpecially not fo as to exclude the Jews, who are own'd by all to have been under the law before that time.

ANNOTATIUNCULÆ
SUBITANEÆ
AD
LIBRUM
DE

Christianismo Mysteriis carente :

Conscriptæ 8 Augusti 1701 *.

L IBER Anglicana lingua scriptus, sæpe auditus mihi, nondum visus, *de Christianismo mysteriis carente,* cum nuper in manus m..as venisset; non potui temperare mihi quin perlegerem statim, & more meo aliquas Notatiunculas in chartam conjicerem inter legendum, quod non rarò facio cum Libri occurrunt singulares. Hunc certè ingeniosè scriptum esse fateri oportet. Et, cùm caritas non sit suspicax, ego mihi libenter persuadeo, scopum

* The celebrated Mr. LEIBNIZ is the Author of these Remarks.

ſcopum Autoris, viri doctrina & ingenio non vulgari præditi, & ut arbitror bene animati, fuiſſe ut homines à Theologia theoretica ad practicam, à diſputationibus circa perſonam Chriſti ad ſtudium imitandæ ejus vitæ revocaret ; etſi via, qua ad hunc ſcopum ivit, non ſatis recta aut plana ubiq; videatur. Equidem Theologiam vere Chriſtianam, eſſe practicam conſtat, & primarium Chriſti ſcopum fuiſſe potiùs inſpirare voluntati ſanctitatem, quam intellectui immittere notiones veritatum arcanarum.

NON tamen ideò negari debet, per Chriſtum nobis revelatas fuiſſe divinas doctrinas quas ratio perſpicere, non poteſt, & cavenda mihi videntur non tantùm quæ ſectarias opiniones Theologorum fovent, ſed etiam multo magis quæ Clerum Reformatum plebi odioſum reddere aut in contemtum adducere poſſunt ; quòd genus ſectæ omnium periculoſiſſimum foret, nam turbas dare poſſet, quibus alimenta ſubminiſtrare alieniſſimum eſſe arbitror à mente autoris, qui ut virum probum decet ſuas cogitationes ad bonum reipublicæ dirigere velle profitetur. Certè errores & abuſus qui irrepſêre in Eccleſiam, non tam cleri artibus, quàm temporum vitio tribui debent; ipſamq; autoritatem Pontificum nimiam, paulatim enatam conſtat circumſtantiis faventibus, & caſu interveniente ut ſolet. Præterea illis temporibus quibus ſolus ſapiebat clerus, cæteri verò omnes ingenui homines militares
erant ;

erant; non abfurdum erat, militare imperium fapientum, id eft cleri, autoritate temperari.

TITULUS ipfe Libri mihi videtur longiùs ire quam par eft, nam ita habet: *Chriftianifmus myfterio carens, hoc eft Tractatus oftendens nihil ineffe Evangelio contrarium rationi, nihil fupra rationem; atq; adeo nullam Chriftianam doctrinam myfterii nomine proprie loquendo appellari poffe.* Equidem omnes fatentur nihil ineffe debere Theologiæ Chriftianæ quod fit contrarium rationi, id eft abfurdum; fed eidem nihil ineffe quod fit fupra rationem, id eft, quod ratione noftra comprehendi nequeat, non video qua probabilitate dici poffit; cum ipfa divina natura, quæ infinita eft, neceffario fit incomprehenfibilis: quemadmodum & in omnibus fubftantiis aliquid ineft infiniti, unde fit ut a nobis perfecte intelligi poffint folæ notiones incompletæ, quales funt numerorum, figurarum, aliorumq; hujufmodi modorum à rebus animo abftractorum. Fateor effe nobis, ut optimè obfervat autor, diftinctam quandam infiniti (per fe fcilicet feu abfoluti) notionem; fed non eft nobis finito intellectu præditis, infinitarum varietatum diftincta confideratio, qua tamen in rebus præfertim divinis comprehendendis perfæpe opus foret. Itaq; miror initio ftatim Libri, in præliminari formatione ftatus controverfiæ, improbari eos qui dicunt: " adorandum effe " quod nequit comprehendi; " quo tamen pronuntiato nihil mihi videtur effe certius: nifi

fcilicet

ſcilicet Comprehenſionem, ut alicubi Cl. Autor facit, (*Sect. 3. cap. 2.*) ita interpretemur, ut nihil aliud ſignificet quàm cognitionem ; qui tamen ſenſus non eſt uſitatus, nec proinde in populari uſu facile adhibendus.

AD SECTIONEM I.

VENIO ad Libri contenta primaria, & Sectionem quidem primam *de Ratione ;* ubi *Capite* 1. autor ingenioſus ait *eſſe in nobis Facultates formandi ideas ac perceptiones rerum, affirmandiq; aut negandi prout eas inter ſe convenire aut diſſidere perſpicimus ; atq; inde amandi ac deſiderandi bona, aut contra odio habendi fugiendiq; mala.* Et legitimum harum facultatum uſum eſſe *Senſum communem* aut *Rationem in univerſum.* Hanc ego Definitionem libenter concedam , quia bonum ſenſum admittit. Tametſi aliquid in ea deſiderari poſſit, dum non explicat in quo rectus ille uſus conſiſtat. Quod tamen hoc loco facilius excuſari poteſt, quia ſcopus autoris non eſt hæc tractare ex profeſſo. *Ideam* definit *immediatum cogitationis objectum,* quod ab aliorum quoq; ſenſu non abhorret.

Capite 2. tractat in quo Ratio conſiſtat; aitq; *Cognitionem* eſſe *perceptionem conſenſus aut diſſenſus idearum:* in quo nonnihil hæreo. Videtur enim mihi id verum quidem eſſe in noſtra cognitione rationali, nempe ex ideis ſive definitionibus deducta, quam dicimus

cimus effe à priori, fed non in cognitione à
pofteriori fumta, five experimentali; ubi fæpe
nullas diftinctas ideas habemus, neq; adeò con-
fenfum aut diffenfum earum percipimus : ita
(ut exemplo utar) experimento quidem cog-
nofcimus acida firupum violarum rubro co-
lore tingere, fed nullam perfpicimus confen-
fionem idearum, quas acidi & rubri & violacei
diftinctas nondum habemus. Solius DEI eft
omnia deducere ex mentis fuæ ideis.   Quæ
adduntur de duplici *cognitione* (rationali fcilicet) *immediata* & *mediata,* laudo; etfi al-
tius penetrandum putem,   ut res fufficienter
explicetur, quod fateor hujus loci non effe.

Caput. 3. fine Annotatione tranfmittere
poffe mihi videor.

IN *Capite* 4. admittere poffum *fundamentum perfuafionis effe evidentiam,* modo
abufus hujus doctrinæ abfit.   Etfi enim id
de quo perfuafi fumus non femper fit evidens;
debet tamen evidentia intervenire in modo
perfuadendi.   Verbi gratia, evidens effe nobis
debet autoritas eorum quibus credimus aliquid
contigiffe, quod tamen quomodo factum fit
non femper perfpicimus.   Ita qui ignorant
quomodo Hydropota intra breve temporis
fpatium ex ore magnam copiam lactis, atra-
menti, cerevifiæ, vini rhenani, vini ex tellina
valle, fpiritus vini, aliorumq; liquorum in con-
fpectu virorum perfpicacium, & de propinquo
intentorum emittere potuerit; rem tamen fac-
                                                        tam

tam esse, non tam mihi (qui bis Hanoveræ vidi) quam tot aliis mecum testibus oculatis credere possunt, eorumque errorem à scriptoribus nonnullis temere defensum deponere, quibus persuasum est non veros esse illos liquores sed simulatos tantùm & in speciem nescio quibus essentiis tinctos. Et hæc *Evidentia* in rebus fidei divinæ inest iis argumentis, quæ vulgò multi Theologi (minùs eleganter quidem) vocant *motiva credibilitatis.* Sed explicandum erat *Evidentiæ criterion :* multos enim vidi ad Evidentiam provocare ubi nulla erat. Itaque in Schediasmate quodam Actis Lipsiensibus inserto *De cognitione, veritate, & ideis,* pro parte supplere conatus sum hunc defectum scriptoribus communem.

AD SECTIONEM II.

CLARISSIMUS Autor *agnoscit neminem Theologorum quos norit, aliquid credendum docere, quod fateatur rationi contrarium ; à plerisque tamen doceri, omnino fieri posse ut fidei dogma rationi contrarium saltem videatur :* quod ipse impugnat *Capite* 1. ubi obiter annoto Evangelicis, quos (invitis ipsorum præstantissimis non paucis) *Lutheranos* appellat, non recte imputari *impanationem,* nec ab omnibus ipsorum Theologis admitti *ubiquitatem,* vel potius omni-præsentiam carnis Christi. Rectè verò culpari *Socinianos* quod *creatum quendam Deum introducunt divini honoris capacem.*

QUOD

QUOD attinet *communes notiones* quibus congruunt aut non congruunt divinæ veritates, jamdudum diftinxere prudentes Theologi inter eas quæ funt metaphyficæ neceffitatis, ubi contrarium implicat contradictionem, à quibus diffidere nulla divina veritas poteft; & inter veritates phyficas, quæ hauftæ funt ab experientia atque ut fic dicam ex confuetudine mundi, cui derogare Deum nihil prohibet, cum etiam in naturalibus tale quid contingere fæpe videamus, ut ipfe Cl. Autor infra agnofcit. Talis veritas eft, maffam ferream fua natura in aqua defcendere; quod tamen cùm non fiat, quoties ea arte in cavum lebetem formatur, quis dubitat multo magis Deo modos præfto effe idem efficiendi, dum naturæ arcana quadam ratione affiftit?

SED hoc miffo, infpiciamus an hîc res eodem redeat, ut ait Dn. Autor, *five contradictio fit vera five apparens.* Id vero ego mihi perfuadere non poffum. Equidem fateor, nobis regulariter fequenda effe quæ apparent; & verorum locum tenere; fed quoties plura apparent inter fe contraria regulam neceffario ceffare; & expendendum effe quænam verifimilitudo magis fit fequenda. Ubi non tantùm fpectandum eft quæ fententia fit probabilior, fed & quæ fit tutior. Veluti fi major mihi probabilitas lucrandi quam perdendi proponatur;

fed

fed lucrum fit futurum exiguum, damnum vero ingens; fitque multo major ratio damni ad lucrum quam fpei ad metum, rectiùs propofita conditione abftinebo. Ita fi verba Domini faveant uni fententiæ, & rerum fpecies alteri, & verbo Domini potius ftando rebus Domini nullum periculum crectur, à verbis autem recedendo periculum accerfatur mihi, profectò rectiùs verbis inhærebo neque recedam ἀπὸ τᾷ ῥητᾷ prætextu τῆς διανοίας. Idque tanto magis verum eft, quanto Dominus prudentior eft & major; cum etiam in re militari miles non impune fit laturus, qui verba mandati ab imperatore fuo profecti fine graviffima caufa deferit. Cæterum *apparentem contradictionem* hic intelligo eam quæ re non fatis difcuffa offertur; veluti fi quis infpectis obiter tabulis rationum ab agente in rebus redditarum, videatur fibi errorem videre aut in calculo, aut in materia calculi: ille huic judicio fuo fidere non debet, nifi examine ut par eft iterato & difcuffione abfoluta confirmetur; cum nihil in rebus impeditis fit magis lubricum quam judicium promtum.

QUOD verò hoc loco dicitur *neminem credere poffe nifi quod animo concipit,* verum eft, fi non nimium extendatur. Verba fenfum aliquem habere oportet, fed non femper neceffarios effe conceptus diftinctos, nedum adæquatos, experimenta oftendunt (qualium & fupra memini) quibus fidem adhibemus tametfi de multis fenfuum objectis imme-

diatis

diatis, (veluti coloribus, odoribufque) diftinctos conceptus non habeamus. Etiam in me-
taphyficis Cl. Autor nofter cum plerifque aliis
loquitur de *fubftantia* tanquam fuftentaculo,
de *caufa,* aliifque multis ; etfi diftinctæ fatis
notiones vulgo fortaffe defint. Immo oftendi
alibi, effe quædam in ipfis primis Geometriæ
notionibus non fatis hactenus à Geometris ex-
plicata. Et quanto quifque in meditationibus
verfatior eft, tanto magis hos defectus agnofcit, animumque ad eam præfertim in facris
modeftiam componit, quæ neque exigat nimium neque polliceatur.

Cap. 2. dicitur *Revelationem effe tantum
modum informationis, non argumentum affen-
fum extorquens ;* cujus pronuntiati fi is eft
fenfus, Revelationem non plus habere auto-
ritatis quam magiftrum cui credimus tantum
quia probat, aut quia rem per diftinctos conceptus explicat, ftare nequit. Nam Revelator
non tantum habet perfonam magiftri aut do-
centis, fed & teftis imò judicis irrefragabilis ;
poftquam fcilicet conftat, quod revelans fit
ipfe Deus. Itaque etiam in humanis non
femper opus eft *evidentia in rebus* (quam
Cl. Autor requirit) modo fit *in perfonis,* ut
de earum fide conftet. Secus eft in doctrinis
quæ ratione conftant, ut fi magifter me do-
ceat Geometriam; ibi enim locum habet, quod
Cl. Autor paulo generaliùs pronuntiare videtur, *fundamentum perfuafionis meæ effe non
autoritatem dicentis, fed claritatem concep-
tionis.*

tionis. Illud utique veriſſimum eſt, nihil eſſe in divina revelatione quod non ſit dignum Deo, qui ſumma ratio eſt : ſed ſcimus tamen etiam in oeconomia naturæ multa nobis viſa eſſe abſurda, ob noſtram ignorantiam, quia in vero centro collocati non ſumus, unde rerum pulchritudo ſpectari debet. Ita Alphonſus Rex, Aſtronomiæ ſtudio inſignis, ridicule credebat melioris Syſtematis ideam ſe daturum fuiſſe, ſi à creatore in conſilium adhibitus fuiſſet. Cum tamen nunc, ex quo nos animo in ſolem (quem deprehenſum eſt centrum eſſe hujus ſyſtematis) transferre didicimus ; manifeſtum ſit pulcherrimam eſſe rerum conſtitutionem.

Cap. 3. concedit Cl. Autor, ut par eſt, *miracula à Chriſto fuiſſe edita :* ſed hoc ipſo, ſi quid judico, etiam concedit eſſe aliquid credendum in Chriſtiana Religione quod ſit ſupra rationem noſtram : quid aliud enim miracula ſunt quàm operationes quæ ex naturæ creatæ legibus quas intellectus creatus quantæcunque capacitatis percipere poſſet, derivari non poſſunt. De cætero bene diſputat contra eos, qui Evangeliſtas & Apoſtolos male & obſcure ſcripſiſſe putant de rebus quas ſcire oportet.

Cap. 4. reſpondet objicientibus *corruptam eſſe rationem noſtram.* Hic mihi videtur rurſus non male diſputare dum diſtinguit inter ipſam *Rationem* & *pravum* facultatis bonæ

e 3   *uſum*

ufum, uti diſtinguimus inter artem & artificem.
Interim non auſim dicere quod habetur §. 31.
omnes noſtras cogitationes plane liberas eſſe;
arbitror enim in quantum noſtra natura in-
firma vel corrupta eſt, in tantum nos ſervituti
obnoxios eſſe. Et cùm mox diſputat pro omni-
moda *arbitrii libertate,* vereor ne longius pro-
cedat quam res patiatur aut ſit neceſſe. Sed ea
quæſtio hujus loci non eſt.

AD SECTIONEM III.

Cap. 1. Autor oſtendit *Myſteria* apud Ethnicos
ſignificaſſe *ritus arcanos in quibus profani aut
non initiati admitti non debebant;* adeoq; *myſterium* olim fuiſſe *rem non intellectam quidem, ſed valde tamen intelligibilem ſi revela-
retur.* Hoc non illibenter admiſero. Genti-
lium enim Religio non tam in dogmatibus
quam ceremoniis conſiſtebat, quæ quiſq; pro
lubitu interpretabatur : unde fiebat etiam ut inter ipſos de religionibus non certaretur.

Cap. 2. obſervat *non ſtatim Myſteria eſſe,
quorum adæquatas ideas aut omnium ſimul
proprietatum notitiam non habemus.* In quo
ipſi libens itidem aſſentior, alioqui enim etiam
circuli & reliquæ figuræ forent myſteria. Sed
illud jam quæritur utrum aliqua ſint Myſteria
in natura ? ubi aio ſi *Myſterii* voce intelliga-
tur quicquid præſentem rationem noſtram ſu-
perat, innumera etiam phyſica myſteria depre-
hendi. Ità ſi quæratur an aquæ interior cognitio

ſit

fit fupra noftram rationem, refpondeo effe fupra præfentem : nondum enim à quoquam ejus texturam fatis expofitam puto ; fed tamen non defpero poffe aliquando explicationem dari quæ phænomenis fatisfaciat. Sunt etiam multa fupra rationem humanam pofita non noftram tantum, fed & pofterorum, feu qualis fcilicet non nunc tantum exiftit, fed & unquam erit in hac vita quam in terris degimus ; etfi fieri omnino poffit, ut ab aliqua creatura nobiliore intelligantur, & nobis etiam in nobiliorem ftatum tranflatis aliquando fint futura intelligibilia.

SED fi quis *Myfterium* appellet quicquid eft fupra omnem rationem creatam ; aufim dicere, nulla quidem phænomena naturalia fupra rationem effe, fed ipfas tamen fubftantiarum fingularium comprehenfiones creato intellectui effe impoffibiles quia infinitum involvunt. Unde fit ut rerum univerfi perfecta ratio reddi non poffit. Et talia nihil prohibet effe etiam dogmata quædam divinitus revelata, ut nulla rationis vi fatis explicari queant etfi animo utcunq; attingantur atq; etiam à contradictionis accufatione rite vindicari poffint. Porro *comprehenfionem* appello non tantum cùm diftinctæ interveniunt ideæ, fed & cùm adæquatæ ; id eft cùm non tantum propofiti termini habetur definitio five refolutio, fed & quivis terminus eam ingrediens rurfus refolutus habetur ufque ad primitivos ; ut in numeris experimur.

Cap. 3. oſtendere aggreditur etiam in Scriptura ſacra & libris primæ antiquitatis *Myſterium* vulgari Theologorum ſenſu incognitum eſſe. Adducit tamen ipſe locum Pauli 1 Cor. ii. 9, 10. ubi dicitur *nec oculum vidiſſe, neq; aurem audiſſe, nec in hominis cor intraſſe, quæ Deus amicis ſuis paravit.* Ubi videtur aliquid intelligi quod nobis ignotum eſt, non ideò tantùm quia nobis non eſt dictum, ſed etiam quia licet nobis diceretur, percipi non poſſet niſi exaltarentur ſenſus noſtri & veniremus in rem præſentem per altiorem quandam experientiam : prorſus ut cæcus de coloribus judicare non poteſt, etſi ipſi colorum doctrina exponatur, niſi oculi ejus aperiantur.

CÆTERUM illud bene notat Autor noſter, multa ignota fuiſſe Philoſophis & nuda ratione obtineri non potuiſſe, non quod eſſent incomprehenſibilia, ſed quod penderent à re facti nonniſi per divinam Revelationem cognoſcenda. In exemplum affert doctrinam de *lapſu Adami,* quæ difficultates tollat de cauſa peccati, quibus Philoſophi exercebantur.

CÆTERUM quod ait §. 30. *nihil magni præſtari ſi reveletur veritas incomprehenſibilis,* non, puto ac ſemper jure dici. Sic in naturalibus quoq; detectio acus magneticæ res magna eſt eritq; etſi operationes ejus perpetuò nobis inexplicatæ manerent. Eodem modo in Theologia veritas cujus ratio reddi nequit

magni

magni tamen ad salutis oeconomiam momenti esse potest.

IN 1 Tim. iii. 16. videtur *Mysterium* etiam aliquid amplius significare quam *rem ignotam quidem antea, sed revelatione facta facilem intellectu.* Nam cùm dicitur *Deum manifestatum in carne, visum Angelis, receptum in gloria,* apparet intelligi quæ naturam creatam, viresq; rationis transcendunt.

OBITER annoto quod ait Dn. Autor §. 39. *veteres in pueritia mundi vixisse, & nos adultiore ejus ætate vivere, adeoq; præsentia potius vetera esse dicenda ;* verissimum equidem esse, & autoritati antiquorum detrahere in iis quæ sunt scientiæ & experientiæ, sed non in iis quæ sunt historiæ ac traditionis. Manifestum enim est remotiores à fonte narrationes vel voce vel scripto propagatas fieri indies imperfectiores.

Cap. 4. Respondet objectionibus à locis scripturæ, item à natura fidei petitis, quibus nunc ut inhæream necesse non puto. Tantum annoto quod dicitur §. 54. *Fidem esse ex auditu, sed si quæ audiamus non intelligantur inanem imo nullam fidem fore ;* esse quidem verissimum : sed multum tamen differre intellectum verborum & comprehensionem rei, ut etiam in naturalibus patet. Sæpe enim vel ideæ quas habemus, vel methodus ex ideis ratiocinandi quam habemus, non sufficiunt ad con-

connexionem subjecti & prædicati intelligendam
etsi aliquam subjecti & prædicati notitiam
præstent. Etiam in Geometria non est cujus-
vis, theoremata demonstrare figurarum distincte
licet cognitarum, quamvis ea theoremata jam
ab aliis sint inventa ac communicata.

Cap. 5. Cl. Autor sibi ipsi prudenter obji-
cit, quod supra objeceram, *Miracula esse supra
rationem.* Definitio *Miraculi* quam exhibet sic
satis ni fallor convenit communi doctrinæTheo-
logorum, ut scilicet sint *super leges naturæ
ordinariasq; operationes.* Recte tamen agnoscit
esse *possibilia & intelligibilia.* Sed eo modo
etiam Mysteria Theologis possibilia & intelligibilia sunt. Quis enim dubitat quin absit contradictio & verba intelligantur, etsi modus
explicandi utrobiq; rationis nostræ vim transc-
cendat. Itaque Vir Cl. objectioni mihi satis
fecisse non omnino videtur. Nihil refert, quod
mysteria sunt *doctrinæ,* & *miracula* sunt *historiæ*; nam miracula sunt ut sic dicam mysteria transitoria, & mysteria aliqua habent quodam modo miraculi durabilis naturam.

QUÆ *Cap.* 6. dicuntur de *introductione
Mysteriorum,& origineCeremoniarum,*brevitatis
causa non persequor, de re ipsa satis fecisse con-
tentus; nam quæ ad Historiam Ecclesiasticam
pertinent latius diffunduntur, quam ut brevi-
bus tractari possint, neq; necessaria sunt ad
scopum nostrum.

IN

IN *Conclufione* fperare jubet Cl. Autor *explicationem intelligibilem doctrinæ Novi Teftamenti.* Talem ego quoque putem dari poffe, imo, (etfi fortaffe difperfam) jam haberi; fi inferiore quodam intelligibilitatis gradu fimus contenti. Sed cum id opus non prodierit, non eft cur rei immorer hoc loco. Itaq; & ipfe finio, tantumq; addo: Philofophos noftri temporis infignes multa in natura agnofcere fupra noftræ rationis vires.

QUIDAM Cartefiani eximii unionem animæ & corporis pro miraculofa habent; alii compofitionem continui, aut conciliationem liberi arbitrii cum divina præordinatione negant comprehendi poffe.

LOCKIUS, magni nominis Philofophus Anglus, cujus fententias Autor nofter paffim probat, cum olim docuiffet omnia corporum phænomena poffe explicari ex foliditate & extenfione & harum modis; nunc in Refponfione quadam ad celeberrimum Stillingfleetium, Epifcopum nuper Wigornienfem doctiffimum, retractat fententiam magna cum laude ingenuitatis, & profundiffimi Newtoni perfuafus argumentis Attractionem cujufvis materiæ partis admittit originariam & a mechanifmo non derivatam, nec proinde ratione explicabilem.

EGO etfi fperem quædam ex dictis explicationem aliquam admittere, cujus & fpecimen dedi

dedi circa unionem animæ & corporis ; aliter
tamen agnofco interiorum naturæ incom-
prehenfibilem fublimitatem ab influxu infiniti
orientem, qui fons eft idearum clararum fimul
& tamen confufarum (quales fenfibilium qua-
rundam qualitatum habemus) quibus nulla
creatura penitus exui poteft, & quas in con-
troverfia inter eximios viros Stillingfleetium &
Lockium non fatis ab aliis difcretas puto. Atq;
hæc quidem omnia fanè oftendunt multo mi-
nus mirandum effe fi in rebus divinis occurrunt,
quæ rationis vires longe tranfcendunt. Quòd
fi ergo funt quædam difficilia & impedita apud
Theologos, non ideò aut ipfis infultandum, aut
Theologica Syftemata (id eft ordinatam doctrinæ expofitionem) rejicienda cenfeo, non magis quàm philofophica aut medica ; fed tantùm
cavendum (ut in medicina) ne nimium difpu-
tando praxin & falutem negligamus.

F I N I S.

BOOKS lately printed, and sold by J. PEELE.

I. THE history of the Conqueft of *Mexico* by the *Spaniards*: tranflated into *Englifh* from the original *Spanifh* of Don *Antonio de Solis*, Secretary and Hiftoriographer to his Catholic Majefty. By *Thomas Townfhend* Efq; In folio.

II. *Joannis Seldeni Jurifconfulti Opera omnia, tam edita quam inedita, in tribus voluminibus; collegit ac recenfuit, Vitam Auctoris, Præfationes & Indices adjecit David Wilkins S. T. P. Canonicus Cantuarienfis, 6 vol. folio.*

III. The Compleat Surveyor ; or, the whole Art of Surveying of Land, by a new Inftrument lately invented, as alfo by the plain Table, the Circumferenter, the Theodolite, as now improved, or by the Chain only. Containing plain and eafy Directions in feveral kinds of Menfuration, and other things neceffary to be known in a Work of this nature. By *William Leybourn*. The whole alter'd and amended, and two entire Books added by the Author long before his death. The fifth Edition, in nine Books. Every Operation, both Geometrical and Arithmetical, examin'd, and an Appendix added to the whole. Confifting of practical Obfervations in Land-Surveying. By *Sam. Cunn.* folio.

IV. A new Syftem of Agriculture, being a compleat Body of Husbandry and Gardening in all the parts of them, *viz.* Husbandry in the Field, and its Improvements. Of Foreft and Timber-Trees, great and fmall ; with Evergreens and Flowering Shrubs, &c. Of the Fruit-garden. Of the Kitchen-Garden. Of the Flower-garden. In five Books. Containing all the beft and lateft, as well as many new Improvements, ufeful to the Husbandman, Grazier, Planter, Gardener, and Florift. Wherein are interfperfed many curious Obfervations on Vegetation, on the Difeafes of Trees, and the general Annoyances to Vegetables, and their probable Cures. As alfo a particular Account of the famous Silphium of the Ancients. By *John Lawrence* M. A. Rector of *Bifhop's-Weremouth*, in the Bifhoprick of *Durham*, and Prebendary of the Church of *Sarum*. In Folio.

V. A general Treatife of Husbandry and Gardening : containing a new Syftem of Vegetation. Illuftrated with many Obfervations and Experiments. In two Volumes. Formerly publifh'd monthly, and now methodiz'd and digefted under proper Heads, with Additions, and great Alterations. In four Parts. Part I. Concerning the Improvement of Land, by fertilizing bad Soils. Of Stocking of Farms with Cattel, Poultry, Fifh, Bees, Graffes, Grain, Cyder, &c. Part II. Inftructions to a Gardener, wherein is demonftrated the Circulation of Sap, the Generation of

Plants,

Plants, the Nature of Soil, Air, and Situation. Of the Profits arifing from planting and raifing Timber. Part III. Of the Management of Fruit-Trees, with particular Obfervations relating to Grafting, Inarching, and Inoculating. Part IV. Remarks on the Difpofition of Gardens in general. Of the Method of managing Exotic Plants and Flowers, and naturalizing them to our Climate. With an Account of Stoves and Artificial Heats. Adorn'd with Cuts. By *Richard Bradley*, Profeffor of Botany in the Univerfity of *Cambridge*, and F. R. S. In two Volumes Octavo. Pr. 12 s.

VI. The Practical Fruit-Gardener; being the beft and neweft Method of raifing, planting, and pruning all forts of Fruit-trees, agreeably to the Experience and Practice of the moft eminent Gardeners and Nurfery-men. By *Stephen Switzer*. Revifed and recommended by the Reverend Mr. *Lawrence*, and Mr. *Bradley*. Adorn'd with proper Plans. In Octavo.

VII. An Hiftorical and Critical Account of the Life and Writings of *William Chillingworth*, Chancellor of the Church of *Sarum*. Wherein are inferted feveral original Letters of that Eminent Divine. By Mr. *Des Maizeaux*. F. R. S. In Octavo.

VIII. The Independent Whig. The third Edition, with Additions. In Octavo.

IX. The Spirit of the Ecclefiafticks of all Sects and Ages, as to the Doctrines of Morality, and more particularly the Spirit of the antient Fathers of the Church examin'd. By Monf. *Barbeyrac*, Profeffor of Laws and Hiftory in the Univerfity of *Laufanne*. Tranflated from the *French* by a Gentleman of *Grays-Inn*. With a Preface by the Author of the *Independent Whig*.

X. The Earl of *Shaftesbury's* Letters to the Lord Vifcount *Molefworth*, concerning the Choice of a Wife, and the Love of one's Country. To which is prefix'd a large Introduction by Mr. *Toland*, giving an Account of Lord *Shaftesbury's* Conduct in publick Affairs.

XI. The Laft Day. A Poem, in 12 Books. By *J. Bulkley* Efq; late of *Clare-Hall* in *Cambridge*, Author of the Letters to the Reverend Dr. *Clark*, on Liberty and Neceffity. The fecond Edition. In Octavo.

XII. Popery againft Chriftianity : or, an Hiftorical Account of the prefent State of *Rome* ; the Election of the late Pope ; the Proceedings of the Jefuits in *China*, and also in *England* and other Proteftant Countries. With an Appendix, containing the Lives and Canonization of the laft four Saints ; and feveral Decrees of Popes contradicting

one

one another. By *Parthenopæus Hereticus.* The second Edition. In Octavo.

XIII. The Case of *Ireland*'s being bound by Acts of Parliament in *England* stated. By *William Mollineux* of *Dublin* Esq; To which is added, The Case of Tenures upon the Commission of Defective Titles, argued by all the Judges of *Ireland.* With their Resolutions, and the Reasons of their Resolutions. In Octavo.

XIV. A Treatise of Laws: or, a general Introduction to the Common, Civil, and Canon Law. In three Parts. I. The Common Law of *England*; illustrated in great Variety of Maxims, &c. Also the Use of this Law; with References to the Statutes in all Cases. II. Of the Civil Law, intermix'd with the Law of Nations, and its Use here in *England*; and a Parallel between the Civil Law and Common Law. III. The Canon Law, and Laws Ecclesiastical; containing the Authority and Rights of the *English* Clergy; Of Patrons of Churches; Courts Ecclesiastical, Tryals, &c. In Octavo.

XV. The Law of Securities: being a Methodical Treatise of all the Laws and Statutes relating to Bills Obligatory, Bonds and Conditions, Judgments, Recognizances, Statutes, Mortgages, Securities Real and Personal, Collateral Securities, and all manner of Engagements for Money; shewing how far Persons and Estates are bound, and the Court of Chancery will give Relief. And also, The Laws and Statutes concerning Pawns, Pledges, and Usury, with the Methods of Prosecution, Pleadings. &c. and proper Precedents in all Cases interspers'd throughout. To which are added, The Laws against Bankrupts; with Variety of Law-Cases, Precedents of Commissions, Assignments of Commissioners, Certificates, Deeds of Distribution, &c. In Octavo.

XVI. The History of *John* of *Bourbon*, Prince of *Carency*; containing a Variety of entertaining Novels. Translated from the *French* of the Countess D'*Aunois.* The 2d Edit.

XVII. The *Dublin* Miscellany: being a Collection of Poems, original and translated. By Dr. *Swift*, Mr. *Parnell*, Dr. *Delany*, Mr. *Brown*, Mr. *Ward*, Mr. *Sterling*, Mr. *Concanen*, and others. In Octavo.

XVIII. A New Treatise of the Art of Thinking: containing a Compleat System of Reflections concerning the Conduct and Improvement of the Mind, in Enquiries into all kinds of Truth: especially such as relate to the Knowledge of Mankind. Illustrated with Variety of Characters and Examples, drawn from the ordinary Occurrences of
Life.

Life. Written in *French* by Monf. *Croufaz*, Profeſſor of Philoſophy and Mathematicks in the Univerſity of *Lau-ſane*. Tranſlated into *Engliſh*, in two Volumes Octavo.

XIX. A Collection of Debates in the Houſe of Commons in the Year 1680, relating to the Bill of Excluſion of the then Duke of *York*; containing the Speeches of the Lord *Ruſſel*, Sir *Henry Capel*, Sir *Francis Winnington*, *Ralph Montague* Eſq; *Henry Booth* Eſq; Sir *Gilbert Gerrard*, Sir *Lion. Jenkins*, Sir *Tho. Player*, Sir *Richard Graham*, Sir *William Poultney*, *Daniel Finch* Eſq; *Hugh Boſcawen* Eſq; *John Trenchard* Eſq; *John Hampden* Eſq; Sir *Roger Hill*, Sir *William Jones*, Sir *Richard Maſon*, *Lawrence Hyde* Eſq; Colonel *Legg*, *Edward Deering* Eſq; Colonel *Birch*, with many more; and a Liſt of the Members that compoſed that Honourable Houſe. To which are added, The Debates of the Houſe of Commons aſſembled at *Oxford*, *March* 21. 1680. as alſo an Introduction, ſhewing the Progreſs of Popery from the Reformation to the preſent Time. In Octavo.

XX. An Hiſtorical Eſſay on the Legiſlative Power of *England*, wherein the Origin of both Houſes of Parliament, their Antient Conſtitution, and Changes that have happen'd in the Perſons that compoſed them, with the Occaſion thereof, are related in a Chronological Order; and many things concerning the *Engliſh* Government. The Antiquity of the Laws of *England*, and the Feudal Law, are occaſionally illuſtrated and explained. By *George St.Amand*, of the *Inner Temple*, Eſq; In Octavo.

XXI. *Cato*'s Letters. With a Preface, containing an Anſwer to the moſt popular Objections to theſe Letters, and a Character of the late *John Trenchard* Eſq; In 4 vol. 12°.

XXII. The Works of the 'Honourable Sir *Charles Sedley*, conſiſting of Poems, Plays, Speeches in Parliament, &c. *viz.* The Mulberry-Garden, *Bellamira* or the Miſtreſs, The Grumbler, *Anthony* and *Cleopatra*, and the Tyrant King of *Crete*, &c. With Memoirs of the Author's Life. In two Volumes 12°.

XXIII. Three Tragedies, *viz.* The Diſtreſs'd Mother; The *Briton*; and *Humfrey* Duke of *Gloceſter*. By *Ambroſe Philips* Eſq; in 12°.

XXIV. Epiſtles, Odes, &c. written on ſeveral Subjects. With a Diſſertation concerning the Perfection of the *Engliſh* Language, the State of Poetry, &c. By Mr. *Welſted*. The ſecond Edition.

XXV. Silk-Worms: a Poem in two Books. Tranſlated from the original *Latin* of *Marc. Hier. Vida*, Biſhop of *Alba*. With a Preface giving an Account of the Life and Writings of *Vida*.

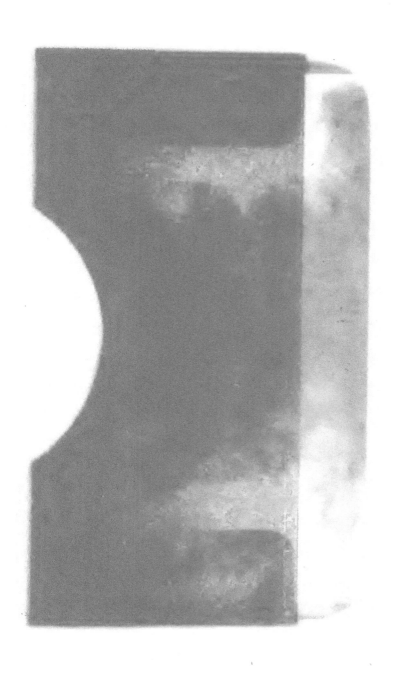

WS - #0057 - 100624 - C0 - 229/152/33 - PB - 9781314257526 - Gloss Lamination

ISBN: 9781314257526

Published by:
HardPress Publishing
8345 NW 66TH ST #2561
MIAMI FL 33166-2626

Email: info@hardpress.net
Web: http://www.hardpress.net